Managerial Comparisons
of Four Developed Countries:
France, Britain,
United States, and Russia

The MIT Press

Cambridge, Massachusetts,
and London, England

Managerial Comparisons
of Four Developed Countries:
France, Britain,
United States, and Russia

David Granick

*Oct.
'73*

To Kitty, Steve,
Bobbie, and Tim

Contents

Acknowledgments

I am most grateful to the following institutions for providing research appointments which made possible work on this book: to the Ecole Pratique des Hautes Etudes, 6e section, of the University of Paris for a visiting appointment as a directeur d'études associé; to the Faculty of Economic and Social Studies, University of Manchester, and to the Simon Foundation for a visiting appointment as a Simon Research Professor; and to the European Institute of Columbia University for a visiting senior fellowship. Additional financial assistance is acknowledged, with thanks, from the Research Committee of the Graduate School of the University of Wisconsin from special funds voted by the State Legislature; from the International Studies and Programs Office, University of Wisconsin; and from the American Philosophical Society. Partial typing services were provided by the International Development Research Center of the University of Indiana.

The following four graduate and former graduate students at the University of Wisconsin have rendered yeoman service: Jean Behrens, Janice A. Johnson, Peter Lundt, and Roger Skurski.

My principal debt is owed to the many senior managers in France, England, and America who spoke to me freely about their own companies. Their names, along with those of their companies, must remain anonymous. I have also been greatly helped by other businessmen, administrators and researchers in various societies, and academics in all three of these countries as well as in the Soviet Union. Of those whose names can be cited, particular mention may be made of André Bougé, Leonard Weiss, the late Dugué Mac carthy, the late Philip Mosely, André Piatier, Michel Wattel, and Bruce Williams. None of these, of course, bears any responsibility for my conclusions.

Vienna
May 1971

Introduction

This book constitutes a study of management as a production factor in the output of large-scale manufacturing enterprises in present-day industrialized countries. Specifically, British and French managements are contrasted with one another against the backdrop of American and Russian practice. Managements are examined through the optic of their willingness and ability to adjust to changing conditions. Factors making for such adaptability are compared for all four countries.

The fundamental assumption of this study is that one can meaningfully distinguish between modal managerial behavior in Britain, France, the United States, and the Soviet Union. On the basis of this assumption, national differences in managerial behavior are related to differences in two other characteristics of management which are themselves treated as independent variables. The first of these independent variables consists of the set of typical value systems of different levels of management in each country; the second consists of the set of representative backgrounds of managers and of the procedures by which managers are selected, promoted, and otherwise rewarded.

The study is restricted to very large enterprises—with one exception, they are among the top two hundred of each capitalist country—for three reasons. The first stems from my interest in adaptation of managements to growth possibilities. Since the largest firms are those least likely in Europe to suffer from lack of knowledge of techniques used elsewhere in the world, from inability to finance the implementation of these techniques, or from incapacity in attracting managers of the desired caliber, it is this stratum of European enterprise that has the greatest advantages in emulating the best performance achieved anywhere. Second, because of the magnitude of these companies, the complex and particularly interesting problems of decentralization of management functions are necessarily posed in each of them. Third, it seems probable that this is the most rapidly growing sector of private enterprise in these countries.

The emphasis throughout the book is upon management of nongovernmental firms in Britain and France. Since I believe that this subject can best be analyzed comparatively, I pay a good deal of attention to American and Soviet management. But the treatment of the United States and the Soviet Union, despite the fact that much new material is presented in Part III, is limited to what is needed for theoretic and comparative purposes.

Since the study is comparative, and intended both to set forth and explain differences in managerial behavior in different countries, I treat the large-scale enterprises in each country as represented by a single ideal type of enterprise. Of course, I do not deny that in each country we can in fact find widely differing patterns of behavior among the individual large firms. Certainly, if we compare British, French, and the American companies, enterprises exist in each country which are better described by the behavior patterns that I attribute to another nation than by those that I regard as typical for that particular country. Nevertheless, modal behavior in each country seems sufficiently different in important respects so that it is meaningful to generalize about national differences between enterprises. It is in this limited sense of comparision of national ideal types that the reader should interpret my comparative analyses throughout this book.

The analytic framework can be depicted by the block diagram of Figure I-1.

No pretense is made that the factors I shall treat as independent variables at each stage of the causal process diagramed in Figure I-1 include all of the most important variables. Rather, the functions implicit in the diagram should be understood as partial correlation functions, with all other major independent variables that act at each stage being held constant.

This treatment creates very serious problems of presentation. The basic independent variables are those normally treated by the sociologist, and my detailed exploration of them is likely to be of only minor interest to economists and students of business administration. On the other hand, the final effect of these variables on economic performance is of more interest to economists than to anyone else. The intermediate treatment of their effect on managerial behavior is more mixed: some of it is reasonably technical economics while other parts of it deal with aspects more commonly considered by sociologists. The result is that the reader from any given discipline is likely

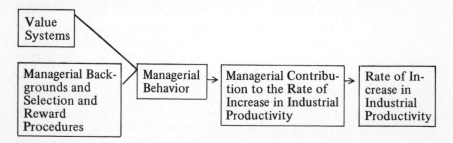

Figure I-1

to find himself bored with portions of the book, and to wonder why so much attention is given to aspects that do not concern him.

The fact is that I hope that this book will appeal to four distinct groups of readers. *The first group* of potential readers is that concerned with economic growth; these readers will be interested in the analysis of a major factor—management itself—in such growth, as it appears among currently developed countries with different social and managerial traditions and different levels of productivity. *The second group* consists of those who are interested specifically in international business; such readers will find here a treatment of various aspects of managerial backgrounds and behavior as revealed primarily in detailed case studies of major British and French firms. *The third group* consists of microeconomists, who will find the problems of internal company planning, investment decision making, and internal pricing treated in terms of the task of reconciliation of the various suboptimization goals of different groups within management. *The fourth group* of potential readers is comprised of industrial sociologists; Part III of this book is devoted to the educational backgrounds, career patterns, and monetary incentives provided to industrial managers in all four countries studied, together with a treatment of the combined effect of these factors upon managerial behavior.

To a considerable degree, the problem of a heterogeneous readership has been tackled by writing various chapters primarily for different audiences. These chapters can readily be skipped, or at most browsed through, by readers from the other disciplines. But, of course, this solution cannot be employed in the core chapters. Here, each reader will simply have to put up with the inherent limitation of this kind of a book.

Part I provides the theoretical foundation for the study. Chapter 1 presents an economic growth model that uses managerial adaptability to change as a key variable, and points to the reasons for believing that French and British industrial growth would have been much more rapid than it has in fact been if it were not for the effect of this variable. Chapter 2 discusses the effect of value systems on managerial behavior, and treats intracompany planning in terms of "satisficing," suboptimization by lower and intermediate managerial units, and the value systems of different levels of management. Chapter 3 explores the effect upon managerial structure and behavior exercised by the variable of national managerial career patterns.

Part II presents nine case studies of large British and French firms. The object of each study is to evaluate, insofar as this can be done qualitatively, the influence of managerial factors upon the improvement of factor productivity in the enterprise during a period of more than a decade. These studies serve as the basic raw material (although they are themselves highly processed) for the treatment of managerial behavior in British and French industry which is carried out in Parts I and IV. As such, they can be skipped by the hasty reader. Their virtue, however, is that they provide the reader both with an empirical means for checking on my own conclusions and with a set of primary data on the actual functioning of these large European enterprises.

Part III supplies sample data concerning the education of managers, the nature of their careers within the company, the level of their earnings relative to that of blue-collar workers, and the nature of the bonus systems under which they work. The various parts of the material relate to different levels of management, but in almost all cases only to those above foreman rank, rather than being restricted to the top officers of the company as is the case in most of the related American literature. Coverage is of large American, British, French, and Russian enterprises; the British and Russian sections rely primarily upon existing studies, but the American and French materials are new. All of Part III can be considered as providing the underpinning for Chapter 3, since it develops in depth the nonbehavioral material that this chapter had earlier related to managerial behavior.

Part IV concerns itself with two problem areas of managerial decision making. Chapter 11 explores national differences in investment behavior which are linked to suboptimization within the large enterprise; it must, however, be considered as limited to the presentation of hypotheses rather than being extended to testing them. Chapter 12 considers national differences in the practices of internal pricing within large organizations, and explains these differences along the lines developed earlier.

Part V includes both a concluding chapter and a brief treatment of developments in large-scale French and British industry since the middle 1960s when the European data were collected.

The chapters can be divided according to the specific audiences to whom they will appeal. This is done according to where the chapters fall in the block diagram of Figure I-1.

Value Systems

Chapter 2   For all readers

Managerial Backgrounds and Selection Procedures

Chapter 10   For all readers

Chapters 7, 8   For industrial sociologists

Reward Procedures

Chapter 9   For business administration specialists and industrial sociologists

Managerial Behavior

Chapters 3, 13, 14   For all readers

Chapters 11, 12   For economists

Managerial Contribution

Chapter 4   For all readers

Chapters 5, 6   For business administration specialists

Industrial Productivity

Chapter 1   For economists

Summarizing this in a different fashion, I recommend that the following groups of readers concentrate on the following chapters:

Economists   Chapters 1-4, 10-14

Industrial Sociologists   Chapters 2-4, 7-10, 13-14

Business Administration Specialists   Chapters 2-6, 9-10, 13-14

The basic materials for this study consist of intensive interviews carried out in France and Britain over a period of eighteen months during 1963-1965. Seven companies in France and three companies in Britain were studied in depth. In each of these, a minimum of some forty to fifty hours of interviews were spent with members of medium and top management, all above the level of foreman. Each company also supplied detailed data as to inputs and outputs of production over the past seven to sixteen years. Briefer interviews, of five to fifteen hours, were conducted in an additional six enterprises. In each of these companies the theme of the interviews was twofold: first, the nature of the most significant factors raising productivity during recent years and the obstacles to such increases; second, the main problems facing the company at the present time and the ways in which the company was proceeding to tackle them.

Each of the ten companies in the basic sample were revisited in 1967 during a six-week visit. Individuals interviewed were selected primarily from among those previously seen. The object of these interviews consisted mainly in observing how both the companies themselves and their managements' attitudes had evolved during the intervening three years.

The second set of original materials consists of a set of much briefer interviews carried out during 1966-1968 in the headquarters of ten large American companies, each in a different industry. The purpose of these interviews was to establish a base from which to examine managerial practices in the British and French firms. Prime emphasis was given to information concerning the career paths of management personnel, the criteria used for evaluating the work of managers, and the incentive systems provided to management personnel.

The third set of original materials consists of some interviews conducted during two weeks in 1967 in the Soviet Union. These covered, although in much less depth, the same questions asked in American firms. Their function in this study is similar to that of the American interviews.

In addition to these original materials, I have leaned in writing this book on a series of brief interviews in a large number of British and French firms which I conducted during 1959-1960 and reported on in my previous book, *The European Executive*.[1] These supplementary interviews have helped me both to place my small sample of European firms into a broader context of European industry and to evaluate the representativeness of my sample of management. Conclusions regarding Soviet industrial management rest primarily on published Soviet materials that I have used and written about over the course of many years, supplemented by the 1967 visit mentioned earlier.

The ten British and French firms are taken as representing the universe of large-scale, nongovernmental manufacturing enterprise in England and France which is completely national in character. The major demands made on the time of senior managers in each of these firms, plus the requirement of willingness to share quite confidential material with the investigator, put out of the question any possibility of sampling this universe in any scientific fashion. In any case, the number of firms studied could not have been expanded without sharply reducing the intensity of study of each company, and a sample of ten is far too small to yield probability results of any great value no matter how the sample might have been chosen. Nevertheless, the broad industry coverage of the sample, the other criteria according to which the companies were chosen, the statistical representativeness of these companies with regard to their industries insofar as profitability and increase in labor productivity are concerned, and the fact that the total universe of firms consists of no more than a few hundred enterprises, all lead me to believe that my sample is reasonably representative. The case for this belief in representativeness is presented in Chapter 4.

The American companies studied are also large, all being among the two

[1] Doubleday, Garden City, N.Y., 1962.

hundred major American firms. They were chosen on the basis of willingness to grant access, of size, of spread among industrial sectors, and particularly of the availability within the company of known data as to career lines of middle and higher managers. To my surprise, it was more difficult to arrange access to American companies than to British and French, and in only three cases was the cooperation as complete. Nevertheless, the American data are broad enough to provide some bases of comparison along a limited number of lines.

The Theoretical Foundation

Part I is the theoretic core of the book. Chapter 1 presents a model in which managerial adaptability to change is a key variable determining a country's rate of economic growth. The purpose of this chapter is to link managerial behavior to economic performance, and thus to justify my study of the differences in managerial behavior between different countries as a contribution to economic analysis.

Chapter 2 is devoted to showing the effect of differing national value systems on managerial behavior in the respective countries. The managerial behavior examined is that of intracompany planning.

Chapter 3 provides the link between the career development of managers within individual companies, combined with the reward system within which they operate, and their behavior. The focus is upon national differences in suboptimizing managerial behavior.

Management in a Model of Economic Development

In considering the question of the relative speed of economic development of different nations, a concept frequently used is that of the "advantage of backwardness."[1] This is the common-sense notion that a country which lags behind the most advanced levels of technology and organization which are known and proved workable can make great strides in productivity by adopting these available techniques. Such a country can be regarded as functioning inside its transformation curve rather than on its border;[2] the greater the degree to which it is operating inside its transformation curve, the larger is its potential for achieving productivity growth. This leads to the expectation that, ceteris paribus, less-developed countries should grow at a faster rate per capita than do the more-developed countries.

It should be noted that this expectation has nothing in common with the view that countries should be expected to grow more rapidly when they are poorly developed than when they are highly developed—relative to some absolute standard—because of the respective levels of their development at different times. When one contrasts the annual rate of growth in gross domestic product per member of the labor force in the United States and western Europe between 1900-1966 and 1950-1966 (see Table 1.2), the growth rate in the postwar years in both geographic areas is so much higher that the difference cannot be reasonably accounted for simply by the effect of the two world wars. There is neither logic nor evidence for the view that it becomes more difficult per se for countries to maintain a high rate of growth as their per capita income level mounts. It is only backwardness relative to those levels of technology and organization which are currently known which would seem to matter.

It is true that a worldwide comparison of rates of growth provides no clear evidence for the view that even relative backwardness is an advantage.[3] But the absence of a higher rate of growth in the less-developed countries can be readily reconciled with the doctrine of the "advantages of backwardness" by pointing to two major peculiarities of many currently less-developed nations:

[1] This was developed by Alexander Gerschenkron. See his *Economic Backwardness in Historical Perspective* (Harvard University Press, Cambridge, Mass., 1962).
[2] A technique is considered more advanced than another only when the first yields a greater output per unit of mix of factor inputs regardless of whether the individual input factors are priced at the shadow prices of the more- or of the less-developed country.
[3] It should be remembered that national income statistics of growth rates are inherently biased upwards for countries emerging into a market-economy stage, due to the fact that no deduction is made for the increased transport, merchandising, and other costs of operating such an economy.

Table 1.1 Annual Rate of Growth in Gross Domestic Product 1950-1966 (Percentages)

	Total G.D.P.	Per Capita G.D.P.
More-developed countries[a]	4.4	3.2
Less-developed countries[b]	4.5	2.2

Source: *Yearbook of National Account Statistics 1967* (United Nations, New York, 1968), Table 6b, pp. 819-823.
[a]Countries of Europe (excluding the USSR and Eastern Europe), North America, Oceania and Japan, and the Union of South Africa.
[b]Countries in Africa (excluding the Union of South Africa), the Caribbean and Latin America, East and Southeast Asia (excluding Japan, mainland China, Mongolia, North Korea, and North Vietnam), and the Middle East (excluding Cyprus and Turkey).

the failure to have reached a point of "takeoff",[4] and the existence of an exceptionally high rate of population growth.

It is thus more interesting to turn to a comparison that avoids these peculiarities. Such a comparison can be made by restricting our universe of countries to those which are relatively developed, and comparing the world leader (the United States) with the major groupings from the rest of the field.

Table 1.2 indicates that the rate of growth of the output/labor ratio over a long period has been no greater in the backward region (western Europe) than in the advanced country. A comparison restricted to the post-Second World War period shows some "catching up," but it still seems slight—at least for western Europe and the Soviet Union—relative to the large degree of backwardness involved.

How can we explain the fact that, within the universe of countries which are all considered developed by international standards, the equalization of income levels has proceeded so slowly? All are fully capable of absorbing the latest technologies. None of the countries has suffered from peculiarly great population pressures. While it is true that the ratio of investment to national income was lower in western Europe than in the United States until after the Second World War, this was compensated for by a much smaller rate of growth in the labor force. Certainly the United States may profit from certain advantages which have not been diminished, such as superior natural resources and the possibilities of greater economies of scale; but it is difficult to believe that these account for a very large portion of the continuing discrepancy.

A useful way of explaining this retardation is by the hypothesis that the

[4]This can be thought of as reflecting both the failure to achieve a viable ratio of net investment to national income and of the inability to overcome many social and psychological obstacles to growth.

other developed countries show a slower speed of adjustment to changing conditions than does the United States. Modern industrial economies are faced with a constantly changing world transformation curve both with regard to new technologies (including organizational methods) and new products.[5] A country that lags in its rate of adjustment will steadily fall behind the leader in its ability to utilize these new possibilities; on the other hand, to the extent that it enjoys the "advantage of backwardness," its exploitation of this resource will provide a compensation in its growth rate. There is no general reason to expect one or the other factor to dominate.

The hypothesis can be described in the model where

$$\frac{dz}{dt} = ax\frac{db}{dt} - (1 - x)\frac{dc}{dt} - (1 - x)\frac{de}{dt},$$

with

z = observed difference between the rates of growth in gross national product per member of the labor force in the lagging country and in the leading country;

a = the degree of backwardness (defined as the intercountry relationship between gross national product per member of the labor force) relative to the leading country other than that accounted for by long-term disadvantages such as inferior national resources and lesser possibilities for achieving economies of scale;

x = the speed of adjustment of the lagging country as a percentage of that of the leading country;

db/dt = the annual rate at which the country would make good its backwardness if its speed of adjustment were the same as that of the leading country;

dc/dt = the rate of expansion of the international transformation curve, assuming both the speed of adjustment of the leading country and sufficient investment to embody the necessary changes;

de/dt = the rate of change in national income due to change in other noninput factors in the leading country—in particular, structural change between sectors and economies of scale; and

[5]See H. Aujac, "Le Passage de l'invention à la production," Congrès des économistes de langue française, May 1966. McGraw-Hill surveys of 1960-1965 showed that new products constitute 10 to 14 percent of the sales of American manufacturing as a whole. (New products are defined as those which meet the twin criteria of not having existed five years earlier and of being considered new by experts in the industry concerned.)

Table 1.2 Comparisons of Production per Member of the Labor Force Among Developed Countries

Measure of Comparison	United States	Western Europe		France	United King- dom	Japan	Soviet Union
		Including United Kingdom	Excluding United Kingdom				
1. Gross national product per member of the labor force, 1966 (U.S.=100)							
U.S. weights	100	58	61	67	49	28	31
Own country weights, non-U.S.	100	43	43	49	41	...	...
2. Industrial production per member of the industrial labor force, 1966 (U.S.=100)							
U.S. weights	100	47	50	55	36	25	...
Own country weights, non-U.S.	100	35	36	40	30	...	...
3. Gross domestic product per member of the labor force, annual rate of growth, 1900-1966 (percentage)							
U.S. weights	1.8	1.7	1.8	...	...	...	...
Own country weights, non-U.S.	1.8	1.7	1.8	1.8	1.2	...	...
4. Gross national product per member of the labor force, annual rate of growth 1950-1966 (percentage)							
U.S. weights	2.6	4.1	4.6	...	...	...	...
Own country weights, non-U.S.	2.6	4.0	4.5	4.5	2.2	7.9	5.0

Table 1.2 (continued)

Measure of Comparison	United States	Western Europe Including United Kingdom	Western Europe Excluding United Kingdom	France	United King- dom	Japan	Soviet Union
5. Industrial production per member of the industrial labor force, annual rate of growth 1950-1966 (percentage)							
U.S. weights	3.1	4.4	5.0	. . .	. . .	. . .	. . .
Own country weights, non-U.S.	3.1	4.3	4.9	4.8	2.2	9.5	7.5

Notes: Western Europe is taken as the weighted average of Belgium, Denmark, France, Germany, Italy, Netherlands, Norway, Sweden, and the United Kingdom—the choice of countries being partly determined by the availability of data. Purchasing power equivalents between currencies are given for 1955 for all west European countries except Sweden in Milton Gilbert & Associates, *Comparative National Products and Price Levels: a Study of Western Europe and the United States* (O.E.E.C., Paris, 1958); for 1960 for Sweden and Japan in Irving B. Kravis and Michael W. S. Davenport, "The Political Arithmetic of International Burden-Sharing," *Journal of Political Economy,* August 1963. The 1966 comparisons between countries as to the levels of gross national product and of industrial production are made by extrapolating the 1955 and 1960 purchasing power equivalents to 1966 by dividing the United States G.N.P. price deflator by each foreign country's G.N.P. price deflator. The summation procedure for western Europe as a whole in foreign country weights rests upon the crude assumption that the price structures of the various west European countries are similar. Basic output and labor-force data are generally taken either from OECD or national economic statistics. Labor force is defined to include the armed forces. However, the source used for the 1900-1966 comparisons is Angus Maddison, *Economic Growth in the West* (Twentieth Century Fund, New York, 1964). Soviet data are taken from the articles by Stanley H. Cohn and James H. Noren for the Joint Economic Committee of the United States Congress, *New Directions in the Soviet Economy* (U.S. Government Printing Office, Washington, D.C., 1966), and from the Joint Economic Committee's *Soviet Economic Performance: 1966-67* (U.S. Government Printing Office, Washington, D.C., 1968).
Postwar annual rates of growth in labor productivity cover, in general, the period 1950-1966. However, the dates vary somewhat by country for three reasons: to eliminate recovery to the prewar level; to allow for business cycle variations; to take advantage of the best statistical sources. Countries for which the period covered is other than 1950-1966 are: Denmark (1951-1966), Germany (1954-1966), Norway (1951-1966), United Kingdom (1951-1966), and Japan (1955-1966). For industrial production only, the Soviet Union is analyzed for the period 1950-1965.

$dc/dt + de/dt =$ the rate of growth in gross national product per member of the labor force in the leading country.

For purely expository purposes, we might assume the following values:

$$\frac{dz}{dt} = 2 \text{ percent per annum}$$

$$a = 0.5$$

$$\frac{db}{dt} = 10 \text{ percent per annum}$$

$$\frac{dc}{dt} + \frac{de}{dt} = 2.6 \text{ percent per annum}$$

Given these values, then x would equal 0.60. If x had equaled unity, and the other values had been the same, then dz/dt would have been 5 percent per annum and the lagging country would have approached the level of the leading country at two and one-half times the assumed rate of speed.

While the above example is only expository, it is not completely arbitrary, being based upon a comparison of the United States and continental western Europe. Employing what are essentially historical data for 1950-1966, and making a quite arbitrary assumption only for the value of db/dt (10 percent per annum), we derive the values of x shown in Table 1.3.

The relative values of x for these five different portions of the world seem quite reasonable. Note that, of the lagging countries, it is only Japan whose value of x is close to unity.[6]

Table 1.3 Values of the Speed of Adjustment

	x
United States	1.0
Japan	0.91
Continental western Europe	0.60
Soviet Union	0.56
United Kingdom	0.31

Note: The data for the various entries is for the following years: United States, 1950-1966; Japan, 1955-1966; continental western Europe, 1950-1966, with 1954-1966 for Germany; Soviet Union, 1950-1966; and United Kingdom, 1951-1966.

[6]In determining the degree of backwardness of the other countries with respect to the United States, own-country weights are used for Japan, the Soviet Union, and the United Kingdom, and the geometric weights of the results obtained from using United States and continental western European weights for this last region. In deriving the value of a for each country, the assumption is made that one-fifth of the backwardness was due to long-term disadvantages.

The above model—which is intended only for secular and not for cyclical analysis—includes a vital assumption as to the degree to which a lagging country can utilize its "advantage of backwardness": namely, that it cannot profitably concentrate all of its technical and organizational effort and its investment resources into improving the areas of existing backwardness at the expense of failing to utilize expansions in world technical knowledge as the international transformation curve moves outward. The justification for this assumption is twofold. On the one hand, the mass of organizational effort available nationally is diversified throughout the economy in the form of the labor force and managerial talent present in each enterprise; it cannot be concentrated. Second, and more important, "catching up" is a sequential process: both because improvements in one enterprise depend on prior improvements in materials, services, and market acceptance by other enterprises and because, within the same enterprise, organizational and technical changes often require prior success in different innovations.

The model also treats gross domestic investment as an implicit dependent variable, being provided in sufficient amounts to support the growth in gross national product which derives from improvements in technology and organization as well as from increases in the size of the national labor force. This implies not only that the level of investment is not a restriction upon a country's increase in labor productivity but also that no gains can be hoped for from the substitution of capital for labor as a result of changes in relative factor costs. The capital/labor ratio is treated as varying purely as a function of the rate of adoption of particular innovations, which happen to be more or less capital intensive. This follows from the omission of capital from my model.

The justification for ignoring the bottleneck aspect of gross domestic investment is that, particularly in economies such as those of western Europe which are reasonably linked to the international capital market, investment will presumably respond to expected profit margins; these, in turn, should be a function of the opportunities confronting the economy and of its ability to take advantage of them. The effect on expected profit margins of different national patterns of income distribution as between wages and profit is ignored. Furthermore, the significance of changing relative factor costs for the combination of factors of production, and thus for labor productivity, is left outside the model on the ground that its quantitative importance is probably secondary among the developed countries that we shall be examining.

The foregoing hypothesis, put in terms of speed of adjustment to change, is primarily a supply analysis. However, as was already pointed out, it also explains the demand for investment resources. Now we can extend the demand analysis to an examination of the balance of trade problem.

In post-Second World War western Europe, it seems reasonable to posit that demand has been secularly restricted below the level needed to ensure full utilization of resources only by the need to protect the balance of payments positions of the nations concerned. If we assume that the prices of export and import goods produced in a country are a function of that country's average unit wage costs, then the evolution of the balance of trade of a country must be a joint function of the changes in the wage level and productivity of that country relative to that of its trading partners.

These assumptions mean that the evolution of a country i's balance of trade is a joint function of db/dt, dc/dt, de/dt, and of the country's values of a_i, x_i, and dy_i/dt relative to its trading partners, where dy_i/dt expresses country i's change in the money wage level. The higher a country's values of a and x relative to its trading partners, the higher the value of dy_i/dt which it can permit itself without the government being forced to depress the country's demand level below that of full utilization of resources. A nation with a relatively low combination of a and x can afford to maintain demand only if it can develop adaptive procedures to restrain appropriately its dy_i/dt growth. Britain is the prime example of a country with a relatively low combination of a and x which has failed to limit its dy_i/dt below that of its trading partners, and which thus has been forced to restrict demand. Demand restriction, in turn, has held down Britain's value of x. The resulting vicious circle can be thus interpreted as a failure in adaptation.

If we compare the present-day problem of "catching-up" to the similar problem facing continental western Europe in relation to Britain or the United States during the pre-First World War era, current difficulties appear substantially greater. This is the case for two reasons.

First, $dc/dt + de/dt$ (the rate of growth in gross domestic production per member of the labor force in the leading country) is substantially greater today[7] and is likely to remain so. The critical reason for this is that dc/dt, the

---

[7]During the period 1870 to 1913, gross domestic product per person of working age increased by an average compound rate of 1.2 percent in the United Kingdom and by 1.9 percent in the United States. (Angus Maddison, *Economic Growth in the West*, Twentieth Century Fund, New York, 1964, pp. 199-209.) Between 1950 and 1966, United States gross national product per member of the labor force increased by an average compound rate of 2.6 percent.

rate of expansion of the international transformation curve, seems to be considerably more rapid today than earlier. For, with the stepping-up both of higher education and of the proportion of research and development expenditures to national income, the pace of technological and organizational advance has accelerated.

With dc/dt higher today, only a compensatingly higher value of x_i (the speed of adjustment of the lagging country as a percentage of that of the leader) could make possible the equalization of the rate at which the continental countries once caught up with Britain. The lagging countries must perform much better in adapting to change than was ever previously necessary in order to equal the historical performance of the half century preceding the First World War.

Adjustment to Change
Adjustment to change can be readily divided into four components, with a fifth component representing all the residual factors. Let these components each be represented by x_j, and comparable components of backwardness by a_j. Then

$$\sum_j a_j x_j \frac{db}{dt} = ax \frac{db}{dt}.$$

The component x_1 is the speed of adjustment of the economy as a whole in the lagging country, relative to that in the leader, in changing sectoral structure in the direction of greater employment in those sectors with higher value added per member of the labor force. Also, x_1 represents adjustment to changing present and forecast demand schedules as well as to international trade possibilities; it requires not only sectoral mobility of labor force and investment, but also business organization and regional mobility as well.

The movement out of agriculture has historically been the prime case of the x_1 type of adjustment. In recent years, $a_1 x_1$ has been of major significance in the continental west European countries and in Japan.[8] But while there remain considerable reserves of a_1 in these nations, the sharp reduction that has already occurred in continental western Europe in the proportion of the labor force engaged in agriculture makes it unlikely that the $a_1 x_1$ component of growth in gross national product in these countries can be maintained.

[8]For continental western Europe, see E. F. Denison, *Why Growth Rates Differ* (The Brookings Institution, Washington, D.C., 1967), p. 215.

The component x_2 is the speed of adjustment of the economy as a whole in eliminating diseconomies of scale that arise from excessively tiny enterprises. The rate of elimination of nonfarm enterprises with no paid employees might be taken as a proxy for this. Here, too, the potential for improvement is rapidly diminishing.

The component x_3 constitutes the macroadjustments by the government to ensure the full use of economic resources. All the countries in our universe have done much better in this regard since the Second World War than was ever the case before. But there seems no obvious reason to believe either that the European countries have done better than the United States in this regard,[9] or on the contrary, that this represents an area of lag on their part. As the situation stands today and in the likely future, x_3 is a neutral force with regard to relative growth rates among the countries in which we are interested.

The component a_4 represents the area of backwardness in technology and organization, aside from those diseconomies of tiny enterprises which are treated under a_2. The relevant x values are labeled as x_{4a} and x_{4b}.

The component x_{4a} represents the relative willingness and ability of nonmanagerial labor to adjust to changing conditions. Willingness and ability to learn new skills, to raise productivity in individual enterprises in line with the potentials of new technologies, to accept employment in different industries and geographic locations and to accede to the working of shifts: all these are involved. The existence of low values for x_{4a} appears to be a major area of weakness of European countries relative to the United States. This is due in part to housing shortages that penalize geographic mobility. It is due in part to lower general educational levels, which make the learning of new skills more difficult. To a marked degree, it is due to working class traditions. But also, to a considerable extent, it is due to the failure of enterprise managements to offer the kind of industrial leadership that motivates and makes technically feasible these adjustments of the labor force.

The component x_{4b} is the willingness and ability of enterprise managements to adjust to changing conditions. This is the component with which I shall be concerned in this book.[10]

---

[9] The lower rates of unemployment do not of themselves indicate superiority, for they often represent no more than underemployed manpower—whether this be spread throughout the economy (as has too often been the British experience), or whether it be concentrated in particular sectors such as agriculture (as in France).

[10] The factors x_{4a} and x_{4b} are obviously closely related to Professor Liebenstein's concept of X-efficiency. His and my approaches share the common features of reflecting

It is x_{4a} and x_{4b} —the micro as contrasted with the macro elements of adjustment—that represent the prime deficiencies in the x factor of the lagging countries. It is their values in particular that will have to be raised significantly if the process of catching up is not to be reduced sharply as the possibilities represented by a_1 and a_2 decline.

The approach of this book is that managements are constantly faced with possibilities, advantageous or disadvantageous, for change; and that the quality of a management's contribution to increases in productivity rests in its ability to respond to these opportunities. The response includes both the specific decisions related to change which are made by management, and the actions which are taken to carry out these decisions.

The managerial function in a modern industrial society is viewed as primarily consisting of adapting the enterprise to changes of all sorts. If demand and supply conditions and the state of knowledge were stable over time, even the poorest management might be expected eventually to stumble into a reasonably satisfactory adaptation to its situation. The differences in quality of management between individual firms that had survived for a long period would not be likely to be great.

From this perspective, management as a factor in the production process differs fundamentally from those of labor and capital as these are traditionally treated in production functions. The usual production-function approach considers that available factors have their full effects either on current production or on production which is a specific number of periods in the future. A country with a lower input of factors than another nation will have lower production; but there is no reason to assume that its rate of growth will be affected. Management, however—like any other factor affecting the x variables—is involved in the adaptation process and thus in the rate of change. It is true that the quality of management can properly be treated as a conventional input into the production function for currently-produced goods; as such, it affects only the production level. But to the extent that it is correct to consider it as primarily consisting of a capacity for adaptation to change, it

a concern with adaptability to change, and with holding to the importance of the fact "that firms and economies do not operate on an outer-bound production possibility surface consistent with their resources." While our analyses are quite different, they are complementary rather than competitive. My interest is the differences between what might be called X-efficiency in different industrial cultures, while Leibenstein has not concerned himself with cultural factors. (See H. Leibenstein, "Allocative Efficiency vs. 'X-Efficiency'," *American Economic Review*, June 1966, pp. 392-415 and "Organizational or Frictional Equilibria, X-Efficiency, and the Rate of Innovation," *Quarterly Journal of Economics*, November 1969, pp. 600-623.)

is an argument in a function which yields the rate of change of production (such as my model above) rather than in a function which provides the absolute level of production in a given period.

The purpose of this book is to study management as a factor of production, viewing the relevant production function as dynamic rather than static.

2 Planning and the "Company Personality"

When one examines managerial behavior in individual companies, one quickly arrives at the conclusion that company policies play a considerable role, for good or bad, in determining corporate actions. The enterprises that we shall examine in Part II are not opportunistic organizations, reacting solely to short-run opportunities and constraints so as to maximize their present financial earnings. Rather, each has its own specific long-run objectives and inhibitions, both those stemming from top-management values and those ingrained in the company's organizational structure and behavior. Nor are these objectives and constraints identical among the various companies, although we do find great similarities among firms within each of the two countries studied. Thus we can reasonably talk of a company having its own "personality."

The notion of individual company personality is one that is familiar to American businessmen, although commonly they have difficulty in delineating the features of the personality of any specific firm. This American acceptance of company personality is a major reason why, in American as contrasted to European business practice, a manager who has been eased out of one firm will not find this fact in itself a significant obstacle to locating elsewhere. It is widely recognized that a particular manager may function poorly within the framework of one company and yet be highly effective in another firm.

Yet, at least to an economist, the reasons for the existence of fairly stable corporate personalities are far from obvious. Why do not firms quickly adjust their organizational and policy emphases to their specific market opportunities so as to maximize the present discounted worth of the company, as is implicitly assumed in neoclassical microeconomic theory?[1] True, this would still leave differences between corporations; but these could be explained by variations in the outside environment which call for differentiated responses.

The analysis of company personality can be divided into two aspects. The first relates to individual company strategies which are long term, and in which differentiation is much greater among firms within a single country than between the industries of different countries. The second is associated with basic values and attitudes that distinguish different cultures, or at least subsets of these cultures, from one another. Both, however, share the common feature that they lead to the development of fairly stable corporate personalities which have a major effect on company operations.

[1]For an interesting formulation of this question, see Michael Gort's review of N. W. Chamberlain, *Enterprise and Environment,* in *the American Economic Review,* December 1968, p. 1470.

Let us begin with the first aspect: differences of strategies. Here I shall deal with the treatment of the problem of uncertainty in choosing among alternative investment projects.

If there were no uncertainty as to the costs and future returns that would result from alternative projects, or if such uncertainty could be expressed in terms of statistical probability matrices, then investment decisions could be handled readily enough by standard techniques. The real decision-making problem arises from uncertainties that cannot be categorized by objective probability functions.

It is to be expected that different companies should follow different investment strategies, both because of the different objective situations in which they find themselves and because of the differing evaluations of uncertainty which are made by the respective managements. But what might be predicted from the standard textbook treatment of investment decision making is that all would employ some form of rate-of-return criterion, and that those projects would be chosen which promise the highest expected rate of return modified by whatever risk factor may be appropriate to the specific financial condition of the individual company. Company strategy would find expression only with regard to the weight to be given to risk and, probably, in systematic biases as to the degree of uncertainty considered to be involved in particular kinds of investments. Both of these, however, should readily be susceptible to a treatment in which lower levels of management could prepare numerical project analyses that are directly comparable with one another. Thus there should be no reason for a company's management to distinguish between different categories of investment, but rather each project should be comparable with all others "on their merits."

In fact, however, this treatment of investment is one that I have encountered in only one company. Instead, all other top managements lean heavily upon the classification of investments.

Thus the corporate comptroller of a large American food company told me that his firm had established a formal requirement of a 30 percent pretax return on investments. But when I attempted to explore the company's actual use of this standard, the comptroller became impatient with my naïveté. For he regarded any such quantitative standard as irrelevant to the more important problems of investment. Only for minor investments, and even here subject to extreme restrictions, could it provide a usable guide to investment policy.

Investment analysis in one large French electrical equipment firm provides the most systematic example of the development of classification criteria which I have encountered in Europe. Although a general rough norm of 20 percent return on investment has been set, more attention is paid to the categorization of investments than to their expected rate of return. Two major categories of offensive and defensive investments were established, and these were divided into five subcategories: strategic investments, expansion of capacity for existing products, building of capacity for new products, investments for replacement of equipment or for improvements of productivity, and investments that are required by law or company policy (for example, safety devices and camps for employees' children) or are motivated by an effort to improve the company's reputation. Investments falling into the first and the last subcategories are considered as lying outside the realm of profit calculation. As for the others, company policy dictates that offensive investments should always be given priority over those intended for purposes of cost reduction. Thus, even in principle, there is no attempt to subject all investment proposals to the test of a uniform rate-of-return requirement. Alternative projects within each of the subcategories are to be compared with one another—but not with projects in other subcategories. In fact, it was explicitly stated in the governing company circular that the criterion of calculated profitability should be determining only in the case of the low-priority defensive investments of the replacement and productivity variety.

In principle in this company, highly profitable divisions are to receive no special treatment with regard to investment allocations. Such privileges do, however, exist. Thus, in deciding whether to build a new plant for the production of an existing product or to subcontract the work outside the company, a profitable division was able to get the funds for construction despite the fact that it itself foresaw no more than a 12 percent return on the investment.

Finally, this company exercises no control after the fact as to what was the actual profitability of given investments. The nearest thing to this is the check by the comptroller's department on the total return to capital in each division. However, not only does this check fail to go down to the level of the individual investment project, but it also deducts as depreciation costs the amount taken for tax and balance sheet purposes. In contrast, the *ex ante* return on investments is computed with deduction only of straight-line depreciation, and the amortization period may extend over a longer period than is utilized for tax purposes. Thus there is no way of knowing whether rate-of-return estimates made for purposes of investment have proved justified, and this fact further reduces managerial confidence in them.

The firm that most systematically uses a rate-of-return criterion is the French metal company F1 described in Part II—the company in our sample which has shown the lowest profits of all. The reason for its ability to use a purely financial standard is that this is the firm which has had by far the largest proportion of investments directed toward the reduction of costs of existing products, and that the bulk of its investment requests have come through the production hierarchy which has made very simple assumptions as to future sales. Even here, however, major allowances are made for risk. Thus the rate of return required on large projects is only 60 percent of that demanded on small ones, this difference being justified on the basis that the former are much more closely studied and that thus the profit estimates are more reliable. Similarly, on the grounds that sales prognostications are more hazardous than productivity-improvement estimates, a higher rate of return is required for offensive investments than for defensive ones. This last is precisely the opposite approach to that of the firm mentioned earlier, and the result has found expression in Company F1's extremely slow and limited expansion into new products.

The French Company F3 stands at the opposite end of the spectrum. When the sales staff at headquarters believes that a new product could be marketed or the sales of existing products expanded, the necessary capital expenditures for production equipment are made automatically and without calculation as to the rate of return. Plant directors put in their requests without even knowing the costs of the alternative types of equipment to be considered, and the vetting at headquarters of these requests has also been done with only the most casual cost calculations. On the other hand, investments for purposes of cost reduction have been almost nonexistent. The head of the firm told me that the company was currently about to engage in an investment with a two-year payoff period, and that he felt sure that the estimate was accurate because the staff had discussed the investment for five years before making a decision. Such total indifference to calculation is an important element in the "personality" of Company F3, and doubtless it helps to explain why its total "productivity"[2] rose by only a 1.3 percent annual compound rate despite a sharp and steady rise in output. Neither the extreme efforts at calculation of

[2]Increases in output measured in constant prices divided by a weighted average of the increase in labor plus capital costs, also measured in fixed prices.

Company F1 nor the absence of analysis in Company F3 appears to have promoted success.

Most typical of the British approach is that of Company B2. Here, investment proposals are drawn up by the divisional management committees and are presented by them to the main board of the company. The main board may reject proposals because the sum of all investment requests is larger than the total funds available, but it has not normally rejected requests on the ground that they promised an unsatisfactory return.[3] Furthermore, it has carefully refrained from pushing divisional managements into investments which they have not themselves proposed.

The divisional managements are judged by their success in achieving targeted returns on capital—and these targets differ as between divisions, depending upon past history and the main board's view as to the differential possibilities of the lines of business in which the divisions are engaged. The significance of this for purposes of investment is that the various divisions employ different standards for judging investments; to the extent that they think in terms of rate of return, the cutoff rate is at the level of the division's targeted profit rate and thus is highest for the most profitable divisions. The obvious implication is that investments for purposes of cutting costs might be accepted in one division which would be rejected in another. While the use of differentiated average rates of return for different divisions, with their different market positions, seems rational enough from the viewpoint of profit maximization, the same is hardly true for the use of differentiated marginal rates of return.

We can see from the preceding examples that company policy has been the determinant factor in the choice of investment projects. Company F1 has given precedence to cost-reduction investments, Company F3 to output-expanding investments, and the French electrical equipment firm to capacity for new products. Company F4 in our case studies of Part II stressed the purchase of equipment in order to reduce marginal costs in the future, even when the return on such investments seemed likely to be negative. Company F6 relies upon a "fair shares" approach for the allocation of investment funds between its various departments. Investments in Division I of Company F5 have been heavily affected by the organizational concept that each major product line should have its own specialized capacity and that, if the line is to prove viable, its sales must be developed to the point where this specialization is economical. In short, the judgment of investments by rate-of-return criteria

[3]See the example cited for this company on page 105.

seems to be a comparatively unimportant factor in investment decisions. It is not just that opportunities have to be evaluated and that different individuals are bound to make varying evaluations; this is inherent. Rather, what is interesting is that different companies employ varying criteria for making these evaluations; policies are laid down which guide the individuals examining investment alternatives, and guide them differently in different firms.

The heart of the matter would appear to be both the degree of uncertainty as to financial results inherent in long-term and even medium-term investments, and the resulting major extent to which investment calculations are subject to a judgment factor. Enterprises might attempt to handle this problem by strong efforts at standardizing the degree of optimism employed by the various proposers of investments, and by studying closely the results of the various investment proposals that are adopted. But this is a most difficult route, particularly because the return from an investment does not only depend upon the quality of the project but very much upon the amount of managerial effort devoted in current operations to realizing the expected return from the individual project.[4] All those companies observed, except for the French firm F1, chose instead to rely primarily upon strategic decisions that amounted virtually to the setting of quotas for different kinds of investments.

Moreover, within a single company, there is great stability over time with regard to the strategic lines followed. Undoubtedly, this is partly because of a stability in the basic market situation facing the individual firm. But much more important, I would hazard, is the difficulty of evaluating the likely success of alternative investment strategies—particularly since all find their justification only in long-run results. Given this difficulty, there is little incentive to change strategic lines once they have been determined.

The comptroller of Division I of the British Company B3 summed up the problem of decision making in the view that the return-on-capital criterion cannot be given operational significance in his division. When considering minor issues of pricing, stocking, and production of individual items, the product range of the company is too large for cost and capital data to be detailed to the level of the individual product except through strong and obviously erroneous assumptions. In such matters, the problem lies in the fact that the accounting data are not sufficiently accurate to be useful. When it comes to consideration of major issues, the accounting data are sufficiently

[4]See B. R. Williams, "Information and Criteria in Capital Expenditure Decisions," *Journal of Management Studies,* September 1964, pp. 116-127, especially pp. 126-127.

reliable; but since they relate to the short run, their implications are completely overshadowed by company policy. Thus the objective of profit maximizing never, in his experience, has provided much guidance in decision making.

Attitudes and Enterprise Planning

Now let us turn to the much more interesting question of the effects of basic values and attitudes that distinguish industries in different countries. This issue will be handled within the framework of company planning and linked to the concept of "satisficing" as it has been developed by Herbert Simon. Beginning with a general treatment of planning within a profit-maximizing context, I shall then examine the different kinds of enterprise planning employed in our four countries.

Satisficing is a construct that has been developed in opposition to the traditional economist's assumption of maximizing. As Herbert Simon has described it: "Administrative theory is peculiarly the theory of intended and bounded rationality—of the behavior of human beings who *satisfice* because they have not the wits to maximize."[5] The crux of it is the notion that firms engage in a process of search for projects which promise to yield them a satisfactory profit, and that they cease the search when they have found a project or a solution to a problem which they believe is satisfactory. The level of what is defined as satisfactory is linked to past experience through the managers' aspiration level. When experience has shown that a brief and easy search will yield a satisfactory solution, the aspiration level will tend to be raised; the reverse is true when a lengthy search process has proved fruitless.[6] The satisficing process approaches maximization asymptotically in static equilibrium.

In the foregoing approach, the term profit is used as a proxy for the matrix of those goals incorporated in the managers' welfare function. If we take the simplest case of a firm that is concerned solely with the interests of its stockholders, profit is used as a proxy for increases in the present discounted value of the expected future earnings of the company. But what happens if we restrict the definition of profit to the operational meaning incorporated in

[5]H. A. Simon, *Administrative Behavior* (second edition, Macmillan Company, New York, 1957), p. xxiv. Emphasis is in the original.
[6]See H. A. Simon, *Models of Man* (Wiley, New York, 1957), Chapter 14; J. Margolis, "The Analysis of the Firm: Rationalism, Conventionalism, and Behaviorism," *Journal of Business,* July 1958, pp. 187-199; H. A. Simon, "Theories of Decision-Making in Economics and Behavioral Science," *American Economic Review,* June 1959, pp. 253-283.

the firm's profit-and-loss statement, and limit it to the short run of one or a few years?

If we employ this restricted definition, it is immediately obvious that successful attempts at profit maximization would keep the present discounted value of the expected future earnings of the company (i.e., present worth, as it shall hereafter be referred to) below the level which could be attained by alternative policies. This is because our definition of profit takes no account of intangible investments. As an extreme example, maintenance would be postponed wherever possible beyond the time period under consideration in the treatment of profit. Since companies do in fact operate with the preceding restricted definition of profit,[7] a maximization strategy would be a decidedly inferior one.[8]

The problem of intangible investments is a difficult one to insert into a profit-maximizing matrix. Physical investments in land, buildings and equipment are nowhere treated as deductions from profits—although the practice of rapid amortization approaches such a treatment. But what is one to do with those expenditures which are written off as current expenses but which are in fact necessary accompaniments of growth or of future improvements in operations? Or how about expenditures undertaken to ensure against possible futurities? All of these constitute expenditures which may be fully justified by their effect on the present discounted value of the expected future earnings of the company, but which can have only a depressing effect on the current profit picture. How far a company should go in pushing ahead with such intangible investments is a decision that is normally never subjected to an accounting test of observed effect on long-term profitability. Yet it is precisely these intangible investments which provide much of the underpinning for the view often heard in Europe that it is the top management of ten to twenty years ago which is most responsible for the financial results currently achieved by a company.

The presence of intangible investments in all spheres of corporate activities, and the fact that normally no attempt is made to isolate them in the accounts from other expenditures that are truly operating expenses, make for great

[7]Or, at best, with minor modifications thereof to take account of such factors as the difference between fiscal and "technical" depreciation.
[8]See the comment of Richard F. Vancil of the Harvard Business School concerning a business case in which quality standards fell: "It may be that part of Pollard's problem is the result of too much pressure on division managers to improve their current profit performance. If the division managers have reacted to this pressure by reducing the quality of their products, the responsibility for their actions can only be traced back to top management itself." (Intercollegiate Case Clearing House, Case 10C55S, p. 4.)

difficulties in attempts to take decisions rationally on the basis of accounting data. The same must apply even to decisions based on approximations to marginal cost and marginal revenue.

Take, for example, a decision as to whether to meet increased demand by an expansion of a factory's labor force or through subcontracting of work outside the company. A comparison of the alternative accounting costs might show that subcontracting would be preferable. But expansion includes costs of hiring new labor, costs stemming from their lower productivity until the additional workers are trained and acculturated to that particular factory's regime, and perhaps discontinuities in expansion of overhead functions: all of which really constitute investments in growth which should properly be written off over an extended period rather than treated as expenses of the year in which they are incurred. Short of an attempt to weigh quantitatively the amount of the additional expenses which should properly be treated as an investment rather than as a current expense, some ad hoc procedure is essential if the investment constituent of the additional expenditures is to be given recognition. "Company policy" is the normal form in which such recognition is given.

It is extremely difficult to estimate the quantitative significance of such intangible investments. However, in the case of one of our French companies which engaged in no research, the *directeur général* made a calculation in one of his reports which indicated that operating expenses linked to growth constituted 7 percent of the firm's total value added. He estimated that 43 percent of these intangible investments were direct results of growth: training of added personnel, development and publicity for new products, and so on. Another 36 percent consisted of the effect of maintaining prices below the level which could have been obtained if expansion had not been a major objective. Finally, 21 percent were due to the wastage of raw materials and to reduced labor productivity which arose from the improvisations required in the interests of expansion. Even this estimate of intangible investments constituted an understatement, since it ignored the effect of expanding the sales force in the provinces as well as in Paris. Both the *directeur général* and the sales manager believed that growth could be just as rapid if the sales force expansion were concentrated in Paris, and that salesmen there would cease to require a company subsidy in addition to their commissions after two years as opposed to five years in the provinces. Nevertheless, expansion in the provinces was viewed as a useful form of insurance, on the ground that provincial customers are more loyal than are Parisians.

A similar example of a sales policy that could be explained only as an investment in security was encountered in a French automotive firm. Exports were pushed by this firm during a period of ten years, throughout which the company could have sold all of its production within France at a higher profit. The sales director who had formulated and executed this policy explained it as essentially due to the desire to protect the company's future by diversifying its markets. In view of the length of time during which this sales policy of "insurance" was continued, it is an excellent example of an intangible investment whose expected payoff was far in the future and was likely to be in the reign of a different *président* than the one who had backed the policy and who paid its costs, which were expressed in the form of a poorer profit record than would otherwise have been attained.

Given the importance of such intangible investments, a company that is under the firm control of its managers and is highly centralized in all of its operations might establish an extremely low aspiration level for its profits,[9] considering profit making simply as a constraint on its efforts to raise the present worth of the company. Thus the aspiration level for profits might be set at no more than enough to pay the minimum dividends which management felt it necessary to provide to shareholders; the level might even be negative for a time. The rise or fall of this aspiration level would not be a function of the ease with which it had been and could be met (as it is in the traditional satisficing model), but would instead be a function both of the future payoff expected from intangible investments relative to that from tangible investments and of the minimum profits believed essential in order to satisfy shareholders, to contribute to cash flow for financing tangible investments, and to attract the desired amounts of new debt and/or equity capital. The setting of too high an aspiration level for profits would have a negative effect on the present worth of the company. The aspiration level would be a target, and the achievement of either higher or lower levels could be regarded as a managerial failure.

Even in a highly centralized company, there would be a major objection to such a treatment of profits; namely, that top management would be deprived of an objective and observable efficiency standard by which it might judge

[9]Obviously this would not depend upon the absolute amount of intangible investments but rather upon the increase in the amount deemed appropriate for a given period compared to what had been realized in the past. In fact, other things being equal, if the monetary value of intangible investments is kept stable over time, one would expect a high level of such investments to be reflected in a high profit rate measured against the book value of tangible net worth. (I am indebted to Leonard Weiss for pointing this out.)

the company's performance and which would alert it to the need for changes in policy. Judgment would instead rest entirely upon the top management's own subjective evaluation of the changes that were occurring in the present worth of the firm. However, to the degree that decisions in the company were decentralized to middle and lower levels of management, the objections to this procedure would become far stronger. For top management would be deprived of a critical objective standard by which to evaluate the performance of its subordinates. Distinguishing between performance failure and a desirable rise of intangible investments would be extremely difficult. Certainly such useful control techniques as "management by exception," which rely primarily upon accounting data, would be ruled out.

How, then, can a company effectively use the accounting figures of profit both for measuring its own total performance and for evaluating the success of its constituent parts without abandoning proper consideration of intangible investments and thus distorting the direction of its activities? The approach commonly followed has been through financial plans. Since American firms have been the world leaders in developing the art of financial planning and comptrollership, we shall first examine the financial planning solution as it has been practiced in several large American firms where I have conducted interviews both in the comptroller's department and among line managers.

The first attempt at resolution of the problem occurs in the formulation of the annual company plan. Here, each division draws up its own plan, indicating among other things the profit it pledges to earn during the year and the other objectives (e.g., sales) which it is to meet. Similar plans are drawn up for the subunits within each of the divisions. Sometimes the starting point is a profit objective set for each division by corporate headquarters; sometimes each divisional general manager sets his own profit objective, but with awareness of the possible range which will be satisfactory to headquarters. In either case, there is likely to be revision and an iterative process of plan reformulation before the various divisional plans are accepted.

The summation of the divisional profit plans which is ideal from the viewpoint of corporate management might be conceived as the maximization of projected profits for the year subject to those constraints accepted by corporate management for reasons which include those of intangible investments.[10]

[10]We here and in the future will abstract from the corporate management's view as to the incentive effect upon divisional and lower management of tight versus loose plans. See Andrew C. Stedry, *Budget Control and Cost Behavior* (Prentice-Hall, Englewood Cliffs, N.J., 1960) and Holland Hunter, "Optimum Tautness in Developmental Planning," *Economic Development and Cultural Change,* Part 1, July 1961, pp. 561-572.

But this view would be mistaken, for at best only a few of the major intangible investments are included as objectives in the annual plan.

Thus one divisional comptroller in a company nationally noted for its development of financial controls argued to me that there is a contradiction between a very ambitious profit plan and the instilling of profit consciousness within management at the divisional level. His example was a cost-reduction project which his division was currently introducing in one plant, despite the fact that it was not included as an objective in the division's plan, and which would reduce divisional profits that year because of the launching expenses (e.g., interruption of production) which were written off to profit and loss. If the profit objective laid down for the division had been overly ambitious, then the division could not have afforded to introduce this project.

Similarly, in another company a plant manager indicated that he would make almost any necessary sacrifice in order to achieve his profit plan. A specific example given was that of eliminating items for control of air and water pollution which are expensed during the current year, regardless of whether he believed that it was preferable from the corporate viewpoint for the money to be spent now rather than in the future. A plant comptroller pointed out that if the plant's purchasing manager were given an ultratight budget, he could scarcely be expected to originate changes in materials specifications if these would raise his purchasing costs, even when the net effect on the plant would be that of cost reduction due to savings in expenditures on processing these materials. A divisional manager remarked that he could raise the year's profits at any time by reducing the number of national meetings intended for all members of management of the division, since the main contribution of such meetings was to morale.

It is perfectly true that all of these items might have been included as explicit objectives in the plans for the appropriate managers. But the difficulty with such a procedure would be fourfold. First, it would force senior management into an inordinately detailed examination of such intangible investments, thus defeating much of the purpose of decentralization of authority within the company. Second, it would rule out those specific objectives for change which had not been thought of at the time of the writing of the annual plan. Third, it must be remembered that units draw up their original annual plan proposals in the light of their knowledge of the profits expected by their superiors. If these expectations are pitched as high as seems normal in American business, the unit managers would not propose intangible investments whose incorporation in their plans might threaten plan realization in case of some mishaps.

Fourth, this procedure would raise a serious problem for the enforcement of priority objectives. As things stand, the profit plan of each unit in American companies seems commonly to be "written in blood"; thus corporate management can be relatively confident that when things go awry each unit will give preference to its profit plan over all its other objectives, and to the other written objectives over those not explicitly incorporated in the plan. If, instead, a whole host of minor objectives were given equal weight in the evaluation of managers, then there would be a much greater likelihood that profit plans would go unfulfilled. Alternatively, the annual plan might be fully specified: that is, drawn up so as to include not only all objectives but also their relative weights in the welfare function of top management. This would eliminate the difficulty in enforcing priority objectives, but it would probably be insuperably difficult for top executives to agree upon this type of completely specified company plan.

Since all intangible investments cannot be incorporated into the annual plan, and particularly not with appropriate priority weights, it would be unreasonable for corporate managements to attempt to design plans which maximize projected profits subject to constraints. Instead, companies typically establish a "satisfactory" level of profits as their profit objective. In the determination of this satisfactory level for any given unit of the company, senior management can of course trade off the prospect of higher profits in the given year against the advantages to be gained in the future from both specified and unspecified intangible investments which would be expensed in the current period. The profit plan as finally accepted can usefully be conceived as representing the result of such a tradeoff on the part of senior management. It is in this fashion that intangible investments are given their due weight in the annual plans.

Viewed from this perspective, "satisficing" takes on an entirely different significance than that given to it by Herbert Simon. In the traditional approach, both satisficing and maximizing are applied to the firm's objective function; thus satisficing is viewed as an operational means for approximating a practicable degree of maximization. In the approach outlined earlier, satisficing and maximization are both applied to the accounting profit data rather than to the objective function which must also, at a mimimum, include the intangible investments. As a result, satisficing and maximizing behavior become operationally distinguishable, since they reflect entirely different attitudes toward intangible investments.

So much for the planning process itself. But what happens in the course of carrying out this plan, when events will inevitably give the lie to many of the specific expectations upon which the plan was based?

It is my impression from those large American companies in which I have held discussions that both the divisions and the lower units typically regard their profit plans as representing simultaneously a minimum and a maximum objective. When things go well, extra income is used for intangible investments.

Thus the comptroller of one large division reported that his division achieved its profit plan in five of the past six years, and in the sixth year missed it by only 10 percent. This was possible because the divisional profits plan always incorporated a hedge against uncertainty. However, despite the existence of this demonstrated hedge, the division never turned in a year's profits that were better than planned—although this did occur for individual parts of the year. In its operations, both the divisional management and the managements of subordinate units treated their profit objectives purely as constraints. Additional funds were used to promote growth, mainly through expenditures on research and on the advertising and promotion of the division's products. This attitude toward profits remained constant despite the fact that there was a high turnover of personnel at both middle and top managerial levels within the division.

In another company, whose business was highly cyclical, a similar situation was observed. But here the profit plan for a manufacturing division did not call for an absolute amount of profit, but rather for a stated variable profit per unit of product. (Here, variable profit per unit is defined as revenue minus fixed costs minus variable costs, all taken per unit. Fixed costs per unit were defined for purposes of the profit calculation as total fixed costs divided by a "normal volume" of output rather than by the actual volume produced.) The statement of the divisional profit plan in these terms is what provided the possibility for the divisional management to take this approach to its profit targets.

It was only in a third company, considerably smaller than the other two and divisionalized for barely some three to four years, that realized divisional profits were allowed to exceed the profit plans. In this company, each division was given a separate budget for each function and was not allowed to exceed any of these expenditure budgets without central corporate approval.

By this device, corporate management could prevent the divisions from expending their "excess profits"; thus it retained control during the course of the year as well as at the time that the annual plan was established. However, decentralization was correspondingly limited, and the situation was probably a transitional one toward truer divisionalization.

We may conclude that, in fully divisionalized companies, senior management above the divisional level seems to have little ability to convert unexpected returns to divisions into above-plan profits for the planning year. The sole exception, important as it frequently is, occurs when the corporate management feels a cash bind and cuts the budgets of all divisions or freezes their manpower levels. Similarly, during the course of the year such senior management has only limited scope for maintaining intangible investments in a division by reducing the divisional profit plan when unexpected events occur. Profit plans are never achieved through the realization of all the assumptions of the plan but rather as a result of counterbalancing unanticipated extra costs with extra savings or earnings. Thus, while corporate headquarters may adjust the profit plan for very major contingencies, the whole host of minor ones are treated as "imponderables" that are to be compensated by unanticipated savings; if any other practice were followed, profit results would always fall below plan. Senior management is forced into a posture of discontinuous control over operations, with its capability for exercising trade-off between profits and intangible investments being largely limited to the period during which annual plans are approved. For the remainder of the year, the profit target of each division and subunit is a relatively untouched satisficing goal; inferior or superior performance or good fortune affects largely the intangible investments rather than the year's profits.

The foregoing limitations on control by top management help to explain why company "personality" is so important in determining the tradeoff between profits and intangible investments which is made when the subunits draw up their annual plans for approval, and even more in explaining which intangible investments are expanded or contracted during the course of the year. One American plant comptroller, for example, believed that a critical aspect of his function was to help assure that the individual department managers in the plant took a view of their function which was consistent with general company policies. As he said, he must watch that the maintenance department does not attempt to establish standards that would be appropriate for a Rolls Royce factory rather than those which the plant can "afford." Obviously, what it can "afford" is a matter of policy.

The real choice is not that of whether the tradeoff between profits and intangible investments as well as between profits and other equally ultimate goals will be made on subjective grounds, but rather that of whether there will be some degree of consistency between the terms of this tradeoff in different parts of the company. It is the role of company policies and personality to provide this consistency.[11]

Satisficing as a Maximizing Model

The foregoing system of satisficing-planning can be described as a system of instructions to the subunits of the firm to operate within a set of constraints: profit, volume of sales, market share, etc. However, although the central planners of the company have an objective function, no such objective function is given to the managers of subunits as guidance in their carrying out of operations.

Another way of describing this satisficing-planning is as a very curious form of maximizing model, in which the managers of the subunits are instructed to maximize the objectives Y under the constraint of reaching established goals for the objectives X. But it is the objectives X that are the critical ones for the enterprise (profit, etc.) and thus are stated in the plan; the objectives Y—which are the ones to be maximized subject to constraints—are all the residual goals of the company central planners, and thus are left unspecified.

If one ignores the organizational aspects of the problem, this would appear on the face of it to be a completely insane solution. It is the less important, rather than the more important, objectives which are to be maximized subject to constraints. Furthermore the plan provides no weighting system according to which the subunit manager can evaluate the relative significance of the various $y_1, \ldots, y_n$ objectives. Each individual manager must provide his own personal weighting system, guided here only by company policy and personality.

This American planning system is in marked contrast to the Soviet, which is a normal maximizing model subject to constraints. There the individual subunits (the enterprises in the Soviet case) are instructed to maximize one or another x_1 objective[12] subject to the restraints of a few specified $x_2, \ldots, x_n$

[11]Philip Selznick has pointed to the importance of an organizational personality and of a "systematic formulation of its own meaning and significance" in the case of the Tennessee Valley Authority. "Inside the organization," he reported, "strenuous efforts are made to indoctrinate all who are involved in administration on a policy-affecting level." (*TVA and the Grass Roots,* University of California Press, Berkeley and Los Angeles, 1949, pp. 21, 30ff., and 50ff.)

[12]Today, this x_1 objective is normally profit; in some cases, it is volume of output.

objectives and of the unspecified y objectives. Substantial and immediate bonuses are paid to the management team of the subunit in direct proportion to its achievement of the x_1 objective, provided that the $x_2, \ldots, x_n$ constraints are met.[13]

Until the end of 1965, the $x_2, \ldots, x_n$ constraints in the Soviet Union constituted a very large number. But, in practice, it proved impracticable to enforce them. If all the constraints stated in the annual plan for the enterprise had been followed, the enterprise management would have had too little room to maneuver in its maximization of its prime objective. Thus both the enterprise management and the plan-enforcing bodies tended to ignore these constraints. At the end of 1965, the system was modified by sharply reducing the number of specified constraints to roughly between four to eight. The result has been that many of the central-planner objectives for the individual enterprises are left totally unspecified and uncontrolled, and even then it has been extremely difficult to enforce the remaining constraints. A system of maximizing the principal objective has proved inconsistent with the desire to pursue other objectives as well.

One way of interpreting this difference between the American and Soviet modal systems of planning is to say that the Russians place their stress on a "logical" organization, in which the maximization process is devoted to the priority criterion, while the Americans are much more intent on developing a system that is less tidy but functions better in terms of human reactions to it. The Russian system follows an engineer's concept of rationality, and attempts to mold human beings to it. American company top managers are much more concerned with human relations problems and with shaping a structure that is adapted to the managers who actually exist. Thus the Russians "maximize" the priority criterion while the Americans "satisfice" with regard to it. This reflects both the differences in education of top managers in the two countries (almost solely engineering in the case of Russians compared to a considerable variety for the Americans), and the traditional Soviet belief in the malleability of human nature.

A supplementary interpretation is that the American corporate planners have greater confidence in their ability to shape rational and demanding plans, and thus are content when their subordinates meet the planned objectives. The Russians, on the other hand, place their stress on "overfulfillment of the plans"—continuing, although in a reduced form, the slogan of the

[13]See the treatment of Soviet managerial bonuses in Chapters 9 and 11.

1928-1932 national plan of "Fulfill the Five Year Plan in four years." Soviet leaders seem to believe that there are substantial resources that remain untapped by the plan; resources that can best be mustered by placing great stress on the exceeding of the planned objectives. Given this view, they are naturally anxious that these "reserves" be devoted to the priority tasks rather than to the subsidiary ones. Thus "satisficing" plays little role in their thinking.[14]

Both the American and Russian approaches, however, share the common feature that they stem from the view that the future is subject to specific analysis and molding. Furthermore, they are both activist in the sense of applying the doctrine that at least the minimum targets for priority objects must be met regardless of the pressure which this places upon managerial ingenuity and upon traditional practices and relationships in all spheres. In sharp contrast, the British firms that I have observed seem to have been motivated by quite a different philosophy in their annual financial planning.

The British firms in my case-study sample are similar to the American in the sense that they have had plans that call for a given profit from each division. But the meaning of these profit targets was radically different, in that central headquarters were quite unable to carry out any rational and detailed trade-off between profits and intangible investments at the time of developing the annual plans. The reason for this was the lack of serious and detailed planning and control by the headquarters organizations. Extreme decentralization was the order of the day, and headquarters staff personnel were numerically few and content to leave most decisions to the divisions.

Thus British profit planning takes two forms. One of these, as exemplified by Company B1, is the setting of quite arbitrary rate-of-profit goals for divisions and subunits—with little analysis of the implications for company profits as a whole of high targets for individual divisions and plants. In this procedure, intangible investments emerge as a residual with no one seriously exercising any informed judgment as to their proper level.

The second form is that of rate-of-return targets which are perceived more as goals toward which the divisions should shoot than as objectives which the divisional managers must meet under pain of dismissal or other punishment. Here, it is the divisions or lower units which exercise the tradeoff between profits in any given year and intangible investments or other goals which the

[14]See David Granick, *Soviet Metal-Fabricating and Economic Development* (University of Wisconsin Press, Madison, 1967), Chapter 7, for a fuller theoretic treatment of Soviet planning.

divisional managements might have. Their financial constraint is, at best, that their average rate of return on assets over an indeterminate number of years must be at a level which will satisfy senior company management. In the case of Company B3, even this constraint seemed to be missing.

In both cases, since central management has made no effort to exercise financial control of the type observed in the American firms, and since it has not been staffed to do so even if it had so wished, decentralized decision makers have had little guidance except for the combination of arbitrary constraints and the direction given by broad company policies. While formal plans exist, either they are not formulated in quantitative terms and with specific dating of the objectives or they are not taken seriously by the company top management. In either instance, their influence seems minimal.

How explain the fact that, in contrast both with American "satisficing" and Russian "maximizing," British company planning seems to be reduced to the minimum needed for coordination? That beyond this minimum, it seems to degenerate into sheer formalism? That, in particular, it is at its weakest in profit planning, despite the fact that profits are taken as the key criterion of success?

The first explanation is that this is part of the general pattern of decentralization of decision making found in large British companies. While, clearly, company-wide strategic decisions must be taken—particularly with regard to investment, dividend policy, and the raising of funds from outside—it is not essential that central headquarters should engage in the detailed analysis and control of its component units which is inherent in serious profit planning of the sort that we see in American firms. It is possible to allow each subunit to proceed on its own within the limits of broad strategic guidelines and of centrally-determined investment allocations, and with cognizance of the fact that headquarters may react by the removal of the top managers of the unit. This appears to be the typical British pattern, and is the form which British decentralization takes.

Such decentralization, peculiar to Britain among the four countries examined here, stems partly from the specific British solution to the suboptimization behavior of middle management which is a result of the career patterns prevalent in British industry. Since this behavior will be discussed in Chapter 3, no further treatment of it will be given at this point.

Also important, however, is the absence of professionalism in British management. As we shall see in Chapters 3 and 7, British top managers have, as a rule, a good deal less education than do those in other countries. Moreover, unlike their American counterparts, their experience tends to have been concentrated fairly narrowly within a single function. They regard themselves as production men, accountants, marketing executives and the like—but only incidentally as managers. Although a good deal of change has occurred in this regard in recent years, British top managers still have the self-image of their job being little more than the top of the ladder in their particular function. Management as such is only slowly coming to be regarded as a profession.

The absence of professionalism finds its expression particularly in the failure to develop systematic plans and controls over the work of other managers, especially over those heading multifunctional units. Not only has there been no feeling of a strong need for such headquarters work, but the know-how to carry it out effectively has been largely lacking.

A second explanation for the absence of profit planning is the attitude toward middle and lower managerial personnel. As we shall see in Chapter 9, British managers at all levels—except possibly the very top—are quite poorly paid compared to those either in the United States or on the Continent. But compensation is found in the reduced work pressure. The British Company B3 is only slightly atypical in that normally no sanctions were employed against managerial personnel at any level who did bad work, and that a division which finally ousted a department head for gross incompetence had to agree to permanently pay one-third of his salary in another division where his new post would not otherwise have permitted the continuation of his previous salary.

As we have seen, an essential part of American planning is that the profit plan of each unit in a company is "written in blood"; it is the extreme pressure upon the managers of the units and subunits to fulfill their "satisficing" targets which makes it possible to have confidence in the plans. Where this pressure is missing, plan targets degenerate into "goals," and no one is shocked when results fall short of them. But the demand for results which American managers expect would be resented by British managers just as bitterly as imposition of an American work pace on the factory floor would be resented by blue-collar workers. British top executives take a relatively relaxed attitude toward both groups. One consequence of this attitude toward managers is the absence of serious planning.

The third explanation lies in the strength throughout the British working force, from top management to unskilled labor, of resistance to rapid change of any sort. One might think that planning would be easier under relatively stable conditions than under highly dynamic ones, and in a sense this is true.

The problem is, however, that no company's plan is ever achieved in any country through the realization of all its underlying assumptions. Things always go wrong; and it is up to management to make unplanned changes in other dimensions of its activities in order to compensate for the failures that have occurred. The greater the resistance to implementing such rapid-fire change, the more severe are the constraints under which the managers of subunits labor in their efforts to fulfill plan targets. When the constraints are as sharp as those in British industry—and we shall see examples of them in the case studies of Part II—it is difficult for anyone to take planning seriously.

If profit planning in the sample of British firms studied has been only formalistic, it has been virtually nonexistent in the French companies. The most that can be said for their use of the profit criterion in planning is that some divisions and smaller product groupings have been under pressure to reduce absolute losses below the level at which they had been previously. Nor, since the French companies operate in a capitalist environment, has any other planning criterion been substituted for profitability at the level of the component units of companies.

One principal reason for this failure to develop subunit plans expressed in terms of targeted profits is the managerial reluctance in large French firms—if not in small ones—to show high profits.[15] The principal ground for this is the fact that top management has been principally recruited from graduates of *grandes écoles*,[16] and especially from those graduates who have first served a span of years in government service. These executives, even after entering private business, remain deeply imbued with the ideals of national service and with the objectives of high rates of investment and of growth in production for the sake of the country rather than for the long-run good of the stockholders.[17] The notion of a "fair return" rather than the maximum feasible

[15]Unfortunately, it is not possible to rely on aggregative national statistics to demonstrate that large French firms in fact earn a lower rate of profit than do enterprises in other countries. The problem is that, as will be seen later, French profit figures are so greatly distorted for tax reasons that it is not possible to compare them to the American or British statistics. However, aggregate balance-sheet data for the four hundred most important French firms indicated that the ratio of net profit to the book value of shareholders' net assets ranged between 3.9 and 4.5 percent during the years 1965-1967. (François Simmonet, "Le financement des investissements dans les grandes entreprises," *Economie & Statistique*, January 1970, p. 28.)

[16]The *grandes écoles* are a tiny number of relatively small higher educational institutions that are outside of the framework of the universities.

[17]See David Granick, *The European Executive* (Doubleday, Garden City, N.Y., 1962), Chapter 5. The dominance of this viewpoint appears to be a post-Liberation phenomenon, and its significance had declined considerably by the second half of the 1960s when it was accepted in big business circles that the realization of the Common Market and the

return to stockholders has remained as the modern counterpart of the Church's earlier insistence upon a "just price."

One top executive whom I interviewed considered that this attitude toward profit represented what he called the postwar socialization of spirit in France. Himself heavily influenced by American business attitudes, he believed that one of his most important functions was to restore the quest for profitability to a major position in the welfare function of the middle managers under him. Yet even this man accepted as basically sound the view that making profits was somewhat shameful; his insistence was primarily upon avoiding the losses with which parts of his company were faced.[18]

This attitude toward profit seeking is most firmly encrusted in the top prestige *grande école* managers of companies in which shareholding is widely dispersed. But, since this is the top prestige group of French management, their acceptance of the "socialization of spirit" ideology gives it considerable status and helps it to permeate even the ranks of family managers. Thus I found it openly expressed by one successful family manager who failed in the competitive *Polytechnique* examinations, had then had to settle for a univer-

---

widening of international capital markets compelled greater attention to profit making. But it was clearly of overwhelming importance through 1964 in most of the firms I have studied, and was still of major significance in 1967.

[18]It is true that French companies have been very deeply interested in their cash flow on the ground that this provided part of the wherewithal for investments and growth of output. (Cash flow equals net cash revenue after the payment of current expenditures, excluding dividends. Depreciation rates, reevaluation of fixed capital or of inventories, and the creation of reserves from income that would otherwise be treated as profits have no effect on cash flow except to the degree that they reduce tax obligations.)

But this interest in the financing of investment has not compelled a deep concern for high profits. Retained profits have been of negligible importance in such financing. (See, e.g., Simmonet, "Le financement des investissements," p. 26. While no evidence is presented by Simmonet for this viewpoint, it is one which seems to be universally held in France.) The sale of stock has been considerably more important, but such sales have almost invariably been on a "rights" basis under which existing stockholders receive the right to purchase additional shares at a price below the market level. So long as these rights have a positive market value, the successful marketing of the additional stock is assured. One company financial director told me that he did not wish to sell new stock at a price below book value, but that this was his only constraint on how low he could allow the company's dividends and thus its profits to fall.

Very important in this regard is the fact that borrowing has been a much more important source of external finance than has the sale of additional stock. For the four hundred most important French firms, only 30 percent of the funds raised from outside the companies during 1957-1967 came from new stock issues, while 46 percent came from increases in long-term and medium-term debt and 24 percent from increases in short-term debt (*ibid.*, pp. 22-23). The strong interventionist role of the French Government in determining the recipients of loans has made the ability of an individual company to borrow relatively independent (compared to the situation in other countries) of its profit position.

sity education, and thereafter had directly entered the firm. Acceptance of this ideology is one means of establishing a link with the truly prestigious elements of French business.

A second reason for the failure to use profit planning within the company is the far-reaching and traditional emphasis within French business on minimizing the tax burden. The 50 percent profit tax in France has an effect in this regard which seems totally incomparable with the effect of the same level of taxation in the United States. When one combines the desire to avoid profit tax, the fear that high profits would only invite socially approved wage demands by a labor force that interprets high profits as proof of exploitation, and the wish to avoid the social disapprobation that would accompany more than "just profits," it is no wonder that profits are heavily "managed."

While small companies can and do widely employ fraud to reduce their declared profits, this is much less feasible for the large firms. Nor is it really necessary. The French tax system not only employs what is now the internationally conventional system of rapid amortization, which permits expected profits in any year to be sharply modified by the amount of investments made in the same year, but it is also replete with various kinds of reserves—payments into which are not counted as profits—and with permissible reevaluations both of fixed capital and of inventories. Since the French company can choose, within limits, the most favorable years both for the reevaluation of assets and for the payment of income into reserve funds, it is only the careless financial director who would show high profits in any individual year.

Thus the showing of large short-run profits is widely regarded in France as evidence of financial incompetence. A significant part of a financial director's job is to assure that declared profits do not exceed a "satisfactory" figure set by top management. As one financial director put the matter to me, the profit figure to be declared for the year is customarily computed at the beginning of the fiscal period rather than at its end. The tax collector's office is said to go along on the grounds that it believes it gains more from the value-added tax on expanded turnover than it would from reducing investment by siphoning off funds when they are earned.

Unfortunately for good business practice in large French firms, these financial manipulations are generally accompanied by the use of only a single set of books. As a result, French methods of financial management provide a highly unfavorable milieu for attempts to judge investment projects or divisional activities according to the profits they earn. While it is feasible to do so on an *ex ante* basis, accounting figures are too widely suspected—within the company as well as outside—to provide a useful basis for evaluation of results; and, of course, *ex ante* analysis has only very limited value when all parties concerned are aware of the fact that it will not be checked on later. Thus accounting procedures reinforce the ideological tendency to denigrate profit making as the prime objective of the enterprise.

Perhaps it would be possible to develop other, nonfinancial criteria of plan fulfillment by subunits within large French companies, but any attempts at such planning would come up against the love of secrecy by upper echelons of top management. Although it is quite true that I have found top French executives surprisingly free in discussing their business affairs with a foreign university professor, such frankness is rarely met with regard to managers in the same company. With good reason—as we shall see in Chapter 3—there is considerable mistrust of the middle levels of management, and information is carefully guarded from them. Thus, in one company that appeared quite typical in this regard, the director of the main plant in his division was allowed to know the profit plan for his factory; but the plan for his division was treated as a company secret which he had no "need to know."

In another enterprise, an annual plan was drawn up for purposes of planning investments and coordinating the financial resources and requirements of the company. This plan document was kept a carefully guarded secret, with only the top fifteen men in the company having access to it. But when I learned that each year the planned investment expenditures were higher than the actual ones, and when I expressed amazement to the company comptroller that he permitted this systematic bias to continue, he assured me that this deviation between planned and actual investment existed only with regard to the formal plan which had to be communicated to the large number of fifteen executives, and not at all with regard to the "serious projections" that were known only by the president and two others.

Thus all French company planning, like French decision making in general, is highly centralized. Of course, annual plans are developed for purposes of coordination of the activities of the company. However, being developed only at a high managerial level, and with only the essential pieces of it being communicated to middle management, this planning bears no real relationship either to the American or Russian setting of targets. Superficially, the system seems most similar to the British; but the two differ fundamentally in that British current decision making is highly decentralized while the French is extremely centralized.

Nevertheless, one might ask whether the French approach does not provide a real advantage over the American. American firms are so organized that, at most, the tradeoff between short-run profits on the one hand and other objectives and intangible investments on the other is determined discontinuously on a once-a-year basis. Even at these times, the profit plans for the year are heavily influenced by the historical record and by a conventional fixed percentage improvement factor. The French, on the other hand, since they either do not develop or do not hold seriously to divisional profit plans, are in a position where they can continuously reexamine the terms of the tradeoff in the light of the changing environment. Thus their approach is more flexible. The high degree of centralization minimizes the danger that the terms of the tradeoff will be greatly different in the various divisions, a type of inefficiency which is apparent enough in the British system.

It is my impression, however, that this French advantage is more than outweighed by the problems involved in departing too far from quantitative analysis. The American emphasis upon meeting specific and ambitious short-run profitability goals tends to compel a serious analysis of policies which appear attractive but which are injurious to short-run profit performance. In the absence of such precisely stated goals that clearly either are or are not met, it is all too easy for managements to avoid grappling with the question of how much they are willing to pay to achieve nonprofit objectives. There is much less pressure upon managements to determine, for example, what they are willing to give up in profits for the safety that may come from a highly diversified product line or from markets in the provinces or abroad. In short, a cost-benefit analysis of different goals and policies is less likely to be developed under the French than under the American system of management.

One might think that we should also point to the greater ease of defining "poor performance" of specific managers under the American type of financial planning, in which profit plans are relatively sacrosanct, than under systems in which the success criteria are considerably vaguer. Certainly there is something to this argument, but I would not give it great weight because of the rapid movement of American managers from job to job within the same company, and the resultant difficulty of evaluating their performance in any single post.[19] Moreover, even in American firms it is difficult to specify the reasons that lead to a verdict of "poor performance."

Up to this point, we have discussed company plans as though they were all

[19]This point will be developed in Part III.

one-year short-term plans. But this is not at all true in the case of the American managements interviewed, where three- to five-year integrated plans have been the rule for some time. On the other hand, such long-run plans are only now coming into fashion in Britain and France, and none of those about which I have heard are taken seriously by their company managements. As of 1967, not one of the European firms interviewed was doing more than experimenting with long-run integrated plans that might or might not become serious endeavors in the future.

Long-run plans provide a guide for such financial policy as that of dividend distribution and the timing of stock and bond issues, and for such personnel policy as the recruitment and training of managerial personnel. But their special significance in the context of our discussion can be treated under two other headings.

The first is that of providing a time period long enough to permit at least many of the intangible investments made in one year to be translated into profits by the final year. Through the use of a multiyear analytic system, the possibility of intelligently exercising a tradeoff between a single year's accounting profits and the same year's intangible investments is significantly increased.

The second is that it provides a sharper focus within which to examine the advisability of change of policy. A company engaged in long-run planning is less likely to keep a profitless venture operating without making a detailed analysis of when its finances are likely to turn around, and the need for making a cost and revenue projection for such a business during each of the following five years leads very quickly to focusing managerial attention on the problem. Similarly, general overhead costs of the company are much more likely to be reduced if a five-year analysis shows little likelihood of the company's averaging "satisfactory" profits than if this is indicated by only a one-year analysis.

The prime significance of these two features is that long-range plans are most valuable for those companies that are relatively willing to undertake significant change in their policies. Long-run planning can be used to suggest that current programs are unlikely to lead to satisfactory profit results, and that either something new must be tried or a segment of the company's existing business should be dropped. In short, a willingness on the part of top management to accept change is essential if the necessary effort involved in developing long-run integrated plans is to prove worthwhile. In the absence of such willingness, managements are much more likely to be impressed with all the inevitable uncertainties inherent in five-year projections and to hold that such plans are too fragile to have any value.

It is the presence of strong constraints on change in the European companies which probably explains the absence of long-run planning there. Thus the top management of the British company B3, with its basic antipathy to "reforming" management at the divisional level, could gain nothing from long-range planning except a sad awareness that the profit picture of its Division I was unlikely to become satisfactory. Similarly, the more the constraints as to reductions in staff or in the number of hourly workers, as to the products which the company can properly produce, or as to the proper locations for its factories—the less can be gained from long-run planning except a feeling of unhappiness. Since the British and French firms studied are far more bound by such constraints than seems to be the case for the typical large American concern, it is understandable that they have not engaged seriously in integrated long-range planning.

One might argue that, in a perfectly competitive economic system, variety in company policies and personalities would be reduced over a number of years or decades by the exigencies of the struggle for corporate survival. Changes in the environment over time reduce the force of this argument. For any actual capitalist economy, the existence of market imperfections further reduces the case. Nevertheless, the survival argument, combined with the spreading of a single managerial philosophy within any given business community, do tend to some degree to standardize company personality within a single country.

However, the force of these arguments is considerably weaker when they are applied to comparisons of different countries. The competition for markets and for capital funds is far milder among corporations based in different countries than is that within a single country. Thus there appears to be a tendency for varying modal "company personalities" to develop in different nations and to be retained there. This, in fact, is what we shall be able to observe in the case studies of Part II.

It is true that the heavy movement of American firms into European operations, combined with the internationalization of capital markets through such devices as the Eurodollar market, may in due course homogenize national differences. But, at least so far as France and Britain are concerned, the existence of modal national company personalities seems still to be very much a fact of life.

3

Reward Systems, Career Development, and Suboptimization

In Chapter 2, I concentrated on organizational policies and procedures used in different countries and linked these to values that are widely held among specific strata of managers. In this chapter I shall examine the effect of motivation and personal experience on the behavior of different levels of management and, because top management is likely to adapt the organizational structure of the company to the behavior patterns which it has come to expect, on the degree and nature of decentralization.

For example, it should be expected that the French national feature of virtually restricting top managerial posts to *grande école* graduates would have its effect upon the career horizons of other company managers, and thus upon both the initiative that they show in their decisions and the degree to which they subordinate personal noncareer goals to what they perceive as company goals. It would seem a reasonable hypothesis that the social fact of restricted promotion within French management should thus influence the decisions and behavior of the company. Similarly, the extreme decentralization of the British companies to be described in the case studies of Chapter 5 is not accidental; it derives, in part, from the managerial traditions of a country in which even today a large portion of top management is recruited from men who had ended their formal education at the minimum school-leaving age, and who are quite aware of the limited scope of their managerial experience and horizons.

It is useful to begin this chapter with a treatment of Soviet industry. This is because suboptimizing behavior on the part of enterprise managers is very richly expressed in both the domestic and foreign literature dealing with the Soviet Union, and because such behavior is peculiarly important in the functioning of the Soviet economy. Since suboptimization is a basic managerial problem in most countries, it is appropriate to begin with a strong case of it. I shall then proceed to examine the same problem in Britain, France and the United States.

Much of Soviet managerial history can be written in terms of the efforts to develop success criteria for enterprise managers which would cause them to act in the fashion desired by executives in the ministries and in other higher organizations. Because the entire Soviet economy is linked administratively into a single organizational network, the problem can properly be viewed as one of suboptimization: Soviet enterprise managers pursue the interests of their individual enterprises rather than that of the larger organization of which the enterprise is only a part. The Soviet leadership has seen one of its major tasks as being that of reconciling the interests of the enterprise with that of the economy as a whole.

The suboptimizing problem takes a wide variety of forms: misleading data and opinion transmitted to higher authorities in the effort to obtain a lower enterprise plan than would otherwise be forthcoming; the slighting of quality in order to reach a higher measured output; the production of undesired proportions of different types of products so as to achieve output and profit targets under conditions of fixed prices that are only weakly related to demand. Investment funds are demanded by all organizations, and many projects are begun with what turns out to be inadequate funding in the justified expectation that more funds will later be added by the state in order to avoid scrapping the project; as a result, investment programs have taken unconscionable periods to complete. Managers have strongly and successfully resisted the starting up of new products in their plants, with the effect that Soviet industry has consistently been slow in adopting product innovations.

The problem has been stated by Evsey Liberman, presumably as a reflection of the orthodox Soviet viewpoint, as consisting of the need to link more effectively the interests of the individual manager to those of society. Certainly this is a correct general statement, but a major portion of the problem can be fully analyzed in more malleable terms: namely, the need for an improved reconciliation of the interests of the manager with those of his organizational superiors. Once described in this narrower fashion, the problem can be viewed as one of managerial organization rather than as one encompassing all aspects of the economy including the satisfying of final consumers.

Writing about internal control within large American companies, Professor Learned and his coauthors have pointed to the "fallacy of the single criterion" (profit in their case) as a means for judging managerial success.[1] They argue that the use of any single operational criterion for measuring performance leads to actions in direct conflict with broader goals held by the senior company management. Any rigid definition of managerial success within the organization results in suboptimizing behavior.[2] Soviet experience appears fully to justify this view.

[1]E. P. Learned, C. R. Christensen, K. R. Andrews, and W. D. Guth, *Business Policy* (Richard D. Irwin, Homewood, Ill., 1965), pp. 684-689.
[2]Richard F. Vancil of the Harvard Business School also writes that "It is fairly easy to make a dramatic, temporary improvement in profits simply by cheapening the product in unobtrusive ways, cutting back on expenditures for research and development and

Top Soviet leadership has consistently, at least since 1940, given primacy to the view that the intensity of managerial effort is the behavioral aspect which most needs encouragement. This view has found expression in the persistence of a system of high bonuses, awarded to all levels of enterprise management on the basis of short-run results. Total monthly or quarterly compensation for engineering and managerial personnel can vary between periods for a given individual by as much as 30 to 40 percent (depending upon the industry), and there have been times in the past when the variation has been even greater.

Soviet managerial behavior would appear to be best described as directed towards maximizing the bonuses received by the enterprise.[3] Partly such behavior is forced upon the top management of enterprises by the need to provide such economic rewards to engineers and to junior and middle management if the better personnel are not to be lost to other enterprises; an enterprise that fails to earn high bonuses is soon bound to become unsuccessful by any standard.[4] Thus Soviet managers seem to have concentrated almost entirely on the achievement of superior performance by their enterprises according to the particular narrow standards used in determining the level of bonuses.

In actual practice throughout the period since the early or middle 1930s, and even in theory since 1965, the position has been taken in the Soviet Union that enterprise performance must be defined narrowly in terms of one or a very few objective criteria rather than through subjective post hoc evaluation by superior executives above the level of the individual enterprise.[5] Presumably, it has been believed that economic incentives will work effec-

---

advertising, and not hiring any new management trainees. The long-term results of these actions may not show up for several years, but in the meantime the division manager who was able to achieve the profit improvement may have moved on to bigger and better jobs, leaving his successor the unwelcome task of trying to equal or better the profit performance of his 'successful' predecessor." (Intercollegiate Case Clearing House, Case 10055S, p. 3.)

[3]Such maximization, however, occurs over a number of periods. Enterprise managements take account of the fact that overly high performance in a single period will lead to an increase in targets set by higher authorities for future periods, and thus in a reduction of total bonuses received during a longer time span.

[4]Personnel in the Soviet Union are free to leave one enterprise for another. Furthermore, standard salary scales—although, of course, with ranges—are set centrally for all enterprises in a given industrial branch; the director of an enterprise has little freedom to use higher salaries as a means of compensation for low average bonus earnings.

[5]As was discussed in Chapter 2, this definition of enterprise performance has called for the maximization of results according to a single criterion (or two at the most), subject to meeting restraints established by only a very few other criteria. The system used in establishing bonuses has been one of "maximizing subject to specified restraints" rather than that of "satisficing."

suboptimization within individual British companies has a content similar to that within the Soviet economy as a whole.

A frequent situation found in British firms, however, is one in which there are a number of functionally integrated units that sell either (or both) to the outside market or to other units within the company. In such a firm, the management of each unit can be judged according to an estimate of the long-run profitability attained. In this case, suboptimization occurs when each unit ignores the contributions—whether they be positive or negative—of its own activities to the profitability of other units of the same company.[7] This kind of suboptimization is rather different from what I have described as applying to the Soviet enterprise.

While suboptimization in the Soviet Union is related to the bonus system employed, the same is not true in Britain. Bonuses play no substantial role in British companies. British suboptimization can, however, be associated with the nature of managerial careers. Since bonus and promotion systems comprise alternative (or complementary) forms of incentive frameworks for managers, the parallel between my previous analysis of Soviet bonuses and my forthcoming analysis of British career patterns is obvious.

Differences between suboptimization in large British, French and American companies correspond to the differences in managerial career paths in these three countries. But, as we shall see, a particular nation's solution to the suboptimization problem can create other difficulties of equal magnitude. It is to an analysis of this situation in the three capitalist countries that I shall now turn. However, I shall deal only very sketchily with the actual career situation in these three countries, since this will be developed at length in Part III.

Management Selection and Replacement

A basic decision to be made in any large company is that of how management is to replace itself: how it is to select new managers for the company and on what basis it is to promote individuals to top positions. It is my hypothesis that the considerable variations in national prototype solutions to this problem are to a substantial degree responsible for national differences in mana-

---

[7]This is a classic problem of "externalities": external to the individual unit but internal to the company as a whole. While in a formal sense it would be quite possible to apply the concept of externalities to Soviet enterprises as well, it does not seem to me that it would be a particularly fruitful approach. This is because of the radically differing nature of prices and of "profits" earned by Soviet enterprises from those observed in a market economy.

gerial behavior. Unfortunately, each country represents only a single observation in my sample: having only four such observations, it is clearly impossible for me to test this hypothesis in any serious fashion. The hypothesis must thus be treated simply as an interpretation of the observed data for four countries, and as still awaiting testing against materials from other nations.[8]

Both middle and upper management in large British industrial companies are recruited to a smaller degree from either a social or educational elite than is the case in any of the other three countries. One large British sample indicated that only 38 percent of upper-middle managers had had either public school or university education—and this in a country where public school education is extremely widespread among the middle classes.[9] In other samples in which almost one-third of the managers had received a university education, the average age at which the managers had started work was eighteen to nineteen; thus many must have stopped their education at or close to the minimum school-leaving age of fifteen. In five out of eight samples, less than 15 percent of middle and top managers had begun their careers in any of the three types of posts of professional, managerial trainee, or manager.

Thus it can be seen that there has been very little preselection at the time of entrance into the firm of those young men who are to constitute the future middle and top management. The characteristics of middle and top managers differ little from those of junior managers, and these in turn are more similar to those of ordinary white-collar employees than is the case in other countries.

British managers appear to be chosen on the basis of their job performance and promoted on similar grounds. Here is an ultrademocratic tradition of promotion according to performance, with performance being judged primarily by the man best placed to evaluate it—i.e., the immediate superior. It is also a very practical tradition, with managers typically spending their entire

[8]One might suggest testing the part of the hypothesis concerning the importance of career patterns for managerial behavior, although not the part dealing with national prototypal solutions, through comparison of different companies within the same country. However, it seems to me that the prototypal solution adopted in a country has greater importance in explaining managerial behavior in a given firm than has the particular solution adopted within the firm itself. This is due to the powerful cultural effect on the behavior patterns of individual managers, and the fact that this cultural effect is determined more by the prototypal solution than by the career patterns found in the individual company. If I am correct in this, then we might expect that, although managerial behavior in an individual firm is affected by that firm's career patterns, the effect is minor and would not become apparent except under more sensitive testing than can be easily done.

[9]The public schools are the private and fee-paying portion of secondary education.

significant career within a single function and narrowly defined industry (since not only interfunctional but also interdivisional transfers appear to be restricted). Thus managers are given the greatest possible experience in the work which they are directing.

The result of this system seems highly effective from a motivational standpoint; since performance on the part of junior and middle managers is rewarded by promotion, it is likely to be forthcoming.[10] On the other hand, this is a system that strongly encourages suboptimization.

The problem here is the need to demonstrate results, and results of a sort which are apparent to one's own immediate superior. As there are many potential competitors for higher posts, these results must be exceptional. Normally, this means results within a manager's own narrow function (which is also his superior's function), or at most within a single narrow product division of the company. The absence of any significant role for headquarters personnel in contributing to the evaluation of performance is an important ingredient in the lack of concern throughout the organization for the good of the company as a whole.

The fact that managers have not had previous work experience in functions other than their own, nor worked in headquarters levels higher than their present one, further contributes to this environment of suboptimization. For neither the manager nor his superior who evaluates and promotes him has been sensitized to the legitimate needs of other functions and units in the company. Thus the manager finds it natural to operate as independently as possible.

The company's top management might either accept this situation or work to integrate the company's activities. Normally it adopts the former posture. For top managers have themselves come up this same managerial route, and view themselves more as practical men specializing in a particular function and product line than as "managers" of a total operation. Having had only limited varieties of functional experience, they are hesitant to interfere too deeply in the workings of the individual units. Moreover, they can observe that the organizational system of the company "works" in the sense that each of the units operates reasonably effectively when judged as an independent entity, and thus they feel minimum pressure to change the system.

Thus British central company headquarters are typically quite weak. Headquarters is often virtually restricted to such policy functions as distributing

[10]However, the low salary differentiation between different levels of managers—at least until one reaches the very top—has a reverse motivational effect that strongly modifies this positive aspect of the career system.

investment funds among units of the company and deciding on dividend policy, and to such technical functions as the handling of company borrowing and of the cash balances of all units. Even with regard to those policy functions that can be fulfilled only centrally, determination of policy often appears quite casual. This is related to the tradition that it is the individual unit within the company which really counts, and that headquarters' functions and personnel should be developed as little as possible.

In short, the procedures used for the selection and promotion of managers in typical large British companies lead to a system of uncoordinated decentralization of operations. To the degree that the different units are structured so that they can function independently without disadvantage, the system works effectively. But difficulties arise as soon as harmonization is necessary (as is clearly the case in Companies B1 and B3 of Chapter 5), and especially when the traditional rights of a single unit should be sacrificed for the good of the company as a whole.

The French solution to the problem of managerial recruitment and promotion is diametrically opposed to that adopted in Britain. The French effectively dispose of the suboptimization problem but only at the price of precipitating other malfunctions.

In the large industrial companies, each managerial rank has virtually its own educational requirement. It is not simply completion of higher education that is demanded from aspirants for middle and top management, but rather graduation from one of a small number of *grandes écoles* that have very difficult competitive entrance examinations. Furthermore, in the case of the most prestigious of these *grandes écoles,* it is not graduation alone which is important but rather graduation within the top 5 to 10 percent of the class.

The degree to which this educational requirement is pushed can be seen from observing the education of the top executive officers (an average of 1.8 per company) in the private firms that are among the one hundred largest industrial concerns in France. After excluding the few companies in the food, textile, and paper industries—industries that are relatively nonprestigious and where top management is heavily chosen on the basis of family—two-thirds of the top executives of the remaining firms were graduates of six fairly small *grandes écoles.* Forty-two percent were graduates of one of these alone, an *école* that had graduated only 0.08 percent of the total French male population over the age of twenty-two. When one considers that a goodly portion of the remaining one-third of the top executives had qualified at least for candidacy status on the basis of their family connections, one can appreciate the degree to which top management is preselected at the time of entry into the firm.

Another way of viewing the same subject is to consider those graduates whose class rankings in the most prestigious *grande école* had made them most eligible for top executive positions. Of the total number of these graduates working anywhere in industry—whether in large or small, private or nationalized companies—one-fifth of the appropriate age cohort held one of the top 1.2 posts in one of the five hundred largest industrial firms in France. It would be difficult for a man with this sort of educational record to end his career with less than a vice-presidential position.

This is a system in which admission into managerial ranks, as well as the level of management to which one can reasonably hope to attain, is virtually predetermined at the time of entry into the company. Evaluation of performance within the firm plays a role only for promotional selection among men with narrowly equivalent levels of education. Competition among managers within the company is at a minimum.

Given this promotional pattern, minimization of the degree of suboptimization seems assured. Graduates of the most prestigious *grandes écoles* are sufficiently few in French industry so that, wherever they may stand in the company hierarchy, they can be assured of the direct attention of the company president. Since they are virtually certain of reaching at least the lower levels of top management whatever they may do, their career ambitions—if they have any at all—are firmly fixed on the top two or three posts. In order to realize this sort of ambition, they must demonstrate from the beginning that they think like a *président-directeur général*. Suboptimizing behavior would be the height of folly for such managers.

Similarly, vigorous suboptimizing behavior should not be expected of the middle managers from the lesser *écoles*. This is true first of all because it is the men of the *grandes écoles* who set the pattern, as it is they who do the evaluating of other managers. But second it is because these lesser managers are effectively cut off from the posts of higher managerial responsibility, and thus no behavior on their part within the company is likely to make a really great difference to their careers. Nor does a system of bonuses exist to inspire them. Thus vigorous suboptimizing is simply not worth the trouble even if it were consistent with the social mores set by the *grande école* executives.

Of course, this does not mean that the managers from the lesser *écoles* carry out their duties in such a fashion as to optimize the economic results for the company as a whole. Rather, being placed in a situation where they feel stripped of the possibility of satisfying career ambitions, and feeling that the traditions of French management provide them with a reasonable shelter against dismissal, they are in a position to exercise their functions in the fashion most appealing to their professional pride. (It is true that they could also choose the solution of doing as little as possible of anything—but this does not, in fact, appear to be a widespread behavioral pattern.) For them, neither the carrot of bonus or promotion nor the whip of demotion or dismissal is sufficiently real to overcome their traditionalist professional approach and to lead them to pursue the goals of the company's top management. Here, in a sense, are the true technocrats of France.

Thus the French promotional system succeeds in avoiding the British sub-optimization pattern. It also brings into the top management posts men who view themselves as managers, rather than as narrow specialists, and who have the self-confidence and experience that permit them to take far-reaching decisions. But the price is high. Middle managers cannot be counted upon to work either for the goals held by top management or for suboptimizing objectives which would at least promote the well-being of the individual units in the company. Instead, their goals seem quite divorced from company objectives of any sort.

In this situation, despite a high level of technical competence of middle managers, French company administration can only be highly centralized. In truth, top managers can trust only themselves and a few younger graduates of their own *écoles*. But since the large French companies are much too big to be run effectively in this manner, they often give the impression of being out of control.

The American solution to the problem of selection and promotion of managers is of a third type, quite different from either the British or the French. Like the French, it squarely meets the problem of suboptimization; but the American disadvantages, while it is possible that they are serious, are quite different from those of the French.

Today, quite unlike the situation in Britain, a college degree is almost a requirement for a candidate for middle or top management in a large American company. In the 1950s and 1960s, the proportion of top executives in large corporations with college degrees was eight to twelve times as high as was the case for all American males of their generation. Furthermore, a substantial proportion of top American executives had done their under-graduate work at one of three schools whose alumni reached such posts in proportions somewhere between three and six times that of alumni of American colleges as a whole.

Here is a far greater degree of preselection of managers than occurs in Britain, but it is still a world apart from the French pattern. When one considers the high proportion of college graduates among American males, and particularly among junior managers, the problem of selecting candidates for higher positions from among the junior management and professional personnel within the company is still a major problem for American managers. The task has not already been done for them by the educational system as is the case in France.

How, then, is suboptimization minimized? One major means is by the frequent transfer of executives both between functions and between units within the company. For example, using a fourteenfold classification system of functions for a sample of middle and top American executives, it was found that 45 percent of those who had been in their company for more than ten years had worked there in at least three different functions.

This frequency of transfer serves a twofold purpose from the viewpoint of hindering suboptimization. The first is that an executive virtually has to succeed in making such transfers if he is to be upwardly mobile; but he has little chance of being acceptable to these other groups if he has been serving his own function and unit exclusively and at their expense in the past. The second is that executives become acquainted with the problems and needs of other company bodies than the ones in which they are currently serving and thus are likely to take a broader view of their tasks.

A second major means of reducing suboptimizing behavior is through the use of headquarters organizations. Quite typically, managers are rotated through either or both divisional and company headquarters at quite an early stage in their careers; while employed at headquarters, they can be judged according to their ability to work successfully as part of a team on interfunctional and interunit problems. Furthermore, even while employed in field organizations, their career route is heavily influenced by the recommendations of headquarters' specialists from different functions. The suboptimizing executive is much more likely to destroy his own career than to promote it.

But this system would be totally infeasible without the rapid movement of the executive from post to post. Of a sample of almost three hundred upper-middle and top executives in a number of large companies, 80 percent had averaged three years or less in each of their positions in the company since the age of thirty-five. Furthermore, this brevity of tenure applied even to such positions as plant manager and divisional general manager, where two-thirds remained for no more than two years. Only with such a rapid rotation policy can there be achieved the extensive cooperation among managers which one sees in American firms.

The costs of this rotation would appear to be twofold. First, everyone is continuously learning on the job and is unlikely to fully master one position before he is transferred. Second, due to the rapidity of transfer, it is extremely difficult to evaluate properly the results actually achieved by an executive in a specific position. Thus, much more than in the two other countries, promotions must be determined on relatively subjective grounds; promotion on the basis of results (à la Britain) is much more difficult to implement. As a consequence, American executives are probably much more sensitive to company politics than are managers in other countries.

Company Planning and Career Patterns

Let us now turn back to the problem of company planning that was discussed in Chapter 2 and see what our examination of managerial career patterns can contribute to the issue of these behavioral national differences.

The formalism of British company planning follows from the acceptance by top management of the extreme decentralization built into the system. Middle management is sufficiently motivated so that it can be allowed to run its own units quite independently. Top managers come to their posts with a narrowness both of education and of career experience which make them reluctant to interfere.

But there is more involved than this. Given the way that British managers are judged for promotion, and the resultant suboptimizing tradition, one might well ask whether more serious planning by headquarters would not do more harm than good.

As was pointed out in Chapter 2, headquarters' plans can never include all of the objectives held by top management. The restricted scope of the plans does comparatively little harm in American firms, where headquarters staffs can directly concern themselves both with those intangible investments that are not covered in the plans and with the degree of cooperation given by units to other functions and units. The way in which promotions are determined in American firms assures that American junior and middle managers will not suboptimize by directing their efforts solely to the plan objectives stated for them.

However, there is nothing similar preventing suboptimization in the British promotional system. Currently, British suboptimization takes the form of attention only to the needs of one's own unit; but at least there is not strong suboptimization in favor of immediate profitability results at the expense of the future. If central plans were both set forth in an ambitious fashion and taken seriously, one might well see much more suboptimization with respect to time. Furthermore, the pressure for still greater suboptimization with respect to other units in the company would be further increased.

The absence in France of planned targets that are widely disseminated among middle managers is partially a reflection of a centralization which is fully justified by the technocratic attitude of middle managers. This attitude, in turn, would appear to be a product of their lack of career opportunities.

In evaluating the absence of American-style planning in France, one should recognize that such planning is a form of decentralization. It amounts to giving targets to individual units within the company, and then providing the unit managers with a good deal of freedom in determining how they will reach these targets. Moreover, it implies that these managers will themselves be allowed to determine supplementary targets of intangible investments. The more detailed the decisions that are taken centrally, the less necessary or meaningful are global targets set for individual managers.

But this type of planning presupposes that unit managers are properly motivated to the achievement of top management's targets. Where this assumption is unjustified—as it would appear to be in large French companies— there is little basis for this or any other sort of decentralization.

The planning observed in American large companies is itself related to a substitute for centralization (alternatively, one might choose to define it as a particular form of centralization) that does not exist in the other countries discussed. This substitute consists of that continual reexamination of managers' potential which is implicit in a system of frequent transfers to different functions and units.

Headquarters staff is heavily involved in this reexamination process. Through its promotional decisions, it provides a constant guidance as to the sort of managerial activity which is desired.[11] In this fashion, functional staff personnel can perform much of the directional role which in other nations can be carried out only by means of instructions from line superiors. This

[11] A striking example of this is the one to be cited in Chapter 10, where promotions of managers in one large American company were found to be totally unrelated to the evaluation ratings given to these managers by their immediate superiors.

system can be used to assure that managers give heed to those company objectives which have not been spelled out in their unit plans.

I conclude that it would be a serious mistake to believe that such a technique as American-style satisficing planning can usefully be transferred—at least in isolation—to other cultural settings: even to those of west European countries such as Britain and France, which are relatively close in overall cultural patterns to that of the United States. American corporate planning has evolved as an adaptation to a very specific managerial environment, and it might be quite out of place in countries with different traditions of managerial rewards and career patterns.

The Case Studies

Chapters 5 and 6 present nine case studies of large British and French firms. They are intended to evaluate the influence of managerial behavior upon the improvement of factor productivity in each enterprise during a period of more than a decade. Taken together, the two chapters display the differences in typical managerial behavior between the two countries and they show the effects of these differences.

The introductory Chapter 4 presents the case for why these nine firms may be considered a representative sample of large scale, private, and purely nationally managed industrial firms of Britain and France; it argues that case studies which constitute such a sample can properly be used as a data source which permits the testing, and not simply the formulation, of hypotheses. It also summarizes the behavioral differences between the two countries which emerge from the case studies of Chapters 5 and 6.

4

The Function of the Case Studies

Part II of this study is devoted to the presentation of nine case studies of British and French companies. But while use of the case-study form is a well-established method of writing about business enterprises, my objective in offering these cases is rather different than the usual one. My claim is that the composite of these cases represents typical behavior on the part of large, private British and French companies, and thus that one can use these cases as a basis for generalization about this universe of firms. Clearly this is a bold claim that requires justification, and much of this chapter will be used for presenting my case. In addition, this chapter will summarize some of the conclusions that can be drawn from the specific cases.

As was explained in the Introduction, the motif of this book is the effect of national value systems and managerial-selection-and-reward systems on the rate of increase in productivity in large industrial companies. The intermediate variable is that of managerial behavior in these companies. Statistical data regarding national differences between managerial-selection-and-reward systems are available, and these will be presented in Part III. Similarly, statistical data regarding national rates of change in labor productivity in industry as a whole were presented in Chapter 1, and these might be used as a rather weak proxy for the variable of changes of labor-plus-capital productivity in large companies. The particular value systems themselves may be taken as "common knowledge" within the countries concerned. But how can we explore the intermediate variable of managerial behavior and of managerial contribution to productivity increase, and how can we examine the effects of one variable upon another?

For the United States and the Soviet Union, neither of which lie at the heart of this study, I have taken a relatively casual approach. Here I rely primarily on the written literature and, in the case of the United States, on a first-hand investigation of only a few highly specific problems in a very small number of firms. But something better was needed for British and French industry.

For these two countries, I have relied upon a highly detailed study of ten British and French companies and a briefer study of six others. In all of these firms, I concentrated upon the examination of managerial behavior itself, upon its links backward to the value systems both of managers and of the society as a whole, and upon its links forward to the managerial contribution to the rate of increase in the company's labor-plus-capital productivity.

Clearly, this raw material is quite subjective, filtered as it necessarily is through my own impressions and interpretations. However, aside from this caveat, I feel no need to defend its use. What other source exists for dealing with these problems?

More serious is the problem of my generalization throughout this book (and especially in Chapters 2, 3, 11, 12, and 13) on the basis of this material. Do the cases analyzed justify the generalizations? It seems only fair to present the reader with as much evidence as possible to allow him to make up his own mind on the matter. This is the prime function of Chapters 5 and 6, although a subsidiary purpose—which I hope will be even more important to some readers—is to present the rich intertwining of factors that lead to the development of specific companies within their specific national environments.

Since this material is one of the two principal data bases of this study, it is essential that *all* of it be presented. Thus I have chosen to burden the reader with the presentation of case studies of individual companies, rather than with a digest of what I feel are particularly relevant aspects of their behavior. It is only in this way that the reader can have any means of evaluating my generalizations from the material.

However, of the sixteen company studies made, only nine are presented. The six companies in which time did not permit of a thorough analysis were eliminated automatically. A seventh firm was also eliminated because statistical data were available only for one plant whose results were quite unrepresentative of those of the company. No further selection has been exercised in determining which company histories to present.

All nine of the case studies presented are treated within the same analytic framework. The company's average annual rate of change in factor productivity (output divided by a weighted average of labor and capital, all measured in constant prices) is presented. (See Appendix A to this chapter for a description of the methodology.) Thereafter, managerial behavior in the company is examined in terms of its effect upon improvement in this factor productivity.

The justification for this approach is obvious enough. Since my eventual interest is in the managerial portion of that chain of behavioral relationships which finally affects the rate of increase of industrial productivity in a nation as a whole, it seems reasonable to approach the problem in the same way on the microeconomic level of an individual company. It is my macroeconomic interest which dictates that the criterion used for measuring managerial effectiveness be the change in factor productivity in an individual company.

However, there are three objections to this treatment which deserve comment.

The first objection is that, whatever the management of a particular company may be trying to attain, improved productivity for its own sake is a most unlikely goal. Is it reasonable to evaluate managerial effectiveness by a criterion other than that accepted by the management itself?

The answer, it appears to me, is that it all depends upon the purpose of the evaluation. If the objective were to give grades to the different managements, then the only justification could be that improvement in factor productivity is a useful proxy for the management's own goals. Indeed, to a limited degree such a justification could be defended. But since my objective is not to grade the different managements, it is perfectly appropriate that I use an external criterion which is relevant to our broad concern, namely, the effect of managerial behavior upon macroeconomic efficiency. (However, in order to provide additional information relevant to evaluation of management by a microeconomic standard, I have also given profitability data where they appear to be reasonably reliable.)

The second objection is that I am inconsistent in my pursuit of the macroeconomic objective. A company of above-average productivity may make its greatest contribution to improving national productivity by increasing its share of the national market at the expense of less productive competitors, rather than by improving its own factor productivity. Yet I ignore completely this issue of company growth in measuring its change in productivity.

This second objection is well founded, and I can only plead practical grounds as an excuse for this inconsistency. I have no means of estimating the overall factor productivity of the industry in a fashion which would be consistent with that used for the individual company, and thus I cannot tell whether a faster than average rate of growth in output by the company represents a contribution to growth in national factor productivity. Thus I have chosen to ignore this issue in general, although I do treat it in the case of Company F1.

The third objection is that the quality of management, like any other factor of production which is left out of a given production function, is relevant to the absolute level of measured factor productivity but not to the rate of change in this productivity. Thus we should not expect managerial behavior to make a contribution to the rate of change in a company's productivity.

This issue has already been dealt with in Chapter 1, and the argument will not be repeated here. The reader should recall, however, that the argument hinges both upon the importance of the speed of adaptation to changing conditions as an influence upon the rate of growth of factor productivity, and upon the peculiar contribution of the quality of management to this adaptation process.

A different kind of problem in the presentation of the case studies is that raised by the need to avoid the identification of individual firms. Access was arranged on the basis of confidentiality, but with the individual firms neither requesting nor receiving any rights of censorship. Despite the self-restraint of the managements of these companies, the problem of confidentiality of data is one with which I have had to wrestle throughout the writing of these cases. Confidentiality is important to the managers interviewed not so much vis-à-vis the general public but more with regard to competitors and potential competitors and in relation to colleagues within their own companies: i.e., to knowledgeable insiders. One manager, for example, objected to the first draft of my case study of his company on the basis that it would permit identification of the firm by some company personnel who knew me by name and were aware that I had visited the enterprise over an extended period during the relevant years. Protection of the identity of the firm against such individuals places severe limitations on what may be written.

The procedure adopted in handling this confidentiality problem was threefold. First, the industry of each firm is identified only very broadly, although correctly; this is essential in view of the fact that all of the companies studied were chosen from among the largest firms in their own industrial branch. Four firms, each of which is in quite a distinct branch, are identified in the respective case studies only as being in the metal industry; "metal" is here defined broadly to include the production of iron and steel and nonferrous metals, the manufacture of machinery and metal products, and the electrical and electronic industries.

This inability specifically to identify the industry imposes some severe limitations. First, it makes it impossible for the reader to relate these case studies to the interesting hypothesis that company organizational structure is greatly influenced by the nature of the technology employed.[1] Second, it prevents me from saying much about the market conditions in the industry.

The second procedure followed is that some of the materials as to managerial background and behavior in individual companies are not included within the case studies but are instead distributed elsewhere in the book without identification of the individual firm even by its code number. The price paid is the impossibility of relating to one another all the different

[1]For the fullest development of this hypothesis, see Joan Woodward, *Industrial Organization: Theory and Practice* (Oxford University Press, London, 1965).

aspects of a given company's managerial background, behavior, and market and production position. This loss of richness in permitting the full re-creation by the reader of individual case studies is regrettable, but it is not serious in hindering an examination of the hypothesis laid down in the Introduction as to the linkage between national differences in managerial backgrounds and behavior. Of course, we are deprived of any information which would permit a differentiation between the two hypotheses that it is national or company differences in managerial background which matter. But, for reasons explained in the Introduction, the raw data themselves would not permit any differentiation between these hypotheses.

The third procedure was that of submitting each of the case studies to the respective company for vetting. This had the additional advantage of permitting the correction of some errors of fact.

Probably the chief loss resulting from the confidentiality problem is the fact that there is comparatively little discussion of the market conditions in which the particular cases are embedded. Market power is a neglected subject. However, while this loss is certainly serious, its significance for our purposes is minimized by the fact that my interest is primarily in relating managerial behavior to changes in factor productivity rather than to profitability or share of the market.

Selection Criteria

The three British and seven French firms that were studied in depth are taken as representing the universe of each nation's large-scale, nongovernmental manufacturing enterprises that are completely national in character. In evaluating the degree to which my sample may be considered representative of this universe, it is useful to begin with a discussion of the criteria that I had in mind when selecting the firms.

These criteria were the following: 1. All of the enterprises were to be in manufacturing and were to be among the largest of their branch in their country. 2. Each firm should be an entirely private as opposed to government-owned enterprise, and its managerial and ownership base should be completely within the country. While it might have subsidiaries abroad, or subsidiaries in its own country which were jointly owned with a foreign company, such joint subsidiaries must constitute a very minor portion of the firm's total activities. 3. The firms as a group should cover a broad gamut of manufacturing. 4. Each firm should be willing to make available to me statistical records of the performance of one or more major, and reasonably homogeneous, sectors of the enterprise. 5. There should be nothing in my source of entry to the firm's management which would raise a question of atypicality. 6. Each enterprise was to be reasonably typical of the larger firms of its branch, both with regard to its economic performance over time and to the backgrounds and attitudes of its top management personnel.

In fact, these criteria were met to the following degree:

1. Of the seven French firms, four were among the top one hundred French industrial firms as measured both by value of sales and value added, and two were among the second hundred largest. The remaining firm had under one thousand employees, but was in a sector of manufacturing where none were much larger. The three British firms were all among the top two hundred industrial companies. All enterprises except for one French firm had more than one plant.

2. All of the firms were completely private, and all had solely national management. Nine had completely national ownership and control; one French firm was subject to a recent substantial minority ownership by a non-French but continental group. Two had subsidiaries that were jointly owned with foreign firms, but in both cases the subsidiaries were of minor significance to the parent firms. Five firms had subsidiaries abroad, but in only one case were these of quantitative significance to the parent firm.

3. Industries represented by the ten firms were of nine quite distinct types. Two were in different consumer industries. Two others were in various light producers' goods industries. The remaining five industries were all within the general category of metal as defined earlier.

Employing a United Nations subdivision of manufacturing into twenty-one sectors, the prime sectors of the firms that were studied totaled 60 percent of the wages and salaries paid in manufacturing in Britain and France. (See Appendix B to this chapter.)

The supplementary interviews conducted during 1963-1964 were with firms in the chemical, automotive, paper, and building materials industries.

For purposes of national comparisions, it might well have been preferable to have studied matched firms from identical industries in each country. This possibility was investigated, but it proved impossible to find such companies which met the other requirements and were also willing to make the substantial effort involved in cooperating with me. Thus I opted for the alternative of breadth of coverage.

4. All firms provided data as to output, labor force subdivided into several categories, fixed capital, and inventories. These were made available on an

annual basis for periods ranging between seven and sixteen years.[2] For five of the ten firms, the activities of the entire company were covered in these statistics, and one of these five also gave data as to a major sector of the enterprise. In the cases of the other five firms, detailed statistics were provided only with regard to a major division; but in all these cases, less detailed data were available as to the progress of the company as a whole.

Of the seven French firms, one is not written up as a case study. The reason is that the usable statistical data from this firm related solely to the seven-year history of a single factory that was built in the first of these years; the period covered was insufficient to provide a meaningful productivity series if this were to be restricted to the stage following the plant's reaching full capacity and overcoming its running-in pains. Treatment of this firm would have given a misleading impression of enormous productivity improvement.

5. My introduction into three of the French firms was from the same source: this was an association of presidents of large French firms. In the other seven cases, my introductions were all from separate sources. In all ten cases, my introductions came from nationals of the country concerned; moreover, in all ten cases, my first contact with the person offering the introduction was also through a national of that country.

6. The economic performance of the firms was compared with that of their respective branches of industry in their own country during the same time span. The average rate of increase in labor productivity was contrasted with that of the companies' respective industries as a whole, while the rate of return paid to investors was compared with that of other firms of their industries listed on the national stock exchange. The average labor productivity of the firms was 109 percent, and the average rate of return was 93 percent, of that of their respective industries. These figures do not differ significantly from 100 percent, although the smallness of the sample and the width of the scatter make the confidence intervals quite wide. (See Appendix C to this chapter.)

Two separate checks can be made of the representativeness of the backgrounds and behavior patterns of the top management personnel. The first exists in the very choice of the enterprises; each was recommended for inclusion in my sample by knowledgeable people in the country concerned,

[2]Four firms provided data covering seven to nine years, but the one whose data were restricted to seven years has not been written up in a separate company history. The data for three firms covered eleven years, and that for the remaining three firms ran between thirteen and sixteen years. The range of years covered by the data was 1950-1966, and for six of the companies it ended in 1966.

who used as one criterion for its recommendation the fact that its management was reasonably typical of those of the larger firms of its industry. The second check exists in the fact that the case studies were submitted to two particularly experienced management specialists from each of the two countries, with a request that they try to identify the companies analyzed. None of the four experts was able to identify any of the firms. One of the British experts suggested several possible candidates for each of the British firms; in fact, none of these guesses was correct. All the experts declared that there were many among the two hundred largest companies of their country which exhibited behavior patterns similar to those of each of the firms described in the case studies.

Hypothesis Testing through Case Studies

The material just presented is the positive evidence justifying generalization from nine case studies to a much larger population of firms. While I believe that the evidence is fairly strong, the unorthodox nature of the approach—and the objections which it has raised in the minds of some readers—seem to require a brief methodological discussion.

It is universally acknowledged that no type of testing can ever "prove" a hypothesis; a proposition can be subjected only to more or less rigid examination of the null hypothesis. But "more or less rigid" is a subjective concept, and it should properly depend upon a good deal more than the limits of confidence felt in the hypothesis. It must also depend upon an appreciation of the likely potential of confidence available from that or any other test methodology.

With specific reference to the value of case studies as a means of supporting the generalizations of this study, it seems to me that four questions must be asked:

1. Are the questions which serve as the basis for this study worth asking? If so, we should use those methods of analysis which are available.

2. Are there alternative feasible research methodologies? Most specifically, can macroeconomic econometric studies be used to answer these questions?

So far as I can tell, the answer here is negative. The nature of the available statistical data is not such as to permit such studies.

For example, an approach which comes immediately to mind as an alternative to the use of case studies is that of elaborating statistical tests of those national differences which may be logically deduced from the distinctions in national managerial behavior which are hypothesized in this study. Indeed, this approach has been followed to a very limited degree in Chapter 13. So far as they go, these tests do confirm the hypotheses. But it cannot be claimed that the tests are at all severe, and no great reliability is claimed for them.

The obstacles to developing convincing statistical tests are twofold. The first deals with the nature of the population studied. The enterprises concerning which I elaborate behavioral hypotheses are solely large-scale, nongovernmental, and completely national in the nature of their management. But the population of firms covered by national statistics is quite different: it includes all enterprises in the industry concerned. Thus we must test statements concerning a narrow category of companies by data that relate to a much broader population.

The second difficulty relates to the nature of the statistical data. For example, a comparision of managerial attitudes toward profit suggests that one would expect the rate of profitability to be considerably higher in Britain than in France. While, indeed, all figures point in that direction, such statistics cannot be regarded as offering any confirmation of the hypothesized difference in attitudes.

This is the case for two reasons. First, it is generally agreed that French firms go much further in hiding profits than do British companies. Second, the rate of profit taxation has been considerably different between the two countries. As a result of the latter consideration, it would not be possible to decide as to whether the proper comparision is pretax or posttax profits unless one makes quite arbitrary assumptions as to the degree to which the profit tax is passed on to the consumer.

3. Can the existing methodology be used substantially more effectively? One of the issues here is whether the problems inherent in the need for confidentiality can be better overcome.

4. Is the evidence presented of sufficient weight to be worth presenting at all? Presumably, if the evidence does not meet some minimum—although subjective—standard, it would be better to treat the subject completely nonempirically.

It is in terms of his answers to these questions that the reader must determine for himself what weight to place upon the case studies as a basis for generalization. In the social sciences, it has long been standard doctrine that it is impracticable to require for hypotheses evidence which has the same reliability as that obtained in the experimental physical sciences. If this demand were to be made, there would be virtually no hypothesis testing at all. Similarly, I would suggest, one cannot properly use the same standards of evidence in the treatment of different questions within the social sciences themselves.

Analysis of the Case Studies

Turning to the British case studies that will be presented in Chapter 5, Company B1 is a rapidly growing and quite profitable firm in a highly competitive industry. Its management appears very typical of the better category of British company: strong at middle and lower levels, but with very weak coordination exercised at the top. In contrast, Companies B2 and the division of Company B3 which is analyzed enjoy strongly oligopolistic market positions but nevertheless have been substantially less sucessful. B3 is particularly interesting because of the total failure of the division's vigorous and well-regarded general manager to draw it out of its sleepy behavior patterns; the managerial environment both above and below him was such that his reforms could accomplish little more than raising overhead and reducing profits.

All three companies have major similarities. In each of the three, the role of company headquarters and company top management is relatively unimportant; each of the companies operates as though it consisted of a host of small firms. The same phenomenon is seen even within the individual divisions of all three firms. In Companies B2 and B3, the functional responsibilities of managers are very narrowly defined, and the problem of their coordination is a difficult one. At least in Companies B1 and B3, the independence of different sectors within a division is a major source of weakness preventing adjustment to changing conditions. Since the division examined in Company B1 is highly successful, while the division in B3 was a flat failure during the years studied, it is particularly interesting that both managements should suffer to a marked degree from the same problem.

Both Companies B1 and B2 share the same financial problem of having difficulty in finding new investment placements for their undistributed profits. Both have been guided primarily by the desire to expand within their own industry so as best to use the know-how of existing management; yet the actual expansions in both have totally failed to meet this latter goal, despite the fact that the price was paid of concentrating investments in relatively unprofitable sectors. In Company B2, various top managers even felt that the same principle dictated the restriction that investments should not be made in other parts of Britain than the one region with which they were most familiar.[3]

Thus the most striking common feature of the three companies is the weakness of top management. It is notable that the only bold central deci-

[3]The parallel is striking between this attitude and that of English workmen who often seem to feel that their real alternatives are between remaining in their own district or emigrating; movement to another region is viewed as bringing all the losses of uprootedness without providing the advantages of a climate or standard of living equal to what

sions taken and executed were in Company B2—and here they consisted only of merger decisions that ended up having little except financial import.

In general, planning has been a highly formal function with little serious content. This is best seen in the case of the division of Company B3, where no dating is employed in the setting of divisional objectives.

Company B1 does use a form of parametric planning which in practice has had real content: namely, the insistence upon a stated rate of return in its major division. But not only was this rate of return chosen quite arbitrarily and never reviewed, but its effects have almost certainly been nefarious: it has led both to an apparent deterioration of product quality and stagnation of market share within the division, and to a much more rapid expansion of the less-profitable divisions of the company than of this relatively closely controlled sector. If this be planning, it is fortunate that British firms do not engage in more of the same.

Suboptimization is quite sharp in Company B1, finding expression both in the prices at which the various divisions sell to one another and in the relations between the various factory managers which leads to the temporary expansion of some factories while others are suffering from partial idleness due to lack of orders. In the division of B3 which was studied, the suboptimization by various functional groups went so far that the general director was hard put to see any solution so long as the division continued to be organized functionally, but because of the nature of its physical plant he saw no way to organize it in another fashion. Sales, engineering, and production all went their independent ways; engineering, for example, was quite uninterested either in the costs of operating newly developed machinery or in the development of new products that could reduce the burden of the division's overhead costs. It is true that suboptimization was not observed in B2, but the strict separation of functions there suggests that this was probably no more than a failure of observation on my part.

Both Company B2 and that division of Company B3 which was studied enjoyed strong oligopolistic positions. Yet neither has been as profitable as B1, which operates in a strongly competitive market. It is difficult to explain the difference except on the basis of the superior quality of management in B1. Yet in most respects, top company and divisional management in B1 was quite as poor as in the other two companies. Its central staff work was

could be attained by going abroad. Similarly, Company B2's management appears to take more kindly to the notion of investing abroad than to that of investing in other regions of Britain.

incompetent, and top management was unwilling either to make decisions and provide guidance to the organization or to reexamine rationally the lines of policy it had earlier laid down.

Rather, the strength of Company B1 was in its lower and middle management, which had made the company into a successful and innovative organization. It is true that the firm's top management must be given high marks for providing an atmosphere in which these levels of managers could exert their best efforts. But otherwise, the managerial accomplishments were all at the lower and intermediate levels. This supports the hypothesis that the vigor of British management in general is found at these levels, and that—given the total managerial environment of British industry—top management is well advised to leave great autonomy to its subordinates.

The French firms of Chapter 6 present quite a different picture.

Company F1 displays the extreme centralization of authority commonly found in *grande école* companies. Functional coordination occurs only at corporate level and there without the significant use of any corporate staff; the result has been an almost total inability to manage the development of the large number of minor products. The company's efforts have been concentrated entirely on the improvement of productivity and the reduction of costs, and not at all upon the marketing function.

At the same time, it should be noted that top management decisions played the key role in the very striking productivity improvements that occurred in F1. It is the reverse position of that in Company B1, where all improvements stemmed from the actions of lower and middle management.

The case of F2 throws a particularly sharp light upon the values held by French business. A merger was negotiated and carried through in a fashion that promised to increase sharply the profitability of the new firm—but at the expense of ruthless elimination both of managers and workers as well as of unprofitable products. The result was the merger's evaluation as a flat failure by those outside the company, and a 48 percent decline over three years in the stock market value of the company. A French top management that strives for profitability alone cannot be accepted, even by the Bourse.

Company F3 is radically different from F1. Top management's interest is in sales expansion, and not at all in cost reduction. But more important, a new administration, although recognizing the inefficiencies of the existing managerial system and resolving to change it, did little about it during a seven-year period. Resolute central decision making is absent here.

Yet the similarities are also notable. Lower and middle management is all purely functional, and coordinated only by the *président*. Although the managerial system that was created discouraged decision making, it stemmed from the attempt of the original *président* to keep all major decisions within his own hands. In order to do this, he fashioned an internal pricing system that he trusted would reduce the number of real decisions to the small number which he could make himself without staff assistance. It is true that the result was great decentralization of a peculiarly chaotic type; but the actual decentralization stemmed from the effort to achieve supercentralization, rather than from the acceptance of an intelligently directed decentralization of authority.

Another feature of F3's management is the distinction made between *grande école* and other managers. Sales is the objective most stressed by top management; any investment made to increase sales is considered warranted, while virtually no cost-reducing investments are accepted. Yet the sales managers are very poorly paid in comparision to the minor *grande école* factory managers, and the former are given a peculiarly inappropriate set of objectives because it is believed that they do not have the education to implement a policy of pursuing more reasonable goals. In view of the nontechnical nature of the sales function, it would have been considered both impracticable and unnecessary to recruit even minor *école* graduates to manage it; but the actual sales managers, because they are not from *grandes écoles,* are poorly regarded by top management and never placed in a position where they could act for the best advantage of the company. The top administration reconciled itself to having the most important company function badly managed, and only at the very end of the period did it begin to consider a change. Even then, it was to be done by linking production and sales so that a *grande école* graduate could be placed in charge of each region.

Company F4 is the only one of the firms that is wholly family owned, medium sized, and with no *école* management at all. The case study shows some of the important features of this kind of enterprise, including the large possibilities for tax avoidance. It also displays the conflict of values between the family owners and the hired manager, who tended to denigrate profitability and strive for the growth objectives so widely emphasized by the *grande école* managements of larger firms.

Company F5 is similar to F1 in that top management decisions (this time at the level of a division) dominate productivity changes; here, a change of the divisional chief is associated with rapid change both in productivity results and with the policy toward new product development. The case is also a study in management values: a policy is followed of diversification of products—with the objective of minimizing risk—rather than the concentration both of investments and of sales and design efforts which top management realized from the start would be needed if the high costs of diseconomies of scale were to be avoided.

Company F6 is of interest because it is highly successful and is run by an essentially non-*grande école* management. It is more decentralized than the other firms, and this is the basis for much of its achievement. But despite the accomplishments of its management system, it was—by the end of the period studied—rapidly turning into a *grande école* company. Similarly, despite its earlier rejection of cartels, it was by then accepting them. As the firm became increasingly important and successful, and so better integrated into the big-business community, it found it more and more difficult to reject the traditional ways of French big business.

Another feature is that F6 is the only one of our companies that is really successful in research and design, and also the only one in which a majority of the professionals and managers in these functions are without a higher education. The linkage of these two features is probably not coincidental. For only in this company is there no serious conflict between the personal values of the designers and the requirements of the marketplace. In the other firms engaged in research and design (F1, F2, and F5), the graduates of minor *écoles* pursue the traditional quality objectives imbued in them during their technical education, and they find no counterbalancing career objectives because of the very limited nature of promotional opportunities. But this group is of comparatively little importance in F6. This sociological advantage of F6's system of staffing seems to have substantially outweighed the fact that its professionals are lacking in theoretic preparation.

Taking the French firms as a group, all of them except F5 show a high degree of centralization of management at the corporate level. This is in sharp contrast to the British firms. However, four of the French firms (F1, F2, F3, and F4) seem to have been quite out of control; top management did not receive enough information to make rational decisions. Despite this major deficiency, top management in four firms were able to make basic decisions and carry them through when the company's or division's affairs were in crisis. (For a fifth firm, F6, no such problem arose during the period studied.) It is true that top management in Company F3 was quite slow in implementing its decisions, but this is because these decisions necessitated a basic reorientation of the attitudes of middle management; even here, more progress was made than in any of the British firms.

In five of the French companies (F1, F2, F4, F5, and F6), one could observe middle managers acting in their own individual interests of professionalism, rather than either suboptimizing or operating in the interests of the company.[4] Suboptimizing behavior was noted in only one company (F3). In sharp contrast to the British companies, middle management seemed a good deal less aggressive and effective than top management.

[4]This behavior is not specifically noted in all of the case studies as they are written up in Chapter 6, but it existed in all the five firms.

The productivity calculations for the individual companies in our sample depend upon the measurement of output and of the two inputs of labor and of capital services. The methods used to estimate these three variables differ somewhat among the various companies, depending both upon what data are available and which series appear most representative and reliable for the individual firm. Alternative methods have been used as checks wherever possible. The procedures utilized for the nine companies are outlined in the following sections.

Output

The preferred estimate is a price-deflated measure of value added, but this could be used for only three companies. The deflation procedure was that of dividing both sales[1] and purchased items by different deflators, and calculating the deflated value added as a residual. Production in physical units was measured directly for one firm. In the remaining five cases, sales[1] in constant prices constituted the measure used; physical output was available as a check in two of these cases, and a value-added measure in a third.

Price deflators that were general to the industry as a whole had to be employed in three cases. In one instance, sales were deflated by a price index specific to the company, and purchases were deflated by indices appropriate to the groups of items purchased. For the five additional companies, it was possible to develop price indices which were quite specific to the particular firm.

Labor Inputs

For eight of the nine companies, annual series listing the number of people in various work-force categories were weighted by their average annual earnings in a base year. Generally, the average annual earnings are those of the company itself; but in some instances, they are those of another company believed to be similar in this respect. In one instance, the number of hours worked each year by manual workers was used as a substitute for the number of manual workers. For the ninth company, labor inputs were measured by the total wage and salary payments of the company, deflated by a weekly earnings index for manual workers for the industry as a whole. In this last case, a check was run by using less reliable data as to the numbers of personnel and their average earnings in the various groupings of

[1]"Sales" here is used as a shorthand expression for actual sales plus the increase during the year in the inventories of finished goods and of work-in-process.

the company's labor force. For all companies, total fringe benefits (including social security payments by the company) are added to the earnings.

Broadly speaking, the labor force categories used are those of manual workers, nonmanagerial white-collar workers, and professional and managerial workers. In addition, because of the sharp differences in their respective earnings, men and women are treated separately in the British firms. The breakdowns of the labor force are reasonably fine; a three-way breakdown is used for four companies, a four-way breakdown for two, a five-way breakdown for one, and a seven-way breakdown for the final firm.

The base year used for weighting purposes differs between the companies depending upon the availability of information, but normally it is 1962 or 1963.

From the foregoing, we can see that the measured labor inputs represent what the total labor costs to the company would have been if each category of the labor force had been paid a constant annual amount. We are able to take account of the fact that, as a rule, professional and managerial employees increased more rapidly than did the number of manual workers.

Capital Inputs

These series represent estimates of the cost of capital services at constant prices. In order that an index of "total input" might later be derived as the sum of labor and capital inputs, the cost of capital services was deflated to the prices of the same year which had been used as a base for measuring the cost of labor inputs.

Capital inputs are defined as the price-deflated sum of capital depreciation, costs of maintaining buildings and equipment, and a rate of return on the amortized value of fixed capital and of stocks of raw materials, goods in process, and finished goods. No account is taken of other current assets or of current liabilities; the justification for this procedure is that these last are purely financial transactions, and do not represent real inputs in the same fashion as does physical working capital.

In calculating capital inputs, the first problem was that of developing a series for fixed capital in constant prices. The procedure used was that of perpetual inventory: starting with a figure for the first year, and then adding gross investments and subtracting depreciation in each following year.

In the case of the French firms, a balance sheet figure for a base year was chosen as the starting point; depending upon what seemed most appropriate for the particular firm, the figure used was sometimes the amortized and sometimes the unamortized value. Fortunately, French firms have revalued their fixed capital to current values[2] sufficiently frequently so that a meaningful capital figure for a base year could usually be chosen.

Investments were added to this figure, after first being deflated to prices of a common year by use of the same price indices for capital which are used by the French insurance companies. A deduction was then made for a similarly deflated depreciation allowance. In the case of four of the French firms, the unamortized value of capital retired or sold off during the year was taken as the measure of such depreciation; in one case, the official balance sheet amortization was employed; for the sixth firm, arbitrary figures of 4 percent for buildings and 7.5 percent for equipment were used.

A similar procedure was employed for one of the British firms and for part of a second. For the remaining one and one-half firms, the companies had themselves calculated "written-down values" of fixed capital, and these values were accepted.

The resulting series of capital values was then used as a base against which to calculate the capital cost of depreciation and of return on capital. The depreciation rates were tailored to the peculiarities of the individual firms and were as shown in Table A.4A.1.

A 15 percent return on capital was charged against fixed capital. (A calculation made later, and shown below in this Appendix, indicates that a figure of 11 or 12 percent would have been preferable.) On variable capital in the form of stocks, a 20 percent rate of return was charged. This return includes the losses from obsolescence and wastage of stock.

Finally, the price-deflated costs of maintaining buildings and equipment were added to the other capital charges. Annual series of maintenance costs exist for five firms. For the other four, it was assumed that each firm had the same average ratio of maintenance costs to total costs charged against fixed capital as was the case for the most comparable of the previous five firms.

Choice of End-Point Years
Since the annual compound rates of change of the various indices were computed from the absolute values for the first and last years, and since short-

---

[2]By the use of price indices, all prior gross investments in fixed capital are revalued to current prices. All past amortization allowances are similarly revalued, and the difference is taken as the revalued amortized worth of fixed capital. The purpose of the exercise is, of course, to increase future amortization allowances and thus to reduce the amount payable as profits tax.

Table A. 4A. 1 Depreciation Rates

Number of Firms	Depreciation Rates Charged on		
	Equipment (Percentage)	Buildings (Percentage)	All Fixed Capital (Percentage)
1	6	2	
4	7.5	4	
1	7.5	5	
1	10	5	
1			10
1			12.5

term productivity changes tend to vary in the same direction as output, it was important to choose the end-point years with care. The criteria of choice were as follows:

1.

As a first approximation, all years for which data existed were used in the series.

2.

Analysis of the annual compound rate of change in output was undertaken in order to see whether the rate was seriously affected by the choice of the particular end-point years.

3.

Further analysis was undertaken as to whether the annual compound rate of change in total productivity was so affected.

Application of criteria two and three affected the starting year for two companies, causing this to be advanced by one year. In no case did the final year have to be altered.

Compensation for the Rise in Real Wages

In Chapters 5 and 6 I shall examine the issue of whether the rise in each company's total productivity was sufficient to cover the increase in real hourly manual wages typical of its industry. The rise in productivity for the nine firms is shown in Table A.4A.2.

The rise in real hourly wages was computed from nominal wages deflated by the cost of living. In calculating the degree of coverage, the ratio of labor payments to the total of labor plus capital costs in each company is calculated as of the original year of the period covered.

Table A. 4A. 2 Rise in Productivity: French and British Firms

	French Firms	British Firms
Covered substantially more than the rise in real wages	3	2
Covered substantially less than the rise in real wages	3	0
Covered none of the rise in real wages	0	1

Of course, the percentage coverage of the rise in real wages indicates nothing as to the change in the financial position of the various companies; for such change is also heavily influenced by the relative movements of the prices of purchases, of final products, and of the cost of living. But it does show how the financial position would have altered if all such price indices had moved together.

Real Profitability of Large British Companies
The purpose of this section is to provide a measure of the ratio of average pretax profits to total net assets earned by large resident manufacturing companies in Britain. This would appear to be a reasonable figure to use in estimating the opportunity cost of capital for our British companies. In order to be consistent with the other calculations made in determining productivity changes, this rate of profit should eliminate the effect of price changes and should take assets valued in current prices as its denominator.

The formula used for the calculation is

$$P = \sum_{i=1}^{n} (P_i^* R_i/n) + (S - I - E),$$

where
P = calculated average rate of real profit on net real assets
P_i^* = rate of profit in year i calculated on the book value of net real assets
R_i = the ratio in year i of the book value of gross assets to the current value of gross assets
S = annual compound rate of growth of stock market values
I = annual compound rate of growth of price increases
E = average annual ratio of retained earnings to the book value of shareholder equity, expressed in current prices
For the years 1951-1964, P = 9.7 percent.

Over the years 1951-1964,[3] the average nominal rate of profit earned by all manufacturing firms quoted on the London Stock Exchange was 16.1 percent.[4] However, this figure was computed against a base of fixed capital measured according to book value, while capital for my firms was measured by its present value. If we assume that net capital measured in book value bears the same ratio to net capital measured in current prices as is estimated to be the case for the gross value of capital,[5] then the average rate of profit falls to 8.6 percent.

On the other hand, there are two reasons why the 8.6 percent rate is too low. The first is that the depreciation rates used by the quoted companies were almost certainly rather higher than those which I have used for my companies. While this reduces both their profit and capital figures, the net effect is to depress the profit rate. The second reason is that return on capital should properly include increases in the real value of corporate shares, but this is not taken into account in the rate of profit quoted earlier. During the same years, the annual compound rate of growth in share prices on the London Stock Exchange[6] rose by 7.5 percent. Even taking account of the rate of inflation[7] and eliminating the effect of retention of corporate earnings,[8] the residual rate of growth in share prices was 1.1 percent.

Thus the proper rate of profit to be applied to our British firms would appear to be the average rate of profit of 8.6 percent, plus the residual rate of growth in share prices of 1.1 percent, plus an allowance for the overstatement of proper depreciation. Since the resultant figure of 9.7 percent which is given by our formula is an understatement of the true value, we may take it

[3]This period was chosen because it is the longest span for which we have all of the necessary data.
[4]The numerator is taken as trading profits after deducting depreciation and other contributions to reserves. The denominator is defined as total fixed assets plus stocks and work-in-progress as of the end of the previous year: the same definition of capital as was used in our calculations for individual firms. (H. M. Central Statistical Office, *Economic Trends*, April 1962, and H. M. Ministry of Labour, *Statistics on Incomes, Prices, Employment and Production*.) Interest on long-term loans is included in trading profits, and such loans are similarly included in net assets. No particular difficulty is created by the fact that interest on short-term loans is excluded from trading profits, since total net assets are roughly equal to the definition of capital which I have employed.
[5]See *Board of Trade Journal*, 11 February 1966, p. 314.
[6]*Financial Times* index of industrial shares.
[7]The inflation rate was 3.6 percent on all final goods and services sold on the home market.
[8]This is the average annual ratio of retained profits and other capital receipts to the book value of shareholder's equity as of the end of the previous year, the denominator inflated to prices of the current year. (*Economic Trends* and *Statistics on Incomes*.) The ratio averaged 2.8 percent.

that an 11 to 12 percent rate of return on capital for British firms would be an appropriate approximation of the true rate.[9]

No reliable profit rate figures are available for France. Thus I have decided to apply the same rate of return to capital for the French firms as for the British. This decision has the advantage of providing homogeneity of treatment between the French and British firms, and this is useful for our purposes of comparing their productivity results.

[9]Of course, the computed rate of return on capital is sensitive to the choice of years used for the comparison, in particular because of the changes in stock market prices. While 9.7 percent is the computed rate for 1951-1964, the rate is 11.8 percent for 1951-1963 and 11.0 percent for 1951-1962. However, the 1951-1964 rate is probably more representative of recent years.

A United Nations' classification of manufacturing industries subdivides them into twenty-one different categories. When we classify each of our companies (or divisions in the cases when our prime emphasis in a case study is upon a single division within a company) into a single category according to its major products, we find that our nine companies fall into eight different categories. The categories covered include the following proportions shown in Table A.4B.1 of all manufacturing in the respective countries.

Table A. 4B. 1 Coverage of Manufacturing

	Coverage of Manufacturing[a] as Measured by		
Country	Number of Employees (Percentage)	Value Added (Percentage)	Wages and Salaries (Percentage)
France	42	46	47
United Kingdom	22	16	17
France and United Kingdom combined	63	58	60

[a]United Nations, *The Growth of World Industry, 1953-65, National Tables* (United Nations, New York, 1967). French data are for 1962, and British data for 1963. Value added for France is computed on the assumption that each industrial category in France has the same ratio of value added to wages and salaries as does the corresponding industrial category in the United Kingdom. French companies are contrasted with the industrial classification data for France, British companies with that for the United Kingdom, and the two together with an unweighted average of the two countries' industrial classification statistics.

The total number of industrial categories for which data exist are twenty for France, twenty-one for the United Kingdom, and twenty-one for the two countries combined.

Profitability

One means of judging the degree to which the firms studied are typical of their country's industry is by examining the returns which an investor would have earned by investing in them compared to those which he would have earned by investing in other companies quoted on the national stock exchange. These data can be presented for five of our six French companies and for two of the three British firms. Unfortunately, the nature of the data that are available compels an asymmetrical treatment of the French and British companies.

For France, I have contrasted each of our companies with a substantial sample of companies quoted on the Paris Bourse which produce the same or related products. The sample was chosen by going through the list of firms described in *Docfin,*[1] whose annual editions present detailed data concerning the more important companies quoted on the Bourse. The relevant industry was represented by a 100 percent sample of those firms described in *Docfin* whose products are such as to make it appropriate to place them in the same industry with one of our companies. Indices for each industry were calculated as the unweighted average of the indices for each of the constituent companies. The time period covered was eight recent years.[2]

Each of the five French firms in our study was compared with its relevant industry in terms of the stock market price[3] of its shares at the final date, plus the dividends distributed over the period,[4] the sum being divided by the stock market price of its shares at the beginning date. In addition, the stock market price index of each company was compared with a general index obtained from *Docfin* for the Paris Bourse as a whole. This second comparison, unfortunately, could take no direct account of dividend distributions. Thus a third index was computed comparing each firm to its own industry with regard to the ratio of dividend distributions in each year to the January prices of the stock, using an unweighted average of the sum of the years. The greater the deviation from unity of the index of the ratio of the firm to that of its industry, the greater is the presumption that the ratio of the company's

[1]Published by Société d'Editions économiques et financières, Paris.
[2]Data availability limited the period to these years. However, a cruder definition of the relevant industries was utilized for a comparison covering three additional years. For none of the companies did it appear that a comparison over the eleven-year period would have yielded different results than those found for the eight years analyzed.
[3]All stock market prices were adjusted for splits, for stock dividends, and for the value of rights to the purchase of additional shares.
[4]The dividends have been discounted by 15 percent per annum to the final date.

stock price index to the general Bourse index misstates the company's market performance because of the fact that this price ratio ignores dividend distributions.

The results for the five companies are presented in Table A.4C.1.

In our analysis of the British firms, we unfortunately have no way of taking account of dividends and must limit ourselves to an analysis of the movement of stock market prices; we can take account only of splits, stock dividends, and rights. In Table A.4C.2, stock performance is analyzed over a twelve-year period.[5] Comparison is made with two industry indices and with a general index of five hundred industrial companies, all taken from the *Financial Times* share indices.[6]

Summarizing these financial results for the French and British firms taken together, two of the seven firms for which we have stock market data showed substantially better than average performance compared to their respective industries, two firms displayed average performance, two were decidedly below average, and the results for one are uncertain depending on which industry sample one uses for purposes of comparison. The two firms for which we do not have stock market data had profit rates that seem slightly on the high side of average for the larger firms of their industries. The average returns to an investor in our companies is slightly (7 percent) lower than what would have been earned by investing in the companies' respective industries, and the spread is evenly balanced. Thus our sample of nine firms would seem to be quite typical of their respective industries in their countries with regard to financial results. Unfortunately, the smallness of the sample and the size of the variance makes for extremely wide confidence limits as to the firms' average as a proportion of that of their industries; with a 5 percent probability of error, these confidence limits are between 44 and 150 percent.

Labor Productivity

A second means of evaluating the representativeness of the companies in our sample is to compare the evolution of their labor productivity with that of each of their industries as a whole in their own country. The results of this comparison are shown in Table A.4C.3.

[5]As was also the case for the French companies, the record of stock-price movements was examined to assure that these end-point dates did not provide a false impression of the evolution of prices.
[6]For a description of the indices, see the *Guide to the F.T.-Actuaries Share Indices* (London, n.d.).

Table A. 4C. 1 Financial Performance of the French Companies (January 1959 to January 1967)

| Company | Firms in the Industry Sample (Number) | Ratio of Company to Its Industry (Percentage) | | Ratio of Company to the overall Paris Bourse Index (Percentage) |
		Value per share to stockholder at end of period (value at start of period = 100)	Ratio of dividends to stock market prices	Value per share to stockholder at end of period (value at start of period = 100)
1	14	155	219	211
2	20	95	129	120
3	14	44	86	101
4	20	42[a]	62	102
5	46	30	44	31

[a]The industry is extremely heterogeneous. If we consider a very tiny industry subsample of firms that produce products similar to those of Company 4, then the ratio would be 253.

Table A. 4C.2 Stock Market Performance of the British Companies

| Company | Market Price per Share at End of Period (Value at Start of Period = 100) (Percentage) | |
	Ratio of company to its industry	Ratio of company to all nonfinancial and non-commodity trading companies
1	171	110
2	111	120

Table A. 4C. 3 Growth of Labor Productivity (Number of Firms)

Country	Faster in Company than in Industry	Slower in Company than in Industry	No Data
France	2	2	2
Britain	1	1	1

These figures would suggest that our sample of companies had a record of increasing labor productivity which was average for their industries. Moreover, when we compare the average annual rate of growth of labor productivity for each firm with that of its industry,[7] we find that the average (unweighted) excess of the companies' growth rates is only 9 percent of their industries' average. But the confidence limits are even wider than in the case of financial results; with a 10 percent probability of error, the limits for the firms' average as a proportion of that of their industries are 23 to 189 percent.

[7]The differences between the company and industry average rates of growth of labor productivity are +5.0, +3.0, +1.5, −2.1, −2.7, and −2.9 percent.

5 The British Companies

Company B1

Company B1 is the first of our British firms, and falls within the textile and apparel group of industries. The technology of the industry is quite conventional, but Company B1 has been in the forefront of those limited changes which have occurred since the end of the Second World War. The company dates back over a century, and is still to a considerable degree both owned and managed by the founding family. It is one of the largest of the companies in an industry in which small family firms still predominate.

During the period for which we have data, Company B1's profit rate, although quite high by the standards of British manufacturing as a whole, appears to have been only slightly on the high side of average when compared with that of the other large firms of its own industry. Its labor productivity increased at much the same rate as did that of the industry as a whole, or perhaps slightly less. It is only in its rate of expansion that the company was unusual, for its sales grew several times more rapidly than did those of its branch as a whole. Even in comparison with its larger competitors, who likewise benefited from the decimation of the tiny firms of the industry, Company B1's growth was quite exceptional. Furthermore, this was accomplished essentially through internal development, very little merger activity occurring.

Over the eight years for which we have information concerning Division I, which was by far the principal division of the firm, the division's compound annual rates of growth were shown in Table 5.1. The differences in the alternative estimates of productivity improvement are substantial, but it would appear that the higher estimates should be relied upon.[1] The increase in total productivity, as measured by value added, was one third larger than what would have been needed to compensate for the increase in real hourly wages in that industry.

---

[1]The methods used for calculating productivity in this, as in the other companies, are described in Appendix A to Chapter 4. It should be remembered that "total productivity" is defined as the deflated value of output divided by deflated labor plus capital costs.

The differences between the lower and higher estimates of each rate of growth are due exclusively to the use of alternative measures of output. The higher estimate of output is founded upon the change in value added in constant prices. The lower estimate is obtained by measuring output in each year by the gross value in constant prices of goods produced and sold by this sector of Company B1, plus the increase in the sector's stocks of finished goods and of work-in-process. Two other estimates, both of which measure gross output in physical terms and which ignore changes in stocks, provide rates of growth intermediate between the two sets presented in Table 5.1.

Table 5.1 Compound Annual Rates of Growth: Divison I of Company BI
(Percentages)

Output	6.7 to 9.1
Labor productivity	0.7 to 2.9
Capital productivity	0.2 to 2.4
Total productivity	0.6 to 2.8

The sales success of the division seems to have been primarily the result of the fact that it acted as a leader in its industry in introducing minor technological product changes, and that these variations improved the quality of the products and gave them greater market appeal. This was complemented by the fact that the company was successful in the design of a number of its products that subsequently did very well in the marketplace.

The improvement shown in productivity is very easily accounted for both by a host of minor changes in the conventional production process, and by the expansion in the use of three major technological developments that substituted one material for another and as a by-product economized on labor inputs. In fact, it seems virtually certain that these changes by themselves must have led to a substantially greater increase in productivity than the 2.8 percent per annum growth which is recorded in the statistics for the division. When we consider that additional increases in productivity should have resulted from the scale effects of the substantial expansion in output of the division, the problem facing us is that of why productivity did not grow at a much more rapid pace.

The only explanation for the failure to show a superior productivity record is the absence of coordination of the activities of the fairly large number of factories within the division. This lacuna appears to be entirely due to a lack of vigor on the part of the top management of Division I, a group of men which substantially overlapped in membership with the top management of the company. Each factory was allowed to go its own way, choosing its own

---

While the differences between the two sets of measures may be due to errors in price deflation, it seems more likely that the differences are explained by the apparent fact that materials declined over time as a proportion of the value of gross output (with both materials and output measured in constant prices). Since there was no change in the sector's degree of vertical integration, this decline represents a reduction in the quality and/or the amount of materials used per unit of output.

In choosing among the various estimates, one might make a case for preferring to measure output either by the value-added measure or by the measure of gross production. But in measuring productivity, the value-added measure of output is clearly conceptually superior and will be taken as the appropriate one in the discussion in the text.

designs and specific products and expanding or contracting its labor force in accord with its success in selling these products to the company's wholesaling organization and, through it, to the outside market. As all factories were interested in expansion, there was considerable proliferation among them of competing products. The result was that lot size of production was much smaller than necessary, and indeed seems to have contracted over time despite the substantial increase in total output. Since economies of scale were positive and were probably much more closely linked to the size of the individual lot than to the dimensions of the factory, this has led to diseconomies of scale over time.

A second difficulty for the division resulted from the fact that predictions of the total sales of the products of each factory taken individually were quite poor. The result of this was that a factory's labor force would frequently be substantially expanded, with all the costs of hiring and training that such expansion implies, and then would be reduced equally sharply when anticipated increases in sales did not materialize. Doubtless a major reason for this failure of sales prediction was that the central divisional sales staff was kept extremely weak and that it did virtually no market research on the prospects for the various components of the national market.

A third difficulty was that no serious effort was made to balance production against capacity between the various factories of the division, although there would have been no major technical difficulty in so doing. As demand fell for one factory's products, it might be able to negotiate with other factories to take over some of their work on a subcontracting basis; but such arrangements were done on an ad hoc basis and by means of interfactory negotiation, with only a minimum of central interference by the divisional headquarters. The result was that one factory could be working short time and suffering from low productivity due to underemployment of the labor force while another, making similar products, was engaging in new hiring and was working overtime.

As one would expect, all of these failures of coordination were relatively unimportant in years when total production increased rapidly. But as soon as the expansion of total output slowed down, and especially in years when total output was stationary, the problem of variance between individual factories became extremely serious. It is the failure to achieve coordination which counterbalanced the large increases in productivity which would otherwise have been shown.

The division thus displays a curious amalgam of managerial performance. I say this because the individual operating units were highly successful. So too were the functional groups at headquarters in their tasks other than those of coordination. At these levels, the company completely justified its reputation as an unusually dynamic British concern.

The division and company were active in searching out international innovations in technology and were among the world leaders in developing these innovations to the operational stage. Individual factories did a superb job in introducing both large and small innovations, and their managers kept in touch with international developments by frequent visits abroad. This introduction of continuous technological change required corresponding reductions in labor costs (measured in constant prices) in order for them to be financially viable. These labor costs were brought down with the aid of a dynamic labor policy of continuous work study, combined with successful persuasion of the trade-union locals that they should permit a piece-rate system based on worker effort rather than on traditional relationships wherein the payment per piece in one kind of operation was based upon the rate for a different operation. Thus jobs were retimed both when innovations occurred and when there were minor product changes, and piece rates for operators were constantly changed on the basis of such time study. Product design, carried out at the individual factory level, was also highly dynamic.

The sales force was similarly quite successful, as shown by the division's fairly steady increase in its share of national market. A strong advertising program provided very useful support. Similar accomplishments were achieved in other divisional and company functional departments.

Thus lower and middle management must be given very high marks for successful dynamism, and top management must be credited with having created a company atmosphere that made such dynamism possible. But the fruits of this success were negated by the utter failure shown earlier either to exercise coordination within the production of sales function or to coordinate the two. Top management policy was that of decentralization to the lowest unit possible, with very little being done at any higher level.

Three further examples might be cited with regard to the issue of top management control. During the final years of the period studied, top management of the division was quite worried over the fact that sales had leveled off. Yet the value of materials consumed per unit of production was 12 percent lower during these years than in the previous period.[2] A fair interpretation of this decline would appear to be that poorer quality materials were being put into the product in order that the factory managers might more readily achieve the profit targets for which they were held responsible. Yet, interestingly, no divisional effort was made to investigate whether this development was a cause of the sales difficulty: materials usage was considered to be exclusively a matter for decision by the individual factory managers. In fact, the divisional top manager most directly responsible stated to me that he had no impression as to whether quality had been improving or declining.

A related example concerns interdivisional pricing within Company B1. Division I sells entirely outside of the company, and its component factories are expected to build quality into their products to the degree that this is consistent with a targeted rate of profit. It buys its materials and components both from inside and outside the company, and has a purchasing manager to handle both kinds of purchases for the division as a whole. Other divisions treat Division I just as they would an outside customer, and try to obtain from it the best price possible.

My interviews in two divisions which sell partly to Division I but primarily outside the company showed that Division I, the leading single customer for both of these divisions, paid lower prices than outside customers in one case and higher prices than some of the outside customers in the other. In neither case did Division I seem to know what price other customers were paying, and the relative prices paid by different customers depended heavily on the ability of their purchasing managers in price negotiations.

Since the degree of quality that is put into the products of Division I is expected to be the maximum consistent with the factories achieving their profit targets, higher prices for major components bought within the company automatically imply a reduction in the quality standards of the factories. But despite its concern over divisional sales, company headquarters leaves interdivisional price setting entirely to the vagaries of the marketplace and to the relative ability of the negotiators for the respective divisions. Thus there is no company or divisional control either directly over quality standards or indirectly through supervision of interdivisional pricing.

The third example concerns the gathering of information relevant to deci-

[2]Both consumption and production are measured in constant prices. No apparent increase in vertical integration occurred during this time span, nor was it apparent that there was any increase in the amount of workmanship going into each unit of the final product.

sions as to investment and marketing strategy within Division I. Since the division contains factories of substantially different sizes, each having production runs of widely varying lengths, one might have expected an effort to learn the nature and extent of the economies or diseconomies inherent both in large production runs and in large factories. However, despite the fact that there was wide disagreement among the division's production managers as to whether or not significant economies existed, that decisions as to building new factories had to be made, and that marketing strategy was strongly influenced by the managerial perceptions of the degree of economy inherent in long runs, nothing was done to investigate these matters until the very end of the period studied. Even then, the investigation was most slipshod and did nothing to resolve disagreement within the company.

Control both by division headquarters and by central headquarters seems to have been limited essentially to the simplest type of financial control: the demand for a specified rate of pretax profits as a proportion of assets. Little investigation was carried out by either headquarters unit as to why individual units succeeded or failed in meeting this target. The magnitude of the target was believed within the company to be of critical importance for Division I and for its subunits, both because this was the only target utilized in setting prices and because it also served as the basic constraint on the quality which could be built into a given product once the price of the item had been determined. The other divisions of the company, on the other hand, were believed to have significantly less control over their financial results than had Division I, and thus the targeted rate of return had much less operational significance for them.

In view of the importance of the target rate of profit, it is interesting to see how this rate was determined.

In the early 1950s, the head of the firm had decided to establish a company-wide criterion of pretax profits as a percentage of assets used. The actual figure was determined by examining the published balance sheets of some thirty or forty firms in the industry; in order to get such a large number of firms, it was necessary to include not only British companies but also American firms that operated entirely outside of Britain. The average rate of return earned by the top quartile of these firms was taken as the company's profit target.

Why this method rather than some other? This procedure was used because top management held the view that a company's efficiency can best be judged by its rate of return relative to that of its industry, and the management felt

that the company belonged in the top quartile of efficiency. Criteria such as
the desire to generate internal funds for growth or to satisfy stockholders
seem not to have played any explicit role.[3] It was for this reason that, in
determining the proper profit target, the chairman was willing to include in
his sample of firms non-British companies that were not competitors on the
British capital market; his interest was in efficiency as measured by the best
international, and not solely British, standards. It was quite typical of the
lack of activity by top management that once a target figure was determined
it should have remained without reexamination for over a decade.

But while the targeted rate of profit served as the main guide to pricing and
quality standards for Division I, this method was not practical for the other
divisions because of the nature of their products and markets. Nor was capital
investment allocated among the divisions in accord with their respective profit rates; over the eight years for which I have data, the correlation between
the various divisions' rates of growth of assets and their average return on
assets was strongly negative. If we can assume that the insistence on a high
rate of profit restrained Division I's expansion below what it would otherwise
have been, then the net effect was to funnel funds into other divisions of the
company which showed a decidedly lower return.

Nor was this accidental. For, in making investment decisions, the top management of the company was bound by two self-imposed constraints. The
first of these was that the proportion of posttax profits to be paid out in
dividends was to be kept exceedingly small. The second constraint was that
all investments had to be made within the company's existing broad industry
classification, this being justified on the ground that every tinker should stick
to his trade and that this was the particular business which the top management understood. Given the amount of profits generated by the company,
and given these two constraints on investment policy and the limited reinvest-
ment possibilities within Division I which resulted from the use of a targeted
rate of profit here, the company's top management had no choice but to
invest increasingly in the activities of the less profitable divisions.

In fact, the constraint that the company should invest only within its own
broad industry made peculiarly little sense in the light of the way that the

---

[3]Thus, although the chairman did argue that the company had the obligation to earn
more for its stockholders from reinvested earnings than they themselves could get if all
earnings were distributed as dividends, he also insisted that one should ignore the issue of
income tax and surtax in deciding whether or not this obligation was being met. His
justification for this viewpoint was that tax angles had nothing to do with company
efficiency.

company's management was organized. As we have seen, top management played such an inactive decision-making role that it was of no great importance whether or not its members were familiar with the industries in which the company was engaged. But even more important, it was the division in charge of foreign operations which was by far the most rapidly growing and which had long shown the lowest rate of profit. Exceptionally little control over operations was exercised by this division, control being pretty much left to each individual foreign subsidiary. Nor, except in the case of one subsidiary that had a catastrophic history, were managers or technicians for these subsidiaries supplied from the British organization. It was believed at the headquarters of the overseas division that the problems of each subsidiary were peculiarly national and that the British headquarters could not understand the problems of each country sufficiently well to permit any useful supervision. Thus, in reality, the company's most rapid expansion was in markets that were probably less understood at company headquarters than would have been home markets in quite different trades. If we use an operational definition of the industries in which the firm was operating, then Company B1 was expanding most rapidly in an industry (i.e., foreign operations) that the top management did not understand and that it found peculiarly unprofitable. Only on the basis of dogma—namely, definition of the company's industry in terms of the nature of the product rather than of the markets or even of the manufacturing processes involved—could it be said that the top management was sticking to its trade. But it was precisely this dogma, in conjunction with the others mentioned earlier, that determined the lines of investment of the company.

While the absence of coordination was most striking at the level of top management, efforts were also made to minimize the necessity for it at middle levels. This was done through extreme decentralization and the reluctance to create middle-level jobs with wide responsibility. Thus, although the leading production man in the division believed that economies of scale were possible in large factories if they could be well managed, he held that factory managers of the proper caliber simply could not be found. For this reason, he preferred to build small factories. Even where relatively good-sized factories existed, they were mostly operated through the establishment of vertically integrated production departments that were virtual replicas of one another and in which diseconomies of scale were fairly obvious. In this way, the challenge to individual managers was kept as narrow as possible.

Company B2

Company B2 is a leading manufacturer of a broad mix of small producers' goods, and in recent years has grown very rapidly through the process of take-over of other firms. These take-overs have led the company into producing an ever-wider product mix, but always within the same relatively low-profit industry. The company's stock is widely held and control is exercised by the management. During a period of twelve years, the value of its stock increased some 20 percent more rapidly than did that of its industry as a whole, and also more than that of the London Stock Exchange as a whole.[4] Similarly, the company's management had the reputation of being rather better than the average for its industry.

We have productivity data for only one medium-sized division of the company. Here, over an eleven-year period, output increased by a compound annual rate of 3.9 percent and total productivity increased by 1.9 percent per annum. This productivity improvement was two-thirds larger than would have been sufficient to cover the increases in real wage rates in that industry over the period.

In the case of this company, we shall not analyze the one division for which we have productivity data but instead shall concentrate on the major developments in the company as a whole over a ten-year period.

The main profit base and center of attention of the company was within a single subindustry in which it held a strong and long-established oligopolistic position in the British market as a whole. Although a number of smaller firms produced an extremely limited range of products within this subindustry, Company B2 and a very few large colleagues were unthreatened in their domination both because of their ability to service customers with a wide mix of slightly differentiated products and because of their traditional reputation for good quality. Despite the fact that profit margins were high, efforts both at serious expansion by the small firms and of entry by others were discouraged by the belief that the industry's leaders had the financial capability and willingness to cut prices as sharply as necessary in order to preserve their market position. As a result of this general belief, the price-cutting potential did not have to be demonstrated. The oligopolists themselves engaged in very little competition with one another, and what competition there was took the form of developing variants of existing products. In short, Company B2 had,

---

[4]This calculation takes account of stock splits and rights issues. Comparison is made with the *Financial Times* indices.

in this subindustry, a secure and profitable base but one which provided little room for expansion.

The management of Division I, which operated the company's facilities in this profitable subindustry, involved a complex but routine set of operations. Production methods remained stationary; only toward the end of the period studied did a member of top management entrust a middle manager with the task of working out some changes in the machinery employed, and this top executive explained his initiative by the fact that he was the only one who was new to the subindustry and thus could make an outsider's evaluation of its conservatism. Pricing policy was also managed routinely. Although the costs of holding finished-product inventories were high, and varied widely between products because of the substantial differences in the rate of turnover of these inventories, the relative prices charged reflected none of these cost differences. The explanation given for this pricing policy was that customers would not understand or accept such a basis for price differentiation among rather similar items. Despite the fact that these products could to a considerable degree be substituted for one another by the industrial purchasers, and a better pricing policy would doubtless have resulted in such substitution and thus in cost savings for Company B2, this pricing policy was perhaps rational in view of the importance of avoiding the risk of price competition among the oligopolists. Rational or not, this conservative pricing policy was in any case simple and routine to administer.

The complexity of operations arose from the fact that literally thousands of product variations were produced in a number of different factories for shipment to warehouses scattered throughout the country. The real problem of the division was that of properly scheduling both production and the holdings of inventories in the warehouses.

Success in this scheduling process was at best mediocre. Over a period of six years, annual total costs of production other than those for the purchase of materials changed only as a result of inflation and random causes, and did not fluctuate with output; thus the marginal value-added cost was close to zero. Yet both in years of increases and of declines in production,[5] 50 to 60 percent of the variation in output was due to changes in inventories rather than of sales. In view of the large number of items produced and stocked, it was perfectly obvious that the scheduling task was one best handled by

[5]Within these six years, there were three periods of increases in production between years and two periods of decline. The last year's production was within 1 percent of that of the first year.

computer. Still, despite preliminary efforts at such computer programming, not even a rudimentary program for scheduling existed in the middle 1960s. The managing director, probably correctly, held that the failure occurred because middle management was not trained to recognize the problems involved in providing the necessary information for such a program.

All in all, the management of Division I of Company B2 made relatively minor demands on the top executives. Being a routine operation, it could be handled quite satisfactorily by the various technical specialists. Nor, given the oligopolistic position of the subindustry, did there appear to be room for aggressiveness on the sales side. It is true that top management could have approached the business more creatively, and almost certainly more profitably; but this would have required a break with traditions in a subindustry whose profits appeared quite satisfactory.

As a result of the nature of Division I's operations, the company's top management found itself faced both with the generation of substantial profits that it could not reinvest into Division I and with considerable excess time on the hands of the top executives. In addition, Division I's foreign markets in the Dominions and former colonies were threatened by rising tariff and quota barriers, and they could be preserved only through the establishment of foreign manufacturing operations. The company responded by expanding abroad as well as by investing in allied subindustries within Britain.

Although during the 1950s and 1960s the company founded a number of foreign subsidiaries that combined both production facilities and sales, fear of managerial problems appears to have exerted a major restraint on the expansion of this program. Top management believed that all management personnel in less-developed countries had to be sent from Britain, and that this was likely to continue throughout the indefinite future. But such personnel would have to be brought back to Britain by the time their eldest children were of secondary-school age, and this necessity posed a dual problem. First, it was necessary to find men of appropriate managerial capabilities who were still in their late twenties or early thirties, and the company was wary of denuding itself of such rare managerial talent. Second, there was concern as to the feasibility of finding posts in Britain for returnees from foreign managerial positions. The combination of these two issues persuaded the company's top executives that they should go slow in expansion into additional less-developed nations. Even in developed countries, although the managerial problems were much less serious and "policy" dictated a reliance on local nationals, the leading posts in each country were in fact filled by Britishers. This, too, was seen as creating managerial problems at home.

In common with the behavior observed in Company B1, top executives did not play a very active role in the management of these foreign subsidiaries—except in the choice of their managers. A striking example of this hands-off policy is the case of a moderately important investment in a subsidiary that had lost money in three of the previous four years. A request came to Company B2's board of directors for an expansion of capacity in this subsidiary so as to complement existing plant. The top company manager in whose hands the decision lay believed that the new capacity would be obsolete and scrapped before it could pay for itself, but nevertheless he supported the request on the basis that it would allow the full utilization of the existing capacity that would otherwise lie partly idle. On my probing, it turned out that he had no idea as to whether subcontracting could be substituted for the requested investment and that no one in Britain was looking into this matter. Despite the fact that the subsidiary's management had a poor record, he insisted that he had to decide on too many such investment proposals for it to be feasible for him to look into the "details" of the individual projects. No staff existed at headquarters which could do even the casual vetting of projects implied by my questions.

Given this approach toward the proper role of the company's top management in supervising foreign subsidiaries, the creation of such firms was in itself insufficient to provide the expansion of Company B2's managerial activities which was desired by top management. Movement into new fields within Britain was thus relied upon as the principal form of such expansion.

Such growth within Britain has been concentrated within the broad industry to which the profitable Division I belonged. Unfortunately for the company, this has not been a particularly profitable or rapidly expanding industry during the 1950s and 1960s. Subsectors similar to those of Division I of Company B2 were either hard to find or difficult to enter. But market orientation was not at all the basis upon which decisions as to expansion were made.

The most important criterion used was that expansion should be in fields as close as possible in product line to the one with which management was most familiar: that of Division I. This judgment was based upon the belief that managerial skills are not transferable across industry lines, and that this proposition applies to top management as much as to lower and middle management. Thus, although it was recognized that the market prospects were not particularly good in these related fields, this fact seems to have been treated as fundamentally an irrelevant consideration. The chief executives believed that they were more efficient than the rank and file of British management in the industry and must inevitably be able to make money in product lines in which other companies were barely making ends meet.

The second criterion, which appears to have been usually but not always followed, was that factory expansion within Britain should be located in the region in which the company had traditionally operated.[6] The logic behind this criterion similarly related to management; the company's managers had their roots in the region, and could not comfortably envision themselves either working elsewhere or having to make decisions about a labor force in other areas of Britain whose traditions and prejudices they would not fully understand.

With all this emphasis upon managerial capabilities and preferences as the key determinant of the direction of expansion, it is perhaps not surprising that one of the motivations for expansion in fields related to that of Division I was that it would provide promotional opportunities for junior and middle managerial personnel. The existence of such opportunities was believed to be particularly important if the company were to be able to continue to recruit youths with good management potential.

Yet, in the actual operation of new facilities that were added by take-over, all of the foregoing emphasis upon better utilization of managers already within the company turned out to be largely irrelevant. For additional management was, of course, taken over along with the facilities. The new management slots created were primarily a very few coordinating positions at company headquarters.

Where managerial posts did open up in the newly added activities, they were filled in almost all cases either by promotion of people who had earlier worked in the companies taken over or by the hiring of managers from outside who had experience in the relevant branch. This practice seems to have stemmed from the basic philosophy of Company B2's top executives: that managerial skills are nontransferable. For, given nontransferability between major branches of industry, why not extend the doctrine to that of nontransferability between subbranches? This extension seems in fact to have

[6]Not all members of the top management of Company B2 were willing explicitly to espouse this viewpoint in conversation with me.

been made in decisions regarding appointments, although the principle of such extension was always firmly denied.

One set of promotions is particularly interesting. In the establishment of one new division, the top managers of companies that had been absorbed were removed or retired early because of the belief that their ineffectiveness had been responsible for the running down of their own firms. The division's top management was created from people who had been second-line managers in the old companies; but things did not improve, and most of these in turn were removed. Men were brought in as their replacements who had had no prior experience in the industry. Why these men instead of managers who had earlier been with Company B2? Presumably because managerial versatility had been trained out of Company B2's own staff; thus, once it proved impossible to hire satisfactory people who had experience with the division's products, only people from companies with a different philosophy could demonstrate the necessary flexibility.

At this point, it is worth examining briefly the backgrounds of Company B2's management and the way in which these people were employed.

Even in the middle 1960s, the basic attitude of the company toward education was negative. The executive at the board level who was in charge of personnel held that the ideal method of training managers was to take men whose personal characteristics indicated high potential and then run them through the company, starting with quite menial tasks. Aside from on-the-job training, it was military conscription that he viewed as having in the past been the most successful form of education. He regarded academic preparation as a handicap, on the grounds that it made men impatient with the elementary work with which they should properly begin until they had proved themselves. I gathered that he believed that the fifteen-year-old school leaver made the ideal candidate for future management, but was reconciled to the fact that he was unlikely to find boys with the proper character and intelligence among this group. Thus he now set his sights on grammar school and public school boys, entering the company at age seventeen or eighteen. Because of the problem of finding sufficient talent even among this group, he was hiring more university graduates than previously, and expected such hiring to expand in the future. But this was solely because of the phenomenon, regrettable in his eyes, that boys of natural talent were increasingly attending universities and thus could most readily be found among their graduates.

As one might expect, this attitude was reflected in the number of university graduates in the company. Although at least two were included among the top managers, there were only some half dozen in the company as a whole who were either managers or regarded as potential future managers. While the company had been chary of employing such people, wishing to keep their numbers down to the small figure that could be given genuine opportunities for promotion, it was found difficult to prevent even those few who were hired from quitting.

By the middle of the 1960s the company was sufficiently aware of its managerial shortages to be providing some selected people in their twenties and thirties with multifunctional experience; yet managerial jobs were still defined quite narrowly. This narrowness is best seen with regard to the role of plant managers in one division (not Division I) of Company B2 which was probably quite typical in this regard.

Here, sales has traditionally been kept outside the purview of the factory managers, although in recent years there has been some relaxation of this policy. Since each factory produces a fairly wide mix of products, this has meant that the factory manager must adjust his production scheduling to the composition of orders imposed upon him. It was only at the level of the division general manager that there was any attempt to match up the three variables consisting of relative pricing of products, the degree of sales effort to be devoted to each of the different products, and the production costs that result from the degree of similitude between the composition of orders and of capacity. Below this level, sales and production have in the past gone their independent ways.

The separation between production and the setting both of cost standards and of work allocations for the manual workers is even stricter. All standards for the factories are established by a functional group working out of divisional headquarters, and the factory managers play no role whatsoever in this. Among other implications of this separation of responsibility is the fact that the plant managers have no authority to alter the production process when this would entail the increase of inputs of any factor of production (even of a highly specific type of manual labor).

Similarly, quality control and accounting are controlled from the functional departments in the division. The people carrying out these functions in the plant are attached to the plant manager only for housekeeping purposes.

Investment decisions are also outside of the jurisdiction of the plant managers. True, a plant manager is permitted to give advice to the general manager as to his preference for retiring equipment or for purchasing one type instead of another; but since, in giving this advice, he is not expected to take any account of the relative monetary cost of alternative solutions, the general manager obviously cannot rubber-stamp requests for even very minor types of machinery.

In the light of these sharp restrictions on the authority of plant managers, it should not be surprising that there is a company policy against allowing the factory managers to keep in their possession the profit-and-loss statements of their own factory. The divisional general manager thinks that he is being very liberal in that he personally goes over these statements with his factory managers, thus allowing them to read the statements under his personal supervision. In another division, the general manager is very careful to be sure that no functional manager knows the profits earned partly or wholly through the efforts of another function. It should also not be surprising that the divisional manager acknowledges that there are continental mills, with similar equipment to that of his own mills, which are substantially more productive.

This sharp delimitation of the authority of managers right up through the level of factory manager seems a reasonable consequence of the fact that the vast majority of these managers have only limited education and narrow experience within the company. It represents an adjustment of the managerial organization to the managerial competencies existing in the company. But, of course, quite aside from its inappropriateness for attaining static efficiency within the company, it deprives these managers of any breadth of experience which would help them to serve effectively in higher posts.

To further complicate the company's managerial problems, there has been a marked reluctance to pay salaries commensurate with special abilities. Thus, if we exclude from the comparison very young and newly appointed managers, the highest paid plant manager in the company earned only some 25 percent more than the lowest paid one.[7] No monetary bonuses, stock bonuses, or unusual fringe benefits were used to increase this differential. Similarly, a highly successful salesman got a "big" increase as a reward for his efforts: but this was to an annual figure of only 223 percent of the annual earnings of the average male operator in the industry! No commissions or bonuses were paid to him. This occurred in the company precisely at the moment when top management was urging that special attention should be given to recruiting and developing top salesmen.

Thus, in practice, Company B2 brought little in the way of management skills to the companies that it took over. Its main managerial contribution

[7]This statement holds for plants of roughly comparable size.

was the broad supervisory talents of the company's top management, and this found expression primarily in a willingness to judge and remove rapidly the top people in those new divisions that performed markedly below expectation. This contribution, of course, should not be minimized—particularly in the British environment, where dismissal of managers is a rare event. Since these managers were new to Company B2, top executives felt themselves morally and emotionally free to remove them. Unfortunately, the later history of these same divisions[8] does not indicate any resultant improvement in performance.

All in all, the expansion and take-overs by Company B2 seem to have done little toward improving the efficiency of the company or of the absorbed organizations. In essence, their effects seem to have been limited to three: (1) A sharp but only temporary increase in the stock market value of Company B2 shares, an increase that appears to have been due to widespread but erroneous expectations as to the beneficial effects of take-overs. (2) The providing of a means for absorbing nondistributed profits generated primarily by Division I. (3) The satisfying of the desire of a few top executives for a broader scope of activities; expansion permitted this desire to be satisfied by means other than grappling with those serious managerial problems of the company which would have demanded creative solutions. Due to the need to handle these wider responsibilities, the top executives could continue virtually to ignore tasks such as those of placing the stock control of Division I onto computer, of rethinking pricing, of establishing a genuine investment control over foreign subsidiaries, and of providing real coordination of the company's various activities through establishing a headquarters staff. Extensive expansion took the place of intensive development of management activities.

Company B3 (Division I)

Company B3 is a leading metal firm, operating both within Britain and abroad in a fairly wide variety of subindustries. It underwent considerable growth during the 1950s and 1960s as a result of take-overs as well as of internal growth. During the eleven-year period for which we have data, the company's stock market performance was typical of that of its industry: first being rather better and then a trifle poorer.[9] Similarly, the company has

---

[8]Here, however, we have data for only a very limited time period.
[9]As was the case for Company B2, the calculation takes account of stock splits and rights issues. Comparison is made with the *Financial Times* index of its industry.

never been singled out for having particularly good or bad top management.

Division I, on which our study will concentrate, is one of the oldest and largest divisions within the company and traditionally has been the major source of the company's top management. Its own management, like that in all the other divisions, acted in a highly autonomous fashion throughout the years under examination.

Over the eleven years, there were only erratic variations in the rates of change in output and productivity. The identical factories kept operating throughout all these years (although their operations and capital equipment were altered substantially), and the division's product mix remained relatively stable. The compound annual rates of growth were as shown in Table 5.2. This poor productivity performance was reflected in profits, with the average profit rate in relation to sales declining by 24 percent between the first five years and the second six.[10] Since the divisions's profit picture had been only about the same as that of the rest of the company during the first five years, the decline in the second period brought it substantially below the company average.[11] This decline was particularly striking because products similar to those of Division I were produced elsewhere in the company during the second period at substantially more than twice the profit rate earned by Division I. Interestingly, these high profits were earned by a group of small organizations which had recently been acquired by the company and were still operated primarily by their former managements.

At the beginning of the time span studied, Division I of Company B3 was a staid and conservative—but quite profitable—organization. Its plant and equipment dated from the beginning of the century. Only two or three men in the division were qualified mechanical engineers. Marketing and sales policy had undergone little change since the 1920s. Virtually no product development was undertaken. Profitability was based on the division's strong oligopolistic position in its principal products and on its well-deserved reputation for being prepared to protect its markets by using the company's financial power to fight off price cutters.

---

[10]Profits as a percentage of assets employed declined slightly more rapidly. Some further evidence is available linking the decline in profitability to the productivity performance; namely, the fact that expenditures on materials declined somewhat as a proportion of net sales. This rise in the ratio of value added (of which wages and amortization were the main components) would argue, although certainly not conclusively, against the hypothesis that the decline in profitability was simply caused by a change from a high-price to a low-price market environment for the division's products.

[11]Profit rate here is defined in relation to assets employed.

Table 5.2 Compound Annual Rates of Growth: Divison I of Company B3 (Percentages)

Output[a]	2.1
Labor productivity	2.0
Capital productivity	−2.2
Total productivity	−0.5

[a]Output is measured by value added, deflated to constant prices, both in the output and in the productivity indices.

Into this situation, a new top divisional management entered at the very start of the period under study. The incoming general manager had a production background in the same division, in contrast to several of his predecessors who had all advanced from the sales function. He in turn brought in as production manager an extremely vigorous man in his mid-thirties who came from an aggressive and efficient company in the same broad industry group. The new production manager was to dominate the division throughout the following years, his vigor and competence being so outstanding within the division as to leave him with no serious competition at the time of his later promotion to general manager. He was fortunate in having a superior who welcomed his ability to initiate change. The history of the following eleven years was that of the changes which he carried through and of their results. His failure—as shown by the decline in total productivity and in the profit rate of the division—represented the inability of even an imaginative and forceful man to make a significant advance in solving the division's real problems, with the result that his changes accomplished little except to pile up overhead costs.

Jones, as we shall hereafter call the production manager, began with changes on the factory floor. Quite correctly, he viewed the existing wage structure as anarchic. In the wages paid for individual jobs, 26 percent of the production workers received "personal allowances" in addition to the rate for the job. Thus varying earnings were received for similar work. Over a period of some six or seven years, Jones eliminated this anarchy of wages. This was done by introducing a system of job evaluation and piece rates. Since the standard earnings at piece rate were set at 32 percent above those paid for the same skill grade at time rates, and since these in turn were 50 percent above the wage rates agreed upon with the union, the new piece rate system was accepted by the men as an acceptable substitute for the "personal allowances."

But the cost of administration was high. A large work-study staff was organized to determine appropriate manning ratios and piece rates. In addition, a complex clerical operation—located to a considerable degree at the shop floor—was mounted in order to calculate earnings. As a result, the number of people involved full time in this wage setting and computation was an enormous 3 percent of the total manual labor force of the division; moreover, this was the case even after payrolls had been shifted to a computer.

Nor was there any real effort to improve work efficiency through this investment in white-collar manpower. The work-study staff did no methods planning. Production by piece workers remained at a remarkably even keel, the normal range among individual workers being no more than 5 to 15 percent. With earnings for piece workers at 200 percent of base pay considered standard, one works manager stated that he was required to explain the reason for any worker earning over 210 percent; if a worker reached 215 to 220 percent of standard, this works manager would automatically ask that the job be retimed and renegotiated with the union. Thus it would appear that the piece-rate system of payment, despite the expense involved in operating it, was not even intended to provide an incentive to workers to increase their effort. Finally, the possible justification for the job evaluation program that it would make easier the shifting of workers to jobs where they were most needed was not borne out in practice. Near the end of the period, the personnel manager of the division stated that workers would accept job changes—either of function or at the identical task in a different building on the same location—only when they believed that they would otherwise lose their employment.

Summarizing Jones's effort at reform of the wage system, it was a response to what was correctly viewed as a chaotic situation. Through considerable effort of production management, and at the cost of building up a large overhead function, the situation was remedied. But there is no evidence that any production efficiencies were gained in return for the cost and effort. Despite this, I have no reason to believe that Jones came to view his reform as having been an error.

Two explanations for the absence of economic results can be given. The first is in terms of the objectives of Jones himself. He evaluated success in terms of the ability to eliminate anarchy in wage payments, and by this criterion the reform was entirely successful. Essentially this was a goal set forth for its own sake on the ground that disorder is an evil. True, Jones rationalized this objective in terms of the effect of the earlier anarchy on worker morale and effort; but no attempt was made to test whether productivity responded positively to the change. (From the statistics of variation in productivity, it is difficult to believe that it had any such effect.) In no significant sense was the campaign linked to any more basic objective of the division such as increase of profits.

The second explanation is in terms of suboptimization. Job evaluation was kept organizationally distinct from the production management of individual works, and the head of work study was judged by his ability to institute order into the wage-payments system. The presence of only a very narrow variance in norm fulfillment by piece workers could be readily interpreted as indicating the objective accuracy of the work norms. Improvement of productivity through methods study was not the task of the time-and-motion crew. Thus the manager of the job-evaluation force had no reason to be dissatisfied with the results.

Similarly, the works managers had no reason for dissatisfaction. Their budgets were not charged with the costs of job evaluation, and the clerical expenditures in calculating individual earnings were treated as a noncontrollable expense. The works managers were not expected to show higher productivity as a result of the job evaluation, and so they felt no need to fight both the union and the job evaluation organization by trying to encourage individual workers with high potential to produce substantially above the norm. By doing this, they would only have stirred up trouble both with labor and with other managers. They could afford to treat job evaluation as a whim of the production manager which was no serious concern of theirs.

Just as Jones strove for order in wage payments, he acted similarly with regard to other administrative functions. His notion was first to bring a number of functions into divisional headquarters under his own supervision in order to straighten out their operations and later to decentralize them once more. But the effect of his efforts was the same as that shown in the case of job evaluation.

During an eight-year period,[12] the division's administrative overhead costs (i.e., all overheads other than selling expenses and depreciation) measured in constant prices increased by 30 percent per unit of product. In view of the fact that these administrative expenses amounted at the beginning of the period to 54 percent of the total of these same expenses plus final divisional profits and to 75 percent of the total at the end of the period, this increase in

[12]This is the number of years for which I have statistics on overhead expenditures.

overhead expenditures was a major reason for the decline in profits during these years.

In addition to the increase in staffing of overhead functions, the division also began a significant investment program at the start of the period and accelerated it during the second half of the period. During the five years prior to Jones's entry into the division, the division's net cash contribution to the company was some 7 percent of divisional sales; during the succeeding eleven years there was a continuous cash drain, which totaled almost as much as the contributions of the earlier years.

The investment program was designed with two objectives in mind. The first was technical efficiency, to be achieved by the installation of new and faster equipment that had been designed by the division itself. The second objective was organizational: Jones was persuaded that production and inventory would be more effectively managed if each factory could handle the entire divisional output of a homogeneous group of products. Due to the large volume of one major product group, such product concentration implied the great expansion of output of one factory and the virtual emptying of another. This increased production in the one factory was to be achieved by the installation of the faster equipment. It was believed that the vacant factory could be filled with new products, whose sales were particularly needed in the later years in order to provide the volume required to "carry" the expansion in overhead expenses which had already occurred.

The justification for the major investment program was thus threefold: (1) labor saving through the substitution of capital in the form of new equipment, (2) organizational, and (3) the freeing of both building space and manpower for the expansion of output. Since the projected savings from improved labor productivity were only sufficient to promise a 9.4 percent return on the investment even when one excluded the costs of amortization, it was justifications (2) and (3) that were critical. In fact, however, there was little reason for confidence in the projections of sales expansion, which indeed went unrealized. For example, a major expansion of equipment for one product group was undertaken in anticipation of a boom of demand which came only six years after the anticipated date.

It is difficult to say why the sales projections were so wildly exaggerated. Doubtless one reason was the paucity and weakness of the market analysts. Much more important was the pressure on these analysts to provide an estimate of sales that would, at least eventually, "justify" the magnitude of overhead expenditures that the division was already carrying. Equally important was the fact that the projections called for from the sales department were for five years in the future, and that no intermediate projections were required to show how these final targets would be realized. In the nature of things, such projections were bound to be highly crude. But the crudeness was accentuated by the fact that the history of the division demonstrated that targets were treated as though they were intended for the indefinite future rather than for the date specified; virtually any sales projections were safe under these conditions.

Furthermore, there was little contact between the sales and production functions except at the very highest levels. Thus works managers requested investment funds and ordered equipment for expansion on the basis of these sales estimates, but without any personal consultation as to the firmness of the estimates for individual products. The result was that investments were undertaken without serious analysis of the very shaky projections that the sales department was forced to make, and without even an awareness of the degree of confidence that the sales department itself had in the individual estimates.

In order to provide the extra sales needed to justify the investments, Jones first tried to persuade the engineering department—in whose jurisdiction the matter lay—to take a serious and creative interest in the development of new products. But the engineering management was interested in designing equipment rather than in developing new products, and Jones was able to move only very slowly in changing this state of affairs. As an alternative, Jones turned to an untapped market that existed for a product which the division could readily produce; this was an item which was currently being produced for their own use by the few large manufacturers in the country who required it as a component in their products.

Jones proceeded to attempt to capture this market through a policy of low prices, and was completely successful in doing so. The only problem was that prices could not be pushed up thereafter or the manufacturers would have returned to individual production to meet their own requirements. So the division found itself with a new major product that showed even lower profits than did the rest of the division's output, and probably did not even cover average costs. Jones indeed continued the same pricing policy in capturing export markets. For it was clear that this product at least helped to cover overhead costs, and its expansion was the only road to the expansion of total sales which Jones was able to follow.

Under these circumstances, it is not surprising that the investment program only worsened the division's profit position. To aggravate matters, the specific types of equipment chosen were designed by the engineering department almost entirely with an eye to the production rate per machine. The result was that the machinery was geared to rather larger lot sizes of production than were currently being produced; thus tooling costs rose sharply and also the stocks of finished goods increased as a concomitant of producing goods in larger lot sizes than formerly. This was a consequence of the lack of communication between the engineering and production departments, and the fact that it was engineering which determined the nature of the machinery to be utilized.

What is most interesting about this history of bold attempts at modernizing the organization and fixed capital of the division, all of which only further depressed the profit rate earned, is that these attempts did not injure the careers of the executives concerned. The general manager of the division went on to the main board of the company, and was finally transferred to the post of general manager of another division that was judged to be in trouble and requiring rescue. Jones was his successor as general manager, and he in turn joined his predecessor on the main board. From the point of view of achieving a successful company career, vigor, personality, and bold ideas were a sufficient substitute for success. Efforts at modernization were welcomed and rewarded by the company's main board, even though these efforts brought only financial deterioration over an eleven-year period.

How is the failure of these attempts at modernization to be explained? Certainly a part of the answer is that some of the attempts were poorly thought out. More significantly, they were not planned in terms of well-specified and dated profit objectives, and programs were not revised when profits failed to materialize. But most important of all were the organizational restrictions within which Jones was forced to work.

As we have seen, within the division there was considerable decentralization by function of the authority for carrying out Jones's various strategic plans. As a result, no one could really be held responsible for the overall effectiveness of any of the undertakings, and no one below the level of Jones had either the task of coordinating or the authority to do so. Jones was kept busy outlining new projects as well as carrying on his normal operating functions, and thus was himself unable to provide the necessary coordination of functions. It is true that Jones could and did both create new staff functions and strengthen old ones, but he did not have the power to give the men in these functions genuine authority over the line managers. Thus the net effect of the expansion of staff was primarily to increase overhead expenditures.

Although Jones was far and away the most powerful figure in the division, he was in no position to move decisively either to remove other divisional executives or to weaken their power. During the eleven years, only one divisional director was forced out of the company—and he into early retirement. In order to accomplish even this, Jones had not only to prove incompetence but also to demonstrate the long-term unwillingness of this director to cooperate with the other divisional directors. A department head, whose position did not rate a directorship on the divisional board, was finally ousted for gross incompetence. But the ouster was politically acceptable in the company only on the basis that he be given an equivalent post in a smaller division, and that Division I agree permanently to pay one-third of his salary there. These two were the total of removals of top divisional personnel during the eleven years.

There was general agreement in the division that sanctions for bad work were normally not employed against managerial personnel at any level. Similarly, policy with regard to nonmanagerial personnel was governed by the doctrine of emphasizing smooth relationships more than efficiency. This traditional no-sanctions attitude of the company was most sharply represented by the chairman of the company's main board, who himself had once headed the division and still maintained a deep interest in its inner workings; he made quite clear his hostility toward "reforming" managers. Even with regard to suppliers and customers, strong forces on the main board ruled out actions to improve efficiency and raise profits at the expense of discomforting these outsiders. Thus Jones had virtually no weapons at his command in fighting against an environment in which managers typically agreed to policies setting forth change in the division, but afterwards effectively sabotaged the changes. Since conservatism and a situation in which each function's management retained untrammeled control over its own affairs continued as the unchallenged order of the day, Jones's efforts at modernizing could only increase costs without showing much in the way of results.

It is probably Jones's acceptance of this situation that explains his unusually rapid career success in the company. On the one hand, he showed initiative and proposed exciting ideas that offered promise of improving the division's position. On the other, he did not push the implications of these ideas so far as to threaten the existing managerial environment. In the light of this combination of progressiveness and absence of attack upon the status quo, the worsening of the divisional financial situation could be forgiven.

By the end of our period, Jones had begun adopting a new approach to the division's problems. He now believed that it was imperative to give one person authority for all the activities involved in producing and selling a small group of homogeneous products; only in this way, he felt, would it be possible to establish truly flexible and responsible management. He had already moved some distance in that direction by reorganizing his factories so that each would produce a homogeneous group of products. But he did not see how it was possible to go further and break down all other functions into similar small units attached to these same products.

His solution was for the division to engage in the purchase of a number of small businesses producing and selling similar products to those of the division itself. These were to be managed independently of the original division, although under Jones's overall supervision. This decision was in fact carried out, and Jones proceeded to devote increasing amounts of his time to the new businesses.

Although Jones did not say so, this approach had two advantages. First, it was a means of coping with suboptimization, even if at the cost of giving up most of the advantages of large scale. Second, it was a method—although possibly not a conscious one—by which to escape from the strains of coping with the existing managerial personnel and organization. Just as American firms have occasionally closed up factories and established others elsewhere in order to run away from a labor force that was encrusted in traditional work-to-rule procedures, here Jones was similarly escaping from the managerial force under him. True, he could not very well give up the existing divisional activities, plants, and organization; but he could pin much of his hopes for overall improvement on what amounted to a new venture.

Company B3 as a Whole

Up to this point, I have centered my discussion entirely upon Division I. But how about the company as a whole, and why did the main board permit the division to evolve in this fashion?

Our concentration upon Division I of Company B3 is explained by the organization of the company's management; namely, that for purposes of management the company has been nothing more than a collection of divisions.

The company's board of directors has been composed primarily of inside, working directors, almost all of whom have simultaneously headed individual divisions. Until recently headquarters consisted of the company's chairman and financial director, and of virtually no staff. Eventually some professionals were recruited into a series of company services in order to provide aid to the various divisions, but they have had virtually no management functions. Thus decisions have been taken by a board consisting essentially of men representing the major divisions. Working committees and their staff were formed on an ad hoc basis from among the managers in the principal divisions, who continued to exercise their divisional responsibilities while working on company problems. Little effort was devoted to evolving common policies for the various divisions, and the company in fact prided itself on the diversity of policies followed in its various segments.

Thus headquarters concerned itself primarily with the treasury function, with handling decisions as to the promotion and retention of top divisional personnel, and with approval of investments. Even with regard to investments, the board's activities were largely restricted to acquisitions. Since the company had a large cash flow and rarely felt it necessary to ration funds, investment requests from ongoing divisions were normally approved so long as they had the backing of the head of a major division. Only toward the end of the period studied did the board even formally insist on a minimum specified anticipated return from new investments in existing divisions.

The main nonfinancial function of the board and headquarters seems to have been to reenforce the status quo in the various divisions wherever it needed shoring. "Reforming" divisional managers would find opposition among their seniors on the main board as well as among their juniors in divisional management. Despite or perhaps because of the fact that the stock of the company was widely held, there was little anxiety over divisional profits.

Thus, in most regards, the company should be considered as a collection of divisions operating under a common corporate umbrella. Of course, the existence of the large company was helpful in reducing the costs of financing and in permitting divisions suffering financial reverses to weather out bad times. Larger investments both in individual divisions and in acquisitions could be financed than would have been possible if the individual divisions had been separate companies. The strong financial position of the company served as a warning both to British and foreign firms that might otherwise have been tempted to trespass in its markets. But from the point of view of managerial control and innovations, it was the divisions rather than the company headquarters that really mattered.

The French Companies

Company F1

Company F1 is a leading French metal firm, producing a rather wide product mix in a number of plants. Much of its technology is fairly sophisticated, and it produces a high ratio of value-added production to total production. Its post-Second World War history is dominated by mergers, with a major effort having been made to use mergers in order to achieve economies of scale and rationalization that had been outside the grasp of the smaller independent companies which were absorbed. The company's management is an absolute prototype of the *grande école* model; this applies equally to management backgrounds, to the fact that headquarters and marketing are centered in Paris while the plants are primarily located in the provinces, and to the fact that the company is heavily dependent upon the French government both as customer and as financier.

In analyzing the company, we shall deal primarily with the overwhelmingly major part of the firm that was incorporated within Company F1 throughout the thirteen-year period under examination. We shall call this portion of the firm Division I. For the nine years for which we have both company and industry data, the output of this portion of Company F1 grew at 84 percent of the rate of the industry as a whole. Yet, despite the fact that we would normally expect output and labor productivity to be positively correlated, its labor productivity grew twice as rapidly as did that of the industry. Total productivity in the division increased at an annual compound rate of 3.0 percent over thirteen years, substantially more than the increase of 2.1 percent that would have been sufficient to compensate for the increase in real hourly wages in that industry.

The history of Division I is best divided into two periods. The first period is one in which the output both of the division and of the industry grew rapidly, while in the second period the division's output barely increased. During both periods, the output of the industry as a whole increased somewhat more rapidly than did that of Division I. In the first period, consolidation of production within the division, so that each of many individual products would be produced in only one or a small number of facilities, was combined with new investments needed to take advantage of the resulting potential economies of scale. The second period saw slightly more real gross capital investment per annum, but was also an era of digestion of the economies which had been made possible earlier. Compound annual rates of growth were as shown in Table 6.1.

What is striking in these figures is the high degree of success in improving

Table 6.1 Compound Annual Rates of Growth: Division I of Company F1
(Percentages)

	Period I	Period II
Output	7.2	0.4
Labor productivity	5.9	7.0
Capital productivity	0.8	−2.5
Total productivity	3.7	2.0

labor productivity during Period II. Normally, the rate of increase in labor productivity is positively correlated with the rate of increase of output, and we would expect such correlation to be particularly strong in France with its social and legal restrictions on reductions of staff. The reversal of such correlation between the two periods (although a weak positive correlation does exist on a year-by-year comparison for the two periods taken together) is a major tribute to managerial success in Period II.

Despite this managerial success in raising total productivity, Company F1—quite typically for its branch—had a difficult financial life throughout. For most of the thirteen years, its prices were sharply restrained either by reasonably effective price controls or by sharp competition within the industry. Thus, although the company's real capital stock increased by 7.5 percent compounded annually (which, while respectable, would scarcely warrant categorizing it as a growth company), only one-quarter of the gross funds[1] were generated internally, another fifth were acquired through additional investments made by the financial groups that were the original dominant owners, and over half came from net increases in outstanding loans and bonds. Given the conditions of the French capital market, this ability to expand through borrowing indicates little about the credit worthiness of the company but much about the ability of the management to obtain the ear of government agencies. Over the period as a whole, internally generated funds plus the minuscule dividends that were distributed in cash fell slightly short of matching even a linear depreciation of the company's assets.

As might be expected, the stock market performance was also very poor. The price of the company's stock, adjusted for stock dividends and after the addition of the discounted value of posttax dividends, dropped sharply during the eight years examined; in contrast, the average for its industry showed a

[1]The calculation is made by including in the total gross funds generated all retained earnings, the increase of reserves, depreciation allowances, accessions in kind through merger, raising of additional equity capital in cash, and net increases in outstanding debt. All contributions are reduced to constant prices.

modest increase. The company did equally badly compared to the Paris Bourse as a whole.

From this financial picture, it is obvious enough that the company could scarcely have continued, let alone have expanded its capital stock as it did, without the receipt of government aid through admittance to a low-interest and restricted-access bond and loan market. Yet even in the light of this government assistance, the new investments in the stock of the company are curious. If one makes the very strong assumption that the market value of the company at the beginning of Period I was zero, and that no debt financing would have been available without the new investments by the original dominant owners, then it is possible to make a calculation as to the rate of return earned on these new investments. Counting the total return as the full gross amount earned by the company in cash flow plus distributed dividends, minus a minimum estimate of 5 percent linear depreciation of only that portion of new investment which was financed from new equity capital, and converting both this return and the new equity investment into francs of constant price, the compound annual pretax rate of return earned was a bare 8.7 percent.[2] It can scarcely be doubted that the actual rate of return earned on new equity capital was substantially less than that.[3]

The low rate of return earned on new investment in this company is highly relevant both to the issue of proper allocation of resources in France as a whole and to productivity in Company F1's industry. The pretax rate of return on total new investment (irrespective of whether this was financed by equity or debt capital) after deflating for price changes in France over the entire period was 4.2 percent, even after making the extremely optimistic assumption of twenty-year life for additions to fixed capital. Even the rate of return on new equity finance was well below the opportunity cost of this money. From this we can conclude that, most clearly from a social point of view but also from a narrowly private viewpoint, the investment in Company F1 was unjustified. Without such investment, and similar expansion of capital in other firms of the industry, major consolidation of production into fewer

[2] The 8.7 percent figure is derived on the assumption that a discount rate of 15 percent should be used as the opportunity cost of this new money. If one were to use a zero rate of discount both for the investments and for the gross returns, the rate of return would rise only to 10.5 percent; thus the rate of return calculation is quite robust with regard to the rate of time discount utilized.

[3] In explaining the substantial equity investments during the period which were made by the financial groups that were the original dominant owners, it is worth noting that stock ownership in the financial groups themselves was extremely widely spread; no single individual stock owner held as much as 1 percent of the shares of these groups.

firms and plants would have occurred in France. It cannot be doubted that such a development would have had substantial positive effects both on national labor productivity and on capital productivity.

It is from this point of view that both French governmental policy and private managerial investment policy must be debited with seriously holding back potential productivity improvement in the industry as a whole. The company's record of a 3.0 percent annual rate of improvement in total productivity now looks considerably less impressive than it did at first sight.

How was the company's rise in productivity achieved? For Period I, it is quite clear that the improvement came from two sources. The most important of these was the consolidation of facilities which was made possible by mergers. Within each plant, much small and obsolete equipment was shut down and their output was transferred to larger units of equipment which were themselves modernized. Where duplicate facilities continued to be operated in two or more plants, the mergers made it possible for each to produce a complementary and smaller product mix, thus gaining the advantages of larger lot size and longer individual production runs. In the case of one process, economies of scale made it economical to close down all existing facilities and to build a single new and modern one.

The second reason for the improvement in productivity was that demand for the industry's products was buoyant. The resultant expansion of output led to a slight improvement in the capital/output ratio, reinforcing the effect of the improvement in labor productivity. This reason for improvement was, of course, quite outside of the company's control.

Thus the improvements in productivity in Period I were due entirely, aside from the phenomenon of general increased demand in the industry, both to the top management decision to engage in major mergers and to rationalize production facilities on the basis of these mergers, and to the government decision to make available the funds to finance this rationalization. Here, the choice almost certainly lay between the imminent closing of the plants and the rationalization which in fact occurred. Three-quarters of the financing of the rationalization came from expansion in loan and bond debt made possible by the government. Nevertheless, top management must be credited with what appears to have been a clever technical scheme of rationalization with a minimum of building of new facilities, and with having had the courage to make the difficult social decisions involved in closing down many individual facilities within plants.

The further rise in productivity in Period II stemmed from rather different causes. It will be recalled that during these years there was virtually no expansion in output, yet labor productivity grew by 7 percent per annum.

The principal reason for improvement was a major effort at the individual shop level. The same products were produced in the same volumes and on the same equipment, but with a steadily declining labor input. Top and middle management inspired this effort through placing increased pressure on lower management both in production and in engineering services, and specifically by demonstrating a readiness to remove individual poor performers among lower management. Top management strategically transferred a fair number of middle managers, and even one member of top management, to staff posts specially created for them so as to make room for more dynamic successors. The seniority route to promotion to middle-management posts was downgraded in contrast with the past, although emphasis upon it remained high if the standard of comparison used is that of American industry.

Three kinds of staff aides were used in this productivity improvement at the shop level. The first of these was cost accounting; a system of standards and variances had been originated in the company in the middle of Period I, and was well into implementation by the middle of Period II. The emphasis here was on the setting down on paper of the technical norms which governed operations in the various shops, but which until then had existed primarily as an oral tradition at foreman and lower-management levels and were thus impervious to examination and change. The systematization in writing of these standards laid them open for analysis and for comparison between shops and plants. Improvement targets could now be set more effectively by both top and middle production management.

The second was the formation in the beginning of Period II of a centralized work-study group, whose members were sent on temporary duty into the individual plants and shops. The members consisted overwhelmingly of new engineering recruits with no experience in industry, who thus had not yet learned the bad traditions of how production was supposed to be organized— but who also carried relatively little authority. This was a staff group viewed by top management primarily as a tool it could employ to bring about change in backward shops. Unfortunately, the resistance by middle management to the employment of this group was considerable. The man in charge of the group stated that about half of the heads of lower production organizations resisted cooperating with the work-study engineers, as they rightly feared providing knowledge to top management which could be used for control purposes. Top management's tougher attitude toward lower-management people doubtless increased this resistance; on the other hand, it was also probably the sine qua non without which the group could not have obtained entrée at all.

The third sort of staff aide, consisting of an operations research group, was also created in the second period. Its work cut across individual shops and even plants, but was still effective only in the narrowly defined production area. Probably its main contribution was that of singling out those key technical "requirements" that served as the bottlenecks to substantial production improvement and then challenging these "requirements" to see whether they were really necessary.

All three of these staff aides played useful functions in improving productivity. But their role should not be exaggerated. It is my impression that the main source of improved productivity was rudimentary pressure from top and middle management. The degree of slack existing in the production organization was such that this was quite sufficient.

The second source of productivity improvement consisted of a whole host of small investments in production equipment. A large part of the total gross investment during Period II was allocated to minor projects that promised a high time-discounted rate of return through cost savings. Individual engineers were encouraged to apply for such funds, and a quite sophisticated methodology was worked out for choosing those projects promising the highest return. Moreover, the procedure was quite well policed, and the promised cost economies were on the whole achieved.

Despite the success of these cost-reducing investments, they should probably be judged as having been prejudicial both to the welfare of the company and to productivity improvement in the industry as a whole. The explanation for this state of affairs is that returns on investment were calculated by the production managers on the hypothesis that all products were to be continued in production even when they were currently being sold at a loss. The reason for this hypothesis will be explained later.

The third and final source of productivity improvement was by far the least significant. One fairly minor process had been abandoned, and thus a few small shops were shut, and there was some continuation of the type of consolidation of facilities between plants which had occurred on a grand scale during Period I.

Although, as we have seen, the reasons for productivity improvement were quite different in the two periods, a major theme of continuity runs throughout both. Namely, in neither period was there a concentration on the more profitable products or on those in which the company showed the highest productivity, a willingness to abandon—with a very few exceptions—even the most unprofitable items, nor a successful development of new products on any significant scale. The successes were all those of production; virtually no contribution was made by marketing policy. The company showed itself totally unwilling or unable to adapt either to shifts in demand for its industry's products or to the emergence of low-cost competitors in any fashion except that of cost reduction. Here was a production-oriented company par excellence.

Let us now turn to the restraints that prevented productivity from rising even more rapidly than it did.

The first restraint was the absence until the last two years of any financial planning by product. Only at the very end of Period II was an effort made to develop one-year cost and revenue projections by product line, and longer projections were still no more than a hope for the near future. Without such projections, it was of course impossible to make rational decisions as to expanding, maintaining, or abandoning individual product lines—and the situation was at its worst for the host of products produced in small volume whose individual importance was not such as to force their way to the attention of the top three or four directors. Little wonder that it was the mass of these minor product lines which were the most unprofitable for the company.

There were several reasons for this absence of financial planning by product line. Many of the products were partially or even primarily sold internally within the company, and there was great scepticism as to the meaningfulness of the intracompany prices. This caused a reluctance to rely heavily on either revenue or cost data by product line. Second, the first priority in developing a cost-accounting system after the middle of Period I was placed on working out cost standards for individual cost centers in the factories. This was rational in terms of the goal of evaluating and bringing down processing costs in the individual shops, but such a system of priorities left little room for the second task of placing costs on a product basis as well. Doubtless cost accounting could have been developed much more rapidly and could have quickly served both functions; but it was treated as an overhead function to which no great resources should be allocated during the perennial financial difficulties that the company was undergoing.

The organizational structure of the company reinforced the nonplanning characteristic of the firm. Production and sales were organized into distinct hierarchies, and these functions were joined together under a single head only at the level of the *président-directeur général*. Thus no one below the level of *président* was responsible for the total financial results of any product line or even group of lines. There was no manager with an incentive to carry out such planning.

Of course, this functionalized structure of the company could have been supplemented by a strong financial planning department at headquarters with the responsibility of integrating the various functional results and plans around individual product groups. But this did not occur. The financial function in the company was limited pretty much to the raising of external funds, and it did not serve the president as a planning and control group. The result of this situation was that no organized procedure existed for regularly reviewing decisions as to the development or abandonment of product lines.

The second restraint on productivity improvement was the previously mentioned system of hierarchical separation of production and sales and, in most cases, of design as well. Although in a formal sense there was coordination of the different functions through consultation at the middle-management level, in fact the real coordination took place only at the level of the *président*. The new functions in the company which might have been developed to play a supplementing central-staff role—namely, cost accounting and operations research—were organized solely within production and never outgrew this secondary position.

One effect of this organizational structure was that investment was primarily directed toward cost reduction. For, given the assumption that no products were to be abandoned, the highest projected return on capital was on such investments. In the absence both of financial planning by product line and of real coordination between sales and production, it was simply not feasible for the production managers to make any other assumption except in the very rare case where the matter was decided otherwise by the *président*. The tendency to invest in this fashion was further strengthened by the fact that it permitted the method of determining investments to appear to be the sophisticated technique of maximizing the discounted return on capital, which appealed to the cult of rationalism of the engineering leadership of the enterprise.

Even the investments directed toward cost reduction were often poorly utilized. This was because of the reluctance during Period II, in the absence of product planning, either to engage in major investments for concentrating and rationalizing production or to reduce total capacity for any product or process by abandoning its output in any plant. Thus small investments were made in each mill in order to reduce costs there. By the very end of Period II, much of this modernized capacity was finally in the process of being abandoned and two new plants were being built; one of these was in cooperation with another enterprise in order to produce, at a larger scale, for the complete needs of both firms.

The separation of functions and the absence of planning made the top management extremely reluctant to engage in investments for the development of capacity of new products. Such investments were regarded as more risky than those for reducing costs, and thus an even higher discounted rate of return was demanded of them. The result was that there was little investment in new products, and what investments of this type were made were aimed at a low level of output. The new products were thus produced at high cost and with insufficiently elaborated design; sales lagged, and the top management's suspicion of sales-oriented investments was further reinforced.

The third restraint on productivity improvement was imposed by the government itself. During Period II, the government often agreed to the issuance of new bonds and to the expansion of loans only on condition that the funds be invested in specific projects which won government approval. Invariably these were projects which, the company's top management believed, promised a lower rate of return than available alternatives. During Period II, one-third of the company's gross investments in Division I went into such investments.

One might question whether the foregoing was really a restraint on productivity improvement. In view of the poor record of the company's management in choosing new investments, one might suspect that the government's choice would be at least as successful. Possibly this would have been true except for the fact that it was the company's management which was entrusted with the task of making these investments succeed, and its suspicion of these investments probably led it to utilize these new facilities less efficiently than would have been the case if management had felt itself responsible for the investment decision.

To sum up, the underlying obstacles to further increases in productivity were fivefold:

1. The company was unwilling to renounce any products, no matter how unprofitable they were and were likely to remain, except under the severest financial pressure. This position essentially arose from a concern with main-

taining employment in each of the factories, and for each skill group within each factory, as long as possible. But it was supported by two additional factors.

The first was that management hoped to negotiate either mergers or agreements with other large companies in which each would produce the full needs of all the linked companies for selected products. In the case of such an agreement, the existence of markets for even highly unprofitable products would be useful for negotiation purposes—since such products might be profitable for one of the other companies or might be made profitable if volume was all concentrated in a single facility.

The second justification was that, when revenue was compared with operating costs defined narrowly so as to exclude even such overhead items as salaries for plant and shop white-collar personnel, very few products were found to be still running a net loss. Thus it appeared that little would be gained by abandoning products. Of course, the implicit and untested assumptions here were that overheads were quite unresponsive to the volume or number of products produced, and that no new products or additional volumes of old ones could be produced and sold using existing capacity.

2. Duplicate facilities in different plants were maintained as long as possible, even when all had to be run well below capacity, and new investments were made in them so as to bring down their operating costs. The essential reason here was the same as in the case of products. In particular, a great effort was made to avoid the firing of workers; thus a major policy goal was to abstain from reducing any plant's employment faster than the natural wastage of the labor force from retirements, deaths, and quits.

3. Decision-making power was very highly centralized at the extreme peak of the management structure. This centralization prevented the creation of bodies that could coordinate the activities of different functions around specific product lines, whether such coordination were to take the shape of forming product groups or of creating substantial staff bodies at headquarters. The result was particularly nefarious with regard to the host of minor products produced.

4. During Period II, management had reached the point of promoting production efficiency by sidetracking or removing ineffective lower managers. But upper management, and even most of middle management in the sales, design, and factory functions, were virtually unaffected by this search for efficiency. At these levels, managerial failure was rarely recognized in any

tangible fashion. Thus there was much less pressure than might otherwise have existed for taking painful decisions in the interest of profitability.

5. Finally, the government approved debt financing by the company only on condition that most of it be employed in specific projects to which the government gave its approval. The underlying government objectives here were those of preserving regional employment. As a result, much of the company's investments were in projects that the management did not believe were warranted even by the company's own, certainly not overly ambitious, standards of profitability.

Company F2

Company F2 is also a major metal firm. Well over 50 percent of the stock has been owned by a single individual who, however, played no active role in the company's management. The top management itself was thoroughly *grande école*. The leading figures in the company were *polytechniciens* who had previously served in high-prestige branches of the French government; but the middle management came in the main from normal engineering schools.

Much less information is available concerning Company F2 than for the other French firms. Specifically, no explanation can be offered for F2's productivity record. Nevertheless, there are several points in its history which are worth noting. In particular, there is the Bourse reaction to the major merger in which it was involved.

We have productivity data for eight years of the company's history. During this period, the compound annual rates of growth were as shown in Table 6.2. The improvement in labor productivity was substantially better than that of its industry as a whole, while its output grew only slightly more rapidly.

Company F2's stock price, adjusted for the discounted value of posttax dividends, moved more poorly than did that of its subindustry. But its stock market performance was about the same as that of the Paris Bourse.

Company F2 attempted to develop product-line departments, organized along profit-making lines in the same fashion as we shall see was done in

Table 6.2   Compound Annual Rates of Growth: Company F2 (Percentages)

Output	12.1
Labor productivity	7.8
Capital productivity	4.5
Total productivity	6.6

Company F6. But here, unlike the case of F6, this effort broke down in practice. This collapse occurred because management believed that many of its product lines could best be sold together in block sales to large customers, and thus a separate department was enormously expanded in order to carry out such design and sales coordination. By the end of the period, one-third of the company's sales were carried out by this centralized organization.

Certainly it would have been organizationally conceivable for this centralized department to have operated as a profit-making unit and for it to have negotiated with the various product departments for internal prices that would have made this feasible. Indeed, in theory this was done. But the company's top management was anxious to see continued rapid growth in sales, and it feared that this goal would be prejudiced if each product department were to decide for itself whether to accept the price reductions needed to make the block sales. Even more to the point, it worried that the various departments would bargain shrewdly over price and would keep cost information bottled up. To avoid such a situation, it allowed the product departments to sell at a profit to the centralized design-sales department, while this department in turn sold to outside customers at a loss. Headquarters consoled itself with the belief that the net effect of these sales was profitable for the company, but it does not appear that any company-wide data existed which could have been used to test this belief. The various product departments were relieved of market pressure, since they could expand their sales to any degree that top management thought appropriate by selling—at their own price—to the centralized design-sales department.

One result of this de facto rejection of product-departmentalization was that sales continued to expand rapidly and that economies of scale were achieved in production and even more in design expenditures. But the cost was both a proliferation of the company's products (since profit control by product group was weak) and a general failure to apply profit tests to decisions as to the continuation of individual products and operations.

An example of the result might be seen in the case of one production shop whose specialized capacity could not be fully used within the company, and which supplemented its intracompany orders by subcontracting its residual capacity on a weekly basis to a neighboring firm that was willing to accept this arrangement because of the low price it paid for the work done. The company had inherited this shop some fifteen years before I visited it, and had been allowing it to contract gradually both because it was unprofitable and because its work did not fit in with the specialty of the plant as a whole. Doomed to disappear, no effort was made to increase its production efficiency although simple and inexpensive improvements were obvious enough to the casual observer. The shop was neither abandoned nor given even the minor attention and investment that could have substantially improved its working. What was striking was that this situation had been permitted to continue for a decade, with no decision being made either "to fish or cut bait."

The foregoing remarks describe the situation in Company F2 prior to its merger. It was obviously a rather loosely controlled company from the point of view of the profitability of operations, but it had shown an abnormally high growth of output and of productivity for its industry. Its stock market record was poor in relation to that of the industry, but not catastrophically so.

The merger was a linkage of two firms of equal size. The majority of their product mix overlapped, and it was believed that major economies of scale—both in production and in design—could be realized by the merger. The other firm was also similar to Company F2 both in that its ownership was highly concentrated and that its management consisted of *grande école* men who had no significant ownership stake in the company.

In many respects, the merger was carried through quite ruthlessly. Although top management was at first constituted from the former top men in both companies, it was not long before the top managers of Company F2 were ousted. Many medium- and lower-management people were forced to change locations and even functions under pain of being separated from the firm, and there was a general bloodletting of managerial and professional personnel.

Similarly, various unprofitable activities of Company F2 were abruptly stopped. Company F2's centralized design-sales department was continued but was forbidden to operate at a loss. It was allowed to engage in block sales only when it could make them at a profit, and thus it was forced to bargain sharply with the product departments over the prices of intracompany sales. The result was, as had earlier been forecast, some bottling up of information within individual departments and a drop in these block sales. Nevertheless, the new company was able to maintain the level of sales of the two merged predecessor firms and in what would appear to have been a much healthier product mix from the viewpoint of future profitability.

Quick action was taken to achieve production economies by combining common products of the previous two firms into the same facilities. This was done on such a wholesale scale that all of the plants of Company F2 either were put up for sale or had their products completely changed. This, naturally, affected heavily the manual workers of the old Company F2, although these workers were affected less than the former managers and professionals.

Only one concession was made to sentiment. The major plant of Company F was located in the provinces in an area where other industrial employment was scarce, and was manned by skilled male workers who were relatively well paid. As its old products were taken away from it, this plant could be provided with work only by supplying it with products which had previously been produced by unskilled and largely female labor. The price of keeping the plant open was a sharp rise in the labor cost of producing these products, a rise which promised to remain permanent. Nevertheless, in the interests of maintaining employment in a region where it would have been difficult for the workers to find other industrial jobs, and which had been the origin of Company F2, this plant was maintained in operation.

Three years after the merger had occurred, the merged company had completed its reorganization. As might have been expected, it had suffered financial losses—but these had financed the complete physical reorganization of the plants of the company. The product mix, labor force, and managerial staff had all been pared to what promised to be a more effective level. True, the company's sales had failed to grow during this period, but that was scarcely surprising. In short, from the perspective of an American observer the merger appeared to have been a highly successful, if quite ruthless, consolidation.

But this was not the way it appeared in France. The stock market value of the company fell over three years by 48 percent, compared to an average drop in Paris Bourse values of only 22 percent during the same period. The merger was described to me by top men in other companies of the industry as a flat failure.

Why this evaluation? I can only explain it by the effects of the merger on sales and on the managerial group and labor force of the former Company F2. This kind of ruthless action was simply not "done" in France.

Thus it would appear that although production and sales agreements, and even "gentlemanly" mergers, are regarded quite favorably by industrialists as a means of bringing French corporate size to the "level of the Common Market," a serious attempt to rapidly achieve the potential advantages of merger is considered quite differently—even by the Bourse, which one would expect to be the least sentimental of institutions. There is little in this experience which would encourage other mergers on an equally ruthless pattern.

Company F3

Company F3 is a consumers' product firm that is one of the two or three leaders in its branch. Although its shares are quoted on the Paris Exchange, the founding family still owns a sufficient proportion of stock to have no reason to fear any shareholder challenge to its managerial decisions—at least so long as the family holds together. The technology employed is fairly simple and classical, and the factories add a relatively small proportion of value added to the raw materials purchased from outside.

During the thirteen years between 1952 and 1965, the sales of Company F3 increased more rapidly than did the French gross national product, although at only 73 percent of the rate of the industry as a whole. Company F3's profitability appears to have been at least average for large-scale French business. On the other hand, total productivity increased by a mere 1.3 percent compounded per annum during the thirteen years: less than one-half of what would have been needed to compensate for the rise in real hourly wages in that industry. The poor total-productivity result was due primarily to a decline in capital productivity, which offset the 3.4 percent annual increase in labor productivity.

Company F3 may be taken as representative of a significant sector of family-controlled and -managed French large-scale industry. In this regard, it differs sharply from F1 and F2.

During several decades prior to 1958, Company F3 was run by its *président-directeur général*—a family member and a graduate of a major *grande école*—without the aid of any real collaborators. Perhaps to keep in his own hands as much power as possible, his headquarters staff was kept relatively powerless. In order to make this system workable, current decisions both as to production and sales were decentralized to the factory and regional sales managers; the two functions were coordinated by means of a pseudomarket relationship between the individual factories and the sales offices, with the managers of each being urged to maximize profits as computed within the system of cost allocation that existed in the enterprise.

Here was a system of interfunctional coordination designed to operate insofar as possible through the managerial mechanism of Adam Smith's "invisible hand." This managerial system is a variant on the model type of the French corporation: dominance by a strong isolated man at the top of the organization, and determination of operating policy with a minimum of face-to-face contact among the managers concerned.

But this internal market situation was considerably falsified by the accounting rules established both for factories and for sales outlets. Let us first examine the situation with regard to the factories.

Profits at the factory level were equal to total funds paid by the sales outlets minus the sum: $\{$ cost of raw materials, power, etc. + wages and salaries + the first year's depreciation of fixed capital + the plant's share of all headquarters and general company expenditures and of capital depreciation beyond that of the first year in all factories of the company $\}$. Not only did the individual factory pay no capital charges on either its fixed capital or its stocks, but it also paid a total of only about 10 percent of its proper depreciation. General company expenditures were allocated among the factories according to a weighted average of their sales volume and profit in the previous year.

The use of this accounting system had two effects that, at least by the middle 1960s, were recognized as pernicious. First, it deprived the factories of all interest in holding down capital expenditures or in operating rational stock policies.[4] Second, it caused factory managers to "manage their profits" so as to show satisfactory profit results but not to display such high profits as to cause a jump in the individual factory's share of general company expenditures in the following year. This "management of profits" took several forms, but one of the more prominent was that of making capital expenditures that were kept hidden from headquarters and were fully written off against current expenditures. Counterbalancing these negative effects, however, it was believed that this costing system led to a strong emphasis by factory managers on growth of production; since only a portion of costs were charged directly to the individual factory with the rest being allocated according to the previous year's results, profits from an individual factory's marginal output were very high—and a factory whose output did not grow in a year in which the other factories sharply increased sales and general company expenditures was likely to suffer absolute losses. Furthermore, this system justified the con-

---

[4]Stock policy was particularly important both because stocks were roughly equal to the value of fixed capital measured in current prices, and because the seasonality of sales of many of the company's products led to a situation of tradeoff between stocks and seasonal irregularity of production.

centration of capital investment and stock decisions at headquarters, where the *président* could have greatest personal control over these key variables of company policy.

In principle, the *président* approved stock levels in each factory each month and made even minor investment decisions. But, particularly because he kept his headquarters staff weak, this was only possible on a fairly arbitrary basis. The result was that both stock and investment policy were virtually out of any-one's control. Thus plant managers originated investment requests, but all cal-culations as to their profitability were made at headquarters—where relatively little information was available. The *président* could and did set investment policy along broad lines and had to approve all specific projects other than those kept hidden from headquarters, but these decisions could only provide the crudest guide to rationality.

Investment policy appears to have had two main facets. The first was to restrict to a minimum any investment not needed for expansion of sales. In general, such an investment would not be made unless it promised to pay for itself within two years—and even then a decision would often be postponed for years in order to make certain that the underlying assumptions were sound. The second facet was to undertake almost any investment in existing factories that was needed to produce new products which the marketing people believed they could sell. For such equipment, plant managers had virtually a free hand to order what they pleased—and, it will be remembered, they paid only the first year's depreciation costs.

One result of this investment policy, combined with the emphasis by plant managers on output and with the system of accounting by which their profits were calculated, was that product proliferation was continuous. New prod-ucts—essentially minor variants on old—were constantly introduced, and new equipment was purchased to make this possible; but older products were hardly ever abandoned. A second effect was that each plant manager at-tempted to expand his output of "profitable" (i.e., generally capital-inten-sive) products, even when the increased output came from diminished sales of the same product by a sister plant within the company. Although efforts were made at headquarters to police such creation of excess capacity and renuncia-tion of possible scale economies, it appears that such efforts were only occa-sionally successful. These two effects seem to constitute the main explanation for the fact that the costs of capital as a proportion of annual output doubled over the period.

While the *président* and his staff attempted to determine stock and investment policy, they tended otherwise to leave production decisions to the individual plant managers. Thus different managers used different equipment to perform identical tasks, simply because of their personal preferences. No effort was made to standardize processes between factories. A striking example of this failure to standardize was the development of a cost-reduction process that was accepted by all except one factory manager but was rejected by him because he believed that it led to a worsening of quality. The headquarters staff found that, in fact, this manager's product was of lower quality than that which other managers produced with the new process; but six years after the cheaper process had been developed, there was still no serious effort made to compel his plant to use it. Here, decentralization to the factory level and the absence of confrontation between headquarters and the factory managers was complete.[5]

Let us now turn from the company's production organization to an examination of the workings of its sales outlets. Sales was the aspect of the company's work which was given most attention during the postwar years. Yet, despite the fact that the company's policy was to concentrate on expansion, this program went in a flatly contradictory direction to that of the personnel policy for selecting managers in the different functions. Factory managers were all graduates of *grandes écoles,* most being from a minor one particularly appropriate to that industry, and they received salaries corresponding to their education. The regional sales managers, to the contrary, were all men without higher education and were primarily recruits from the rank-and-file sales force. Those with the highest total earnings still earned less than a factory manager, and two-thirds earned less than factory-management people two levels below the factory managers. Their promotion possibilities were nil. Headquarters' view of the capabilities of these sales managers was quite compatible with their level of earnings.

These regional sales managers were paid primarily by bonuses attached to their sales volume. They also received a bonus linked to their profits, but this averaged only 10 percent of the bonus received for volume. Yet these sales managers were virtually uncontrolled as to which products they pushed, and it was they who placed orders on the factories for specific volumes of particu-

[5]It is this last element which sharply distinguishes this policy from managerial decentralization as normally carried out in decentralized American companies. In a decentralized American company, it would be quite normal for different factory managers to make opposite decisions concerning the introduction of a new process; but headquarters would certainly impose its will if one manager wished to maintain an older process once experience within the company had clearly shown it to be less efficient.

lar products. The only real restraint on their activities was that their selling prices were determined by headquarters.

The relative lack of attention to profits in the sales managers' compensation presumably had two causes. One was an awareness by headquarters of the fact that the accounting definition of profits was misleading, in that the sales organizations were not charged for the costs of holding inventories and that many of the outlets bore no capital costs. Second, and doubtless much more important, was the belief that the sales managers did not have the education or experience needed to operate successfully a policy of attention to profit maximization. It was believed that the best they could be expected to do was to carry out a policy geared to expansion of total sales.

The results were what might have been expected. Sales managers steadily increased the variety of products ordered from the factories, seldom abandoning orders for a product as they added new and competing items to their stocks. Products were pushed because of their contribution to volume, and their profit contribution—not only to the company as a whole but even to the sales organization—was largely ignored. The company's sales mix was totally out of control.

As was pointed out above, selling prices were determined by headquarters. These prices were always set higher than those of competitors, presumably to provide an assurance that the output emphasis of both factory and sales managers would not lead to unprofitable operations. Given a situation in which the costs of individual products were unknown, and in which the product mix was out of control, this was not an unreasonable precaution. Such a pricing policy still permitted sales to grow more rapidly than France's gross national product. But the fact that the firm's share of the national market declined is probably not unrelated to this policy.

To sum up, Company F3's organization displayed many of the features of traditionally managed French enterprises. "Major decisions" (in Company F3, these covered pricing, stock levels, and investment) were highly concentrated in the hands of the *président-directeur général.* This organizational system was made practical by decentralizing to the field the actual decisions regarding current operations and company development, and no real effort was made to coordinate the work or interests of managers of different functions. Face-to-face contacts, both among managers of different field functions and of these managers with headquarters personnel, were minimized. Suboptimization was the guiding principle for each of the functional managers, but even such suboptimization was difficult to achieve because of the rudimentary character of the accounting system. Finally, despite the fact that the company's emphasis was entirely on sales expansion, it was production men rather than sales managers who were recruited from the minor *grandes écoles*—and their relative compensation was entirely commensurate with the sources of recruitment.

In 1958, the *président* retired and was succeeded by a team of top managers who were all members of the same family. They quickly became aware of the fact that the company's operations were uncontrolled, and they determined to take action to counteract this state of affairs. Furthermore, since there was no longer a single dominant company leader, the former reason for the fear of a strong headquarters staff had disappeared. Let us now turn to the changes which were introduced by the new management over the period of the following seven years.

The prime effort was put into developing a central set of records on how much of each type of product was sold in each region and to which sorts of customers: in short, the most basic information needed for any kind of marketing analysis. Second, work was done in developing a cost-accounting system for groups of products in both the sales organization and in the factories. Third, a beginning was made toward introducing capital charges into the cost function of both regional sales outlets and of factories; but after seven years, this introduction had still only been carried out in well under half of the company and even there the capital charges were set at the pitifully low rate of 7 1/2 percent per annum.

Seven years after this effort had begun, practical effects had only started to be felt—and these solely in one functional area. Headquarters was pressuring the sales outlets to reduce the number of lines of products that they handled, and had in fact cut the number by three-quarters. This was done primarily by compiling regular data on the volume of each line that was sold, and this systematic compilation gave headquarters for the first time a handle to the problem. But the products eliminated were almost entirely those for which the sales outlets acted as wholesalers, rather than those produced in the company's own factories. Thus rationalization reduced sales costs but had no effect on manufacturing expenses.

This effort to reduce the variety of products sold was accompanied by a change in the principle of payment of the regional sales directors. There was a slight increase in the importance of profits, as opposed to sales volume, in the determination of their bonuses; but, primarily, the accent on sales volume was reduced through sharply abating the proportion of bonuses in the total compensation of these managers. This shift in method of payment helped to make acceptable the reduction in variety of products.

However, seven years was considered insufficient time to have done anything in the direction of repricing products for greater profitability or to have redirected marketing effort toward the more profitable products. Although it was believed by headquarters that sales to many small customers were unprofitable, no decision had yet been taken to drop small-bulk individual customers or to increase the prices charged to them. Not even a start had been made toward standardizing production methods in the factories or toward redistributing the production of products between plants along cost-reduction lines.

The relation between headquarters and the sales outlets had changed, with headquarters playing a more active control function. But nothing comparable had occurred between headquarters and the factories. Doubtless the difference was that the regional sales managers were regarded as men whose backgrounds really prevented them from fitting the image of a proper managerial type, while the factory managers were *grande école* graduates deemed worthy of respect.

In part, change was slow because of the time required to develop and exploit cost-accounting procedures. But of considerably greater importance was the reluctance to change the occupants of managerial postions, although this was recognized as an essential prelude to enforcement of major policy changes. The best example of this is the case of the heads of the major functions at headquarters. During these seven years, all of these heads had retired. But in each case, the man was succeeded by his former assistant—also an older man who was considered to have earned the right of succession. Only on their retirement was it likely that major change could be implemented by headquarters.

This is not to say that there was no thinking about change in personnel policy. Consideration was being given to a shift to a regional linkage of production and sales under a single manager in each district, with his being a graduate of an *école* comparable in status to the minor *grande école* which currently supplied the factory managers. Even more heretical, the question was being posed whether such men should not be people with some commercial education rather than those coming from a purely technical school. By the seventh year, one such regional director had in fact been appointed. But clearly it would be a long time, if ever, before the company's management would be significantly transformed in this fashion.

Aside from such developments, one important technical change had occurred. Prior to 1958, the production facilities of the company had expanded solely by enlarging existing plants and by purchasing and reconverting old factory buildings elsewhere in France. Now, for the first time in the company's history, expansion took the form of a new single-story factory that permitted considerable economies in materials handling that until then had been no more than a dream. Moreover, it meant that the factory could be located in the most advantageous region of France, rather than—as previously—wherever a cheap building was available at the time of the investment decision. This expansion represented a change in investment policy, in that it meant giving more consideration to long-run profitability than to the search for an immediate "bargain."

Looking at this seven-year development since the new management took over, we do indeed see change. But what is particularly striking is both the hesitancy with which it has been undertaken and the lengthy gestation period involved. A traditional company is not being modernized overnight.

Company F4

Company F4 is a leading firm in a producers' goods industry with an exceptionally light capital structure and with a great many customers who must be visited by salesmen. It is the sole relatively small firm in our sample and has less than one thousand employees. Yet, in an industry composed of small firms, it is still one of the two largest in the country in its principal speciality. Considering our ten-year period of study as a whole, its output increased considerably more rapidly than did that of its industry.

With regard to productivity improvement, this is the least successful of all the French firms we shall examine—one of two whose total productivity was virtually stagnant. Compound annual rates of growth were as shown in Table 6.3.

But while the productivity results were most meager, the financial results were excellent by French standards. Over the entire period, officially declared

Table 6.3   Compound Annual Rates of Growth: Company F4 (Percentages)

Output	+ 8.6
Labor productivity	+ 0.6
Capital productivity	− 0.4
Total productivity	+ 0.3

gross returns were 7 percent of total turnover, and only in two years did they run below 6 percent.[6]

Actual returns were substantially higher. If we use an estimate worked out for me in detail for a single year by the firm's management, gross returns were 129 percent of what was declared for tax purposes, pretax net profits were 263 percent, and posttax net profits were 430 percent. On the basis of this estimate, and adding to it the effect of a tax device used in a different year which made it legally permissible to amortize virtually all fixed capital twice over, it would appear that real posttax net profits averaged about 12 percent of the market value of capital over the entire period.[7]

Company F4 is in many ways typical of much of French medium-size industry. Wholly owned by a single family, whose control over this 250-year-old firm goes back half a century, it is quite clear that long-run financial returns constitute the basic goal of the owners. Concern for stability of employment of the company's workers, which played such a critical role in the decision making of the *grande école* managers of Company F1, does not seem to be given a thought in this company. Partly this is because F4 is located in Paris, where alternative employment is plentiful; partly it is because the company is not so large that the government feels motivated to take an active interest in its employment policy; but primarily it is due to the personal value system of the owner-*président*.

The products are sold at high prices, and there has been little worry as to efficiency so long as the industry's prices remained sufficiently high. On the other hand, taxes are a major concern; the family frowns on receiving more than nominal dividends, since these would have to be paid from declared profits subject to a 50 percent profits tax as well as to personal income tax. Part of the earnings are taken in high managerial salaries for family members and in payments to the family board of directors; but, primarily, untaxed

[6]Gross returns are defined as net pretax profits, amortization, interest payments, and net increases in reserves held against possible future costs. Turnover is defined as excluding sales tax.

[7]Since interest payments are included in gross returns, bank debt is included in capital; however, neither were substantial. Capital investment includes stocks and net trade debt.

Of the 330 percent difference between actual and declared posttax profits in the one year studied, some one-third was due to such normal and legally permissible devices as the use of rapid depreciation instead of straight-line depreciation. (In fact, the company appeared to be rather below par in its employment of legal methods of tax avoidance.) But two-thirds of the difference was due to tax evasion techniques such as the payment of exceptionally high salaries to family members for managerial services. The results of these tax-evasion techniques entirely ignore certain elements such as the overstatement of expenses for family managers.

returns are plowed back into the business as investments. Thus growth is highly prized by the owning family not, as is the case so often with *grande école* managers, for its own sake and for *"la gloire de la France,"* but simply as a device for tax avoidance. Sometimes, indeed, the owners of this firm wonder whether the various tax advantages encouraging high investment do not really constitute a trap laid by the French treasury.

The owning family has a second business of much the same size. But still it is careful to keep much of its funds in lands and villas—traditionally favored forms of property for the Parisian bourgeoisie. Thus the family's fortunes are partially insulated from any conceivable business catastrophe.

The members of the owning family who are active in the business are not themselves *écoles* graduates. While reserving for the head of the family the position of *président,* they have for a long time hired a *directeur général* from outside as the operating manager. Since the family is active in the business and the industry is not an *"industrie noble,"* it is not too surprising that the *directeur général* throughout the period observed was also other than an *école* graduate. This was despite the fact that his salary plus bonus totaled what would have been a very substantial sum even for a *grande école* manager in a big firm. Interestingly, however, his career pattern followed that of many of the *grande école* managers in that his exposure to this industry began only two years before he became *directeur général* of this firm.

One of the most striking features of the company, and one which did not change particularly throughout the nine-year period, is the existence of organizational chaos and the absence of any real effort by top management to exercise control. On the most primitive level, only 50 percent of orders were shipped out on schedule. No one had any notion as to the degree of labor absenteeism, despite the fact that it appeared high. Workers could leave the factory premises without being checked at the gate, although the existence of multishifts and split shifts meant that workers might legitimately be coming and going at any hour. In an important segment of the business, salesmen's incentives were such as to lead them to ignore the maintenance of orders from existing customers and, instead, to concentrate entirely on gaining new customers; yet management made no effort to verify the effect of this incentive system by keeping records of the degree to which old customers' business was retained. Although the company bid for orders on a cost-plus basis, there was no attempt to compare these cost estimates with the actual costs incurred.

This chaotic situation, and the failure to make any improvements in it, seems sufficient immediate explanation for the fact that virtually no net productivity increases were attained. But why this acceptance of chaos? What is interesting is that it stems directly from the strategy of the *directeur général*. His failure, and his resultant eventual ousting at the end of the period, was not at all the result of stupidity or laziness; rather, it was the direct outcome of his managerial philosophy.

The *directeur général* held to the view that the company's immediate objectives should be twofold. First was continued and rapid expansion of output. The company's main product line, although unprotected by any patents, was highly profitable; moreover, there was the expectation that its national market would grow at a rapid rate for a decade or more. The high and rising demand, relative to national supply, made it urgent to produce at maximum capacity so long as these profit conditions continued.

The second objective was protection against the evil day, which could not be many years off, when national supply would have greatly expanded as a result of the profitability of the product line. It was imperative, believed the *directeur général*, to place the firm in a strong position for the battles to come.

His approach to achieving this second objective was two-pronged. First, efforts at improving factory performance should be concentrated on the raising of quality standards. True, the product was a fairly simple one whose quality improvement could be only of minor interest to industrial customers. Nevertheless, such high quality would distinguish this company's output from that of its host of competitors at a time when any distinction would be vital. Workmen, foremen, and lower management should all be oriented primarily to this effort in what was considered as an investment to be needed only in the future.

Second, material investment should be concentrated on relatively capital-intensive machinery that would both raise the quality of the product and sharply reduce the variable costs of production once this machinery was run in. Thus only the most technically advanced foreign equipment should be purchased. The hope was that later, when competition became severe, the company's low variable costs would allow it to bid for orders at a price which would drive smaller competitors out of this product line. At that point, it would be too late for many competitors to follow suit in investment policy. First, profits in the industry would no longer be sufficient to finance such purchases quickly; second, the price situation would make it a financially painful period for other companies to go through the slow process of learning how to use the new machinery effectively. Third, his own company would know more about using modern equipment than any other French firm in the industry and thus would be able to proceed to still newer equipment that the other firms would be technically incapable of handling.

In examining this strategy, it is difficult to be certain as to how to evaluate the dual strategy of concentrating on quality improvement and on investment in capital-intensive equipment. It is possible that the *directeur général* viewed this approach as offering the greatest likelihood of maximum profits over the long pull. However, in the light of his expectation of greatly increased competition in the future, this does not seem probable. More likely, his analysis amounted to applying subconsciously a substantial negative rate of time discount to future earnings.

It is clear that the business values of the *directeur général* were centered on the expansion of output and the later maintenance of it in the face of tougher competition. He did not have in mind any new product lines that might in the future grow sufficienctly to replace his principal one once this would become less profitable. Thus it was critical for him to place the company into a position where its marginal costs would be low, so that the owners' best profit strategy in the future era of low prices would be to meet the competition head on. Investment now in capital-intensive equipment would constitute sunk costs that would substitute for higher variable costs in the future. Concentration on quality improvement now would provide additional salability in the future at no increase of costs at that time.

In the eyes of the *directeur général,* increased current profits were much less important than that the firm should have a secure position in the future. Current "real profits"[8] were now quite satisfactory; there was little reason to give up anything important in order to raise them. Thus it seemed perfectly reasonable to him to adopt a strategy that amounted to maximizing the expected value of the firm subject to an implied negative real rate of time discount for future earnings. In the very year in which the company's output in constant prices was reaching its peak, the *directeur général* calculated that real posttax profits could be increased by 28 percent if it were not for the operating expenditures linked to growth. He was perfectly willing to make

[8]This is defined as a calculation that was made for managerial bonus purposes rather than as part of the regular accounting system.

this sacrifice, even though he himself received a substantial bonus linked to "real profits."

I have no doubt that the *directeur général* believed that this strategy was in the best interests of the firm. It would have been difficult to make a forecast of future prices and costs and to calculate the effect of the strategy on profits over a long period. Certainly no such effort was attempted even in the crudest fashion. But this was unnecessary, for two axioms of "well-managed" French business were sufficient to justify the strategy. The first axiom was that continued rapid growth was a number one goal, for only the largest firms in each industry would be able to survive in the future. The second axiom was that it was essentially immoral for a company to earn too high a profit; it was clear that the company was already stretching the limit of morality. Finally, this policy posed no threat to the future financial stability of the company, since growth was to be financed almost entirely from internally generated funds and thus no burden of fixed interest charges was being incurred.

The task of selling this strategy to the owning family was enormously eased by the fact that the company was using the system of rapid amortization under the tax laws and that a reduction of annual investment would have inevitably implied an increase of taxable declared profits. It has been accepted as axiomatic in French business that such an increase is virtual proof of financial mismanagement and is to be avoided at almost all costs. Thus high investments were quite acceptable to the family; the only relevant question was the form which these investments should take.

In understanding the strategy of the *directeur général*, there is one final feature to consider. This was his personal philosophy that a company organization should concentrate on a very limited number of goals at any moment. If additional goals were also pursued, he felt, there would be less success in achieving the primary ones. It was as a deliberate result of this philosophy that he made no serious effort to eliminate the organizational chaos which surrounded him. For, as he saw the matter, such chaos had its effect primarily in increasing current operating costs and in reducing the current gross returns. But the *directeur général*'s eyes were fixed firmly on the future. Once the company had learned to handle the new equipment and had raised the quality of its products, it would be a relatively quick operation to reduce sharply the dimensions and costs of the disorganization. In this last belief, of course, he was accepting the stereotype that improvement of technology is the all-important and really difficult task.

This view as to the critical importance of choosing priority goals is exemplified by his attitude toward waste of raw materials. He believed that a great deal of unnecessary loss of raw materials took place in the process of fabrication, and two years earlier he had for a short time tried an allocation of materials to a sample shop on the basis of reducing the loss allowance by an arbitrary 20 percent. The shop produced as normal and without complaints. If the company had successfully applied this reduction across the board, as the *directeur général* believed was possible, "real profits" posttax would have increased by 9 percent. As he himself told me, there was a potential gold mine here.

However, once having established the existence of this potential saving, the *directeur général* purposely ignored it. He believed that an effort by the shops to reduce materials wastage would interfere with their efforts at mastering new equipment and improving quality. The first would only provide current profits, while the second two were building the future of the firm. Nor could the conflict be resolved by hiring additional managerial personnel, since these would have to be supervised and trained. So the *directeur général* put off the entire matter for what he thought would be four years or so; his only care was to see that the *président* did not hear of the experiment, as he feared that the *président* might insist on pursuing this immediate profit gain.

The results of this policy of concentration upon the future by the *directeur général* yielded financial results satisfactory to the owning family until the last few years. By this time, however, competition had increased sharply while demand was increasing more slowly than in the past. The result was that prices of the main product line were depressed, and the company could not continue to expand its real output without bidding for orders at prices which the *directeur général* turned out to be unwilling to quote. Thereafter, sales in constant prices were stable at the same time that the *directeur général* continued to expand investment ever more rapidly—reacting to competitive pressure by trying to speed up the tempo of arriving at a stage where variable costs would fall sharply. In the meanwhile, however, productivity gains from new equipment were fully counterbalanced by losses from gaining experience with the very newest acquisitions. The proportion of orders shipped on time did not improve, for too many orders were run on the newest equipment whose operation had not yet been mastered. Finally the company encountered a quarter with an actual loss, and the *directeur général* was dismissed. The *président* shifted to a policy of concentration on immediate cost reduction.

In looking back at the history of the firm over these years, it is evident that the *directeur général*'s extreme emphasis on preparation for the future stemmed from the currently profitable market position of the firm combined with a minimizing of the psychological value of those current profits which exceeded a norm of what was "reasonable." In this rejection, the *directeur général* reflected the mores both of French "progressive" business and of the total society. His method of preparation for the future—concentration on the mastery of advanced technology rather than on the establishment of order and managerial control in the company—also reflected the traditional French respect for advanced technology in comparison with the development of managerial control devices for better employment of existing resources.

The personal failure of the *directeur général*, in the form of his dismissal, stemmed from the fact that business conditions worsened a few years earlier than he had expected. Until this happened, the strategy was perfectly acceptable to the owning family.

Company F5

Company F5 is a multiplant metal firm. Top management is firmly in the hands of two branches of the founding family, despite the fact that the family has long held only a minuscule proportion of the company's shares. Although there are *grande école* managers in the company, the management can still be characterized as of family type.

The company as a whole had a stock market record which was only slightly poorer than that of its industry, and was a great deal better than that of the Paris Bourse as a whole. It is not possible to develop any profitability data restricted to the single division to be discussed below.

The productivity study of this firm is concentrated on two provincial plants which constitute the original base of the company, dating back to the mid-nineteenth century. During the second period of our study, they were jointly administered by a single family member who had been granted great autonomy in their direction. The eleven years for which we have productivity data concerning what we shall call Division I are best divided into two equal periods. Compound annual rates of growth were as shown in Table 6.4.

In order to analyze the two periods, it is useful to examine the productivity changes of four all-inclusive categories of employees. Compound annual rates of growth analyzed in this way are given in Table 6.5.

Improvements in productivity were aided during Period I by the fact that Division I's output increased very rapidly (although only about 10 percent

Table 6.4 Compound Annual Rates of Growth: Division I of Company F5 (Percentages)

	Total for Years Studied	Period I	Period II
Output	+ 2.5	+ 6.8	− 1.6
Labor productivity	+ 0.9	+ 4.5	− 2.5
Capital productivity	− 0.8	+ 2.9	− 4.4
Total productivity	+ 0.4	+ 4.1	− 3.1

Table 6.5 Compound Annual Rates of Productivity Growth for Different Categories of Workers: Division I of Company F5 (Percentages)

	Total Years Studied	Period I	Period II
Productivity of labor as a whole	+ 0.9	+ 4.5	− 2.5
Operators[a]	+ 2.6	+ 8.2	− 2.7
Auxiliary blue-collar workers[b]	+ 8.8	+ 8.9	+ 8.6
Ordinary white-collar workers[c]	+ 0.8	+ 3.0	− 1.4
Managers and engineers[d]	− 5.2	+ 1.6	−11.6

[a]All blue-collar workers engaged in direct production operations as contrasted with those in such auxiliary operations as inspection, materials handling, maintenance and cleaning (*ouvriers directs*).
[b]All other blue-collar workers (*ouvriers indirects*).
[c]*Employés.*
[d]*Cadres.*

more quickly than its industry's output). While production was mostly in fairly small lot sizes, its composition remained relatively stable and consisted primarily of product lines which were well into production before the beginning of the period. These conditions made some improvement in productivity almost automatic.

What was far from automatic, however, was the rate of productivity improvement for blue-collar workers as a whole (8.4 percent per annum during Period I, and double the rate achieved on an average in Company F5's industry). This was a direct result of managerial concentration during these years upon holding down production costs through reducing the absolute numbers of blue-collar workers despite the expansion in output.

Piece-rate payment for operators was widely introduced during these years, and this introduction was accompanied by a good deal of methods study at the levels of the shop and of the individual work position. The analysis and introduction were carried out primarily by a consulting firm, and management's decision to call in these consultants and support their authority was fundamental in achieving the operators' productivity improvements. In addition, methods studies plus a concentrated managerial effort made possible a one-third compression of the numbers of unskilled auxiliary workers.

The resulting sharp improvement during Period I in blue-collar productivity appears to have been a direct result of management's decision during these years to concentrate its attention on shop floor efficiency. It is interesting to note that this managerial emphasis created no serious social conflicts and did not run counter to any aspect of the managerial value system. It is true that the trade unions in the factories opposed on principle the switch to piece-rate payments, but the change-over met with general worker approval in view of the fact that it was accompanied by a rise in earnings. This increase in earnings was particularly sharp because the host of continuous minor changes in product design made it possible for the workers to bargain individually for increased standard-times on tight jobs, while unquestioningly accepting whatever loose times were set for other jobs. Well before the period ended, the plants were among the highest paying in the area.

The small decrease in the number of operators created no difficulty because firings and "compulsory quits" were not necessary in order to achieve this. It was only the unskilled workers who were sharply reduced in number, and this group was in any case one with a high turnover and little rapport with the other workers.

It might seem that this change in shop floor organization would have run counter to the French managerial value of avoiding close face-to-face contact between different levels of the hierarchy. In fact, however, it was only the foremen's position which was affected by the methods studies. While the power of the foremen was weakened through the creation of functional methods groups, all levels of management, even the lowest, were left untouched. Thus the groups concerning which top management was really sensitive—the managers and engineers—were unaffected by the changes. Moreover, it was not they who had to carry out this interference with traditional foremen's rights, but rather outside consultants who were specialists in this task of disrupting power at the foreman level and who were used to accepting the social consequences of their work.

In contrast with the developments during Period I, the productivity of all categories of employees except auxiliary blue-collar workers fell during

Period II, although labor productivity continued to rise in the industry as a whole along with the industry's output. Again, decisions of the top management of the division appear to have been directly responsible.

Period II began with the division facing a difficult sales situation. The market for its products had deteriorated, and only its single major product line remained profitable; even this line, constituting under 50 percent of the division's total sales, seemed likely to be faced in the future with a slowly declining, although still profitable, volume of demand. This situation resulted in part from changes in the total French market which were quite outside of the control of Company F5, but partly it was a result of a failure to modernize the design of the division's products. It was at this point that a family member came in to head the division and to decide what was to be done with it.

The new chief of the division took the view that all efforts should be made to maintain the total volume of production and employment. This, he believed, could best be done by concentrating on superior design of old products and on the rapid development of new lines. Second, he held that the optimum organizational strategy was to divide up the division along product lines and to place a single manager in charge of sales, engineering and production for each such line. In this way, he hoped, coordination of these functions would best be achieved; for it would depend much less upon voluntary team cooperation among functional managers holding equal rank—a type of cooperation which he believed was peculiarly antipathetical to the French character. Although there were obvious diseconomies and duplications, stemming from the relatively small volume of sales of each product line, which were implicit in such an organization by product, he felt that this restructuring represented an investment in organization which would make feasible both the development of higher quality products and the sales effort needed for successful expansion of markets.

This creation of product sections would appear to run counter to the French tradition of centralization of authority in the hands of one head. Certainly the new division chief was personally inspired by what he believed to be the American example, even though he was responding to what he perceived as the specific inability of French middle managers to function as a team. However, as the organization evolved throughout Period II, only limited powers and responsibilities were in fact given to each product-sector chief. Each was pressed hard by the division head for immediate results, and was neither encouraged nor given time to plan the future of his product-sector. All decisions with clear long-range implications remained firmly in the hands of the division head.

Unfortunately, the goal of profitable sales expansion had still not been realized by the end of Period II. Seventy percent more engineers than at the beginning of Period II were employed within the division, essentially in design and sales; fairly heavy investments had been undertaken and the new equipment and buildings were already fully in use; major efforts had been made in a variety of products. Yet still only the original major product line was in a stable and profitable condition. As of that point, design development and diversification had yielded no significant fruits; nor was it obvious to me as an observer that any payoff could be expected in the future.

The sharp decline in the productivity of engineers during Period II followed inevitably from the failure to expand output as the number of engineers hired to work on design increased. But how explain the changes in productivity among the other three groups in the labor force?

With regard to the operators, the expansion in the product mix while total output declined had a negative effect. But much more important was the fact that the new division head was fundamentally uninterested in operator productivity.[9] He took the position that the upsurge of the division would come about through improving design and so selling engineering services in the form of new products. Concentration of managerial attention on production efficiency was, from this point of view, simply a diversion of managerial attention—and one which had cost dearly when followed by the previous division chief. The fact that the heads of the newly formed product sectors were all managers who had formerly been in charge of design or sales functions only reinforced this bias. Furthermore, since the production shops were being reorganized to fit in with the new product organization of the division, and since it was planned to reorganize them still further as soon as volume of production increased, there seemed to be little potential gain in striving for greater efficiency in the shops as they were currently organized.

The sharp increase in the productivity of auxiliary blue-collar workers represented the result of a tough managerial decision: to slice costs where it could be done without the use of much managerial time. Thus, in a series of connected decisions, the absolute number of auxiliary blue-collar workers was

[9]This was despite the fact that, at the beginning of Period II, two-fifths of the division's labor force was composed of operators.

slashed by 40 percent during Period II, the number of nonmanagerial white-collar workers in preexisting functions was also reduced somewhat, and wage increases of blue-collar workers as a whole were restrained to the point where the division quickly lost its position as one of the highest-paying firms in its region.

The decision to reduce sharply the number of auxiliary blue-collar workers was particularly courageous in the French industrial setting since it could not be done at the expense of unskilled workers, whose number had already been pared to a minimum. Long-service skilled workers had to be gotten rid of, and it was essential to persuade remaining workers to change their accustomed work practices. Fortunately from the point of view of the company, the operators and the trade unions shared a distaste for "overhead" and thus did not resist too strongly.

Here was a tough top management decision, since it went strongly against the normal French managerial value system of avoiding firings at almost all costs—particularly in provincial areas of France. Management justified the decision, both to itself and to its workers and the public, on the grounds that the division was suffering financial losses and had to reduce costs or eliminate its unprofitable products, and that elimination of products would have led to much sharper cuts in employment.

While recognizing that this decision went against the management's value system of preserving employment, it should be pointed out that this method of cost reduction had its attractive features. Although it required the acceptance and manipulation of a difficult social situation, otherwise it was extremely simple to implement. A major manpower reduction could be undertaken at once and from fairly obvious sources. No significant investment of managerial time was required. All that was needed was the hiring of a tough personnel director.[10]

The reduction had to be carried out cleverly in order to yield its maximum financial results. Mass dismissals would have resulted in public protests and would probably have caused government pressure for cancellation. At the least, it would almost certainly have necessitated expenditures for the "early retirements" of employees over sixty years of age.

Instead of this, the personnel director persuaded a sufficient number of workers to resign. By a combination of offering additional financial payments supplemental to the contractual ones, of making a cash payment in lieu of the

[10]There was a 25 percent reduction of auxiliary blue-collar workers during the eight months after the new personnel director was brought into the division.

contractual notice, and by threats of down-gradings, formal dismissals were avoided at an average cost of two and one-third months' pay per resignation. The regional labor market was such that all who resigned were able quickly to find work elsewhere, but often in small firms and at substantial reductions in earnings.

The number of nonmanagerial white-collar employees in traditional functions were compressed in the same fashion as were the blue-collar auxiliary employees.[11] But since the number of engineering and managerial personnel rose sharply during Period II, new white-collar positions were necessary to provide support personnel for them. The net result for Period II as a whole was close to stability in the numbers of these white-collar employees.

So much for the changes in productivity in both Periods I and II. It is clear from the foregoing discussion that the major changes, both positive and negative, were direct results of the interaction of the decisions and attitudes of the successive top managers of the division with the national market conditions. (It was these latter which permitted rapid increases in sales during Period I, while making similar increases much more difficult to achieve in this industry during Period II when the industry's expansion was appreciably less and the competition stiffer.) Both the early improvement and the latter worsening of productivity can be explained without any major reference to either the accomplishments or failures of lower managers or workers.

What remains to be explained is both the decision of the division's chief during Period II to expand the product range of the division and the reasons for the failure of this policy.

When the family member took over the division early in Period II, his first task was to decide on its future path of development. One alternative was to reduce the division's sales by more than half, thus getting rid of the unprofitable products. A second alternative was to choose one of the near-profitable product lines, or some new one, and to concentrate on developing it in order to replace the various unprofitable lines. A third approach was to continue with all the unprofitable lines and to develop additional new products—thus trying to cover overheads by expanding total output.

The new chief was unusually profit oriented for a French businessman, and the first alternative was tempting. He had once roller-coasted the employment of a large plant in the company, cutting it by half during less than a year. But

---

[11]The difference between the maximum and minimum employment levels of nonmanagerial white-collar employees taken as a whole was 16 percent of the original maximum during a single year.

there were two critical reasons for not following the same path in this division. The first, and it was this which he stressed in conversation with me, was that these plants were the original ones of the firm; he viewed this region as the true home of the firm, and thus could not see himself bringing it heavy unemployment. The second reason was more pragmatic. Two-thirds of the company's sales consisted of two complex product lines of widely disparate types, and these lines shared the common feature that the clientele of each was limited to a few large customers. If the division abandoned its unprofitable products, the sales of the company as a whole would be even more concentrated. A wide divisional product range was viewed as representing security, even if much of it was unprofitable for the time being.

The same emphasis upon security dissuaded the new head of the division from attempting to follow the second alternative of picking a likely product line and investing in it heavily. He felt that the company could not afford to risk the magnitude of investments in a single product line which would be necessary if the division were to hope to attain a design and cost position from which it could quickly capture a sufficient volume of sales to replace the existing unprofitable lines.

Thus the new division head decided to follow the third approach, and this choice seems to have been followed through intelligently. Negotiations were undertaken with a number of foreign concerns for the creation of joint sales companies, in order that their designs and sales know-how could be made quickly available on a partnership basis. However, although the joint companies were formed, and still other products were pushed independently by the division, none was particularly successful.

A fundamental reason for the failure would appear to be that the strategy was not appropriate to the changing conditions of the French metal industry. In the past, the total market had been growing rapidly and, generally speaking, none of the competitors had had sufficient volume in any product line to achieve major economies of scale. But the situation was changing in Period II, and the refusal to concentrate efforts on a single product line foreshadowed the failure to achieve either production economies or such product designs as would be both peculiarly modern and appropriate to the potential market. In this period of difficult market conditions, the traditional search for security through diversification doomed these expansion efforts to failure.

Company F6

Company F6 is another major metal firm, but in a product area that has seen rapid market expansion. The company's own rate of growth of sales has outpaced even that of its subindustry, and this has been accomplished without mergers or acquisitions; the few minor exceptions have been transformed into affiliates rather than joined to the firm proper. Although the groups of products produced by the company are technologically quite conventional, design has evolved fairly rapidly, and thus a high level of technological competence has been a requirement for success. The company is comparatively young, having been formed after the First World War, and it still has a family and regional base; but it appears to be in the process of development toward a Paris headquarters and a *grande école* management.

Company F6 is the only one of our French firms whose stock market record has been clearly much better than that of its industry. During eight years the price of its stock, adjusted for stock dividends and after the addition of the discounted value of posttax dividends, increased at 178 percent of the rate of the industry as a whole. Since the industry's market performance was substantially better than that of the Paris Bourse, this made F6 a very good performer.

Over the thirteen-year period for which we have data, the growth of output and of productivity was continuous. The compound annual rates of growth are as shown in Table 6.6. Total productivity increased 70 percent more rapidly than would have been sufficient to compensate for the increase in real hourly wages of that industry during the period.

The foregoing high rate of productivity improvement was mainly a result of the thorough redesign of each of the products every seven years or so, with the redesign being primarily geared to cost reduction. The head of one of the two largest product groupings in the company estimated that such redesign was responsible for some two-thirds of his division's total cost reductions.

Examination of a specific example of redesign indicates the sources of the

Table 6.6   Compound Annual Rates of Growth: Company F6 (Percentages)

Output	10.1
Labor productivity	4.8
Capital productivity	1.0
Total productivity	3.6

savings. Of the 30 percent total reduction in costs[12] of this important product, 10 to 15 percent stemmed directly from the increase in the volume of output. The volume expansion had made it economical to produce the product with different equipment, and this possibility was utilized through the reengineering both of parts and of the total assembly. Another 5 to 8 percent saving was due to greater design attention to the problem of minimizing production costs than had been the case when the item was first placed on the market, a care that was now warranted by the current production volumes. Finally, an additional 7 to 15 percent was a result of the combination of the borrowing of technology previously unavailable in France and of the application of a value-engineering team approach to design. This latter involved cooperation by sales personnel in providing a judgment as to which features were really of importance to the purchasers, and by the purchasing department in determining how redesign might best take advantage of the relative costs of alternative purchased materials and of specific low-cost manufacturing capacities of subcontractors.[13]

The preceding example illustrates the great significance for cost reduction of the fact that the company's sales increased rapidly and consistently, at the same time that the range of product mix remained limited. Partly this was due to the good fortune of the company in being part of a subindustry whose markets were rapidly expanding. But it was also due to the company's success in restricting its product range and in going to considerable lengths to produce even this range from standardized subassemblies. Furthermore, the company's emphasis on the export market, which it penetrated by accepting much lower prices than it demanded within France, was also of major importance in building volume.

Considerable success in executing the design function was also, however, of major importance. Substantial funds were spent on this function: some 9 percent of total company current expenditures. But equally important was the fact that design appears to have been successfully tied to the achievement of sales targets. The starting point for the design of a product was always an average cost objective, determined by a process that took as its starting point the price which the sales executives believed they could get on the market.

[12]Costs as defined here include all materials purchases and direct labor employed in producing the product, as well as the amortization of all equipment used in its production. Other overhead costs are excluded.
[13]This analysis of the relative importance of the various sources of cost reduction is of course approximate; it was supplied by an upper-middle-management participant in this exercise in redesign.

Although managers complained that designers tended to emphasize quality for its own sake, it is clear that F6 had gone further than most French companies in successfully combating this tendency. Increased volume provided the basis for reductions in direct costs, but these were achieved primarily through the active route of design change.

A second, but much less important, source of cost improvement was investment in superior capital equipment; the amount of capital per manual worker increased at an annual compound rate of 4 percent. One of the top managers estimated that this betterment of equipment was responsible for one-sixth of the total productivity increase.

Finally, progress in organization and improved production methods were believed to provide an additional one-sixth of the growth in productivity.

Top managers of the firm, in their talks with me, spoke as though they believed that the principal cost-reducing advantage of sales expansion was that it permitted the spreading of overhead personnel functions across a larger volume. In fact, however, the productivity of manual workers increased virtually as rapidly as did that of white-collar employees and of professionals; for management increased the numbers of designers, researchers, and sales personnel much more speedily than it expanded the product range. Throughout the period, the company used its growth in gross revenue to concentrate ever more intensively on the design and sales of its limited range of products.[14]

In explaining the success of design in bringing down costs so sharply and continuously, it seems to me that three phenomena are important.

First is the fact that the company is organized into fairly narrow product-group departments. Each of these handles its own production, methods studies, design, and sales, as well as some of the administrative functions for its own department. In addition, there are both headquarters personnel and a separate company-wide sales force. The significance of this departmental organization is shown by the fact that, even if we ignore production *cadres* who are all attached to some department, some 60 percent of the managerial and professional personnel of the company are located administratively within the departments. If we deduct from the total those *cadres* in the separate sales force, the proportion rises to three-quarters.

The strength of this type of organization is that it creates a number of small

---

[14]The relevant measure of such intensity is the expenditure per subfamily of products rather than the expenditure per million francs of sales. Expenditure per million francs of sales (both measured in constant prices) fell off sharply.

managerial groups, each of which combines various functions. This maximizes the likelihood of professionals from the various functions having in mind their common product-group interest rather than the independent performance of their individual functions. The pressure to work as a team has been further reinforced by the fact that the vast majority of the professionals seem to spend their entire career within the same department, except perhaps for the first few years during which they may change departments once.

The second phenomenon is that the sales function is the dominant one within each of the various departments, except for those departments that sell only within the company. This is because it is the sales engineers who are the professionals with the greatest theoretic knowledge of the industry's technology and who are graduates of the stronger engineering schools. It is from their ranks that the heads of departments are usually recruited, and it is they who are eligible to move into the more prestigious company-wide sales force. Thus, within the departments, the probability is that leadership will be exercised by these sales engineers.

Finally, a substantial majority of the professionals and managers both in production and in design, as well as many in the broader applied-research function, are people without a higher educational degree. These men have been advanced from technician ranks, and their careers have been much more successful than they had any reason to expect when they left school.[15] The presumption is that such professionals would accept the cost-emphasizing values of the sales engineers with whom they work because they themselves have been accustomed throughout the earlier parts of their careers to accept the orders of graduate engineers, because respect for graduate engineers is inbred in the mores of French industry in general, and because the sales engineers have an obviously superior theoretic technical knowledge. Finally, and perhaps most important, these former technicians are much less likely than are graduate engineers to have had instilled in them through their education a regard for high quality per se irrespective of the actual needs of the customers. Their internal value system is less in conflict with the demands of the market.

Doubtless, this type of recruitment for design and applied-research work has its disadvantages for the company. One might expect graduate engineers on the average to be more imaginative because they are more theoretically

[15]Nevertheless, there is a definite ceiling on the progress of their careers within the company. Of the top forty men within the company, only one does not have a higher educational degree.

informed. Nevertheless, it would appear that the gains from F6's pattern of recruiting predominate. Furthermore, management has tried to reduce the costs of this policy by normally choosing only graduate engineers for the top posts in these departmental functions.

Although F6 has had more than average financial success, the emphasis on expansion of sales as the basic company goal seems to apply to the top level of the company as well as to the departments. Even in the financial function of headquarters, profits are viewed simply as a necessary means to the achievement of the desired growth in volume. As I was told by one of the company's top financial managers, the company is judged by its customers, its competitors, and its possible future partners both in mergers and in production and sales agreements according to its rate of expansion rather than by its rate of profit.

The financial results of the company appear to have reflected this emphasis. If we compare balance sheet and profit-and-loss data for two end-point four-year periods, both of which had high rates of return relative to the intervening years, the latter period showed an average rate of return on the book value of equity which, according to various measures, can be estimated to be only between one-half and two-thirds of that of the earlier period.

This decline in rate of return is particularly striking not only because of the sharp increase in total productivity in the company during the total period but also because of the sharp rise in the ratio of medium- and long-term debt to the book value of equity capital: from 11 to 54 percent. As was pointed out earlier in the discussion of Company F1, such debt capital is financed at rates of interest that are artificially low in the light of the rate of inflation. Although the industry as a whole suffered from unfavorable price movements, it thus would seem likely that the policies of Company F6 contributed to its own decline in rate of return.

These policies were twofold, but both were directed toward the expansion of the company's sales. The first was an acceptance of a much faster rate of growth in the sales of the low-profit sector of products than in the high-profit one. The rate of growth in the high-profit sector probably could not have been increased, but the company need not have continued to expand its capital investment in the low-profit products. Second, exports were enormously developed, despite the fact that they had to be sold at an average of 15 percent less than the price received inside France. Management rationalized that these exports were financially justified because they were sold at more than direct costs, and that overhead expenditures on personnel (especially for research and design) need not rise with the increase in sales. In fact, however, the company—as we saw above—maintained a virtually stable ratio of overhead personnel to manual workers.

Although these financial data are insufficient to demonstrate that, as a direct result of its sales policy, the company in the latter period earned a lower rate of return than it might have, certainly they point in this direction. Particularly given the explicit view of top management that profits were a means rather than a goal, it seems fair to conclude that rate of return was sacrificed for expansion. The various product departments were pressed to show a profit, but the amount of their profits was considered to be far less important than the rate of their sales expansion. As one might imagine, department heads who came from the sales function needed little urging in this direction.

Turning back to the previously-mentioned issue of company organization, the importance of product departments has implied a fair degree of decentralization. But the extent of this should not be exaggerated. The limitation on independence is best seen in the departmental budgets.

Individual departments have separate profit and loss statements and are operated according to annual budgets. But the budgeted costs are themselves somewhat unreal; for the allocation of general company overhead is set so as to weigh disproportionately heavily on the more profitable departments,[16] and in principle to be least of a burden on the most rapidly expanding departments. Both of these distortions are the results of conscious policies by the comptroller; the first is a result of his recognition that department heads are satisfied with minimum profits but sweat uncomfortably over losses; the second is his means of encouraging an expansionary policy by all departments. The obvious significance of this policy of distortions is the headquarters' belief that department managers will make decisions in relation to their effect on the department budgets, and that implementation of top management policy can be furthered through the budgetary process.

On the other hand, the comptroller has been quite explicit in saying that he does not judge department heads by their results relative to budgets. Partly this is because he is primarily concerned with seeing that the departments present accurate annual forecasts of their activities and profits to top management, and he believes that this accuracy would be prejudiced if the performance of these departments were to be judged against these plans. Second, and equally important, he believes that evaluation of departments against bud-

[16]The purpose of this is to reduce departmental resistance and efforts to get around the internal transfer price system described in the Appendix to Chapter 12.

gets could not be implemented unless the top management adopted a hands-off policy toward operating decisions during the course of the budget year; this is a restraint that top management is unwilling to impose on itself. Thus cost accounting has significance to the department heads only in the sense that they should beware of absolute losses; but comparisons with plan do not seem to be of great importance. Under these circumstances, top management is not only free to interfere in current operating decisions but is virtually compelled to do so.

Top management does not even present all known and relevant data to the department heads. Thus, while the comptroller's office processes aggregative national and industry data in order to make annual market projections, the department heads are not considered sufficiently "mature" to be given the full conclusions; it is feared that they would overreact to projected cyclical swings. In short, although Company F6 is relatively decentralized by French standards, it is still managed in the tradition of maintaining considerable concentration both of information and of power.

However, as is again common in French firms, headquarters seems to possess inadequate data to serve as a basis for genuine financial control. For example, the monthly budget statement of each department is supposed, in theory, to include as production only those goods actually billed to customers during the month. But since in fact there are often both relatively large accumulations of work in process and delays between shipment and billing dates, the department head is allowed to modify his report of billing to take account of these variances whenever he thinks it desirable to do so. The comptroller's department simply receives without challenge the subjectively determined "production" figures.

As to long-run planning, it was only at the very end of the period that top management was beginning even to try to plan for longer than one year at a time.

Investment allocations are determined centrally but primarily on a "fair shares" approach to the various departments. No effort has been made to distribute investment funds in such a way as to maximize return on capital. Indeed, it was only at the very end of the period that an attempt was made to introduce common standards across department lines for deciding even on those investments whose sole purpose was cost reduction.

Thus, as we have seen earlier in other French companies, concentration of power at headquarters has not implied that this influence has been used to exercise rational financial control—or even that it could have been so used in the light of the lack of detailed and reliable financial information available to headquarters.

Company F6 has traditionally had the reputation of a dynamic firm, jealous of its independence and fighting shy of production agreements with other companies in order to maintain its ability to expand rapidly. But as the company grew in national importance, such a position proved difficult to maintain. At the very beginning of the period we are studying, market-sharing agreements were signed with two other leading French firms of the industry. These accords took the form of each company renouncing the production and sale of an important subfamily of products in which it was currently weak. For F6, this amounted in practice to giving up some items on which it had only recently embarked but which were closely related to existing major products. At the end of the period, further agreements were signed: partly for specialization by product families but, more significantly, for joint design and research work on products common to the firms involved. These latter agreements were cemented by the other firms purchasing a substantial interest in the shares of F6. Yet, such was the reputation of Company F6 for dynamic management, that it was this firm which took the leadership in the work which was common to the corporations involved.

As the company has grown in significance, its earlier rejection of the *grande école* prototype of management has become increasingly difficult to maintain. During the company's earlier years, the use of managers who were graduates of minor and average engineering schools was a natural one for a small and regional firm. The fact that the family *président-directeur général* is not a *grande école* graduate has further reinforced this tradition. But by the end of the period studied, 40 percent of the vice-presidents (*directeurs*) of the company were *grande école* graduates. One of the *directeurs* who was not himself a *grande école* graduate expressed the belief that it was almost inevitable that top management would evolve increasingly in the direction of the *grande école* pattern.

This is an interesting example of a phenomenon that I have observed in other large French firms as well: that top management becomes increasingly dominated by *grande école* graduates as the company grows in importance and becomes increasingly integrated into the big-business community. Despite some claims that French management is becoming increasingly democratized,[17] the traditional structure is still extremely powerful and well established.

[17]See, e.g., H. van der Haas, *The Enterprise in Transition* (Tavistock Publications, London, 1967), p. 87.

The Managers

Chapter 3 expounded the hypothesis that international differences in managerial behavior are, to a considerable degree, explained by the variations in the reward systems for successful managers and in the nature of the career experiences of such managers. Part III presents in detail the nature of such variations among the four countries we are examining.

Since the principal reward available is that of promotion to more responsible positions, Chapters 7 and 8 concentrate upon this. Stress will be placed first upon the degree to which de facto educational requirements limit the career competition among junior managers, and then upon the nature of managerial careers within single large industrial enterprises. Attention will also be given to the role of headquarters in affecting the standards by which managerial success is judged.

A subsidiary element of the reward system for managers is monetary. Chapter 9 deals with the salary differentials between different levels of management and with the system of managerial bonuses.

Chapter 10 summarizes the data of Chapters 7 and 8, and analyzes them from a different point of view than that taken in Chapter 3.

American managerial patterns are studied first and at greatest length, and are taken as a standard against which to examine the managerial characteristics of Britain, France, and the Soviet Union.

7 Aspects of Prior Selection of Managers

There is considerable variation among the countries studied here—particularly between France and Britain—in the degree to which enterprises select the serious candidates for higher management from those who possess particular characteristics at the time of entry into the organization. The more restrictive a given nation's normal criteria for viable candidates are, the less fierce the competition among those who meet these criteria is, and the less burden must be placed upon techniques for determining promotion on the basis of past performance in company posts. The counterpart of this, of course, is that restrictiveness limits the size of the pool of company employees eligible for promotion, and thus leads to the passing-over of men with superior potential.

In the United States, France, and the Soviet Union, the principal prior qualification for consideration for middle- and upper-management posts is that of higher education. Communist Party status should be added to this in the case of the Soviet Union. Unquestionably, the social class position of parents is also relevant; but since this is highly correlated with education, and since it is much more difficult for companies to observe and use directly, I shall not treat it as an independent factor.[1] For Britain, where comparatively few managers have received a higher education, "public school" secondary education can be treated as a proxy for social class. Stock ownership as well as family connections with existing top managers in the organization are also obvious qualifications; these, however, are much less important in the large enterprises with which I am concerned than in smaller companies. Criteria such as race and religion still exert an influence, but at most these disqualify only relatively small minorities of the population. Sex, while a very important criterion, plays a similar role in all four countries (although less in the Soviet Union than in the others). Thus it is not unreasonable to focus attention on education.

The original data presented in this chapter relate both to all management in France and to other than the very top executives in the United States. Except for these groups, the published literature will be relied upon almost exclusively.

United States

The proportion of top executives in large American corporations with college degrees is shown in Table 7.1.

[1]Social class data are provided in many of the published studies to which reference will be made. However, because of the aggregative fashion in which the figures have been reported, partial correlation techniques cannot be applied to most of them.

Table 7.1   Proportion of American Top Executives with College Degrees (Percentage of Sample)

Type of Degree	Narrowly Defined Category of Top Executives			Broadly Defined Category of Top Executives
	1950[a]	1952[b]	1964[a]	1954[c]
First degree	62	65	74	57
Postgraduate degree			22	

[a]Mabel Newcomer, *The Big Business Executive* (Columbia University Press, New York and London, 1955), p. 68; *The Big Business Executive/1964* (Scientific American, Inc., New York, 1965), p. 36. Coverage in the 1964 sample includes the chairman of the board, the president, or the principal vice-president in each of 593 of the largest nonfinancial corporations.

[b]"The Nine Hundred," *Fortune*, November 1952, p. 135. Coverage is of the three highest paid officers in the 250 largest industrial corporations, the 25 largest railroads, and the 25 largest utilities. Data were available for 90 percent of the group or 832 executives.

[c]William L. Warner and J. C. Abegglen, *Occupational Mobility in American Business and Industry* (University of Minnesota Press, Minneapolis, 1955), p. 108. Coverage is of the largest companies in each sector of business, but all vice-presidents are included as well as company secretaries, treasurers, and comptrollers. There are 8,300 executives in the sample.

Of the broader category of top executives, 7.7 times as high a proportion had college degrees as was the case for all American white males of their age group; for the more narrowly defined category, the figures ranged between 10- and 12-fold.[2] Unquestionably this bias in American corporations toward demanding a college education of top executives has been a formidable barrier for most of the entrants into the company's labor force; but it must be acknowledged that it has left a substantial number of potential competitors.

As one would predict, further selectivity has been working among the college graduates in favor of the private schools on the two coasts. Table 7.2 shows that 16 to 32 percent (depending on the sample) of those top executives in large companies who had attended any college had done their undergraduate work at Harvard, Yale, or Princeton, and 30 to 53 percent had attended one of nine colleges as an undergraduate.[3] Since only 4 to 5 percent of all American male college students of their age group had attended the first three colleges, selectivity was working in favor of those who had been stu-

[2]Data for the American white male population are for those with four years or more of college in the group aged 55 to 64 in either 1950 or 1960, depending upon the average age of the executive sample with which they are contrasted. If comparision of the executives is made with the total American male population, the ratios increase by approximately 5 percent. (Data taken from the U.S. Census Special Reports.)

[3]Sample 4 is ignored in analyses of colleges other than Harvard, Yale and Princeton, since it contained no data for three of the remaining six.

dents at Harvard, Yale, or Princeton to the tune of between 3.1 and 6.2 to one compared to students at American colleges as a whole. For the other six schools, the selectivity ratio fell to between 0.9 and 1.9.

One might have expected that the most significant selectivity would be with regard to those who attended graduate or professional schools at the prestigious universities. But as Table 7.3 indicates, less than one-third of the top managers surveyed attended any graduate or professional school whatever. This proportion was approximately nine times as large as the proportion of the managers' age group in the total American male population: i.e., somewhat less than was the proportion with regard to first degrees.

Of course, Table 7.2's figures as to undergraduates represent much more than simple corporate bias. If we consider all graduates of those American colleges that contributed five or more names to the new entries into *Who's Who in America 1966-1967*, 11 percent came from the first three schools and 10 percent from the second six.[4] The selectivity ratio was 4.0 for Harvard, Princeton, and Yale and 2.0 for the others.[5] It might be presumed that graduation from one of these colleges would not per se, and simply because of selection procedures by employing or other organizations, have very much of an influence upon the probabilities of a person being listed in *Who's Who*. Yet the selectivity ratio from these nine colleges was much the same for the *Who's Who* entrants as for the top executives, suggesting that much or even virtually all of the edge in big business in favor of graduates of these schools is due to a combination of the colleges' admission standards and of the quality of their education. But this is irrelevant to the fact of interest to us: namely, that graduation from one of these schools acts as a partial screening device for candidates for top corporate management.

Similar results to those just outlined for top executives have been found for a rather broader group of executives in three large companies in the food, paper, and oil industries. Since I shall often refer to this sample, a reasonably full description of it seems warranted.

In these firms, full personnel records were made available for the top 322 executives as of 1967-1968. For one company (which yielded 62 percent of the total sample), there is full coverage of all the upper managers working at

[4]*Who's Who in America 1968-1969* (Marquis-Who's Who, Chicago, 1968), pp. 22-26. While it is true that the *Who's Who* total excludes some college graduates, and thus overstates the true selectivity ratios for the prestigious colleges, 237 colleges are included in the count of this study.
[5]In computing these selectivity ratios, it is assumed that the new entrants into *Who's Who in America* graduated from college during the decade of 1930-1939.

Table 7.2 Undergraduate Colleges of Top American Business Executives

	Top Executives Who Were Undergraduates at Listed Colleges as Proportion of All Top Executives Who Attended Any College							Undergraduate Degrees for Males from Listed Colleges[a] as Proportion of All American Undergraduate Male Degrees[b]		
	Samples							Age Group of Samples		
	Narrowly defined category of top executives					Broadly defined category of top executives				
	1	2	3	4	5	6	7	5, 6, and 7[c]	1 and 3[d]	2 and 4[e]
	Percentage of Sample									
Harvard, Yale, and Princeton	17	16	23	18	32	16	26	5.2	4.0	4.6
M.I.T., Cornell, Stanford, Pennsylvania, Dartmouth, Columbia	14	16	19	7	21	13	12	13.0	10.2	11.6
Total	31	32	41	25	53	30	38	18.2	14.2	16.2
Sample size of all attending college (number)	897	364	803	95	75	505	1205			
Executives who attended any college as proportion of total sample	90	83	80	90	71	...	51			

Sample 1: Chairman of the board, president, or principal vice-president in 593 of the largest nonfinancial corporations, 1964, from Newcomer, *The Big Business Executive/1964*, pp. 36 and 40-41.
Sample 2: Top two executives of the one hundred largest nonfinancial corporations, 1955, 1961, and 1964, in George W. Pierson, *The Education of American Leaders* (Praeger, New York and London, 1969), p. 113.

Sample 3: Chief executive officers of the 500 largest industrial firms and 50 each of the largest banking, insurance, merchandising, transportation, and utility companies, 1963, *ibid.*, pp. 106-107.

Sample 4: Top two executives of the 53 companies with 1 billion dollars or more of sales, 1961, *ibid.*, pp. 104-105. No data are available for Pennsylvania, Dartmouth, or Columbia, but this is because of the paucity of executives from these colleges.

Sample 5: Top two executives of the 66 companies with 1 billion dollars or more of sales, 1952, *ibid.*, pp. 94-95.

Sample 6: Chairmen, presidents, vice-presidents, company secretaries, treasurers, and comptrollers in the largest companies in each sector of business, 1952. Of the total sample of eight thousand three hundred executives, a random subsample of five hundred and five college graduates were chosen. W. L. Warner and J. C. Abegglen, *Big Business Leaders in America* (Harper & Brothers, New York, 1955), pp. 50-51.

Sample 7: Chairmen, presidents, directors, and other officers of the one hundred largest corporations, 1952. The low proportion of executives indicated as having attended college suggests that many may have attended but not have been identified as doing so. Thus the proportion having attended the selected colleges may be exaggerated. Pierson, *Education of American Leaders*, pp. 96-98.

[a]Pierson, *Education of American Leaders*, p. 257 provides total average annual enrollments during these decades. Since females are not counted, one-third of the enrollments at Cornell, Stanford, and Pennsylvania are eliminated. It is assumed that degrees equal one-fourth of enrollments. While this makes no allowance for students who withdrew, this overestimate is offset by two factors. The first is that some of these were only three-year programs. The second, and more important, is that some of our top executives attended more than one of the colleges being studied, and no allowance was made for such duplication.

[b]U.S. Department of Commerce, Bureau of the Budget, *Historical Statistics of the United States: Colonial Times to 1957* (Washington, 1960), pp. 211-212.

[c]Degrees awarded during 1910-1919.

[d]Degrees awarded during 1920-1929.

[e]Arithmetic average of the two decades.

Table 7.3 Postgraduate Education of Top American Business Executives (Percentage of Samples)

	Top Executives with Postgraduate Education as Proportion of All Who Attended Some College			
	Samples			
	Narrowly defined category of top executives			Broadly defined category of top executives
	1	2	4	7
Those who attended any graduate or professional school	30	32	29	31
Those who attended Harvard, Yale, or Princeton	7	10	8	12
Those who attended M.I.T., Columbia, Cornell, Stanford, Pennsylvania, or Dartmouth	6	6	4	6

Note: The sample numbers are the same as those used in Table 7.2. The last figure for Sample 4 is slightly understated for the reason given in Table 7.2.

corporate headquarters and of those in one division working either at divisional headquarters or in the field. The number of managers at this level in the company at that time constituted approximately 1 percent of the company's labor force. In a second company, there is complete coverage of the top 107 executives, who constituted about 0.5 percent of the total labor force. In a third company, only the top 15 executives are included. In each of the companies, all those executives at or above a specified level in the relevant subunits are included.

Within this sample, each person has been categorized as belonging to one of three levels.[6] The top level begins with minor corporate vice-presidents and the treasurer and comptroller, and rises to include the chief executive officer. The second level begins with regional sales managers and the second-in-command in major factories. The third level includes the remainder of the managers in the sample. The results are shown in Table 7.4.

The proportion of executives with undergraduate degrees from prestigious institutions is, as one would expect, considerably below that shown in Table 7.2; for even the top-level category of executives treated here is much broader than the category treated in the earlier table. Three times as high a proportion

[6]Almost all of the managers were categorized according to level by their own companies. On the basis of these company categories, I reconciled the differences between the company measures and reduced them all to a common system.

Table 7.4 Education of Sample of Executives from Three Large American Industrial Companies

Category of Executives			Characteristics				
			Undergraduate Degree		Graduate Degree		
Managerial Level	Function	Age (Years)	None (percent)	From prestige institution[a] (percent)	None (percent)	From prestige institution[b] (percent)	Sample Size (Number)
All	All	All	17	13	72	8	322
		35 and under	11	2	59	7	44
		36-55	15	10	72	8	202
		Over 55	29	15	78	7	76
Top	All	36-55	12	19	63	19	64
	Technical	36-55	0	11	67	0	9
	Nontechnical	36-55	10	15	65	25	20
Middle	All	36-55	16	6	78	5	93
	Technical	36-55	7	4	68	4	28
	Nontechnical	36-55	19	7	81	7	59
Lower	All	36-55	17	7	76	2	45
	Technical	36-55	12	6	69	0	16
	Nontechnical	36-55	21	7	79	3	29

Note: Technical functions are manufacturing, engineering, and research and development. All others are called nontechnical functions, except for a third category that is not listed separately. The third category consists both of those carrying out either general management or administrative functions and those who are in "assistant to" positions intended primarily for training. This third category is numerically important only for the top level of management; for this level, it shows an exceptionally high proportion (23 percent) who attended prestige undergraduate colleges. However, the proportion with no degree is also rather higher (17 percent) than is the case for the other members of the top level of management. The graduate education of this group is quite similar to that of the top-level managers in nontechnical functions.

For undergraduate degrees, a calculation has also been made by level of management for all executives regardless of age. The results are quite similar to those obtained for those thirty-six to fifty-five years of age.

[a]These are the nine listed in Table 7.2.

[b]These are: for business administration degrees, Harvard, M.I.T., Pennsylvania, Carnegie-Mellon Institute, Stanford, and Chicago; for law, Harvard and Yale; for engineering and science, M.I.T. and California Institute of Technology.

of the top-level executives as of those in the other two levels went to prestige colleges. When we restrict ourselves to those executives aged thirty-six to fifty-five, a slightly larger percentage of the top-level executives received a college degree; but this difference is quite unimportant.

The proportion of executives with graduate degrees is higher for the top level; but even here, only 37 percent of those aged thirty-six to fifty-five had such degrees. The difference between levels is, however, quite marked for those with graduate degrees from prestige institutions; this distinction is caused entirely by degrees in the fields of business and law.

Data for the entire group taken together show that the proportion of those with an undergraduate degree from a prestige college increases sharply with age. Since all the executives in any level of the sample can be considered as managerial successes, it would seem that possession of a degree from a prestige college is playing a diminishing role in managerial careers.[7]

Britain

The proportion of top executives with college education in large British companies is substantially lower than in the United States, and the same is true of the proportion with elitist education. Of course, college education is much less common among British males than it is among Americans in the same age groups; still, it remains a fact that education serves in only a minimal fashion as a preselector of viable candidates for British top management (Table 7.5).

It is quite true that, as is shown in Table 7.6, the selectivity ratios are higher in Britain than in the United States for all university graduates, although not for those from elite universities. Nevertheless, the fact remains that only 7 to 14 percent of the top executives have a truly elitist university education,[8] in contrast to close to three-quarters of the entries into the British government Administrative Class during the mid-1950s, and only a heavily overlapping 11 percent of the business executives have an elitist secondary education.[9] A

---

[7]The changing proportion is, of course, strongly influenced by the relative growth in the total number of graduates from nonprestigious compared to prestigious colleges.

Examination of the significance of age for the proportion with undergraduate degrees from prestigious colleges is strongly confirmed by the data for the top-level executives alone. (This is the most interesting level, since it is the only one from which the "successes" are not promoted out as they grow older.) Here, 34 percent of the executives over fifty-five were from prestige colleges, as against 19 percent for those younger than fifty-five. When we examine the two lower levels, the highest proportion of those from prestigious colleges is for those less than thirty-six years old; but the differences by age are not striking in these levels.

[8]That is, they attended Oxford or Cambridge arts.

[9]An elitist secondary school is defined as one of the small groups of nine major public schools which are called the "Clarendon Schools." Public schools in general are both

Table 7.5   Educational Qualifications of Top Executives in Large British Companies (Columns are ranged from left to right in order of the degree to which the sample can be categorized as consisting of top executives of large firms)

	Sample 1	2a	3	4a	5	6	7	Range of samples 1-7	8
Percentage of Sample									
All university graduates	23	36	29	34		31	31	23-36	38
University graduates under the age of fifty	38		31	43		38		31-43	38
Oxford and Cambridge arts graduates (percentage of total university graduates)						25			38
Former students of any public school				50		34	31	31-50	26
Former students of major public schools				over 8		11	11		
Those with professional qualification:									
Narrow definition		23				25			15
Broad definition	50		45						
University honors degree or higher professional qualification[b]					52				
Number in Sample	290	120	493	1243	532	455	110		61

Table 7.5 (*continued*)

	Sample 1	2[a]	3	4[a]	5	6	7	Range of samples 1-7 / 8
Period covered by the questionnaire	1959	1968	1959	1951	1968	c. 1954	1954-55	c. 1963-64
Size of companies	Very large	Very large	Very large	Very large	Very large	Exceptionally large	Large	Wide range
Level of management	Managing directors	Managing directors	Full-time directors other than managing director	All directors	All full-time directors	Managers closely below the director level	Full-time directors and managers closely below the director level	Directors[c]
Geographic location of the sample	Anywhere in Britain, biased to be near London	Anywhere in Britain	Anywhere in Britain, biased to be near London	Anywhere in Britain	Anywhere in Britain	Anywhere in Britain	Manchester courbation	Manchester conurbation

Notes: Sample 1: Study of managing directors and other full-time directors who listed themselves as "general managers" of companies with a capital of more than £1 million. Sample chosen entirely from among members of the British Institute of Directors, and study conducted by the Institute. See David Granick, *The European Executive* (Doubleday, Garden City, N. Y., 1962), p. 356. Sample 2: Study of managing directors of the five hundred largest British companies. The rate of response to questionnaires plus two follow-up letters was only 24 percent, by far the lowest of all the studies. See D.J Hall and G. Amado-Fischgrund, "Chief Executives in Britain," *European Business*, January 1969, pp. 23-29.

Sample 3: Study of all full-time directors except those listed in Sample 1 from companies with a capital of more than £1 million. Sample taken from the same study by the Institute of Directors. Same source.

Sample 4: Study of directors of companies listed on the London Exchange and with more than £1 million nominal net shareholder assets in 1950. Eighty percent of the respondents claimed that one of their directorships was a full-time activity. Rate of response to questionnaires was only 37 percent, the second lowest of all the studies. See George H. Copeman, *Leaders of British Industry* (Gee and Company, London, 1955).

Sample 5: Stratified sample study of seventy-two nonnationalized industrial and commercial firms, chosen to represent the three hundred largest companies or groups. See National Board for Prices and Incomes, Report No. 107, *Top Salaries in the Private Sector and Nationalized Industries*, (Command Paper 3970, Her Majesty's Stationery Office, London, 1969), p. 68.

Sample 6: Study by the Acton Society of manufacturing firms with over ten thousand employees. Twenty-seven of the roughly sixty-seven such companies in the United Kingdom participated. See the Acton Society Trust, *Management Succession* (The Acton Society Trust, London, 1956), and also Granick, *The European Executive*, for some of the results of the study which were not published by the Acton Society but were kindly put at my disposal.

Sample 7: Study of four firms, each with over three thousand employees. See Roger V. Clements, *Managers: A Study of Their Careers in Industry* (George Allen & Unwin, London, 1958).

Sample 8: Study of thirty-six manufacturing enterprises, chosen so as to represent a cross section of manufacturing in the Manchester conurbation. One third of the firms employed under one thousand employees (the smallest having six hundred), and one sixth had over ten thousand. See D. G. Clark, *The Industrial Manager* (Business Publications, London, 1966).

[a]These two samples had by far the lowest response rates, at least as these were reported by the authors of the respective studies. They should thus be treated as the least reliable.

[b]University honors degrees cover a wide range of standards, and are obtained by the vast bulk of university graduates.

[c]There is no indication in the source as to whether only full-time directors are included.

much coarser educational screen is represented by all universities taken to-gether in the case of higher education, and by all public (i.e., nonstate and fee-paying) schools for secondary education. Of the executives in sample 6 of Table 7.5, only 38 percent had attended either a university or a public school.[10]

Another way of evaluating the strength of the educational screen for top management in British industry is to compare the educational levels of senior and junior management. From Table 7.7 one can see that the screen certainly exists; on the other hand, it can have not more than minor significance in selecting the candidates for top management. Nor does the pattern change very much if we restrict our comparison to the younger top executives and to their age group among the junior executives.

Of course, there is no intention to argue that class consciousness is weak in British society and that it is this which explains the relatively minor role of proxies for class in screening top management candidates.[11] Rather, the ex-planation lies in the fact that business is still a comparatively low (although rapidly rising) prestige area in British society, and thus that upper-class Englishmen tend to be repelled from it.[12] One indication of this phenomenon is the fact, shown in Table 7.6, that males who have had the most prestigious type of higher education have the same selectivity ratio for top industrial management in Britain as do all others with higher education, a situation in very sharp contrast to that in the United States or in France. Similarly, there is no higher selectivity ratio for the graduates of elitist secondary schools than for the alumni of other public schools. Clearly this is because of the British preference for nonindustrial careers.

France

In order to examine the education of top executives in large French firms, it has been necessary to develop my own sample.[13] Those eligible for inclusion

nonstate and fee paying, and are members of the Headmasters' Conference. Since there were about one hundred twenty such schools in Britain at the time when these execu-tives attended school, they must be considered as class selective but not really elitist.

[10]While it is a minimum of 62 percent for the managing directors in sample 2, the low response rate of those questioned makes this figure suspect.

[11]Attendance at a public school, and especially at a major public school, is probably the best such proxy.

[12]See the discussion in David Granick, *The European Executive* (Doubleday, Garden City, N. Y., 1962), Chapters 7 and 9.

[13]See also Nicole Delefortrie-Soubeyroux, *Les dirigeants de l'industrie française* (Li-brairie Armand Colin, Paris, 1961). Unfortunately, the group she studied is quite hetero-geneous both with regard to the size of firm and to the level of management; one-quarter of the total are not managers at all, but are rather nonmanager members of a board of directors.

Table 7.6   Education Selectivity Ratios for Britain, U.S., and France

	Britain[a]	United States[b]	France[c]
Proportion of all former public school boys among managers divided by proportion among male population of their age group:			
All top management	13-21		
Proportion of all former major-public-school boys among managers divided by proportion among male population of their age group:			
All top management	16		
Proportion of all higher educational graduates among managers divided by proportion among male population of their age group:			
All top management	15-18	7.7	
Very top management only	12-19	10-12	28
Proportion of all managers graduating from higher educational institutions who went to elite institutions compared to the same proportion for the male population of their age group:			
All top management	1.0	3.1-5.0	
Very top management		3.7-6.2	15

[a]Managerial data are from Table 7.5. Samples 3-7 are treated as "all top management," and Samples 1 and 2 as "very top management." Elite higher education refers to Oxford and Cambridge arts graduates.
British data for the relevant male age groups are approximated from the following sources:
1. Public school and major-public-school students: from the *Public Schools Yearbook* for 1914, 1921, and 1923, supplemented by T.J.H. Bishop, *Winchester and the Public School Elite* (Faber and Faber, London, 1967), pp. 45, 61, and 80.
2. Male university graduates from all British universities: from the University Grants Committee, *Returns from Universities and University Colleges in Receipt of Treasury Grants* (Her Majesty's Stationary Office, London, annual reports for 1922/23 through 1926/27).
3. Oxford and Cambridge male arts graduates: *ibid.*, 1927/28 and 1928/29.
[b]Data are based upon Table 7.2. Elite higher education refers to undergraduate attendance at Harvard, Yale or Princeton. Samples 6 and 7 are considered as "all top management," while Samples 1 through 5 are considered as "very top management".
[c]Data are from Table 7.8. Elite higher education refers to Polytechnique. Comparison is made between the managers and all males over the age of twenty-two; this reduces the French ratios rather substantially below what they would have been if comparison had been possible with the proper age group.

Table 7.7 Comparison of Educational Qualifications of Top and Junior Executives in British Companies

	Exceptionally Large Firms[a]		Wide Size Range of Firms[b]		Division of One Very Large Firm[c]
	Top Executives	Junior managers	Directors	All Managers	All managers
	Percentage of Sample				
All university graduates	31	8	38	35	25
Same for managers under the age of 50	38	19			37
Oxford and Cambridge arts graduates	7	2	15	8	
Same for managers under the age of 50	10	2			
Former students of any public school	34	9	26	12	22
Same for managers ages 30-49	39	16			27
Former students of major public schools	11	1		3	
Same for managers ages 30-49	13	2			
Possessors of professional qualifications[d]	21	9	15	21	49
Same for managers under the age of 50[e]	29	14		23	49
	Number in Sample				
	455	984	61	686	83

[a]Companies treated in Sample 6 of Table 7.5. Junior managers are at the level of technician, assistant accountant, shift manager and section head. Top executives seem to average only a few years older than junior executives: those between the ages of thirty and fifty-nine, the difference in average age is only 2.5 years. (Top executives as a group average 2.2 years older than those between the ages of thirty and fifty-nine.)

[b]Companies treated in Sample 8 of Table 7.5. Although we have no data for junior managers as such, 84 percent of all managers were at levels below that of the top managers of Sample 6; thus the group of "all managers" is distinctly junior to the directors. There is no indication as to whether all the directors are full time.

[c]This is a 100 percent sample of all managers except for a few of the lowest paid. Managers constitute 4 percent of the division's labor force.

[d]Primarily, members of professional societies which require examinations for admission.

[e]The age limits used for the first two groups of firms differ slightly from this.

in the sample were the top executive officers (an average of 1.5) in the five hundred largest industrial firms, but with these firms essentially restricted to those whose shares are quoted on the Paris Bourse or which are nonmonopolistic state owned companies. After excluding nine non-French nationals, 682 names could be identified out of those occupying these posts in 1963; these comprise our sample.[14]

Analysis of the biographical data showed that there is a significant degree of heterogeneity among the top executives; this heterogeneity could be appreciably reduced by a classification of the executives' firms according to size and to the nature of the industry, particularly the latter. Executives (20 percent of our sample) in the least prestigious industries were placed into a separate category.[15] Both the size of the firm and the nature of its industry are important indicators of its prestige and thus of its ability to recruit members of the French educational elite.

Forty-five members of the sample were top executives of firms in which identified foreign interests owned at least 30 percent of the shares.[16] Executives of these firms had a slightly less elitist education than did the executives in purely French companies, but the difference is insufficient to warrant

[14]The firms are taken from the listing in *Entreprise,* October 27, 1966, which ranks the firms according to the book value of shareholders' capital. Both nationalized firms and foreign subsidiaries are included. The names of all *présidents* and *directeurs généraux* of these firms who were also members of the board of directors of the same company were taken from the *Annuaire Desfossés 1964,* Volume 2 (Société d'éditions économiques et financières, Paris, 1964); thirty-four additional names were taken from the 1966 edition of the *Annuaire Desfossés,* this being done when no names were given in the 1964 edition. Biographical data were then looked for in *Who's Who in France* (Editions Jacques Lafitte, Paris). Some additional names and brief biographical information were found through a first-hand search by Michel Wattel of *Who's Who in France.*

[15]The industry classification of the firms was taken from *Entreprise.* The eleven industries treated there were grouped into two classes, based on the proportion of top managers who were graduates of Polytechnique or other *grandes écoles,* who had been members of a *grand corps* in the civil service, or for whom there was evidence of any higher educational degree. The size category of the enterprise, and whether or not it was nationalized, was held constant in making a judgment as to the relative proportion of top managers in each industry who fitted into these elite categories.

Combining these standards, the food and textile industries could be categorized as clearly nonprestigious. Of the other industries, the evidence was most ambivalent for the paper and automotive industries. Paper was grouped with food and textiles, and its top executives constitute 12 percent of the nonprestige category. The automotive industry was grouped with the prestige industries, and its executives constitute 4 percent of this category.

[16]Data were taken from *Les liaisons financières des entreprises françaises* (Société d'éditions économiques et financières, Paris, second edition, 1967).

separate treatment.[17] On the other hand, executives in nationalized firms[18] do show an above-average degree of educational elitism, and thus are treated separately.

Tables 7.8 and 7.9 analyze the characteristics of these top French industrial executives. However, since French firms are smaller than either the American or British, it is the category of very large, nonnationalized firms which best bears comparison with our tables for American, British and Soviet industry. Within this category, it is the subgroup of very large, nonnationalized firms of prestige industries which are headed by men with a highly exclusive educational background by all international standards.[19] It is in these companies that the preselection of top managers, prior to their having achieved any record of performance within the enterprise, goes the furthest.

In order to place into perspective the educational data of Tables 7.8 and 7.9, it should be noted that graduates of French higher educational institutions constituted in 1962 about 2.6 percent of the total French male population over the age of twenty-two.[20] Those with complete secondary education comprised only an additional 3.7 percent of the male population of the same age,[21] and it seems probable that this second group constitute the majority of the top executives without higher education. For French males over the age of forty-four (the best approximation we can make to the age group of our French executives), the respective figures are 2.1 and 3.2 percent.

[17]A separate analysis was made for firms with 30 to 49 percent foreign ownership and for those with over 50 percent foreign ownership.
[18]Defined as those in which the government owns 30 percent or more of the shares. *Nomenclature des entreprises nationales, année 1966* (Imprimerie nationale, Paris, 1966). For executives in these companies, size was not a relevant variable.
[19]To the best of my knowledge, Japanese companies are the only competitors with the French in regard to such exclusivity.
[20]Graduates are defined as those with diplomas from an engineering, commercial, or military *école* as well as those who received a *licence* (the first full university degree) from a French university. The principal counteracting biases in the percentage figure derive from the assumption made in the calculation that no graduate of an *école* also earned a *licence,* and from the fact that graduates of nonengineering *écoles* were ignored.

According to the March 1962 census, 3.3 percent of the male population over the age of twenty-four had received a higher educational degree. However, this figure includes university degrees that are below the level of the *licence,* and thus is too comprehensive for comparison with our managerial data.
[21]Completed secondary education is here defined very liberally to include those who had passed only the first part of the *baccalauréat* and also those had received the *brevet supérieur.* To the figure given in the census for those over age twenty-four is added the difference between the census percentage of graduates of higher education institutions and our own percentage. See Institut National de la Statistique et des Etudes Economiques, *Recensement général de la population de 1962, Résultats du sondage au 1/20ᵉ,* Volume 1 (Imprimerie Nationale, Paris, 1964), Table R11, p. 24.

Table 7.8 Education[a], Prior Career, and Family of Top Executives in the Five Hundred Largest French Industrial Companies (Percentages are of the total sample except where otherwise stated)

| | All Nationalized[b] Firms | | All Private Firms | | | |
| | | | In Prestigious Industries[c] | | In Non-prestigious Industries[c] | |
	Number	Percentage	No.	Perc.	No.	Perc.
Size of sample	35		509		138	
A. Education						
1. Graduates of Polytechnique, members of the Corps des Mines	5	14	28	6	0	0
2. Graduates of Polytechnique, all others	14	40	137	27	6	4
3. Other members of *grands corps*[d]	3	9	8	2	1	1
4. Graduates of Centrale, Mines, Ecole Normale Supérieure, St. Cyr, Hautes Etudes Commerciales	6	17	100	20	23	17
5. Subtotal of 1-4 (after excluding duplication)	28	80	272	53	30	22
6. Graduates of other *écoles*	10	29	62	12	18	13
7. Graduates of universities[e]	0	0	52	10	15	11
8. Total graduates of higher educational institutions (1 + 2 + 4 + 6 + 7)	35	100	379	74	62	45
9. No higher educational degree	0	0	14	3	3	2
10. No complete data[f]	0	0	116	23	73	53
11. Engineering or science degrees	25	71	312	61	31	22
12. All other degrees	10	29	67	13	31	22

B. Former Careers in Government

Table 7.8 (continued)

| | All Nationalized[b] Firms | | All Private Firms | | | |
	Number	Percentage	In Prestigious Industries[c] No.	Perc.	In Non-prestigious Industries[c] No.	Perc.
13. Civilian engineering *corps*						
a. *Polytechniciens*	11	31	56	11	0	0
b. All others	0	0	1	0	1	1
14. Military engineering *corps*						
a. *Polytechniciens*	4	11	27	5	0	0
b. All others	0	0	2	0	1	1
15. Other civilian government service						
a. *Polytechniciens*	2	6	5	1	0	0
b. All others	8	23	17	3	2	1
16. Military, nonengineering						
a. *Polytechniciens*	0	0	2	0	1	1
b. All others	1	3	5	1	2	1
C. Prominent Fathers[g]						
17. (percent of all *polytechniciens*)	4	21	17	10	0	0
18. (percent of all non-*polytechniciens*)	2	12	31	9	14	11
D. Elite Education and Prominent Fathers						
19. Those in educational categories 1, 2 or 4 and others with prominent fathers	27	77	292	57	43	31

[a]An individual is placed in only one category as to education. When he fits into more than one, he is put in that category which is highest in prestige ranking—as shown by its order in the table.

[b]These constitute twenty-five companies in which the government owns 30 percent or more of the stock. All of these companies are in prestigious industries.

[c]Nonprestigious industries are defined as including food, textiles, and paper. All other industries are treated as prestigious.

[d]The *grands corps* are defined very restrictively as the Corps des Mines, the Inspection des Finances, the Conseil d'Etat, and the Cour des Comptes.

[e]Only those with a *licence* or a higher degree are included.

[f]No one in this category is a graduate of Polytechnique, Centrale, or les Ecoles des Mines.

[g]Almost all of these fathers held top positions either in the French government service or in very substantial private companies. Levels included in the government, for example, are those such as general or cabinet minister, but not senator or deputy.

Table 7.9 Education[a], Prior Career, and Family of Top Executives in the Largest Non-nationalized French Industrial Companies (Percentages are of the Total Sample Except Where Otherwise Stated)

	Very Large Firms[b]				Large Firms[b]		Medium Size[b] Firms	
	Prestigious Firms[c]		Nonpres-tigious Firms[d]		Prestigious Firms Only[c]		Prestigious Firms Only[c]	
	No.	Perc.	No.	Perc.	No.	Perc.	No.	Perc.
Size of sample	121		12		153		235	
A. Education								
1. Graduates of Poly-technique who are also members of the Corps des Mines	13	11	0	0	6	4	9	4
2. Graduates of Poly-technique, all others	38	31	2	17	48	31	51	22
3. Other members of *grands corps*[e]	2	2	0	0	5	3	1	0
4. Graduates of Centrale, Mines, Ecole Normale Supérieure, St. Cyr, Hautes Etudes Commerciales	26	21	1	8	28	18	46	20
5. Subtotal of 1-4 (after excluding duplication)	79	65	3	25	86	56	107	46
6. Graduates of other *écoles*	11	9	1	8	19	12	32	14
7. Graduates of universities[f]	12	10	1	8	16	10	24	10
8. Total graduates of higher educational institutions (1 + 2 + 4 + 6 + 7)	100	83	5	42	117	76	162	69
9. No higher educa-tional degree	0	0	0	0	6	4	8	3
10. No complete data[g]	21	17	7	58	30	20	65	28
11. Engineering or science degrees	88	73	3	25	94	61	130	55
12. All other degrees	12	10	2	17	23	15	32	14

B. Former Careers in Government

Table 7.9 (continued)

	Very Large Firms[b]				Large Firms[b]		Medium Size[b] Firms	
	Prestigious Firms[c]		Nonpres- tigious Firms[d]		Prestigious Firms Only[c]		Prestigious Firms Only[c]	
	No.	Perc.	No.	Perc.	No.	Perc.	No.	Perc.
13. Civilian engineering *corps*								
a. *Polytechniciens*	22	18	0	0	17	11	17	7
b. All others	0	0	0	0	1	1	0	0
14. Military engineering *corps*								
a. *Polytechniciens*	5	4	0	0	14	9	8	3
b. All others	0	0	0	0	1	1	1	0
15. Other civilian government service								
a. *Polytechniciens*	3	2	0	0	1	1	1	0
b. All others	4	3	0	0	7	5	6	3
16. Military, non- engineering								
a. *Polytechniciens*	0	0	0	0	0	0	2	1
b. All others	0	0	0	0	3	2	2	1
C. Prominent Fathers[h]								
17. (percent of all *polytechniciens*)	7	14	0	0	4	7	6	10
18. (percent of all non- *polytechniciens*)	11	16	1	10	10	10	10	6
D. Elite Education and Prominent Fathers								
19. Those in educational categories 1, 2, or 4 and others with promi- nent fathers	86	71	4	33	91	59	115	49

[a]An individual is placed in only one category as to education. When he fits into more than one, he is put in that category which is highest in prestige ranking—as shown by its order in the table.

[b]Very large firms are defined as those ranked Number 1 to 100 in size. Large firms are those ranked Number 101 to 250, and medium firms those ranked Number 251 to 500.

[c]Nonprestigious industries are defined as food, textiles, and paper. All other industries are treated as prestigious.

[d]Despite the small size of this sample, it is included in order to show the similarity of this group to the larger sample of top executives from all nonprestigious industries.

[e]The *grands corps* are defined very restrictively as the Corps des Mines, the Inspection des Finances, the Conseil d'Etat, and the Cour des Comptes.

[f]Only those with a *licence* or a higher degree are included.

[g]No one in this category is a graduate of Polytechnique, Centrale, or les Ecoles des Mines.

[h]Almost all of these fathers held top positions either in the French government service or in very substantial private companies. Levels included in the government, for example, are those such as general or cabinet minister, but not senator or deputy.

Thus one sees that at least 68 percent of the top executives of all the leading 475 nonnationalized industrial firms, and 74 percent of the subgroup in prestige industries, had an education equalled by only 2 percent of the French male population of their age group. Even these educational figures for top managers are understated, due to my assumption that all of the managers for whom there was no educational data had failed to complete higher education.

This, however, is only the beginning. Of Frenchmen with higher educational degrees, only about 2.8 percent had degrees from Polytechnique—as contrasted with 42 percent of the top managers with higher educational degrees in the very large, nonnationalized firms in the prestige industries. For the engineering schools with the next highest prestige,[22] the corresponding figures are roughly 4.5 and 21 percent.[23] Furthermore, the recruitment of industrial managers throughout French industry primarily from among graduates of engineering *écoles* rather than from among university graduates is only a very partial explanation; for over one-third of all French males with higher educational degrees are engineers.

Polytechnique is extremely selective in its choice of students. Would-be candidates for admission first study an average of two years in a post-*baccaulauréat* program, with considerable screening preceding entrance into this program. The candidates are then further screened for entrance to Polytechnique through written and oral competitive examinations. Thus the students must all show a high degree of intellectual competence, particularly in mathematics and physics. But still further screening occurs upon graduation. The best eight to fifteen students typically go on to the Corps des Mines (the technical civil service with the highest repute) after first passing through the Ecole des Mines, and most of the other superior students go into another civilian or military-engineering *corps*. This is true regardless of whether these students intend to make a career within the government or in the private sector.

The degree to which government service is viewed as a proper early career stage for the stronger graduates of Polytechnique is indicated by the jobs held in 1958 by the 180 French students who graduated in 1949. Of the top 20 students, nine were in the Corps des Mines, ten were in two other civilian *corps,* and one was in the most prestigious of the military-engineering *corps.* On the other hand, none of the bottom 20 worked in either a military-engineering or a civilian *corps.*

[22]The Ecole Centrale and the Ecoles des Mines.
[23]For the number of living graduates of engineering *écoles,* see *Id,* March 1968, pp. 1-10.

With this background, we can appreciate the significance of the fact that, although only 22 percent of all *polytechniciens* working in industry in 1958 had previously belonged to a civilian or military-engineering *corps* of the government, 53 percent of the *polytechniciens* who were top executives in our firms of prestigious industries had been in these *corps*. (See also Table 7.10.) If we assume that the figure of 22 percent held for the age cohort of the top executives, this entire group of *polytechniciens* in industry numbered only 475.[24] Thus, out of those *polytechniciens* in industry whose education and ranking in class made them highly eligible for top executive posts, 21 percent of the appropriate age group held such a position in one of the five hundred largest industrial companies in France.

Another way of approaching the same question of disproportionate selection of *polytechnicien* top executives from within the top group at graduation is to examine their rank in class at Polytechnique. Since the *Journal Officiel* did not begin publication of class ranks until 1927, we have data only for those *polytechniciens* who were about fifty-eight years or younger at the time of the study. This group comprised eighty-four people, or 44 percent of our total sample of *polytechniciens*. Taking the class size to be the average of the classes graduating between 1927 and 1935, I find the proportions given in Table 7.11.

The degree of selection of top executives according to their education is particularly amazing when we remember that a large number of the five hundred largest French firms are still controlled, either through stock ownership or through tradition, by individual families. Thus we might expect that many of the top executives who do not have an elitist education were selected for their posts as a result of their family connections. Unfortunately, I have no direct method of estimating the number of these "family" top executives. An inadequate estimate of this can be obtained from the count of the non-*polytechniciens* whose biographies indicate that their father held very important positions (almost entirely either in very substantial private companies or within the French government service). These totaled 9 percent of the chief executives of the very large private firms in prestigious industries; added to the *polytechniciens* heading these companies, they comprise 51

[24]Although the mission of Polytechnique is primarily that of preparing government officials, both civilian and military, it can be estimated that 45 percent of its graduates still in active professional life from the age group of our top executives are engaged in industry. Yet this group comprises no more than 2,200 people in total. (Data on the occupation of graduates are for 1958; see G. Chevry in *La Jaune et la Rouge,* June 1960, p. 61. The basic age group is taken to be those between the ages of fifty and sixty-nine, but allowance is made for those both older and younger.)

Table 7.10   Proportion of the French Population with Specific Education or Government Careers (Percentage)

	French Male Population Over Age Twenty-Two	All *Polytechniciens* Working in Industry	Chief Executives in Total Sample of Private Firms in Prestigious Industries	Chief Executives of Very Large Private Firms in Prestigious Industries
Higher educational degree	2.6	100	74	83
Graduate of Polytechnique, Centrale or Mines	0.19	100	49	63
Graduate of Polytechnique	0.07	100	33	42
Polytechniciens who are former members of civilian or military-engineering *corps*		22	16	22

Note: All chief executives for whom we have no information as to education are treated as though they did not have a higher educational degree. Thus the proportion with such a degree is underestimated to an unknown degree.

Table 7.11   Class Rank of *Polytechniciens*

Rank in Class at Graduation	Percentage of Top Executive *Polytechniciens* in the Five Hundred Largest Firms	Percentage of all *Polytechniciens*
1 - 10	36	4
11 - 15	6	2
16 - 52	17	16
53 - 230	42	77

percent of the total. If we add the graduates of the major *grandes écoles* (Centrale, Mines, E.N.S., St. Cyr, and H.E.C.), we reach a figure of 71 percent.

There is no point in saying anything about the social origins of the top executives except that it is quite elitist. Of the 682 top executives in the 500 firms, none described his father's occupation as that of manual worker, 6 described it as that of farmer, and 10 described it as that of a minor white-collar worker in either private or government service. But since I have no data for 264 executives, the true figures may well be much higher. One hundred seventy-three (41 percent of those providing information on this subject) gave their father's occupation as that of businessman, but the enterprises were undoubtedly of a wide range of size and the positions may have been as low as that of middle-level executive.

In order further to pursue the topic of the preselection of top managers in French industry, it will be valuable to examine the educational attainments of different levels of management in individual nonnationalized companies. Data concerning all, or virtually all, of the managers at selected levels are available for sixteen companies; discussion will be restricted to these firms. While the details are left to Appendix A of Chapter 7, the results can be summed up as follows:

First, the proportion of all the *cadres* with higher education is very large and, in the one case for which we have data, half of the remainder had completed secondary education. Nevertheless, it is perfectly clear that men with neither higher education nor family connections can rise above the foreman level even in high-prestige industries. But normally they do this toward the end of their career, and they are quite unlikely to move beyond junior or middle management.

Second, within the educationally select managerial group, it is apparent that the average educational level increases very sharply between management levels. This is true even when we restrict our comparison to a contrast between the two top levels which together constitute 1 to 9 percent of total management (see Companies 1 and 5 especially, but also Company 3). In view of the fact that future candidates for top management are among those who are currently at lower managerial ranks because of their age, these materials provide strong confirmation of the high degree of preselectivity between levels. Only a relatively few managers at middle levels have the family connections or educational background necessary to make them serious candidates for promotion. In considering managers for advancement, as well as in considering nonmanagers for admission into the managerial category, French industry need pay much less attention to the success of these men in their earlier careers than is the case in America or Britain. Barring the unusual case, only a relatively few candidates who pass through the educational screen for the next managerial level need be examined as individuals.

Soviet Union

Since the beginning of the Five Year Plans and the expansion of the economy beyond the level reached in 1913, two quite distinct generations of top management have run Soviet industry. The first consists of "Red directors" who were largely swept away in the purges of 1936-1938. The second consists of their immediate successors; most of these had reached top executive status by 1941, and were still holding down their jobs in the middle 1960s. The two differ sharply in their characteristics.

The first generation is effectively described by five Soviet sample studies of 1934 and 1936 which cover managers in heavy industry, a sector of particular priority and of large-scale enterprises (Table 7.12).

Of these Soviet industrial managers of the mid-1930s, the top group was selected out of a very small body of people who met the educational and political qualifications. It was drawn heavily from the tiny body of Old Bolsheviks with higher education.[25]

On the other hand, the enterprise directors were drawn from a considerably wider body of potential candidates. Although these directors were only slightly younger than the branch heads, the differences in education and in the period of joining the Party were significant. Education, in particular, was a much less stringent prior requirement for the directors; only one-quarter had attended normal higher educational institutions, the rest of those with higher education having been sent to the industrial academies for the brief and inferior education that was provided there. The principal prior qualification for the position seems to have been political: three-quarters had joined the Communist Party during the years when this was a risky venture and could be taken as significant evidence of political conviction. Since there had been only a total of some 515,000 members and candidates of the Party at

[25]The official estimate of the number of Party members as of January 1917 is twenty-four thousand. In the fall of 1927, only 1.4 percent of the members of bureaus of Party cells were Old Bolsheviks. See Leonard Schapiro, *The Communist Party of the Soviet Union,* (Methuen, London, 1963), pp. 170-171 and 310-311. No data are available as to their education.

Table 7.12 Qualifications of Soviet Top Executives of Heavy Industry in 1934 and 1936

	Branch[a] Heads	Assistant Branch[a] Heads	Enterprise Directors	Heads of Departments in Enter-prises
	Percentage of Sample			
Education				
a. Attended a higher educational institute	59-66	50-100	26-44	57-81
b. Primary education only	21	0- 12	40-49	8-20
Communist Party membership				
a. Members	97	58-73	97-100	50-51
b. Joined pre-1917	33-45	6- 7	9-11	. . .
c. Joined during the Civil War	55-62	45-72	60-65	. . .
White-collar social origin	56-71	67-88	23-37	46-70
Age				
a. 31-50 years	88-90	83-92	92-95	83-86
b. Of this, 31-40	33-41	40-46	48-50	52-60
	Sample Size (each individual sample)			
	32-39	40-84	457-944	267-343
	Number of Samples			
	2-3	2-3	2-4	2

Source: See David Granick, *Management of the Industrial Firm in the USSR* (Columbia University Press, New York, 1954), pp. 290-291, where the sources of these data are described.
[a]*Glavk.*

the end of the civil-war years, and since a goodly number of these had left the Party by the middle 1930s, the political requirement was fairly restrictive.

Most of this generation of top managers disappeared in the purges of 1936-1938, and a younger group replaced them. These were better educated, but this fact did not indicate an equivalent increase in selectivity since a larger percentage of their age group had also received a higher education. Although a few of them were Old Bolsheviks, and most were too young even to have entered the Party during the days of the civil war, the branch heads of the early 1940s had demonstrated their political activity by an exceptionally early age of admission to Party membership. Most had worked for several years prior to beginning higher education and had been selected for this schooling both because of their political reliability and their demonstrated ability (Table 7.13).

While presumably all of these branch heads were Party members, this was a very common qualification in the Soviet Union. In March 1939, when these men had had an average age under forty, about 7 percent of Soviet males over the age of twenty-nine were full Party members. Similarly, almost 5 percent of the males of their generation had completed higher education,[26] and the two groups heavily overlapped. Although it is true that most or all of the branch heads with higher education were engineers, about 50 percent of all males receiving higher educational degrees in the same years as these men had similarly earned engineering degrees. The most uncommon statistical feature was probably the early age of admission to the Party of the branch heads of 1941; but this identifying characteristic had disappeared among the branch heads appointed during the 1950s.

The further data shown in Table 7.14 concerning the education of these branch heads indicates that some 84 percent of those who graduated from higher educational institutions appear to have been full-time students. Thus the proportion with the inferior evening- or correspondence-school higher education is quite small.

Good data are available as to the higher educational institutions from which these branch heads graduated, but unfortunately I know of no figures as to the total number of students graduating from each type of institution. Nevertheless, it seems significant that only a small proportion of the branch heads graduated from the single most prestigious scientific institute in the country.

[26]Schapiro, *The Communist Party*, pp. 436 and 439; TsSU, *Itogi vsesoiuznoi perepisi naseleniia 1959 goda* (Gosstatizdat, Moscow, 1962) pp. 13, 17, 49 and 74.

Table 7.13   Characteristics of All Soviet Branch[a] Heads of Industry and Construction

	In Office June 1941	In Office Oct. 1952	In Office Oct. 1965	New Heads Appointed	
				In 1940s	In 1950s
Education					
a. Attended a higher educational institute (percentage)	71	100	94	100	100
b. Average age at graduation	30	28	26	27	26
Party membership					
Average age of entry	22	25	27	24	29
Age					
Average year of birth	1901	1904	1909	1906	1906
Sample size (number)	21-23	19-27	33	12-17	20-25
Sample as a percentage of the relevant population (percentage)	75-82	68-96	100	52-74	67-83

Source: Jerry F. Hough, *The Soviet Prefects* (Harvard University Press, Cambridge Mass., 1969), pp. 47 and 76.
[a]Ministry.

The nearest proxy that can be readily used for other high-prestige institutes consists of those institutes that are physically located either in Moscow or in Leningrad: some 53 percent of the branch heads graduated from these. While it is true that a very substantial proportion of all engineering graduates in the country came from the Moscow and Leningrad institutes, it would appear that, as we might expect, branch heads are likely to be chosen from among the alumni of the more prestigious institutes. Nevertheless, it seems fairly certain that there has not been any of that concentration on the graduates of a very few schools which characterizes the top management of French industry.

Turning from recent branch heads to enterprise directors, those of the 1950s and 1960s have almost all been Party members. Yet, in a sample of ninety-eight men who were directors of the larger plants in the country during 1957-1965, and who were of much the same generation as the branch heads appointed in the 1950s, the average age at joining the Party was two to

Table 7.14   Educational Characteristics of all Soviet Branch[a] Heads of Industry and Construction Appointed after the Purges of the Late 1930s

	Total	Appointed before the 1960s	Appointed during the 1960s
Of those graduating: (percentage)			
Were full-time students	66	59	78
Probably were full-time students	18	25	4
Total (percentage)	84	84	83
Sample size (number)	67	44	23
Sample as a percentage of the relevant population (percentage)	62	57	82
Of all branch heads: (percentage)			
Graduates of the most prestigious institute[b]	7	8	4
Graduates of all other Moscow and Leningrad institutes	53	55	48
Graduates of all other institutes	26	20	41
Graduates of universities	1	0	4
Graduates of correspondence schools or of the Industral Academy	3	3	4
No complete higher education	9	13	0
Sample size (number)	88	61	27
Sample as a percentage of the relevant population (percentage)	73	66	96

Source: Data supplied privately by Jerry F. Hough.
[a]Ministry.
[b]Bauman.

three years older than for the branch heads. Thus there is no indication that unusual political activity marked the early years of their careers.[27]

With regard to the education of directors it is true that, for all of the enterprise directors in the country as a whole in 1966, one-third had neither a higher nor a specialized secondary education.[28] But the percentage of graduate engineers among directors was far higher in the larger plants; of the sample already referred to, 97 percent of the directors had engineering degrees and only 4 percent had earned these degrees late in their careers. In general, these directors seem to have gone on directly from high school to a higher educational institute.[29]

Since Party membership is a virtual requirement for top management in Soviet industry, while this is not the case for managers below the level of enterprise director, Party membership serves as one criterion for preselecting those managers who are to be considered for top positions. But the criterion is not a very stringent one. In 1939, as we saw earlier, some 7 percent of all Soviet males above the age of twenty-nine were Party members. By 1959, the figure had risen to 12 percent. As of 1934-1936 in plants of heavy industry, members and candidate members comprised 30 to 35 percent of all those in that managerial category with the lowest proportion of Party membership.[30] Doubtless the proportion is a good deal higher today. Thus perhaps only one out of two middle managers in Soviet industry are excluded from promotion to top management on the ground of not being a Party member.

With regard to education, unfortunately, data limitations force us to lump together three widely disparate levels of education: degrees, incomplete higher education, and specialized secondary education. As of 1959, about 21 percent of the male population between the ages of twenty-five and fifty-seven had had one of these types of education.[31] Applying this figure to 1966 (it is unquestionably an underestimate for that year), we find that the proportion of directors of all enterprises in the Soviet Union with such an education was 332 percent of the proportion in the relevant male population. The proportion of enterprise managers with this education in 1966 was as shown

[27]Jerry F. Hough, *The Soviet Prefects* (Harvard University Press, Cambridge, Mass., 1969), pp. 49, 61-62, and 373.

[28]TsSU, *Trud v SSSR* (Statistika, Moscow, 1968), p. 297.

[29]Hough, *The Soviet Prefects,* pp. 49, 61-62 and 373.

[30]Sources referred to in Table 7.12.

[31]TsSU, *Itogi,* page 74. Twenty-five is taken as the lowest age because those in age categories below this had not completed their education. Fifty-seven is taken as the highest, as representing those males who had not yet retired in 1966, the year for which we have educational data relating to managers.

in Table 7.15. Although these educational data are much more broadly grouped than would be desirable, they do suggest that education is even less effective than Party membership as a preselector of those junior and middle managers to be considered for promotion. My impression as to the proportion of managers at different levels who are graduate engineers is that such data, if available, would give rise to the same conclusion.

If one assumes that the directors of all large enterprises had engineering degrees, then the population from which they were drawn (males between the ages of forty-five and fifty-nine in 1959 with a higher educational degree) is still very large: 5 percent of that male age group.

To sum up, the qualifications shown by Soviet top industrial managers prior to beginning their serious careers (or, with regard to joining the Party, qualifications which are independent of career success) are only slightly more restrictive than are those of American managers. The one exception was for the branch managers of the middle 1930s, who demonstrated a combination of political and educational qualifications which was and is extremely rare.

Conclusion

It is quite clear that, in the case of all four of the countries studied, men with particular kinds of precareer qualifications have a much greater statistical probability of achieving managerial status than has the run-of-the-mill male adult. The same is true with regard to reaching the status of a top executive compared to the position of a junior or middle manager.

However, there are three clearly distinct patterns for the top managers in our four countries. The United States and the Soviet Union constitute one pattern: that of high educational qualifications in countries where these are not rare either among adult males as a whole or among lower managers. The

Table 7.15   Advanced Education Among Enterprise Managers in the USSR

	Index (Directors = 100)
Chief engineers	128
Department heads and their assistants	103
Ordinary engineers	118
Technicians	84
Foremen	74

Note: "Advanced Education" here refers to degrees, incomplete higher education, and specialized secondary education.
Source: TsSU, *Trud v SSSR* (Statistika, Moscow, 1968), p. 297.

British pattern is that of recruiting some half to two-thirds of top executives from men without either a public school or university education. The French pattern is that of demanding, at least in large companies, an exceptional type of higher education for the substantial bulk of all managers above the foreman level. Furthermore, slightly over half of the top managers of the 335 large private firms in French prestigious industries are recruited from men with an education that is extremely uncommon among junior and middle managers.

For my purposes, the three national patterns can be consolidated into two. British, American, and Russian large industrial organizations are all of a fairly "open promotion" type, in which the force of the preentrance qualifications is relatively weak. In all three countries, the enterprise management faces the task of considering a very substantial body of men when making promotions to middle and upper managerial posts; the converse of this is that large numbers of junior and middle managers can legitimately aim for promotion to senior positions.

In contrast, large French enterprises have a "closed promotion" character, and the task of selecting men for promotion according to their performance within the company is greatly simplified. Far more than is the case in the other three countries, the selection job has already been done at the moment of a man's entrance into the firm. At each managerial level, there are only a few viable candidates for promotion.

**Appendix A
to Chapter 7**

**Educational Attainments of
Different Levels of French
Management**

The data presented in this appendix are for sixteen large nonnationalized companies. In each case presented, the figures cover all, or virtually all of the managers at the selected levels.

The first company has over fifteen thousand employees, is in a prestige industry, and its shareholding is widely diversified. Five percent of its employees have the status of *cadres,* i.e., of managers and professionals above the level of foreman. Educational data for the various groups of *cadres* are given in Table A. 7A.1.

Even this highly stratified picture understates the reality, since young managers who graduated from the more prestigious *écoles* are unlikely to have yet worked themselves up to the top levels of management.

Out of the "all other managers" category, I have a subsample of twenty-seven men; this subsample is chosen from among the top one-third or so of those in this category, and all work in the factories. Six of these men (22 percent) had not completed higher education, but at least two of them had completed secondary education. One (4 percent) had a university degree. The remaining 74 percent were graduates of *écoles.*

The second company has seven thousand employees and is also in a prestige industry. Its *cadres* comprise 8 percent of the labor force. However, this is a family-dominated company and the *président,* while he did have a higher education, was not a graduate of a *grande école.* In this type of firm, as one

Table A. 7A. 1 Education of *Cadres* in a Large French Company of a Prestigious Industry

Management Level	Number of Cadres at that Level as a Percentage of All Cadres	Higher Education (As Percentage of All at a Given Managerial Level)				
		Polytechnique and Corps des Mines (1)	Polytechnique, all others (2)	Centrale, Mines, and Ecole Normale Supérieure (3)	Subtotal, cols. (1)-(3)	Universities
1st	0.7	50	17	17	83	0
2nd	2.8	0	30	22	52	9
3rd	4.8	0	10	31	41	5
All others	91.7	0	0.8	7.1	8	...

Note: Here, as elsewhere, any manager who attended more than one higher educational institution is listed under the most prestigious one. The category "Polytechnique and Corps des Mines" refers to *polytechniciens* who had served in this most prestigious of government engineering *corps.*

might expect, the selectivity in education of top management is much lower than in the first company. Yet the differences between management levels are still striking despite the fact that 81 percent of the total managerial staff has at least a complete secondary education, in comparison with 6 percent of the total French male population over the age of twenty-two (Table A. 7A.2).

The third company has well over twenty-five thousand employees, is also in a prestige industry, and its shareholding is widely diversified. Nine percent of the labor force consists of *cadres*. Educational data are available for the various managerial levels, but unfortunately the different higher educational institutions are grouped very grossly and one major *grande école* is even placed in the second category of institutions. This gross grouping of *écoles* makes the variation of education between managerial levels appear much less than it is in reality (Table A. 7A.3).

More detailed educational data are available for the top five men in the company. Three are graduates of Polytechnique, and the two others are from other *grandes écoles*. Four of the five had previously worked in civilian *grands corps* of the government.

Some materials are also available concerning previous careers in government of the top *cadres*. These are given in Table A. 7A.4.

Table A. 7A. 2 Education of *Cadres* in a Family-Dominated French Company

Management Level	Number of *Cadres* at that Level as a Percentage of All *Cadres*	Higher Education (As Percentage of All at a Given Managerial Level)			No Completed Higher Education	
		Polytechnique, Centrale, and Mines	Education superior to that of the *président*	Education equal to that of the *président*		Of this, less than completed secondary[a]
Top	5.4	26	32	54	4	...
All others	94.6	1	Over 1[b]	Over 31[b]	38	19
Top quartile	23.2	...	...	...	17	...

[a]Second *baccalauréat*.
[b]Information is not available for all of the relevant *écoles*.

Table A. 7A. 3   Education of *Cadres* in a Very Large French Company

Management Level	Number of *Cadres* at that Level as a Per-centage of All *Cadres*	Higher Education (As Percentage of All at a Given Managerial Level)			
		1st rank schools	2nd rank schools	3rd rank schools	No completed higher education
1st	3.0	62	30	6	2.1
2nd	5.8	48	34	1.1	16
3rd	16	31	28	12	28
4th	30	16	21	16	47
5th	37	9	24	10	57
6th (new recruits)	8.5	20	63	16	1.5
All *cadres*	100	19	28	12	41

Table A. 7A. 4   Previous Government Careers of the Top *Cadres* in a Very Large French Company (Percentage)

Government Service Prior to Joining the Company	Top Sixteen Men in the Company	Sample Drawn from the Top 8.8 Per-cent of *Cadres* (Sample Size = 33)
Civilian service	31	15
Professional military service	19	18
None	50	67

The fourth company has some four thousand employees, of whom 3 percent are *cadres*. However, not only does it have family management and ownership but also it is in a nonprestigious industry; the educational qualifications of its management reflect these two factors (Table A. 7A.5).

This company is the only one of those five for which we have data as to the educational qualifications of all managers in which there is no correlation between the gradation of these qualifications and the management levels. The explanation clearly lies in the family nature of the firm combined with the nature of the industry. Yet even in this company, the top nonfamily executives have a high educational level relative to the others. Furthermore, the factory directors and their chief aids are almost entirely recruited from the prestigious institution of the industry—while very few if any other managers at any level were recruited from this institution.

The fifth company is the last for which I have educational data concerning all managerial personnel. It falls into the top stratum of our "very large" size category of Tables 7.8, and 7.9, is in a prestigious industry, and its shareholding is diversified. Seven percent of its employees are *cadres* (Table A. 7A.6).

Table A. 7A. 5 Education of *Cadres* in a Family-Managed and -Owned Company in a Nonprestigious French Industry

Management Category	Number of *Cadres* in that Category as a Percentage of all *Cadres*	Higher Education (As Percentage of All in a Given Managerial Category)			
		Polytechnique	Other major *grandes écoles*	One minor *grande école*	No completed higher education
Family members at top	5.0	0	17	0	83
Top non-family *cadres*	3.3	25	50	0	25
Factory directors and their assistants	10	0	17	83	0
Sales heads	36	0	0	0	100
All others	46	0	24	. . .	. . .

A sixth company is in the "large" size category and in a prestige industry but is under the ownership control of a family that also dominates other large firms. The three top executives are all *polytechniciens*. There are only two other *polytechniciens* in the company, and both are at the level immediately below.

For six other companies, I have data concerning the top five to ten executives in each company. All six companies are in prestige industries; three are in the "very large" size category, and three fall into the "medium" size category. Grouping these companies, the educational levels shown in Table A.7A.7 appear.

Finally, I have educational data for a sample of well over two-thirds of the

Table A. 7A. 6   Education of *Cadres* in One of the Largest French Companies

Management Level	Number of *Cadres* at that Level as a Percentage of All *Cadres*	Higher Education (As Percentage of All at a Given Managerial Level)				
		Polytechnique and Corps des Mines	Polytechnique, all others	Centrale and Mines	Other *grandes ecoles*	No completed higher education
1st	0.375	67	0	0	0	0
2nd	0.750	17	0	33	17	0
All others	99	0	3	13	. . .	. . .

Table A. 7A. 7   Education of Top *Cadres* in Six French Companies

Type of Company	Number of Executives in Sample	Higher Education (As Percentage of Top Executives from each Type of Company)				
		Polytechnique and Corps des Mines	Polytechnique, all others	Centrale, Mines, and Hautes Etudes Commerciales	Universities	No completed higher education
Nonfamily, nonforeign controlled	10	70	10	20	0	0
Family	14	0	14	21	7	7
Foreign controlled	16	0	12	12	19	12

Table A. 7A. 8   Education of Top Managers of Four French Plants (As Percentage of Total Sample)

Polytechnique	Centrale and Mines	Universities	No completed higher education
2.7	35	8	0

Note: Size of sample = 37 managers.

top group of managers in four plants, three of which are in prestige industries.[1] The number of employees in each plant is between eight hundred fifty and nine thousand nine hundred (Table A.7A.8).

[1]Three of the four plants are from a two-thirds sample of all top plant *cadres* in selected iron and steel plants. See Jean E. Hamblet, *Les cadres d'entreprises* (Editions Universitaires, Paris, 1966), pp. 118, 134, and 138.

The four countries differ sharply with regard to the type of higher education which appears to be considered appropriate for management, at least insofar as this is revealed by the nature of the degrees which managers possess. These differences, however, are not related to the degree of educational selectivity in the various countries.

It is quite clear that an engineering education is most omnipresent in the Soviet Union. If one assumes that all graduates of engineering institutes studied engineering,[1] and that all others received a nonscience diploma, then 90 percent of the graduates among branch heads appointed since the purges of the 1930s had an engineering education. It seems quite probable that close to the same percentage figure applies to all managers in industrial enterprises, although undoubtedly the proportion is quite a bit lower among junior and middle managers in organizations above the level of the enterprise.[2]

France is a close competitor in its emphasis upon science and engineering, at least in the prestigious larger companies. For the top executives of the 500 largest industrial firms discussed in Chapter 7, Table A. 7B.1 gives the proportion of all degree holders who have an engineering or science degree.

Data are also available for a broader group of managerial and professional employees in two large companies. In one firm, 92 percent of a 100 percent sample of the top *cadres* (here, top *cadres* constituted 6 percent of all the *cadres*) had an engineering or science degree. Out of a sample of those at the next level, 90 percent had this kind of degree. Similar data for a second company are shown in Table A. 7B.2.

The American pattern of education is radically different. To show this, I shall turn to the study of the top three hundred twenty-two executives in three large companies which was reported on in Chapter 7. Neither the age nor the level of the executive is particularly significant in predicting his undergraduate major; but, as we would expect, there is a sharp distinction depending upon his present function. Table A. 7B.3 shows that, for all executives, there is a fairly even split between business and economics on the one hand[3] and engineering and the natural sciences on the other. Only some 14 percent of executives had other majors.

---

[1]This is perhaps a slight exaggeration, as courses comparable to industrial engineering—which, after all, is related to business—can also be taken there. On the other hand, some of the graduates of industrial academies and institutes are presumably engineers.

[2]Here we would find many more industrial engineers and graduates of applied-economics institutes.

[3]The logic behind combining the two fields is that many executives must have attended colleges where business was not offered as a distinct field.

Table A. 7B. 1   Proportion of French Top Executives Holding Engineering or Science Degrees to All Degree-Holding Top Executives

	Engineering or Science Degree (Percentage of Degrees whose Field is Known)	Any Degree whose Field is Known (Percentage of Total Degrees)
All five hundred firms	77	70
Of these:		
Nationalized firms	71	100
Private firms in prestigious industries	82	74
Private firms in nonprestigious industries	50	44

Table A. 7B. 2   Proportion of Engineering or Science Degrees among *Cadres* of a French Company

	Percentage of Degree Holders with Engineering or Science Degree	Percentage of Sample Possessing a Degree	Percentage of all Company *Cadres* at the Indicated Level	Number in the Sample as Percentage of all *Cadres* at the Indicated Level of Management
Top managers	90	95	8	89
All *cadres*	91	64	100	100

Table A. 7B.4 gives the pattern of graduate education. Business rises sharply in importance compared to its role in undergraduate education, and law also becomes important; these gains are made at the expense of graduate work in engineering and the natural sciences. As one would expect, business degrees decline significantly as a proportion of the total as age increases: while 60 percent of all graduate degrees held by executives of all ages filling nontechnical posts were in business, the figure is only 20 percent for those over fifty-five years of age. Legal degrees are very heavily concentrated at the top level of management; 34 percent of all graduate degrees at this level are in law, while the figure is only 6 percent at the other two levels.[4]

In view of the interest in recent years of both graduate business schools and companies in having engineers take masters degrees in business administra-

[4]This many be partly an artifact of the higher average age of executives in the top level, but the sample size is too small to reveal whether or not this is the cause.

Table A. 7B. 3 Undergraduate Major of Sample of American Executives from Three Large Industrial Companies

		Executives Currently Filling	
Undergraduate Major	All Executives	Technical posts	Nontechnical posts
	Percentages of All with Undergraduate Degrees		
Business	28	14	36
Economics	10	3	12
Engineering	26	49	13
Natural sciences	14	29	8
All others	14	1	23
Unknown	7	4	7
Business and economics	38	17	48
Engineering and science	40	78	21
Sample size	267	72	141

Note: For the definition of functions, see Table 7.4.

Table A. 7B. 4 Graduate Major of Sample of American Executives from Three Large Industrial Companies

		Executives Currently Filling	
Graduate Major	All Executives	Technical posts	Nontechnical posts
	Percentage of All with Graduate Degrees		
Business	45	14	60
Law	17	5	19
Engineering and science	24	67	5
Other	14	14	16
Sample size	86	21	43

Note: For the definition of functions, see Table 7.4.

Table A. 7B. 5   Education of Top-Level American Executives

	Top-Level Executives of Sample of Three Companies in 1967-1968		Two Hundred Top Executives in One Hundred Corporations in 1964	
	Percentage of sample	Size of sub-sample	Percentage of sample	Size of sub-sample
Total undergraduate degrees	88	64	75	150
Of these, in				
Business	25		1	
Engineering	27		15	
Total graduate degrees	28	35	26	51
Of these, in				
Business	37		19	
Law	34		38	

tion, it is interesting that only 14 percent of the M.B.A.'s in the sample had undergraduate majors in either engineering or science. None of the law degrees had been taken by scientists or engineers. Moreover, although the sample is too small to be significant in this regard, there is no indication of more crossing of disciplines by the younger executives.

Finally, comparison can be made between the educational pattern of the top-level executives in this sample with that of the two hundred top executives in 1964 in the hundred largest American corporations.[5] If one takes both studies at face value, and remembers that the top-level executives in the sample treated earlier include executives down to the level of lesser corporate vice-presidents, one can see that degrees in business—both undergraduate and graduate—are much more prevalent when the "top-level executive" category is defined broadly (Table A. 7B.5).

British executives must be considered in a different fashion than that applicable to their colleagues in the other three countries, since only in Britain is the proportion of executives with higher education relatively low. Thus the nature of this higher education is much less important for an understanding of management in Britain than elsewhere.

[5]Study conducted by the Council for Financial Aid to Education and reported in *Business Week*, 21 November 1964, p. 202.

Table A. 7B. 6 Holders of First Degrees Among Managers of Very Large British Industrial Firms

	Degree in Scientific or Technological Speciality (Percentage of All Holding Degrees within the Respective Management Level)
Top managers closely below the director level	55
Middle managers	68
Junior managers	79

Table A. 7B. 7. Education of Top British Executives

	Science, Technology, or Engineering Qualification (Percentage of all with Qualifications within the Respective Managerial Level)
Full-time members of the board of directors	
Nationalized firms	44
Private firms	36
Senior executives directly below board level	
Nationalized firms	41
Private firms	39

Source: National Board for Prices and Incomes, Report No. 107, *Top Salaries in the Private Sector and Nationalized Industries* (Command Paper 3970, Her Majesty's Stationery Office, London, 1969), p. 68.

Table A. 7B.6 gives a breakdown of first degrees for a sample (c. 1954) of all managers in exceptionally large industrial firms.[6]

Data for 1968 exist for a stratified sample of enterprises chosen to represent both nationalized industry and the three hundred largest industrial and commercial private companies. Those with known "professional and academic qualifications" (which are often rather less than a higher educational degree) may be categorized as shown in Table A. 7B.7.

[6]These materials were prepared by the Acton Society Trust for its *Management Succession* (London, 1956), but were not published there and were kindly placed at my disposal.

Thus the proportion of top executives in Britain who have a scientific or engineering education in comparison with some other type seems to be much the same (or even higher) than in the United States, but is considerably below the French or Russian levels. It would appear that those with scientific degrees are considerably better represented at junior than at senior levels of British management, a result which is quite consistent with the traditional high standing of an Oxford or Cambridge arts degree in large British firms.

Managerial Careers within the Enterprise

The pattern of managerial careers in the large industrial enterprises of different countries is, as one would expect, related to educational requirements. "Open managerial" systems display quite different patterns than does the closed French system. But in addition, American companies employ a unique institutional innovation: namely, the use of headquarters posts as an early- and mid-career socialization, training, and observation device.

This chapter concentrates primarily upon career patterns within given organizations rather than between organizations; this is a subject which has had very little treatment in the literature concerning any country. The main sources used will be the personnel histories of executives in the individual companies studied. The American materials are the fullest, and will be taken as the base against which to analyze the careers in other countries.

United States

This section is composed of two parts. The first consists of a statistical analysis of the careers of different strata of managers in six large industrial companies. The second takes the individual company as its unit of analysis and covers ten firms including the earlier six. Of the ten, four are among the twenty-six largest industrial companies in the United States, five more are within the top one hundred and fifty, and one is a large utility.[1]

The principal sample (Sample 1) of the first part, and the one to which the data will refer unless specific mention is made to the contrary, consists of 322 executives in three companies.[2] Sample 2, which will be combined with the first for certain purposes, consists of 116 executives from three additional firms. The career histories for this second sample are both less complete and less reliable, as they were assembled through interviews with personnel managers rather than from records. Both of these samples consist entirely of executives within the upper 1 percent level of the companies' labor force. The firms in the first sample are in the food, paper, and oil industries, and those in the second in the drug, chemical, and large-volume metal-fabricating industries.

Sample 3 consists of a complete count of all managers and professionals (i.e. all, including foremen, who are exempt from the provisions of the Wages and Hours Law) in the chemical company of the second sample who were either promoted or were transferred between subunits (narrowly defined)

---

[1]The ranking follows *Fortune's* listing of industrial firms according to sales in 1966.
[2]This sample was discussed in Chapter 7. The method there described as having been used for categorizing these executives according to the level of their position in the company was also applied to Sample 2.

during 1967 or 1968. This group constitutes between one and three thousand individuals. Unlike the first two samples, it was drawn from a very wide category of personnel constituting 22 percent of the company's total employees.

As a prelude to discussion of career patterns within a given company, let us examine both the age of entry into the company and the previous experience of the executives in Sample 1.

From Table 8.1, we can see that two-thirds of all the executives entered their present company before the age of thirty-one, and have thus spent the substantial bulk of their career within it. It is interesting to note that the proportion entering before the age of twenty-six is considerably higher for the top executives than for the others; this is despite the fact that a larger proportion of the top executives had undergraduate and graduate degrees and thus began their working careers later. On the other hand, as we might have expected, late entrance after the age of forty is important only in the case of the top executives.

Previous experience can be viewed from the perspective of elitism. The closest American parallel to prior service by French executives in a government *corps* is earlier experience in legal, advertising, and accounting firms. While American executives with this background are fairly rare, they are much more common in top-level management than in the next two levels (Table 8.2).

Table 8.1   Age at Point of Entry into the Company

	Level of Management	
Age at Entry	Top	Middle and lower
	Percentage of Executives	
Less than 26 years	46	33
26-30	16	37
31-35	16	19
36-40	8	8
Over 40	13	3
	Sample Size	
	99	222

Note: Managers who had previously worked for firms that have been bought up or merged into their present company are considered to have entered this company at the age at which they joined the original firms.

Table 8.2   Managers' Experience Prior to Entering the Company

Current Function of Manager	Earlier Experience in Specialized Legal, Advertising, and Accounting Firms	
	Managers who have had such experience (percentage of all in the relevant function)	Sample size of all managers in the function (number)
Marketing, advertising, comptrollership, finance, and legal		
Top-level management	23	26
Lower two levels	10	111
General management		
Top-level management	11	61
Lower two levels	5	22

One might argue from the figures in Table 8.2 that these specialized firms play the same role for American business as does the government for the French: acting as a vetting agency for those moving to the top. This is true to a limited degree in the specialized functions treated above (particularly that of law). But the analogy breaks down both because it is primarily only the top nontechnical functional specialists who enter American companies by this route, and because the American specialized professional firms have not exacted the extremely stringent entrance qualifications that the French government *corps* have demanded.

Turning now to careers within the managers' current company, the first problem to investigate is the rate at which positions are changed within the same company. Here I have considered only the jobs held after the age of thirty-five, basing this decision on the ground that one is safe in assuming that, for the people who eventually mounted high enough to get into our Sample 1 or Sample 2, these were responsible positions that had to be filled effectively if the company were to prosper.

The influence of two characteristics appears clearly from Table 8.3. Current age is important in determining the probability of an executive having averaged over three years per position in the company. So, also, is whether or not he has earned a graduate degree.

But much more important is the basic similarity: that the average number of years per position is no more than four in even the oldest category (Table 8.4).

Tables 8.3 and 8.4 deal with a sample composed of individuals, and count

Table 8.3 Proportion of Executives Averaging More than Three Years in Any One Position

Characteristics	Executives Averaging More than Three Years per Position (Percentage)	Sample Size (Number)
Total of those for which there is age information	20	274
Age		
36-45 years	2	96
46-55	15	103
Over 55	51	75
Possession of a graduate degree		
Top level management		
with degree	5	33
without degree	24	66
Middle-level management		
with degree	17	29
without degree	24	99
Lower-level management		
with degree	8	13
without degree	11	37

Table 8.4 Average Number of Years per Position

	Average Number of Years per Position
Total	2.9
Age:	
36-45	2.0
46-55	2.8
Over 55	4.0

even minor posts so long as they were held after the age of thirty-five. Table 8.5 is restricted to the major positions in the companies, and a unit in the sample is a given position during the period that it is held consecutively by a single individual.

Table 8.5 shows that in all these leading positions except those of functional vice-president, president, and chairman, some 72-87 percent of the posts were held by a single occupant for three years or less. Even in the case of functional vice-presidents, only 10 percent of the posts were held for longer than five years by the same man. Thus job mobility is extremely rapid in all positions below that of president. Moreover, there is a fair degree of circulation of executives to multiple jobs within the same category. For the six categories treated in Table 8.5, the average number of positions held by

Table 8.5 Distribution of the Number of Years that a Given Post is Held by a Single Individual

Positions	Number of Years (Percentage)							Sample Size (Number)
	1	2	3	4-5	6-10	11-15	16-20	
Plant manager	25	32	16	16	0	8	4	76
Regional sales manager	30	41	15	2	11	0	0	46
Posts reporting directly to a divisional general manager	36	32	11	18	3	1	0	103
Divisional general manager	42	25	11	11	9	0	1	80
All other corporate vice-presidents and comptroller	36	11	13	30	6	3	1	94
President and chairman	25	17	0	25	8	25	0	12

Notes: Table 8.5 utilizes data from both Sample 1 and Sample 2 companies.
Rounding of time periods is to the nearest year, except that periods of less than one year are considered as one year. One might think that the distribution is biased downward by the inclusion of time periods for posts that are still currently held. However, a comparison of those currently holding the post of plant manager with those who had held it earlier shows that the average time period is slightly longer for current managers. (This comparison was restricted to the companies of Sample 1 since their data are most inclusive.)

the same man within the same category was 1.6. The range among categories fell between 1.2 for plant managers and 2.2 for functional vice-presidents.

Data from Sample 3 makes possible examination of the same issue of job mobility as it relates to all managerial and professional employees, and not solely to their upper stratum. Of the total number of such employees, a minimum annual average of 20 percent of those who did not leave the company changed position within it.[3]

Having shown the degree of job mobility within companies, I shall now turn to the nature of this mobility. Here, the first question is that of the degree of mobility between functions during the period of an executive's career. For this purpose, I have grouped the positions held while a manager or professional into fourteen functions.[4] Table 8.6 shows the total number of different functions in which executives worked during their careers within the company.

Of all those who had been in the company for more than ten years, 45 percent had worked in three or more functions. Of those in the company for over twenty years, 26 percent had worked in four or more functions. Holding constant the number of years employed in the company, there is no difference between executives currently at different levels of management; but, of course, one must remember that the entire sample falls within the upper 1 percent of the total labor force.

Moreover, the length of service in functions other than the executive's principal one (defined as that in which he spent the longest number of years) was substantial. Table 8.7 shows that, of those in the company for more than twenty years, 65 percent had worked for more than five years in these secondary functions and 40 percent had worked there for more than ten years. Of those in the company for over thirty years, only 45 percent had worked consecutively for more than fifteen years within a single function.

Sample 3 contains data as to the proportion of job changes (for all managerial and professional employees during a two-year period) that involved functional changes.[5] These are presented in Table 8.8. The proportion rises

---

[3]The actual figure may be considerably higher, as no information is available concerning those who changed positions within the same subunit and without promotion.

[4]These functions are: 1, manufacturing; 2, engineering; 3, research and development; 4, sales; 5, marketing; 6, advertising; 7, personnel; 8, accounting, comptrollership, and economic analysis; 9, finance; 10, purchasing; 11, legal department; 12, public relations; and 13, catchall category of general management and administration. The last function, 14, is that of assistant to a major company official when this is clearly a training post.

[5]Positions here are divided into eleven functions, plus a twelfth miscellaneous category which is ignored in the calculations. When the same individual changed jobs more than once within the period, the second job change is ignored.

Table 8.6 Total Number of Different Functions in Which a Given Executive Was Employed during his Career within a Single Company

Years Employed within the Company (Number)	Number of Different Functions (Percentage)					Sample Size (Number)
	1	2	3	4	5-7	
0 - 5	74	20	6	0	0	50
6 - 10	41	38	18	4	0	56
11 - 20	19	39	24	14	4	74
21 - 30	24	31	20	19	6	90
Over 30	13	15	42	19	10	52
Total	32	30	22	12	4	322

Table 8.7 Length of Service within the Company in Functions Other than the Executive's Principal One

Years Employed within the Company (Number)	Years of Service in Other Functions					
	0	1-2	3-5	6-10	11-15	Over 15
6 - 10	41	34	23	2	0	0
11 - 20	19	15	30	34	3	0
21 - 30	24	10	7	26	27	7
Over 30	13	4	8	23	15	37

Table 8.8 Functional Changes as a Proportion of Job Changes for All Managerial and Professional Employees within a Two-Year Period (Percentage)

Classification	Proportion Changing Function	Group as Proportion of Total Sample of Job Changes
All managers	18	100
Original level of manager		
Lowest	13	41
Middle	17	40
Highest	31	19
Original function of manager		
Manufacturing or engineering	21	37
Research and development	25	18
Sales	9	19
Nontechnical, nonadministrative	9	16
Administrative	23	11

Note: Data taken from Sample 3.

systematically with the managerial level of the manager prior to his job change, and it is lowest for those beginning in sales or in other nontechnical, nonadministrative functions.[6] But it is the average proportion which is most interesting: 18 percent of the job changes were also functional changes.

Now that I have looked at job mobility from the viewpoint of changes of function, I shall examine it with regard to the degree of movement between units of the company. Each division is treated as composed of two organizational units: field (lumping together all manufacturing, sales, and research locations) and divisional headquarters. In addition, corporate headquarters is considered as a separate unit. The sample consists of two of the three companies in Sample 1, the third being omitted because it was only recently fully divisionalized.

Table 8.9 shows the number of different organizational units in which the executives served.[7] As one would expect, the number increases with the total years in the company. But what is interesting is that it is the higher executives who have served in the most units; thus transfer between units appears to be a device used to provide seasoning. Of the top executives who had been in the company for over twenty years, 60 percent served in more than three units and 36 percent served in more than five.

Table 8.10 shows the average length of time which executives spent consecutively within the same unit. (The significance of consecutive service is that it indicates the maximum length of time in which an executive was part of a particular management team and could be evaluated as such). Here, managerial level is irrelevant; only the length of service in the company distinguishes among the different executives. It would appear that the average length of stay within a given unit is shortest within the first decade to decade and a half of service—precisely the period when evaluation of managers is most important and difficult. But even for those in the company for more than twenty years, one-third had averaged five years or less consecutively per unit.

Having shown the considerable degree of interunit movement within the company, let me now examine its significance with regard to mobility between organizational levels of the company. Table 8.11 presents the results as they relate to movement between field, divisional headquarters, and corporate headquarters. The sample consists of the total number of job changes,

---

[6]The proportion of managers in these functions is much the same for all levels; thus the percentages are not affected by any correlation between level and function.
[7]A unit is counted only once, even if an executive moved in and out of it several times.

Table 8.9 Number of Different Organizational Units within the Company in Which the Executives Have Served

Managerial Level	Years Employed within the Company (Number)	Number of Organizational Units (Percentage)			Size of Sample of Executives (Number)
		1-2	3	4-7	
Top	11-20	20	13	67	15
	Over 20	20	20	60	25
Middle	11-20	46	38	15	26
	Over 20	11	47	42	19
Lower	11-20	55	27	18	22
	Over 20	55	36	9	11
All	Any over 0	59	20	21	215
	11-20	43	29	28	63
	Over 20	24	33	44	55

Note: Data are from two companies of Sample 1. The definition of an organizational unit is given in the text.

Table 8.10 Average consecutive Service within the Same Organizational Unit

Years Employed within the Company (Number)	Average Number of Years Per Unit (Percentage)					Sample Size (Number)
	Less than 3	3-5	6-10	11-15	Greater than 15	
6-10	17	48	35			52
11-20	3	52	30	8	6	63
Over 20	15	18	44	15	9	56
Total	16	44	29	7	4	215

Note: Data are for two companies of Sample 1. The definition of an organizational unit is given in the text.

rather than the total number of executives. This explains the fact that 79 percent of the moves represented no change in organizational level.[8]

The intriguing finding in Table 8.11 is that a full 40 percent of the moves between organizational levels were downward. The fact that the figure for those currently at the top managerial level (not necessarily the top organizational level) is 37 percent strongly suggests that relatively few of these moves should be considered as demotions or as sidetracking of executives. Instead, movement back and forth between different organizational levels must be regarded as a normal part of a successful executive's career. "Seasoning" can be viewed as consisting not only of exposure to different functions and to different organizational units but also of service in both divisional and corporate headquarters prior to the stage in his career at which the executive is permanently attached to headquarters.

The timing of this last type of seasoning is clearly of importance both for the nature of the evaluation which can be made of the rising executive and for his socialization to the corporate goals espoused at headquarters. Table 8.12 shows the proportion of executives in all six of the companies in Samples 1 and 2 who had served in corporate or divisional headquarters at a youthful age. Unfortunately, the base of the proportions shown has to be taken as those executives who, at some time in their career, served in either corporate or divisional headquarters; this is because there is no information as to service in headquarters for many of the executives in Sample 2. Because of the inclusion of Sample 2, with its incomplete information, the percentages of those entering either headquarters below the age of thirty-six must be taken as minimum estimates.

Of those joining the company by the time they were thirty, 65 percent had served in divisional headquarters by the age of thirty-five, and an overlapping 59 percent had served at corporate headquarters by that age. It seems clear that a substantial proportion of all executives who join their company early and later rise to the top 1 percent bracket of the corporation's labor force serve at either or both divisional and corporate headquarters while still in the

[8]Table 8.11 is based upon the job moves throughout their career in the company of only those executives who, at the time of the study, had been with the company for over twenty years. There were fifty-six such executives in the sample. If, instead, data for all executives had been presented, the results would have been much the same with regard to the proportion of interorganizational moves that fell between specific levels; 42 percent of these moves were to a lower organizational level. The only significant difference would have been that only 12 percent—instead of 21 percent—of total job changes would have been shown as accompanied by a change in the level of organization. The sample size of job changes accompanied by change in the level of organization would have risen from 129 to 289.

Table 8.11 Job Changes Accompanied by Movement to a Different Organizational Level within the Same Company (for executives who had been in the company for over twenty years at the end of the period)

Classification	Proportion of Total Job Changes (Percentage)	Proportion of Job Changes Resulting in Organizational Change (Percentage)	Sample Size (Number)
Job changes accompanied by change in the level of organization	21	100	129
Of these job changes:			
From field to divisional headquarters		28	36
From field to corporate headquarters		8	10
From divisional headquarters to corporate headquarters		24	31
From divisional headquarters to field		13	17
From corporate headquarters to field		8	10
From corporate headquarters to divisional headquarters		19	25
Total of movements to a lower level of organization		40	52

Note: Data are for two companies of Sample 1.

Table 8.12 Executives Serving at Headquarters at Various Ages (For Executives Who Had Been in the Company for Over Ten Years at the End of the Period)

Age at Time of Joining the Company (Years)	Age at Which First Entered							
	Divisional Headquarters				Corporate Headquarters			
	Under 30 (%)	31-35 (%)	Over 35 (%)	Sample Size (Number)	Under 30 (%)	31-35 (%)	Over 35 (%)	Sample Size (Number)
30 or less	41	24	35	78	40	19	41	118
31-35		72	28	18		29	71	21
Total of 35 or less	33	33	33	96	34	20	46	139

Note: Data taken from both Samples 1 and 2.

first years of their career. Presumably, a large proportion of those executives joining the company later were previously in a headquarters organization of another company.

Confirming data with regard to moves to corporate headquarters are available from Sample 3. During a two-year period, 11 percent of all managerial and professional personnel who were either promoted or transferred to another subunit moved into or out of corporate headquarters. For those in the highest level (0.5 percent of the labor force), the figure was 31 percent. However, for the total group the proportion of transfers into or out of corporate headquarters differed radically depending upon the manager's function at the beginning of the period. Thirty-six percent of the managers in nontechnical (other than sales) or administrative functions were transferred to or from headquarters, compared to only 2 percent for those in technical, research and development, and sales functions.

The greater degree of movement of administrative and nontechnical managers for purposes of "seasoning" is supported by the fact that 25 percent of their promotions and transfers were transfers unaccompanied by any promotion whatsoever. In contrast, the figure was only 10 percent for the managers in technical, research and development, and sales functions.

To sum up: this statistical material concerning executives within the top 1 percent earnings bracket of their company's labor force, corroborated by data for all managerial and professional employees who were promoted or who changed subunit during a two-year period, shows an extremely high rate of job turnover within the same company. This high rate applies not only to their careers as a whole after the age of thirty-five, but similarly to their rate of movement between high company posts right through that of vice-president. Job mobility took the form of moves both between different functions and between major administrative units of the corporation. It also made possible extensive movement between posts in the field, in divisional headquarters, and in corporate headquarters; moreover, a substantial proportion of the executives worked both at divisional and corporate headquarters as a prelude to more responsible posts at lesser organizational levels.

Since it is to be expected that managerial career patterns will differ between companies, it is useful to examine the subject by taking the individual company as the unit of analysis. The categorization of ten companies presented in Tables 8.13-8.16 rests primarily upon analysis of specific careers in each firm; the incompleteness of data forces only a roughly qualitative treatment.

(See Appendix A to this chapter for a more detailed discussion of each of six of the companies.)

Table 8.13 makes reference only to genuine managerial rather than training experience at corporate headquarters which is a prelude to further posts in the field. One can see the close links of common experience which exist between managers in corporate headquarters and in the field in a high proportion of our sample companies.

Table 8.14 excludes from its definition of change in function all progression to such a general-management post as head of a product department or of a

Table 8.13   Managerial Experience in Corporate Headquarters at an Interim Career Stage

Managerial Level	Proportion of Managers with Such Experience	Number of Companies
All managerial and professional	High	1
Of managers within top 1 percent of labor force:		
All	High	3
Top-middle levels and/or the most prestigious functions	High	3
Top level	Moderate	1
All	Unknown	2

Table 8.14   Degree of Mobility of Managers between Functions within the Company

Managerial Level	Level of Mobility	Number of Companies
All managerial and professional	High	1
Of managers currently within top 1 percent of labor force:		
All	High	1
Top-middle levels	High	3
Top-prestige function	High	1
Top-middle levels from the top prestige function	Intermediate	1
All	Low	3

Table 8.15   Age of Reaching Post of Divisional General Manager

	Number of Companies
Young: normally by middle forties at latest	4
Medium: few above age fifty	2
Older	2
Unknown	2

division. Although a high degree of functional mobility is probably relatively uncommon for most of the managers within the top 1 percent of the labor force, change of function is quite a normal experience in two-thirds of our companies for those who move to the upper levels of this 1 percent category.

Table 8.15 indicates the accent placed upon early promotion to top managerial posts in half of our companies. There are several explanations for this policy. The first is a strong emphasis upon having men who are still in their full vigor in top operating posts. The second is the important role given to corporate headquarters, and the room that this provides for promoting divisional general managers to top corporate positions. The third, and perhaps the most important, is the desire to nurture a number of candidates for the top two or three positions in the company, and the wish to observe their behavior in important independent managerial posts over a period of time. Linked to this last reason is the belief that a viable candidate for corporate president should have first obtained a variety of experience in posts equal to or above that of divisional manager.

One consequence of this policy of rapid promotion is the need for freeing posts of their current occupants when these are not to be promoted further. In one company, this occurs primarily through resignations. In a second, it is done through demotions. Two others employ extensively the policy of early retirement. A fifth has had sufficiently rapid growth both through mergers and by expanding the marketing function so that the problem does not arise. For the remaining five companies, the situation is unknown.

An article on demotion among managers in one large industrial company is particularly interesting in this regard.[9] Out of a sample of seventy middle managers located in two different divisions of the company, 61 percent expressed the belief that there was a good chance that they would be demoted

[9]Fred H. Goldner, "Demotion in Industrial Management," *American Sociological Review,* October 1965, pp. 714-724.

Table 8.16   Role of the Manufacturing Function as an Avenue to Top Management

	Number of Companies
High role	3
Medium to low role	1
Low role	3
Unknown	2
Irrelevant (utility company)	1

sometime during their company career. Even more impressive was the fact that managers who saw no likelihood of their being demoted and those who foresaw a good chance of demotion did not differ with regard to the probability which they attached to a promotion during the coming two years. The likelihood of future demotion seemed to be an accepted part of this company's way of life even for those who believed that they were currently on the upswing of their career.

Table 8.16 casts light on the value which American industrial companies place upon the manufacturing function. In four of the seven companies for which we have information, the valuation is on the low side. None of the remaining three single it out as the prime function from which to draw top management; they only choose not to discriminate against it.[10]

How is this to be explained? It would appear to be due to the belief that, although an efficient manufacturing operation is essential, it is nevertheless something that a well-run company can expect as a matter of routine. It is not from this function that the impetus need come for those changes that determine a company's future. Thus manufacturing can get along with managers who are stolid and efficient but who do not have the imagination or breadth demanded of really top management. Furthermore, because of the nature of the function, the native daring and imagination of its managers is not challenged and thus tends to disappear.

This situation seems to reflect the current attitude of much of American big business. Static efficiency is both demanded and expected. But the real managerial challenge is not considered to lie here; rather, it is assumed to lie in the conception and institution of change.

[10]Paul R. Lawrence and Jay W. Lorsch report a similarly low status for manufacturing in six plastic companies that they studied. Their explanation is the relatively high degree of certainty ("you have the facts there") available in production as compared with the research and marketing areas. See P. R. Lawrence and J. W. Lorsh, *Organization and Environment* (Graduate School of Business Administration, Harvard University, Boston, 1967), p. 28.

Britain

British managerial careers have their own very distinctive national characteristics. Most striking is the early age at which most managers begin work, and the concomitant feature of their starting in a position which is neither managerial nor even that of a managerial trainee. This pattern has been changing since the Second World War, but it is still quite pronounced in contrast both to the United States and to France.

From Samples 1-9 of Table 8.17 one can see that both managers and directors began work at an average age of eighteen—i.e., immediately after completion of secondary education. Despite the fact that one-third to one-half of the managers had spent their entire careers in their current company, it is still true that the average age of joining it was eight to ten years after the age of beginning work. Experience in other firms was important: 25 to 40 percent of the managers had been hired into their current company at a point when their career was already developed. Of the chief executives in Sample 5, some 35 percent had transferred in after reaching a top management position in another firm.

The evidence is somewhat mixed as to the proportion of managers who started their careers either in managerial positions or in posts which assured that they would eventually become managers. Most of the samples show a fairly low proportion, but Sample 6 (taken, however, from only four companies) indicates that over half of the top managers began their industrial career in such a post. Only for one company do I have data as to the original position in the current company, and here some two-thirds of the middle and top managers started as managers, professionals, or managerial trainees. It is probably reasonable to conclude that less than one-third of managers in large British firms began their careers assured of managerial status, but that a majority started in their current company with such assurance. Thus a substantial proportion of managers—but probably a good deal less than a majority—had to be selected out from a broader group within their current company for promotion to managerial status.

Finally, if one uses a broad classification scheme for work functions, a substantial majority of managers never changed functions throughout their career. Using a set of narrower definitions, however, evidence from the very small Sample 2 suggests that top managers changed functions within their current firm appreciably more often than did middle managers.[11]

[11]It is true that the first group averaged three years older than the second, and had been in the current company for three years longer. But these differences seem hardly sufficient to account for the observed variation in change of functions.

Particularly interesting is the high mobility of managers between posts within the same firm, especially, as one would expect, in the larger companies. Using the same sample numbers as for Table 8.17, the results of Table 8.18 appear.

For the middle and top divisional managers in Sample 2, I can also point to the average time spent in each post held in the company since the age of thirty-five. (This age cutoff is chosen arbitrarily as being one after which a man's nonmanagerial and managerial-training career is behind him, and is the same used in the American analysis). Using data for fifty-five posts, we find that the average time spent in each was 3.6 years. Divisional directors had spent a somewhat longer time in each post than had middle managers: 4.3 years compared to 3.0 years.

Finally, I have career data over a period of two and one-half years for upper and middle managers of one division of another large company. Out of a sample of eighteen who were in the company at the beginning of the period, one had left the company by the end of the period, two had moved to other divisions, and four had changed posts within the division. Thus, of those who remained within the company, 35 percent had changed positions within two and one-half years.

For two companies (Sample 2 and the firm above) I have data as to the tenure in post of fifteen factory managers, who together had held twenty-five positions as heads of individual plants. The plants were medium size, ranging from two hundred to one thousand employees each. Five of the posts (20 percent) were held for more than five years, and only one of these for more than ten years. The average number of years in post was three. This brief tenure is particularly interesting because many people expect (erroneously) that the position of factory manager tends to be held for an especially long time.

Unfortunately, very little systematic data are available concerning transfers between headquarters and the field. However, even defining headquarters to include divisional headquarters, it appears that the transfer is almost entirely unidirectional: from the field to headquarters. I have clear information in this regard only for the fifteen factory heads mentioned earlier. Two of them had served at headquarters (both at divisional headquarters) sometime prior to taking their last post as plant manager. Both of these had worked at headquarters for a few years when they were first employed, and were then sent into factory posts below the level of plant manager. The remaining 87 percent worked exclusively in factories, at least until some of them were promoted to posts above the plant-manager level.

Table 8.17   Career Characteristics of Managers in Large British Companies (Samples 8 and 9 are Taken from Firms of Various Sizes)

Characteristics	Sample					
	1			2		3
	a	b	c	a	b	
Average age at which managers started work				18	19	18
Average age at which managers joined their current company[a]				28	28	
Average number of years managers have spent in their current company				21	18	
Average age at which became a manager						
Managers who have spent their entire career in their current company (percentage)		44		40	31	41
Managers who have worked only in their present company after the first ten years of their career (percentage)				60	69	65
First full-time occupation was that of manager or managerial trainee (percentage)[c]	12	14	6	60	62	22+[d]
Family members of a family firm, whatever the initial position: not counted above (percentage)						
Managers who never changed their work function within industry (percentage)[e]						
a. Broad definition of work function[f]	86	89	89	60	65	

Table 8.17 (continued)

Sample							
4		5	6	7	8		9
a	b				a	b	
							18
28	30						26
19	27	24			23	20	20
			33				34
		42	49	47	34	38	33
							75[b]
			55		11	12	31
			1				1
					62	72	73

Table 8.17 (continued)

Characteristics	Sample					
	1			2		3
	a	b	c	a	b	
b. Narrow definition of work function[g] 1. Since age 35, for managers				30	54	
over that age				44	83	
Number in sample	455	1870	984	10	14	1243
Period covered by questionnaire	c. 1954			1967		1951
Size of companies	Exceptionally large	Exceptionally large	Exceptionally large	Exceptionally large	Exceptionally large	Very large
Level of management	Managers closely below the director level	Middle managers	Junior managers	All divisional directors	Middle managers	All directors
Geographic location of the sample	Anywhere in Britain	Anywhere in Britain	Anywhere in Britain	. . .	Anywhere in Britain	Anywhere in Britain

Notes: Sample 1: Study by the Acton Society of manufacturing firms with over ten thousand employees. Twenty-seven of the roughly sixty-seven such companies in the United Kingdom participated. See the Acton Society Trust, *Management Succession* (London, 1956), and David Granick, *The European Executive* (Doubleday, Garden City, N. Y., 1962), for some of the results of the study which were not published by the Acton Society.

Sample 2: One very large division. The sample constitutes 100 percent of the divisional directors and 43 percent of the remaining top third of the division's managers. All managers together constitute 4 percent of the division's labor force.

Sample 3: Study of directors of companies listed on the London Exchange and with more than £1 million nominal net shareholder assets in 1950. Eighty percent of the respondents claimed that one of their directorships was a full-time activity. There was only a 37 percent response to the questionnaires. See George H. Copeman, *Leaders of British Industry* (Gee and Company, London, 1955).

Sample 4: Stratified sample of seventy-two nonnationalized industrial and commercial firms, chosen to represent the three hundred largest companies or groups. An average of seven full-time directors and thirteen managers immediately below the directors were studied. See National Board for Prices and Incomes, Report No. 107: *Top Salaries in the Private Sector and Nationalized Industries* (Command Paper 3970, Her Majesty's Stationery Office, London, 1969), p. 57.

Sample 5: Study of managing directors of the five hundred largest British companies.

Table 8.17 (continued)

Sample							
4		5	6	7	8		9
a	b				a	b	
532	920	120	110	120	61	686	646
1968		1968	1954-55	1966-67	c. 1963-64		1954-55
Very large	Very large	Very large	Large	Large	Wide range	Wide range	Wide range
All full-time directors	Managers immediately below directors	Managing directors	Full-time directors and managers closely below the director level	Middle managers and up	Directors[h]	All managers	All managers
Anywhere in Britain	Anywhere in Britain	Anywhere in Britain	Manchester conurbation	Anywhere in Britain	Manchester conurbation	Manchester conurbation	Manchester conurbation

The response to questionnaires was only 24 percent. See D. J. Hall and G. Amado-Fischgrund, "Chief Executives in Britain," *European Business,* January 1969, pp. 23-29.

Sample 6: Study of four firms, each with over three thousand employees. See Roger F. Clements, *Managers: A Study of Their Careers in Industry* (George Allen & Unwin, London, 1958).

Sample 7: One hundred percent sample of the students attending three twelve-week middle-management courses at the Manchester Business School. Students were almost all sent by their company and were primarily from large industrial firms. These figures were provided by courtesy of the Manchester Business School.

Sample 8: Study of thirty-six manufacturing enterprises, chosen so as to represent a cross section of manufacturing in the Manchester conurbation. One-third of the firms employed under one thousand employees (the smallest employing six hundred), and one-sixth had over ten thousand. See D. G. Clark, *The Industrial Manager* (Business Publications, London, 1966).

Sample 9: Twenty-eight manufacturing firms in the Manchester conurbation. No sampling procedure was employed. Seventeen firms had less than one thousand employees, one having as few as thirty-two; six companies employed between three thousand and ten thousand. See Clements, *Managers.*

[a]Managers in Sample 4 who had previously worked for firms that have been taken over or merged into their present company are considered to have entered this company at the

age at which they joined the original firm. The same is true for at least most of the executives in Sample 2. No information is available with regard to Sample 9.
bThese are all those who did not both enter their current company from another firm and do so in a managerial position.
cProfessional, manager, or managerial trainee. This is the total of those whose entering position designated them as present or future managers. For Samples 3 and 8, the first full-time occupation in the manager's entire career is considered. For Samples 1, 6 and 9, it is the first full-time occupation in industry. The data for Sample 2 are not at all comparable, relating to the first job in the current company only.
d"Trainee for an executive post" only.
eFor Samples 1 and 8, data are available as to the number of work functions throughout the manager's entire career. For Sample 2, data are available only for his current firm. It is not clear from the source which situation applies to Sample 9.
fFor Sample 1, functions were classified four ways: sales, personnel, production and technical, and clerical and administrative. For samples 2 and 8, a five-way classification scheme was employed: the production and technical function was divided into production on the one hand and technical and development on the other. For Sample 9, a six-way scheme was used: commercial, personnel, works, works service, technical, and office.
gThe definition used here is intended to be sufficiently narrow to reflect changes which the manager himself would consider to be functional moves. Thus training is distinguished from other personnel functions, and maintenance from manufacturing operations. These figures are narrower than the ones used in the American section of this chapter and are comparable to that used for French companies in Appendix B to this chapter.
hThere is no indication in the source as to whether only full-time directors are included.

This completes all of the systematic data at my disposal which relate to managerial careers in large industrial firms of Britain. The samples of managers in large British companies seem to contain a sufficient number of people to be convincing for all questions other than that of the number of years in which a given post was held. For this last issue, unfortunately, I have data for only eighty-eight managers in large companies; but even here, the consistency of results among my three samples is reassuring.

France

The significant role that prior governmental careers played in the credentials of *polytechniciens* who came to the top of one of the five hundred largest industrial firms in France was noted in Chapter 7. Of the *polytechnicien* top executives, 57 percent had had a professional government career, although the same was true for only 8 percent of the non-*polytechniciens*. It is those with a previous government career who travel the royal road in French management.

Moreover, this service is more than purely nominal in terms of length of time. I have data on the age at which the top executives left the government service for 62 percent of the *polytechniciens* and for 78 percent of the non-*polytechniciens*. The figures are given in Table 8.19. One can see that a

Table 8.18   Length of Service in Current Posts in British Companies

	Large Companies				All Sizes of Companies[a]	
	Sample 2			Sample 7	Sample 8	
	Top management	Middle management	Top and middle	Middle management and up	Directors	All managers
Held current post for less than five years (percentage)	70	93	83	83	47	46
Held current post for more than ten years (percentage)	10	0	4	2[b]	29	29
Number in sample	10	14	24	46[c]	61	686
Average number of years in company	21	18	...	_[d]	23	20

[a]Many of these firms are relatively small, thus reducing the possibilities for changing position within the same company.
[b]More than nine years.
[c]Data are available only for participants in one of the three courses reported on in Table 8.17.
[d]Fifteen percent had been in their current company for less than five years, 70 percent for more than nine.

Table 8.19   Age at which French Top Executives Left Government Service

		Left Government at Age (Percentage of sample)			Was in Government Service during
Education	Size of Sample (Number)	Under 35 years	35-44 years	Over 44 years	Interims of Industrial Career (Percentage of Sample)
Polytechnique	67	43	31	22	3
All other	31	35	29	34	3

substantial majority of the group who followed this most prestigious of industrial careers remained in the government at least until the age of thirty-five. As would be expected, these people generally "parachuted" directly into fairly important industrial posts.

Information as to the nature of careers within the companies themselves is drawn essentially from two firms. One hundred seventy-eight managerial positions are covered, comprising the top 2.2 income percentile of the labor force in one company and the top 0.6 percentile in the other. A further breakdown within this group is given for thirty-five members of top management. One of the firms is a *grande école* type with widely diversified shareholding, while the second has a management with a lower educational level and is family dominated. In view of these differences between the companies, the similarities in career patterns are striking.

Details of managerial careers in the two companies are reserved for Appendix B to this chapter. The analysis can be summed up in the following four conclusions.

First, the truly striking result in comparison with American career patterns is the length of time which managers spend in a single post. This is even more true for top executives than for middle and junior managers. The inevitable result of this phenomenon is that opportunities either for promotion or for the broadening of experience by movement between functions and between the factories and headquarters is quite limited. No particular effort is made to compensate through lateral job changes for the fact that slow promotion opportunities restrict the possibilities for broadening types of job experience.

Second, in the company where major *grande école* graduates dominate the top positions, a high proportion of the few job openings at higher levels are filled by recruitment from outside. In both companies, a much larger proportion of the occupants of top positions than of those in the second level posts joined the company when over thirty years of age. This common method of filling senior positions further restricts the opportunity for promotions at all levels of management.

Third, even in such an organization as the second company in which one-fifth of all managers have an education level less than that of a university *license,* 78 percent of the senior and upper-middle management[12] were recruited into the company at the *cadre* level. Thus the opportunity to reach

[12]This is defined as the top 8 percent of the company's total number of managers and professionals.

the upper levels of management is extremely limited for those who begin their careers as ordinary white-collar employees or as foremen, let alone for those who begin as manual workers.

Fourth, managers move between companies only very rarely after the age of about thirty. Changes of company are not at all uncommon in the first years of an engineer's industrial experience, but thereafter they virtually cease except for an occasional *grande école* graduate.

Soviet Union

The pattern of Soviet industrial careers changed radically between the 1930s and the 1950s and 1960s. In the earlier years, there was very high job mobility that seemed to exceed even the American tempo. Since the middle 1950s, to the contrary, job stability has been much like that of French industry.

Table 8.20 shows that in the 1930s, even prior to the beginning of the political purges of management, a mere 0 to 15 percent of the samples of top managers both at the industrial branch and the enterprise level had held their current posts for more than five years. Well over three-quarters had been in the same position for less than three years. Clearly, this situation demonstrated the existence of substantial promotional opportunities.

It is only for enterprise directors that I have data concerning previous and following jobs. Table 8.21 shows that the proportion of demotions was quite extraordinary by the standards of any other country, constituting two-fifths of those who changed job from that of enterprise director. There was also a high rate of transfer in both directions between positions at the enterprise level and posts in higher organizations which are comparable to "headquarters" in large capitalist companies.

The purges of the late 1930s swept away this pattern. For they brought into office a group of young executives who remained in their posts during the following decades, clogging up the channels of promotion for those below them.

Of the twenty-eight men who were ministers of heavy industry, light industry, and construction in June 1941, 52 percent of those who were alive fourteen years later still held the identical post (Table 8.22).

Just as striking are the data for the thirty-three ministers of industry and construction in February 1968. Despite the fact that all of industry and construction had gone through two major reorganizations in the previous eleven years, 36 percent had been ministers in 1957. Eighty-eight percent of

Table 8.20 Mobility of Soviet Top Executives of Heavy Industry in 1934 and 1936

	Branch Heads	Assistant Branch Heads	Enterprise Directors	First Assistants to Enterprise Directors	Heads of Departments in Enterprises
	Percentage of Sample				
Number of years' service in the specific industry					
Less than 5	22	8	37	16	. . .
5 to 10	19	27	39	36	. . .
More than 10	59	65	24	48	. . .
Number of years in the same post[a]					
Less than 1	9-32	35-43	25-34	19-28	22-25
1 to 3	44-64	45-61	40-56	44-64	46-53
3 to 5	3-28	0-18	16-20	13-21	16-18
More than 5	0-15	0- 3	3- 8	4- 9	6-14
	Sample Size (Of each Individual Sample)				
	32-39	40-84	457-944	240-670	267-343
	Number of Samples				
	1-3	1-3	1-4	1-3	2

Source: Described in David Granick, *Management of the Industrial Firm in the USSR*, (Columbia University Press, New York, 1954), pp. 290-291.
[a]It seems likely that the length of time in the same post is slightly understated for branch heads and their assistants due to reorganizations. These men may have earlier held virtually identical posts under different titles.

Table 8.21   Careers of Directors of Soviet Enterprises of Heavy Industry in the 1930s

	Director Anytime During the Prepurge Period of January 1934 to March 1937	Director Anytime between January 1934 and June 1941
	Percentage of Sample	
Position held immediately prior to being named as director		
Post below that of director in some enterprise	33	36
Enterprise director elsewhere	31	38
Post in an organization above the level of the enterprise	35	26
Position held immediately after that of director		
Dismissal or transfer to an enterprise post lower than that of director	39	41
Enterprise director elsewhere	35	30
Post in an organization above the level of the enterprise	18	23
Other post	8	7
Sample Size		
	49-51	89-90

Source: Granick, *Management of the Industrial Firm in the USSR*, pp. 292-296.

Table 8.22   Posts Held over a Fourteen-Year Period by Soviet Industrial Commissars

	1955 Posts of the 1941 Commissars (Percentage)
Held the identical position	43
Held a very similar post in the same branch	7
Headed a different ministry	7
Demoted to post of deputy minister or director of a very large enterprise	18
Died	18
Died and were ministers at the time of death	14
Unknown	7

Source: Hough, *The Soviet Prefects,* pp. 365-366.

those who were ministers in 1968 had held posts of enterprise director or higher for at least seventeen years.[13]

By the 1960s, directors of important enterprises seem to have shown much the same continuity in office as did the ministers, although this represented a substantial change from the situation of the early 1950s. Out of a sample of one hundred seventy of the largest enterprises in the Soviet Union, the average time spent in the post by the current occupant was as shown in Table 8.23. The tenure in office seems to have increased steadily from the middle 1930s to the 1960s, ending up at only perhaps 10 percent less than the high level of the top stratum of French industrial managers.

This lengthening of tenure appears to have been a general phenomenon in Soviet society. Between January 1955 and April 1968, for example, the proportion of first *oblast* (regional) secretaries of the Communist Party who had held their post for over five years increased by 2½-fold, ending up at 53 percent—virtually the same figure as applied to directors of major enterprises.[14]

The same lengthy tenure in post seems to apply to lower managerial personnel as well. A Soviet study of more than two hundred junior and middle executives over the age of thirty in a large factory in the mid-1960s showed

[13]J. F. Hough, *The Soviet Prefects* (Harvard University Press, Cambridge, Mass., 1969), p. 75.
[14]*Ibid.*, p. 71.

Table 8.23   Continuity in Office of Enterprise Directors in the USSR

| | January 1953 | | Average of January 1962 and January 1967 | | Both Periods |
| | Percentage of | | Percentage of | | Number of Enter-prises |
	Total	Known Periods	Total	Known Periods	
Less than 3 years		57		30	
3 to 5 years		11		18	
5 to 10 years		· · ·		29	
Over 10 years		· · ·		23	
Over 5 years		32		52	
Unknown	33		34		
Total sample size					170

Source: Hough, *The Soviet Prefects,* pp. 49, 61, 368, and 377.

that only 45 percent had been in their post for less than five years, and that 29 percent had held the same position for more than ten years. This was despite the fact that 40 percent of these managers were under the age of forty. A similar picture as to tenure in post was said to apply to a second large enterprise which had also been studied.[15]

Furthermore, a study carried out in the spring of 1965 of personnel in seven metal-fabricating enterprises of Leningrad showed that the average age of all managers above the foreman level was forty-two years. Only 10 percent of these managers were under the age of twenty-five, and 75 percent were thirty-five years or older. The authors of this study drew the conclusion that one of the main criteria for appointment to a managerial position is age and length of service, and stated that this conclusion is supported by other data relating to Soviet industry as a whole.[16]

Conversations with Russian industrial administrators and scholars in 1967 have confirmed the reasonableness of generalization to Soviet industry as a whole of the impressions given by these statistics. Even in the case of clear failure to perform successfully as an enterprise director, demotion would not

[15]Cf. an opinion survey of a sample of junior and middle management personnel in 10 Soviet enterprises and design bureaus, where the "possibility for promotion" scored as least satisfactory among all the conditions of work. (A. A. Zvorykin and A. M. Geliuta in G. V. Osipov and Ia. Shchepan'skii, eds., *Sotsial'nye problemy truda i proizvodstva,* Mysl', Moscow, 1969, pp. 170-173.)
[16]A. S. Bliakhman, B. G. Sochilin, O. I. Shkaraman, *Podbor i rasstanovka kadrov na predpriiatii* (Ekonomika, Moscow, 1968), pp. 58-59.

normally occur until the executive had held his post for four or five years. In view of the dearth of promotion opportunities, it is small wonder that a Soviet interview-study of one thousand engineers showed that relatively few wished to work in line operations in the factories, preferring instead to engage in research or design. In fact, since 1960 a higher proportion of engineers have been employed in research or design organizations than in all of the industrial enterprises of the country,[17] and a substantial proportion of those in the enterprises also carry out design functions. Despite the fact that applied research and design organizations are regarded as a favorite area into which to place demoted enterprise directors, and that their employees are well off the main track for promotion to high posts in industrial administration, these organizations are popular with engineers because of the nature of the work and the relative lack of pressure. In an economy where promotion is slow, most engineers can relatively easily place their preferences as to type of work above career ambitions.

Movement between plants and headquarters organizations is also quite limited. Junior executives may start work in the ministries or their subdivisions, but it is rare for them then to be willing to move out to the plants. Plant executives do indeed move up to headquarters organizations, but such a move normally occurs after the age of forty and is a once-and-for-all career development.

At the same time, the top men of the ministries and their subdivisions almost always are promoted from the plants of the same industry. A successful enterprise director may be promoted to an important ministerial post, but he will come there without having had headquarters experience earlier in his career.

Table 8.24 shows the high proportion of all industrial and construction ministers at the national level who had previously held top enterprise posts. For all those ministers appointed since the purges of the late 1930s, only 15 percent had not previously held a post as either director or chief deputy director of an enterprise. Of this fifteen percent, moreover, half had held major posts in either research or design or in the Communist Party.

The unimportance of research and design as a route to the ministerial level is shown in Table 8.24. Only 7 percent of the ministers had been in charge of research or design work carried out above the level of the enterprise, and a mere 12 percent additional had had major responsibility of this sort at the

[17]TsSU, *Trud v SSR* (Statistika, Moscow, 1966), pp. 268-269.

enterprise level.[18] In fact, 71 percent of the ministers seem to have had no exposure whatsoever to either the research or design functions. Moreover, two-thirds of the group with such experience above the enterprise level had also been directors of enterprises, and seven-ninths of those with such major experience at the enterprise level had also been either directors or chief deputy directors of enterprises. In sum, only 6 percent of the ministers had earlier been in charge of research or design work but had failed to hold a major operational command position in an enterprise.

Published biographical information show that at least 31 percent of the ministers had held full-time positions within the apparatus of the Communist Party, and that 16 percent had held very important Party posts. However, only 9 percent had held major Party posts without also having been director of an enterprise.[19] Thus, although the Party hierarchy is a significant source of recruitment of future industrial and construction ministers, few are transferred directly to the ministerial rank without first having been placed in charge of an enterprise.

Not only is recruitment to the level of minister made almost entirely from among those who have been directors or chief deputy directors of enterprises, but lengthy plant experience is generally a prerequisite for any important headquarters position.[20] This latter is shown by the careers of the five men who headed one major industrial ministry in 1967. Unfortunately, the career histories begin only with the attainment of a reasonably important post; but it may be presumed that the earlier experience of all of them was entirely outside of headquarters and was probably limited to the enterprise level.

Of the five men, the minister had had the most unusual career; for he was the only one who moved back to an enterprise after having been at headquarters. From being the first assistant to the director of a plant, he became first assistant to the head of a ministerial subdivision. Then he moved back into the field as director of a second enterprise, became director of a third enterprise, became head of a *sovnarkhoz* (a regional organization existing during 1957-1965 and comparable to a ministry), and then was appointed minister.

---

[18]However, the proportion having one or the other of these types of experience rose sharply among the ministers appointed during the 1960s as compared to those appointed earlier: from 16 percent to 28 percent.

[19]Even of this last group of eight ministers, six had been graduates of higher-educational engineering institutes, one had completed a correspondence course, and only one appears not to have completed higher education.

[20]The post of personnel head of a ministry seems to be an exception, with people from the Party hierarchy being natural candidates.

Table 8.24 Previous Career Characteristics of Those Soviet Ministers of Industry and Construction Appointed after the Purges of the Late 1930s

		Appointed Before the 1960s			Appointed during the 1960s
	Total	Sub-total	Heavy Industry	Light, food, and Construction Industries	
Earlier Career in Enterprises (percentages)					
Was director of at least one industrial enterprise	76	80	78	83	68
Was not above, but was the chief deputy[a] of an enterprise director	9	7	10	0	12
Neither	15	13	12	17	20
Sample size (number)	79	54	42	12	25
Sample as a percentage of the relevant population	66	59	65	44	89
Experience in Research or Design Work (percentage)					
Head of a research or design institute or of important research/design work in a ministry	7	5	9	0	12
Major research or design responsibility in an enterprise	12	11	14	5	16
Minor research or design responsibility in an enterprise	9	11	14	5	4
None of above	71	73	63	90	68
Sample size (number)	80	55	35	20	25

Table 8.24 (continued)

		Appointed Before the 1960s			Appointed during the 1960s
	Total	Sub-total	Heavy Industry	Light, food, and Construction Industries	
Sample as a percentage of the relevant population	67	60	54	74	89
Earlier Career in the Communist Party (percentages)					
Major Party post[b]	16	15	9	26	19
Party organizer in an enterprise	1	2	3	0	0
Political work in the military	2	4	0	10	0
Party or Comsomol post before entering a higher-educational institute[c]	11	17	20	10	0
None of the above	69	63	69	53	81
Sample size (number)	80	54	35	19	26
Sample as a percentage of the relevant population	67	59	54	70	93

Source: Data supplied privately by Jerry F. Hough.
Note: Overlap has been eliminated among the various categories. A minister is counted within each attribute solely in the highest level to which he belongs.
[a]Chief engineer.
[b]First secretary of a city or *oblast* Party committee, the industrial secretary (or head of the industrial department) of an *oblast* Party committee, and the head of a department within the Central Committee of the Party.
[c]Those who held quite minor Party posts, and did not attend an institute, are also included here.

His move back into the field was at a very high level, and doubtless was accepted by him in order to gain the experience of independent command which is regarded so highly as a qualification for the top position in the industrial branch.

The second man had been the head of a major function in a major plant of the industry, and was promoted to the post of first assistant to the director of the same enterprise. From there he moved to the second post in the ministry.

The third man had been director of an important enterprise, then head of the ministerial subdivision directing his industrial subbranch; after this he advanced into the third spot in the ministry.

The fourth man had been director of a significant enterprise, then first assistant to the director of a far more important enterprise, then director of this same enterprise, finally moving into his current position in the ministry.

The fifth man had been director of one of the most important enterprises of the industry immediately before moving to his current post in the ministry.

To sum up the careers of these five men, only the minister had moved back from a headquarters to a field position. All five had worked for a long time at the enterprise level: four had been enterprise directors, and the fifth had been first assistant to the director of his enterprise.

When one inquires as to the promotional opportunities of enterprise directors, the prime one appears to be that of going into the ministry of the enterprise's own branch. This has been true in the Soviet Union for a long time: even when one looks back at the ministers of industry and construction in 1941, the vast majority had worked a stint as director of one of the most important enterprises of their industries.[21] But the opportunities at the ministry level are limited, since only a really important position here would constitute a promotion for an enterprise director.

A second possibility is transfer to a larger plant as director. Of the five top men of one ministry who were described above, two had directed two different enterprises. But such moves are also restricted; one former Soviet enterprise director told me that, in his opinion, men would refuse to serve as directors of more than two or three different enterprises.

The third possibility is that of entering into work within the Communist Party apparatus. Of the first secretaries of the Party committees of the twenty-five most industrialized *oblasts* (regions) in the country in 1962, five

[21] Hough, *The Soviet Prefects,* p. 40.

had earlier in their careers been directors of major enterprises.[22] It would appear that transfer to the Communist Party apparatus is even more common for directors of minor enterprises than for those who head major plants. However, this appears to be an unusual career change.

All in all, then, men who reach the post of enterprise director can normally regard this post as their last. Nevertheless, almost all of the top posts at the headquarters level are filled by men chosen from among these directors, and the new ministerial appointees normally come with very limited experience other than that of manufacturing in the field.

To sum up, Soviet careers of the middle 1930s were highly mobile and apparently included a good deal of movement in both directions between enterprises and higher organizations. By the 1960s, to the contrary, tenure in post throughout industry had become extremely lengthy, and shifting from ministerial headquarters to enterprises had become rare. Promotional opportunities were scarce, and the position of factory director was normally a terminal one. Yet the proper career route for an ambitious manager was still through the factories.

Conclusion

Since the material of this chapter will be reviewed in Chapter 10, there is little need for a summary at this stage. But it is worth pointing to the fact that national differences with regard to managerial careers within the enterprise are quite as great as the national differences in managerial education. The continuum of career stability runs from France to the Soviet Union in the 1960s to Britain and, finally, to the United States. But the appropriate grouping is clear: France and the Soviet Union on the one hand, and Britain and the United States on the other. The real surprise here is the Soviet Union; not only is the career stability in this country quite different from what one would have predicted from its educational pattern and the "open" character of its managerial recruitment, but it is also radically at variance with the Soviet pattern of the 1930s.

[22]*Ibid.*, pp. 64-65 and 373.

Of the six companies treated here, only the second and fourth were included in the samples used in the statistical analysis of the text. The other four were excluded because of the unavailability of detailed individual biographical material. All of the American firms for which sufficient data are known are examined in this appendix.

The first company is a large electronics firm. It is very much a young man's company, its division general managers being in their thirties or forties. The company is extremely market oriented, and the vast majority of the divisional chief executives come from the sales and marketing function.

As one would expect in a firm where the rise to top managment occurs very rapidly or not at all, a high proportion of the forty-one top executives have a university degree: between 88 and 98 percent. Forty-seven percent of the highest degrees earned by these executives are in business; another 33 percent are in engineering, natural science or mathematics. Thirty-six percent of those with bachelor's degrees have a higher degree as well.

Yet in manufacturing—which in this company is the least regarded of all the major functions—a study in one large plant showed that half of the recent promotions among managers were of people without any university degree. This appears to be the only function in which such promotion still occurs.

I have no general information as to movement of managers between functions. But the most prestigious function can be treated: movement out of marketing seems to occur only at the highest levels where men may be put in charge of other functions. Others leave this function only through resignation from the company. Movement into the function is limited, and seems to be concentrated among men who transfer in at the lowest level and remain there.

One top executive, thinking particularly of the marketing function, held that a man is either recognized as having significant managerial potential within his first five years in the firm or he is permanently missed. This seems inevitable if the top divisional posts are to be held by men in their thirties and forties. For a man to be selected as having such potential, unusual ability in one of his first professional posts seems essential. But no level of performance is in itself sufficient. Rather, a salesman who substantially overfulfills his quota gets an opportunity both to attend conferences that would otherwise be closed to him and to speak at and chair meetings. Here he has the opportunity of impressing higher managers—but only if he does so is he likely to move further. Thus high performance at this level is relevant only as a means by which a salesman can call attention to himself; what happens thereafter has nothing to do with his performance as a salesman.

At a somewhat higher level, even average performance is not essential. Mention was made of a headquarters man with a bright future who had been rather a poor field manager, and who would eventually have been demoted or have resigned if he had stayed at that level. Nevertheless, he was one of six men in the company recommended for a challenging headquarters post; and he was picked for it simply because he made the best personal impression on the interviewer.

In the sales and marketing function, no second-level manager is appointed unless there is the expectation that he will later be a viable candidate for a higher position. (Only 5 percent of the employees in this function are at this second level or higher.) Yet, in fact, the second-level manager who performs well but is not to be promoted is allowed to remain indefinitely in his post; roughly half of these second-level managers thus become "career men" in their job, while only 5 to 7 percent are demoted or encouraged to resign.

Thus we can see that tenure in these second-level management positions is treated in a compromise fashion. Since the post is a necessary stepping stone for people moving higher, it would be undesirable to allow all of these positions to become filled with semipermanent tenants; this is why no one is appointed unless he is expected to have a reasonable chance of moving further. On the other hand, there are enough such posts so that not all of them need be used as stepping-stones.

Third-level posts, however, are treated as "test jobs" in which no one will stay more than three years. This is because there are only twenty of these marketing posts in the company. Most of the occupants are in their early thirties, and perhaps 80 percent move on from there to lateral headquarters posts or to higher positions. The others are demoted or resign.

Here, then, is a company in which movement upward in the prestigious function is either very rapid or does not occur at all. Demotion is also common, and seems to be accepted by most executives. Certain very important positions are reserved almost exclusively as a testing ground. Out of twelve divisional general managers in the company at the time when I was interviewing, seven had followed the outlined route in the marketing function. Four of the remaining five were heads of functional divisions and had come up through the function of which they were currently in charge.

Unfortunately, I have no general information as to the movement back and forth between field and corporate headquarters. But the one career of which I do have a record is revealing. A current top executive began in the field as a salesman and stayed there for three years. He then moved to headquarters for three years as one of three administrative assistants to a vice-president; he regarded this as the greatest educational experience in his career, as it was here that he learned to work with managers in other functions. He then was transferred back into the field in three successive marketing posts at rising levels, and ended once again in headquarters in charge of the marketing function. His most recent position, held in his middle forties, was that of general staff advisor on managerial problems at corporate headquarters. What is most interesting in this career is the early three-year stint at corporate headquarters prior to being appointed to any significant managerial post.

The second company is a large machinery firm engaged in large-volume production. Here the key function, in the sense of being the most highly regarded, is comptrollership. To the limited extent that managers in this company have transferred between functions, it is the comptrollers who have branched out to take management posts elsewhere. It is comptrollership that is the royal route to the top, and it is managers in this function who—along with those in personnel—have made the most moves back and forth between the field and corporate headquarters.

Why the peculiar success of this function in establishing and maintaining dominance in the corporation? Partly it is because it has been especially well led and has done peculiarly well in recruiting men of talent. But doubtless a major contributing factor has also been the fact that it is this function which has given its managers the broadest background available in the company, and has done this by revolving them through positions at different field and headquarters levels.

Manufacturing is the reverse type of function. Although one-third of the factory heads have had some experience at divisional headquarters, these factory men are mostly shirt-sleeve managers. Of all current factory heads in the company, 53 percent do not have a college degree; even among those appointed within the past five years, 30 percent do not have degrees. In contrast, all the other functions are manned at this management level virtually entirely by college graduates.

It is true that tenure in the plant manager post does not tend to be long: of a sample of twenty-six plant heads, 50 percent had been in their current post for no more than three years, and only 8 percent had been there for over ten. But this is primarily because of the length of time required to reach the position of plant manager, and additionally because the company follows a policy of lateral movement of managers between plants. Of a sample of twenty-one factory heads, 62 percent were fifty years of age or older and considered as probably too old for promotion. (Thirty-eight percent were beyond fifty-five, and were assuredly too old.)

The result of this pattern is that there is a complete absence of men at top management level who have had manufacturing experience. The company was feeling this lack seriously at the time I did my interviewing; it was proving impossible to bring the production function into decision making at the top councils of the corporation. The company was belatedly trying to remedy this by guiding across divisional lines a few of the executives in manufacturing, with the expectation of eventually giving them top posts in other functions and bringing their manufacturing background to bear on broader problems. But this move occurred only when the company felt itself already seriously injured by the lack of cross-functional experience.

The third company is a large utility firm, and is interesting because of the extensive role of corporate headquarters which is manned essentially by people brought on loan for two years from the various divisions. At any time, some 20 percent of the top 12 percent of managers and first-line supervisors are on duty at company headquarters. This is the first career stage at which managers are brought to corporate headquarters, but virtually all of these upper-middle managers get this experience.

The fourth company is a large firm in the oil industry. Five years is considered as a long time for a manager to stay at a single post. Two top men in personnel spoke of the company's desire to keep men in a given job for at least two years so that they may establish a record of performance which can be judged, but they acknowledged the difficulty of implementing this policy of "stability." The consequence of rapid upward mobility is the extensive use of early retirement (at age fifty-five).

The company's top personnel executives spoke of the difficulty of rationally ranking managers' current performance, let alone their potential. At best, they thought that individual managers could be ranked according to job performance into the bottom, middle, or upper third of all managers at their level; but this was all they really hoped for from evaluations. For, although the company has a full-blown evaluation system, they held that evaluations are so subjective that they tell more about the evaluators than about the managers being evaluated.

The high rate of managerial mobility within the company was explained as necessary not so much in order to broaden the manager's experience as to provide them with a testing ground. Since there are no objective criteria for evaluating managers, they said, the best one can do is to move managers frequently so that they will have many superiors, all of whom will be called upon to evaluate them. (This was the only company in which this was explicitly stated as a reason for high mobility.)

The fifth company is a large one in the electrical equipment industry. Here, the high cost of rapid managerial mobility was explicitly recognized; it was accepted that a manager would not carry out his functions in a fully competent fashion until he had worked in the specific post for some time. Nevertheless, the best that the company could do was to refuse to consider a man for transfer until he had been in his job for one year; and even in this regard, exceptions are made.

Despite this explicit recognition of the costs to the company of a high transfer rate, this firm has an explicit requirement intended to discourage inbreeding within product departments. In considering an appointment for any of the top five to ten posts within any department, at least two managers who are currently working outside of that department must be formally considered.

The sixth company, engaged primarily in heavy chemicals and textiles, is particularly interesting because of its explicit policy of shifting "comers" both between functions and between different types of businesses. This policy is closely policed by corporate headquarters, which had at first to overcome strong resistance from product divisions to giving up "essential" men and taking on others with no experience in their industry. This resistance was couched in terms of division heads declaring that they could not take responsibility for profits when these managerial changes were forced upon them; corporate headquarters responded by compelling the early retirement of some divisional general managers. By the time I interviewed in this company, 90 percent of the division chiefs were graduates of the system and opposition had completely broken down.

While these functional and product shifts mostly occur before the age of thirty-five, the moves are made into responsible managerial rather than into training posts. The only factor which eases the problems of implementing this policy is the fact that virtually all of these managers, regardless of the function or industry into which they were originally recruited, have a similar education: a college degree in chemistry or engineering.

Of course, this policy does not apply to all managers. Many remain in the same function and product line throughout their career; but none of these men are regarded as competitors for top positions in the company.

The most comprehensive data available are for the first French firm of Appendix A to Chapter 7; this company is nonnationalized, is among the one hundred largest in the country, is in a prestige industry, and has a *grande école* management. I can trace the careers over a five-year period of all the occupants of posts which constituted 45 percent of the total number of *cadres* employed in a large portion of the company at the beginning of the period. These posts comprise a 100 percent sample of all management jobs in the top 2.2 income percentile of the labor force.

First, it should be noted that the length of tenure in a single post is very high in comparison with the American and British patterns. For those managerial positions that continued unchanged throughout the five years, there was one occupant throughout in two-thirds of the cases (Table A. 8B.1).

One can see that, while there was considerable job stability throughout management, it was a good deal higher in the more desirable headquarters and sales functions than in the factories. This impression is confirmed by looking at the reasons why people left their posts and at the sources of recruitment to fill the open positions (Table A. 8B.2).

The data used to prepare Table A. 8B.2 also makes possible an analysis of the five-year job history of the individual occupants at the end of the period both of the old positions and of the ones newly created during the period (Table A. 8B.3). Those few individuals who changed jobs more than once are counted twice.

Thus a situation prevailed in which not only was movement between factory and headquarters positions virtually nil, but in which there was also very little movement between functions at the same broad managerial level (only 7 percent of the job histories were of this latter type). It can be said that the

Table A. 8B. 1 Transfers among Top Management Jobs During Five Years in a French Company

	Headquarters and Sales Positions		Factory Positions		Total Positions	
	Number	Percentage	Number	Percentage	Number	Percentage
Size of sample	41		97		138	
One occupant throughout		83		53		62
Two occupants		17		42		35
Three or more occupants		0		5		4

Table A. 8B. 2   Reasons for Leaving Posts and Sources of Recruitment

	Headquarters and Sales Positions		Factory Positions		Total Positions	
	Number of Managers	Perc.	Number of Managers	Perc.	Number of Managers	Perc.
People leaving posts	8		49		57	
Left the company[a]		75		22		31
Changed positions		25		78		69
People assuming posts[b]	24		71		95	
Entered the company in that post		62		20		31
Changed positions		38		80		69

[a]Two individuals counted here changed jobs shortly before retirement.
[b]Forty additional posts at the same managerial levels were created during the five years. These are included here.

Table A. 8B. 3   Five-Year Job Histories of Those Who Were Managers at the End of the Period

	Number	Percentage
Total number of individuals	161	
Held the same position throughout		53
Entered the company in the post		10
Promoted		18
Moved at the same managerial level		7
Demoted		5
Change in managerial level unknown		7
For all individuals changing positions within the company	60	
New post was within the same function, very narrowly defined, as the previous one		63
Among these, the new post was the next highest position in the same function and in the same suborganization as the previous post		37
New post was in a different function from the previous one		37

company virtually never moved the upper half of its professional and managerial staff between positions in order to broaden their experience; changes of functions were almost always due either to demotions or to the existence of openings for promotion.

With regard to the posts of directors of the three major plants of the company, I can take a longer time horizon of thirteen years. During this period, there were seven occupants of the three posts. Two of the four changes are accounted for by one man who was first moved from the directorship of one of these plants to that of another, and then at the age of fifty-five went to head a smaller company that is under the same financial control as that of the company he left. A third change is due to another man leaving at the age of forty-four for a superior position in another company under the same financial control; he had spent only four years in the first company—all of them as plant director. The fourth change was a retirement. Of the four who took on these posts, one was shifted between the plants at the same level, two were hired directly from outside, and only one was promoted.

The average time spent as director of a single plant was five and one-half years, even ignoring occupancy of the post prior to the beginning of our thirteen-year period. This compares with three and one-half years for the American sample treated in Table 8.5. But what is more striking is that not a single one of the directors was moved within the company except to another plant, and that only one of the replacements came from another post within the company other than that of plant director. Clearly, promotional opportunities within the company were extremely meager at this level.

Finally, I can trace the careers over a period of eight years for the final occupants of sixty top management positions. (These constitute an 88 percent sample of the highest 8 percent of management posts.) These sixty positions can themselves be divided into groups. Sixty-four percent of the higher group, and 49 percent of the second, were probably held by the same man throughout the eight years. Only 20 and 31 percent, respectively, of the posts were filled during the period through promotion. Changes in function ran 12 to 14 percent; none of the top group and only 11 percent of the second group moved between the plants and headquarters (Table A. 8B.4).

The other company for which I have good statistical data is the second firm of Appendix A to Chapter 7; it is in a prestige industry, but it is only half the size of the first firm and is family dominated. The educational level of the managerial staff is considerably below that in the first company. The figures to be presented exclude the two positions held by family members.

For this company, the sample constitutes 89 percent of the 8 percent of the managers in the top two levels in the company, i.e., of the top 0.6 income percentile of the labor force. Despite the fact that this firm is radically different from the first with regard to the education of its very top managers, the careers within the company look quite similar (Table A. 8B.5).

The first and second firms are also very similar with regard to the number of years which executives spend in the company (Table A. 8B.6). In both cases, the very top group joins the company at a somewhat older age than does the stratum immediately below it.

Finally, I have data over a five-year span for one large plant in a third company. The history of this plant was exceptional, because its personnel almost doubled over this period. Furthermore, it was in a very large and rapidly growing company in a prestigious and rapidly growing industry. Thus the opportunities for promotion of the *cadres,* both within the plant and outside, were quite exceptional.

Under the circumstances, the degree of career mobility, although greater than in the other two companies, is not inconsistent with the earlier data in the overall picture presented of French industry. Furthermore, our figures for

Table A. 8B. 4 Eight-Year Job Histories of the Final Occupants of Sixty Top Management Positions of a French Company

	Top Posts of the Company		Second Level Posts of the Company	
	Number	Percentage	Number	Percentage
Number in sample	25		35	
Posts that existed throughout the period				
Same man in post throughout		44		23
Entered company in that post during the period		4		6
Entered company in a lesser post during the period		12		9
Promotions of men who were in company throughout		0		11
Demotions of men who were in company throughout		0		9
Posts created during the period				
Post created through merger, and man entered company in that post		20		26
Post created through merger, and man promoted		8		11
Man moved at the same managerial level		12		6
For all individuals changing positions within the company	8		16	
Man changed function		38		31
Man moved between plant and headquarters		0		25

Table A. 8B. 5   Job Mobility among the Managers of a French Company

	Top Level	Second Level
Sample size (number)	10	30
Average period per post in the company (years)	7	9
Men joining the company at the rank of *cadre* (percentage)	90	77
Average number of changes of function in the company throughout career (number)	0.5	0.8
Of these, average number of such changes through lateral moves at the same managerial level (number)	0.0	0.2

Table A. 8B. 6   Age at Joining the Firm and Number of Years Spent by Executives in Two French Companies

	First Company		Second Company	
	Top Level	Second Level	Top Level	Second Level
Average age of joining the company (years)	34	28	32	28
Men joining the company over the age of thirty (percentage)	60	37	50	27
Average period in the company (years)	21	22	20	23

this plant include the most junior *cadres;* one would expect them to show a higher level of mobility than do the data of the first two companies, which are restricted to middle and senior management. The figures of Table A. 8B.7 indicate the changes of position for a 100 percent sample of all the *cadres* who worked in this plant at the beginning of the period.

It is only for the nine persons who changed posts within the same plant that I have information about the new function. Six of the nine did not change function at all, and one changed only in the sense that he was promoted to a post where he was in charge of his old function as well as of others. Thus only two people changed functions in a significant sense.

This exhausts the statistical career data at my disposal. However, data for various individuals in other companies suggest that these results are quite typical of careers in large industrial companies. Only one other firm (number

Table A. 8B. 7 Job Changes of *Cadres* in a Plant of a Rapidly-Expanding French Company

	Number	Percent
Number in sample	41	
Held the same post throughout		37
Changed position within the company		49
Of this:		
Changed positions within the plant		22
Transferred to another plant		12
Transferred to company headquarters		5
Transferred to another non-factory position		10
Left the company		7
Died or retired		7

four of Appendix A to Chapter 7) warrants mention as demonstrating a somewhat different pattern. This is a large company in a nonprestigious industry, which has a quite small proportion of *cadres* who are graduates of true *grande écoles.*

Mobility between posts is slight in this company, and movement between functions even less. The difference from the pattern of our other firms is the unwillingness to hire nonfamily managers from outside. As one of the company directors told me, hiring an outsider as a plant manager would constitute a revolution. During the remembered history of the firm, only one future plant manager joined the company past the age of twenty-three—and he was a *polytechnicien.* The company would go outside only to hire an occasional rare specialist when there was no one working in that function within the company.

This peculiarity appears to stem from the fact that this is a family firm in a nonprestige industry, and thus does not staff its top posts from the major *grandes écoles.* Since it is primarily such men who move into firms at the level of middle management or higher, it is not surprising that such a company should look only inside its own ranks for its managers.

I shall concentrate in this chapter on two aspects of monetary incentive systems. The first is the degree of inequality in total compensation between upper-management personnel and the rank and file. The second is the system of bonuses (including stock options).

It seems probable that managers in all four countries consider promotion as a more significant operational goal than financial reward per se. Quite correctly, they believe that their total compensation will rise over their lifetime primarily as a result of such promotion, and that enlightened self-interest is better served by attention to promotional opportunities than to possibilities for higher immediate compensation. Nevertheless, they are more likely to sacrifice personal inclination and nonbusiness objectives in the interests of promotion when the structure of compensation is highly inegalitarian. Similarly, the nature of managerial actions is likely to be affected by the promise of higher immediate compensation in the form of bonuses. Thus, while I do not hold that financial incentives as such have a motivating force equal to that of the search for promotion, nevertheless they deserve attention.

Total Compensation of Management
The method that I shall use for measuring inequality of income in industrial enterprises is to compare the lower limit of total compensation of upper management with the average earnings of male manual workers in manufacturing. The appropriate comparison for all countries except the Soviet Union appears to be with average male manual wages in manufacturing as a whole rather than in the industries of the specific companies studied, since the relevant market for management personnel is the national one.

Upper management will be defined for this purpose as constituting the highest paid 1 percent or so of all company employees. Concern with the lower bound of an upper management which is so broadly defined has two advantages. The first is that, by dealing with a group that is lower in the organization than either the chief executive or the most highly paid three to five executives, it provides a better indication of the sort of income inequalities that are relevant to the aspirations and behavior of a broad group of managerial and professional personnel. The second is that it allows us to avoid the difficulties involved in considering stock options and deferred compensation, since these are relatively unimportant at this level of management.

No attempt will be made here to take account of differences in income tax between the various countries. Similarly, the only nonsalary benefit that is considered in total compensation is average annual bonus. However, one ex-

Table 9.1   American Upper-Management Earnings

Size of the Managerial Group Treated (Percentage of the Total Labor Force)							Annual Earnings of the Lowest Paid People in the Managerial Group Treated (Index: Average Annual Earnings of all Manual Workers in Manufacturing = 100)						
Company							Company						
1	2	3	4	5	6	7	1	2	3	4	5	6	7
3.6							279						
	1.5							362					
		0.9							435				
			0.9							447			
				0.9							460		
					0.3							418	
						0.2							586[a]

[a]Stock options are also received by this group but are not included here.

ception is necessary: this is the inclusion of family allowance in France, where it reduces income inequality.

Data are available for seven American industrial companies in 1967 (Table 9.1). Unfortunately, American statistics for average manual worker earnings in manufacturing—unlike the British and French statistics—do not distinguish between male and female workers.[1] Since average male earnings are higher than female, this biases upwards the American base in comparison with the British and French.

It would appear that the lowest earners within the top 1 percent of the company labor force receive roughly some four times the amount gained by an average manual worker, and probably about three and one-half times the earnings of an average male manual worker.

Comparable detailed data are available for four British companies. The figures are for late 1964 (Table 9.2). The lowest British earners within the top 1 percent of the company labor force receive only two to three times the amount gained by an average male manual worker.

In the case of France, I have detailed data for only three companies. However, two supplementary sources are available as corroboration. The first is average income of the top 5 and 7 percent of the labor force in two additional firms. The second is a study of minimum and maximum salaries of

[1]A study of 1970 incomes showed, however, that full-time year-round male operatives in manufacturing earned 16 percent more than the average of similar workers of both sexes. (See U.S. Department of Commerce, Bureau of the Census, *Current Population Reports,* Series P-60, No. 80, 4 October, 1971, tables 55 and 60.)

Table 9.2   British Upper-Management Earnings

Size of the Managerial Group Treated (Percentage of the Total Labor Force)				Annual Earnings of the Lowest Paid People in the Managerial Group Treated (Index: Average Annual Earnings of all Male Manual Workers in Manufacturing = 100)			
Company				Company			
1	2	3	4	1	2	3	4
		4.0				282	
1.6				242			
	1.1				212		
		0.5				353	
			0.5				302
			0.2				353
	0.2				363		

Table 9.3   French Upper-Management Earnings

Size of the Managerial Group Treated (Percentage of the Total Labor Force)					Annual Earnings of the Lowest Paid People in the Managerial Group Treated (Index: Average Annual Earnings of all Male Manual Workers in Manufacturing = 100)				
Company					Company				
1	2	3	4	5	1	2	3	4	5
7.3			7.3		320			285	
	5.2					290			
				5.0					385
4.0					405				
	2.6					352			
2.4					500				
		2.1					354		
	0.9					444			
0.8					635				
		0.5					996		
	0.3					584			
0.2					816				

managers at varying grade levels in fourteen large French companies. Both sets of supplementary sources indicate that the figures from the three companies are in the correct ranges. Data are for 1963 (Table 9.3). From this, it would seem that the lowest earners within the top 1 percent of the French company labor force receive four to six times the amount gained by an average male manual worker.

When we turn to the Soviet Union, we face the problem that the relevant comparison is between top managerial personnel at all levels of Soviet industrial administration—including those bodies superior to the enterprises—and the top managers in capitalist companies. Unfortunately, I have no data as to the number of high-income industrial officials working above the level of the enterprise. As a result, I shall have to rely entirely upon enterprise figures.

Three Soviet sources present recent earnings of managerial and professional employees in particular industries. The results are presented in Table 9.4.

It seems reasonable to assume that, on average, it is the heads of the enterprise's administrative units who constitute the lowest earners within the top 1 percent of income recipients in the industry as a whole (including units above the enterprise level). This group appears to earn some two to three times the sums received by manual workers in their own branch of industry.[2]

A British source[3] provides data concerning directors of five Leningrad enterprises. The data are base salaries for 1962-1963, and I have adjusted them using the assumption that the directors received the average percentage bonuses earned in all industry in 1961 and 1964 (Table 9.5). These figures seem quite in line with those of Table 9.4.

A final source[4] dealing with the middle 1950s presents higher figures for directors' earnings as a proportion of those of all manual workers in Soviet industry (Table 9.6).

The difference between these figures and the ones previously cited seems to reflect the movement toward greater equality of earnings which has been occurring in the Soviet economy since the late 1930s. Earnings of all man-

[2]The combination of low mobility of managers across branch lines and the substantial degree to which higher education is specialized by branch lead me to believe that managerial earnings are more proportional to those of workers in the branch than to those of workers in industry as a whole.

[3]Mary McAuley, *Labour Disputes in Soviet Russia 1957-1965* (Clarendon Press, Oxford, 1969), pp. 74-77.

[4]D. Granick, *The Red Executive* (Doubleday, Anchor edition, Garden City, N. Y., 1961), p. 92.

Table 9.4 Earnings of Soviet Enterprise Managers as a Proportion of Average Manual Worker Earnings in Their Branch of Soviet Industry (Percentage)

Industry	Approximate Date	Director	Chief Engineer	Head of One of Enterprise's Administrative Units	Head of Production Department	Foreman
Construction materials	1959	360	331	264	237	177
Auto transport	1964	323	310		227	
Metal fabricating	1964	434		282	261	165
Textiles	1964	317		207	193	158
Food industry	1964	276		186	179	137

Note: The original sources give managerial base-salary schedules in relation to that of technicians. Total income ratios must have been much the same, since bonus rates for all managerial and professional employees have been roughly proportional to base salaries since 1959. It has been calculated that total earnings of technicians were equal to the following proportions of the average earnings of manual workers in industry: 1959—115 percent, and 1964—103 percent. (This calculation is based upon an expansion of the basic salary paid to technicians in these industries by the bonus rate earned by all managerial and professional employees throughout industry in the relevant year, and by "other earnings" received by the same group in 1955. Comparison is then made with total manual earnings in all industry.) In all cases, I have used as the basis for analysis the largest size-grouping of enterprise or subunit, and thus the one whose managers are best paid. Since ranges are given for salaries in a given post, I have taken the midpoint of each range; as ranges are narrow, this does not constitute a problem.

Sources: Construction materials: G. M. Batekhin, N. P. Nevolin, I. A. Kleinfel'd, *Organizatsiia zarabotnoi platy na predpriiatiiakh promyshlennosti stroitel'nykh materialov* (Gosizdlit po stroitel'stvu..., Moscow, 1962), pp. 178-186. Data are given for six sub-industries, and I have taken an unweighted average of them. Auto transport: V. N. Mizinov, V. F. Dement'ev, M. P. Dubnikova, N. A. Cherke, *Organizatsiia truda i zarabotnoi platy na avtomobil'nom transporte* (Transport, Moscow, 1965), pp. 187-188. Metal fabricating, textiles, and the food industry: E. A. Lutokhina, *Oplata truda inzhenerno-tekhnicheskikh rabotnikov* (Ekonomika, Moscow, 1966), p. 65.

Table 9.5   Earnings of Directors of Five Leningrad Enterprises

Number of Employees in Enterprises	Industry	Director's Average Earnings as a Percentage of:	
		All Manual Workers in Soviet Industry	All Manual Workers in that Enterprise
5000	Textile machinery	373	360
2500	Metal fabricating	340	307
1900	Precision measuring instruments	340	336
10,000 plus	Shoes	340	375
1800	Candy	283	333

Table 9.6   Directors' Earnings as a Percentage of All Manual Workers' Earnings in Soviet Industry, Mid-1950s

Major steel enterprises	703-879
Leningrad food enterprise with 1100 employees	528
Normal earnings in enterprises of two hundred to one thousand employees under the administration of the Moscow City Council	223-528

agerial and professional workers taken together as a proportion of those of manual workers declined as shown in Table 9.7.[5]

Since it seems likely that the relative earnings of top managers has been declining along with those of managerial and professional workers as a group, the current ratios are probably quite different from what they were even as recently as the middle 1950s.

To sum up, top managerial monetary compensation relative to the earnings of manual workers appears to be highest in France and lowest in Britain and

[5]Data for 1935 from E. A. Lutokhina, *Oplata truda inzhenerno-tekhnicheskikh rabotnikov* (Ekonomika, Moscow, 1966), p. 80. Data for all other years from TsSU, *Trud v SSSR* (Statistika, Moscow, 1966), pp. 138-139.

Table 9.7   Changes in Pay Differentials in Soviet Industry

Year	Index of All Managerial and Professional Workers (Manual Workers = 100)
1935	236
1940	213
1945	230
1950	176
1955	166
1960	148
1965	142
1966	144

the Soviet Union.[6] The lowest earners within the top 1 percent of income recipients in large industrial companies (industries in the case of the Soviet Union) appear to receive:

France	Four to six times the income of male manual workers
United States	Four times the income of all manual workers and three and one-half times the income of male manual workers
Soviet Union	Two to three times the income of all manual workers
Britain	Two to three times the income of male manual workers

When we consider the effect of income tax laws in the four countries, the foregoing differences between France, the United States, and Britain are further increased; but the Soviet Union is pushed upwards in the table to greater inequality.

Bonuses in American Companies

The descriptive and analytic literature that relates to American incentive payments has dealt primarily with those received by the one to five top officers of large companies. In the economic literature, the concern has been with the question of whether or not total compensation of these executives is geared so as to yield them greater rewards for growth of the company's sales,

[6]It is true that the above comparisons (except for the Russian) are based upon data received from a small number of firms in each country. But the companies are all large and thus tend, at least in a rough fashion, to be knowledgeable of and to take steps competitive with managerial salary developments in other companies; thus they can probably be considered representative of large industrial companies with regard to their earnings differentials. Furthermore, general discussions with informed managers in the respective countries confirm the relative ranking of the different western nations' earnings differentials.

of its total profits, or of its profitability. The subject takes its significance from the fact that a compensation system based primarily on size of operations, rather than on the excess of total profits over what is normally earned on capital invested at similar risk, would indicate a division of interests between top executives and the stockholders. Unfortunately, the studies to date have been quite inconclusive on this matter.[7]

The prevalence of bonus schemes in American firms has similarly been studied only insofar as it relates to the three highest paid executives. In 1967, 63 percent of the manufacturing companies listed on the New York Stock Exchange had such schemes—an increase from 44 percent in 1962. Over 78 percent of the companies had a stock option plan.[8] Thus the vast majority of large manufacturing firms have one or both of these incentive schemes for their very top management. Presumably almost all of these schemes cover a considerably larger number of managers than just these top three executives, but no information is available as to this.

In order to study the scope and characteristics of such incentive schemes, I asked about them in the large industrial corporations in which I did interviewing. The results were obtained in 1967 and 1968 and are presented in Table 9.8.

The companies described in Table 9.8 are all among the top one hundred and fifty American firms ranked according to sales in 1966, and they include one-fifth of the top twenty-six companies. There seems no reason to believe that they are unrepresentative of the population of large industrial companies with executive bonus plans.

Taking an unweighted average of the figures for all the companies, 1.2 percent of all employees—and 5.1 percent of all managerial, professional and sales personnel—were covered by the bonus plans. (Excluded are bonuses intended purely for sales personnel in lieu of commissions.) The annual basic salary for the lowest-paid bonus recipients (barring a few exceptional individuals) ran about $20,000 in 1967.

Thus, by and large, practice is consistent with the generally espoused doctrine that bonuses should be limited to those in a position to affect signifi-

[7]See David Roberts, *Executive Compensation* (The Free Press, Glencoe, Illinois, 1959); J. W. McGuire, J. S. Y. Chiu, and A. O. Elbing, "Executive Incomes, Sales and Profits," *American Economic Review,* September 1962, pp. 753-761; Robert J. Larner, *Management Control and the Large Corporation* (Dunellen, New York, 1970); and Wilbur G. Lewellen, *Executive Compensation in Large Industrial Corporations* (National Bureau of Economic Research, New York, 1968), pp. 244-248.
[8]Harland Fox, "Top Executive Compensation," in National Industrial Conference Board, *Studies in Personnel Policy,* No. 213 (New York, 1969), pp. 10, 13, and 18.

Table 9.8   Bonus and Stock Option Schemes in Large American Manufacturing Companies in 1967-1968 (Number of Companies)

Characteristics	Companies for Which Data Exist	Threefold Classification Answer to Questions			Percentage								Annual Base Salary ($1,000)		
		Yes	No	Intermediate	Less than 0.5	0.5 to 1.5	2.5 to 4.9	5 to 6	8 to 9	Less than 10	15 to 35	More than 800	15 to 18	20 to 25	Over 50
Bonus system exists	10	10	0												
Proportion of total company labor force which receives bonus[a]	9				2	6	1								
Proportion of total company managerial and professional personnel[b] which receives bonus	7				1		2	2	2						
Annual salary for lowest-paid bonus recipients, barring a few exceptions	8												2	5	1
Bonus is substantial as a proportion of base salary[c]	9	6.5	1.5	1											

Performance of the division in which the manager is located is important in determining his bonus[d]	7	1.5	5.5
Performance rating of the individual is important in determining his bonus	8	6	2
Stock option system exists	8	8	0
Proportion of stock option recipients to all those receiving bonuses	7	2 4	1

[a] Sales bonuses, granted in lieu of commissions, are not included. The test of whether a bonus is to be included is that everyone in the company at that grade or higher should be eligible for consideration for the bonus.

[b] These are all those exempt from the provisions of the Federal Wages and Hours legislation. They include all salesmen.

[c] In the firm for which bonus is considered to be low, it ranged between 5 and 15 percent of base salary. In the firm in which it is considered intermediate, it ranged up to 40 percent of base salary, but the vast majority of recipients received between 10 and 25 percent. In a third firm, bonus averaged only some 3 percent over a five-year period for 86 percent of the bonus recipients. However, bonuses there ran up to 50 percent for the top executives (0.7 percent of all managerial and professional personnel).

[d] In one company, divisional performance is considered for the top six or so managers in each division but not for the bonus recipients below their level.

cantly the profit position of their unit in the company. Furthermore, bonuses are restricted to those whose salaries are sufficient so that they can gracefully accept some reduction in total compensation in years of poor profits. Both principles not only apply to bonus recipients as a whole but are also applicable as between bonus recipients in that, within each individual company, normal bonus as a proportion of salary almost invariably rises with base salary.

The National Industrial Conference Board study referred to above indicated that in 1967, for the three most highly paid executives in each industrial firm listed on the New York Stock Exchange, bonuses did not constitute a simple addition to total compensation. Basic salaries were lower in companies with bonus plans than in those without, although total compensation was higher.[9] From scanty evidence in a few firms, I would think that the same is true for bonus recipients as a whole in the group of companies which I studied. Despite the viewpoint of many personnel specialists that basic salary should be the same regardless of whether or not a bonus plan exists, it is not surprising that the pressures of the marketplace prevent this.

Generally speaking, the bonus earned is paid out over the next several years rather than in a single year. This practice has three advantages. First, for the company, continued payment is usually linked to the individual remaining in the employ of the company, retiring, or at least not entering into a competitive business. Second, it provides some minor tax advantages for the bonus recipient through the smoothing of income receipts among successive years. But the greatest advantage to the bonus recipient is that this practice cushions the effect on his total income of bonus fluctuations; in any given year, he receives, say, one-fifth of the bonus earned over each of the previous five years. This would seem particularly important in making serious fluctuations in bonus socially acceptable, particularly to the lower-paid executives covered by the bonus scheme. On the other hand, this practice runs in the face of the orthodox notion expressed in incentive schemes intended for manual workers that supplemental pay should be received soon after the supplemental effort for which it compensates. Clearly, executives are implicitly considered to be more rational than manual workers and to have longer memories.

---

[9] *Ibid.,* p. 16. The study employed a crude implicit model holding, as a first approximation, that total compensation is affected only by the volume of sales of the company; it then tested as to whether the presence or absence of bonus and stock option plans were also relevant variables. No account was taken of profitability as a possible factor independently affecting compensation.

As one would have predicted on grounds of economic rationality, stock option plans are much more restrictive in coverage than the bonus plans: only about one-fifth of those earning bonuses also receive stock options. In only one of our companies is the relationship reversed; but here no more than some 0.02 percent of all employees receive bonuses.

The reasons are straightforward and fully recognized. As an executive's salary plus normal bonus increase, stock options represent an increased tax advantage to him; it is also easier for him to raise the funds needed to take up options, and he can better afford to accept the risks involved in having a large investment in a single company. On the other hand, the cost to the company's stockholders of granting stock options is the same regardless of the income bracket of the recipient: putting aside the issue of risk, it is twice the cost of granting an equivalent pretax number of dollars in the form of bonus, since bonus payments are treated in corporate income tax law as an expense while stock options are not. It is thus not surprising that, on average, only about 0.2 percent of company employees receive stock options.

On the whole, normal bonuses have been substantial. This is true for six of the nine companies for which I have information, and for a seventh for its top executives alone. Both of the firms in which bonuses were either low or intermediate in level had installed their bonus schemes only two years earlier; thus it is quite possible that their present schemes will prove to be only transitional in character. Examples of substantial bonuses are found in three companies in which some 5 to 9 percent of all managerial, professional, and sales personnel receive bonuses. In the first firm, normal bonus for the lowest grade of bonus recipients is about 20 percent of base salary; for those at the level of plant managers, it rises to between 60 and 90 percent. In a second firm, normal bonus averages 36 percent of base salary, ranging between 28 and 60 percent depending on the place of the recipient in the managerial hierarchy. In a third firm, the normal bonus also averages 36 percent of base salary; but the lower end of the range is down to 10 to 12 percent for those in the lowest positions. It is clear that bonuses of these magnitudes are sufficient to have a potentially large incentive effect on the managers concerned. Whether or not this potential is realized would seem to depend upon the methods used in determining the distribution of bonuses.

Normally, although not invariably, a bonus pot for the entire company is established as a share of profits. One example, which seems quite representative in character, is that a reserve for bonuses is set aside in the company's books equal to a percentage of the pretax profits earned during the previous year, after first deducting from such profits an amount equal to 10 percent (14 percent in another firm) of the capital employed. Although this reserve need not be fully distributed in any given year, and in many companies can be drawn upon in a low-profit year to supplement the amount that would otherwise have been available for bonuses, there seems no question that bonus awards in all of the companies studied are heavily dependent on the profits earned by the firm during the previous year.

Aside from the rules for the creation of the total bonus pot, it is interesting that the very criteria used in determining the allocation of bonuses are not infrequently kept fairly secret from the mass of bonus recipients. In view of this secrecy, it is certainly possible that I have been misled as to the criteria actually used in some of the firms where I did interviewing. However, in all cases where I received information my source was an individual in a position to have accurate knowledge, and I believe that the data are fairly reliable.

In all except one case, the prime factor determining the distribution of bonuses is the managerial level of the recipients. The exception is a company with a rule that each large division can submit for bonuses the names of only two-thirds of the people filling posts which make them nominally eligible under the bonus plan. But even here, once a person is placed upon the bonus list, he will normally continue receiving a bonus thereafter. Thus, to a considerable degree, bonus earnings depend primarily upon the level of corporate profits and on a proxy for the individual's base salary. This implies that some significant portion of bonuses really amounts to no more than delayed salary payments.

It is interesting that five companies pay no attention at all to the profits earned by the division in which the individual bonus recipient is located. In one of the two cases where such divisional performance does play a role in the distribution of the bonus, this is true only for the top half dozen or so men in each profit center.

The justification given for this neglect of divisional profit performance is threefold. First, there is the view that the profits earned by any given division are heavily affected by special situations of patents and markets. In one company, for example, it was pointed out that the sales and profits of one division could be increased sharply except for the corporate policy of protecting competitors so as not to incur the attention of the antitrust division of the Department of Justice. Second, profits earned by a division in a given year are heavily influenced by past divisional actions; thus it would be unfair to men newly transferred into a given division to hold them responsible for that division's profits, and linking bonuses to divisional profits would sharply restrict the ability of the corporation to transfer managers freely between divisions. Finally, bonuses are regarded as a means of attaching the financial interests of managers to the well-being of the company as a whole rather than to that of individual subunits.

Although I find it impossible to assign relative weights to these three reasons, the effect of attaching bonuses to the profits of the company rather than to those of any small subunit is to make bonuses an instrument of company policy combating rather than promoting suboptimization. It is true, however, that this effect might be negated by the methods used in determining individual ratings for bonus allocation. Unfortunately, there is little information available concerning this.

In six of eight companies for which we have data, the performance rating of the individual plays a significant role in determining his bonus. This is also true in a purely formal sense in a seventh company, but here the chief executive is highly skeptical as to the objectivity of such performance ratings and so in practice ignores them in determining bonus allocations. Generally, the performance rating is given by the manager's immediate superior and then requires approval all the way to the chief executive officer. Normally, this means that only two levels of superiors examine the performance rating in the light of knowledge of the specific man concerned; the reviews of the higher echelons are primarily intended to assure consistency of the ranking methods used within the different units.

Detailed data with regard to the significance of individual ratings are available for only one company. This is one in which over one thousand people receive bonuses annually, the bonus group constituting about 9 percent of the total number of managerial, professional and sales personnel.

Table 9.9 indicates the average bonus as a percentage of base salary over a

Table 9.9   Average Bonus Payments in One Company

Managerial Level	Average Base Salary, 1967 ($1,000)	Bonus Awards as Proportion of Base Salary, Five-Year Average (Percentage)	Extremes of Bonus Awards as Proportion of Base Salary, 1967 (Percentage)
1	40	48	20-70
2	25	36	
3	20	26	
4	17	16	
5	15	11	5-30

five-year period for five different levels of management. (All managers receiving bonuses are included except for the top three to ten company executives.) It also shows the range of the bonus as a percentage of base salary in the last year (which was a typical one) for the two extreme levels. The table suggests that performance evaluations have an enormous influence on bonus receipts by individuals, since the proportion of bonuses to base salary overlaps even between managerial levels one and five.

However, the significance of these performance evaluations can only be properly evaluated once we see the distribution of the ratings (Table 9.10). Six different ratings are employed, but the lowest (which excludes the recipient from any bonus that year) is rarely given. Over a period of two years, only five managers received this lowest rating; in addition, some ten to twelve others had tentatively received this rating but had left the company prior to the date of bonus distribution.

Over a three-year period, the distribution of managers among the five ratings which are consistent with continued employment was as shown in Table 9.10. There was some bias toward giving higher ratings to managers at higher levels, but the bias is much less than might have been expected (Table 9.11). (Data are for a single common year.)

How do individuals' performance ratings change from year to year? Over at least a twelve-year period, there was never a case of a manager's rating

Table 9.10 Bonus Rating Distribution

	Rating				
	Top	2nd	3rd	4th	5th
Percentage of total bonus recipients	3	29	45	21	3

Table 9.11 Bonus Rating Distributions in Upper and Lower Managerial Levels

	Rating				
	Top	2nd	3rd	4th	5th
Percentage of bonus recipients in the top three managerial levels	3	41	46	9	1
Percentage of bonus recipients in the lowest two managerial levels	1	20	51	27	1

changing by more than two grades between successive years; moreover, only about 1 percent of the managers change their rating by two grades in either direction in successive years.

Thus, for all practical purposes, an individual's rating remains either constant or changes by only one grade between years. But even this last is a significant figure. For a $15,000-a-year executive, it amounts to ± $1,250. For a $40,000 man, it comes to ± $6,800. At the same time, performance ranking is clearly of much less significance than managerial level in determining bonus. In years of sharp changes in the profits earned by the firm, this factor can also swamp the influence of the performance rating.

To sum up, it would appear that executive bonuses in large American companies consist to a considerable degree of nothing more than delayed salary. However, they are also significantly affected by annual variations both in the profits earned by the company and in the performance ratings of the individuals concerned. Thus, while it is true that a good part of the bonus element is facade, much of it is real. The genuinely flexible portion of the bonus is distributed in such a way as to encourage both high individual performance (however this may be evaluated by the manager's superiors) and attachment to the optimization of total corporate profits rather than those of any particular subunit.

It would appear that American bonuses encourage suboptimization in only one respect—i.e., with regard to time. They emphasize the importance of current profits rather than giving due weight to future discounted profits. On the other hand, those executives who are most likely to be able to make decisions involving such tradeoffs are precisely those who are also mostly recipients of stock options. Thus the negative suboptimizing effect of bonus schemes is not likely to be great.

Bonuses in British and French Companies

Bonuses appear to play a reasonably significant role in British managerial compensation. This is indicated by a stratified sample study of seventy-two nonnationalized industrial and commercial firms, chosen to represent the three hundred largest private companies or groups, and covering the situation in 1968. Data were compiled for two different groups: full-time members of the boards of directors who controlled less than 5 percent of their companies' common stock, and senior executives who were directly below the board level. For these two groups, bonuses paid in 1968 were as shown in Table 9.12.

Table 9.12   Bonuses in British Companies

Categories of Executives	Executives Receiving Bonuses as Proportion of All Executives (Percentage)	Average Bonus as Proportion of Base Salary (Percentage)		Number in Sample
		All Executives	Executives Receiving Bonus	
Full-time directors	25	6	24	1733
Senior executives	41	7	17	2962

Source: National Board for Prices and Incomes, Report No. 107, *Top Salaries in the Private Sector and Nationalized Industries* (Command Paper 3970, Her Majesty's Stationery Office, London, 1969), pp. 55-56.

During the previous three years, there had been a decline both in the proportion of directors who received bonuses and in the total amount of bonuses paid; but the amount of these declines was not specified.

Comparing the British and American situations, executive bonuses seem rather less important in Britain. For, in 1967, 63 percent of American manufacturing firms listed on the New York Stock Exchange had bonus schemes covering at least their three most highly paid executives. In 1967, those three executives who received any bonuses were awarded a median bonus of 37 percent of their base salary.[10]

A more significant difference between the two countries, however, is that stock option plans, as a result of tax laws, are virtually nonexistent in Great Britain.[11] Thus variable compensation as a whole is considerably less important in Britain than in the United States.

Turning to individual British companies for which I have data, two have executive bonus plans and one of these firms also has a stock option plan.

The first of these firms distributes bonuses to its managers down to the level immediately below that of the divisional directors. (In the division studied, these bonus recipients comprise about 1 percent of the total number of employees.) The bonuses vary from about 3 percent of salary as normal bonus to some 12 percent for those showing outstanding performance.

However, these bonuses—distributed at Christmas time—seem to represent more of a Christmas present than anything else. The amount is quite indepen-

[10]Fox, "Top Executive Compensation", pp. 13-14.
[11]National Board for Prices and Incomes, Report No. 107, *Top Salaries in the Private Sector and Nationalized Industries* (Command Paper 3970, Her Majesty's Stationery Office, London, 1969), pp. 7-8.

Table 9.13   Bonuses Paid in a British Company in a Good- and a Bad-Profit Year

	Percentage of Base Salary	
	Good Year	Bad Year
Eighty-six percent of bonus recipients (percentage of bonus depended exclusively upon recipient's managerial level)	8-28	2-6
Others, other than company directors	55	12
Company directors	72	15

dent of profits, whether those earned by the division or by the company as a whole. Furthermore, no systematic procedure is used to choose the high-bonus managers. There is no indication that these bonuses act as an incentive to managers: no one in the company except the divisional general manager mentioned them to me, and he only in response to a direct question.

The second firm pays substantially higher bonuses, and these go to 1.6 percent of the employees in the division studied.[12] Bonuses can reach a maximum of 85 percent of base salary for members of the board of directors of the main company, and the bonus rate is sufficient so as to be fairly meaningful for even the lowest managerial level of recipients. Bonuses depend exclusively upon the level of management of the bonus recipient and upon the profits earned by the division in that year. Bonuses paid in two consecutive years, one of which was very good and the other very bad, are shown in Table 9.13.

In addition, stock options are paid to the top 14 percent of the bonus recipients, excluding those who are members of the family owning most of the company stock. At the time of my interviewing, these stock options had been even more financially rewarding than the bonuses.

In looking at this company's incentive system, one should note that it differed sharply in two respects from those employed in the vast majority of the American firms studied. First, it took no account of individual performance in the preceding time period. Second, the bonus scheme, although not the stock options, was attached to divisional profit performance rather than

[12]Since company-headquarters employees and directors are counted as being in one division or another, this divisional figure is probably fairly representative of the company as a whole.

to corporate performance; thus the bonus scheme tended to encourage sub-optimizing at the divisional level.

In this company, approximately 0.3 percent of the total number of employees received substantial bonuses in good years. However, the existence of these bonuses and stock options seems due to the fact that the company is still heavily dominated by a single family. (Seventy percent of the company's directors were members of this family.) These rewards were intended to provide a stake in the company's well-being to the nonfamily members of top management. This explains the fact that variable compensation is pitched at a level which seems unusually high by British standards.

French executive bonuses are less important than British. It is true that it is customary to pay *cadres* a salary for a "thirteenth month"; but since this payment is dependent on the performance of neither the company, subunit, nor individual, it is not a bonus in any significant sense but rather simply a delayed salary award. Payments other than this appear to be negligible.

In addition, stock options are extremely rare—so much so that I did not hear of any in the companies in which I carried on interviews. For all practical purposes they can be ignored as a part of executive compensation.

Of the six French companies for which I have bonus data (see Appendix B to Chapter 9), there is little significant bonus variation in five of them; both the level of company profits and individual performance make for only slight differences in payments. Barring a very few exceptions in the sixth company, a 5 to 10 percent differential in total compensation is the maximum that occurs. The second company is the only one in which bonus matters: even here the genuine incentive situation has been limited to a single man in a family-owned company.

Two French vice-presidents explained very aptly the executive bonus situation. The first argued that a choice must be made between equity and stimulation; high and varying bonuses would be unfair both because of the difficulty of comparing individual managers and because a company's profit level in any year is so heavily determined by factors outside the control of management. In the choice between equity and financial stimulation, he said, French companies opt for equity.

The second stated his belief that upper management would refuse to accept the idea of sharp swings downward in their total compensation; thus substantial and varying bonuses are out of the question.

To sum up, the United States, Great Britain, and France appear to represent a continuum with regard to the importance of those bonuses that depend upon some combination of company financial success and of the evaluation of individual executive performance. But the continuum is probably a highly skewed one, with British and French industrial firms bunched together away from the American companies. If one considers the significance of total incentive payments, including stock options, the difference between the American and European firms is even more marked.

Bonuses in Soviet Enterprises

Bonuses for Soviet managerial personnel in industry appear extraordinary by international standards on a number of counts.

1.

They reach down to include all professional and managerial personnel. In fact, since 1959 it has been forbidden for bonuses awarded to top management at the enterprise level to be higher as a percentage of base salary than the average for white-collar workers as a whole in that enterprise.[13] This contrasts sharply with American practice under which apparently only about 1 percent of a company's labor force is included in bonus schemes.

2.

The proportion of total earnings which is paid through bonuses is quite high.

3.

Bonuses are heavily linked to specified performance indices of the enterprise or of its subunits, rather than being paid either automatically (as a delayed salary payment) or on the basis of the judgment of superiors.

4.

Bonus payments do in fact appear to vary sharply as a percentage of base salary for given individuals, and major movements downward as well as upward are commonly observed.

Table 9.14 illustrates the second point for Soviet industry as a whole over a long period. Since 1940, the proportion of earnings paid to professional and managerial personnel in the form of bonuses appears never to have fallen below 8 percent. Furthermore, for the period up to late 1959, bonuses played a more important role in the earnings of middle and upper management than in those of the total group of managerial and professional employees.[14] The decline shown by the table since 1959 seems to have been reversed after 1965 or 1966, when it is said to have become normal in those enterprises trans-

[13]See *Sotsialisticheskii Trud,* 1969, No. 7, pp. 141-142 and S. I. Shkurko, *Formy i sistemy zarabotnoi platy v promyshlennosti* (Ekonomika, Moscow, 1965), pp. 276-278.
[14]See Shkurko, *Formy i sistemy,* pp. 274-275.

Table 9.14 Bonuses as Proportion of Total Earnings for Managerial and Professional
Employees[a] of All Soviet Industry

Year	Percentage
1934 (September-October)	4.2
1940	11
1944	26
1947	33 (almost)
1950	15.8
1955	12.2
1958	13.9
1959 (March)	18.9
1960 (March)	8.3
1961	7.8
1964	8.9

[a]*Inzhenerno-tekhnicheskie rabotniki.* This group rose as a proportion of the total
industrial labor force from 8 percent in 1940 to 11 percent in 1966. (TsSU, *Trud v
SSSR,* Statistika, Moscow, 1966, p. 84.)
Sources:
1934: Sample of 84,160 individuals from five major branches of heavy industry.
TsUNKhU Gosplana SSSR, *Zarabotnaia plata inzhenerno-tekhnicheskikh rabotnikov i
sluzhashchikh v sentiabre-oktiabre 1934 g.* (Soiuzorguchet, Moscow, 1936), pp. 12 and
22-25.
1940, 1944: E. A. Lutokhina, *Oplata truda inzhenerno-tekhnicheskikh rabotnikov* (Ekonomika, Moscow, 1966), p. 92. While it is said that data are for the entire Soviet
economy, figures quoted in the same paragraph for 1955 and 1966 are identical to those
quoted elsewhere for industry alone; thus it may be assumed that the 1940 and 1944
figures also apply to all industry. In taking these percentages, I assume that total earnings
are equal to the total wage fund.
1947: J. S. Berliner, *Factory and Manager in the USSR* (Harvard University Press, Cambridge, Mass., 1957), pp. 30-31.
1950, 1955: V. I. Markov, *Planovoe regulirovanie zarabotnoi platy inzhenerno-tekhnicheskikh rabotnikov i sluzhashchikh* (Gosplanizdat, Moscow, 1961), p. 120.
1958, 1961: Lutokhina, *Oplata truda,* 77. Data are for all industry under the *sovnarkhozy.* The same assumption as to the wage fund is made as for 1940 and 1944.
1959, 1960: Shkurko, *Formi i sistemi zarabotnoi platy v promyshlennosti* (Ekonomika,
Moscow, 1965), p. 284. Data are for all industry under the *sovnarkhozy.*
1964: *Vestnik Statistiki,*1965, No. 10, p. 90.

Table 9.15 Bonuses of Managerial and Professional Personnel in Soviet Heavy Industry in September-October 1934

Personnel Covered	Bonuses as Percentage of Total Earnings	Percentage of Personnel receiving any Bonus	For those receiving bonuses, bonuses as percentage of total earnings	Sample Size (Number)
A. Those working at level of production departments within enterprises				
Total	5	18	26	63,131
Heads and assistant heads of departments	8	24	30	9,055
B. Those working at level of plant administration				
Total	2	7	26	21,092
Second in command of enterprise and top technological personnel	4	13	28	747
Grand total	4	15	26	84,223

Note: Both bonuses and earnings relate to a single month. Original data are given separately for each of five industrial branches, and have been combined through using weighted averages.
Source: TsUNKhU, *Zarabotnaia plata*, pp. 12 and 22-25.

ferred to a new premium system to set bonuses for plan fulfillment at three or more times the level established after early 1959.[15] (By late 1969, the overwhelming majority of managerial and professional employees in industry were working in such enterprises.)

Throughout Soviet history bonuses have generally been awarded on the basis of monthly results.[16] Thus, Table 9.15 is particularly revealing because it is based on the monthly figures. It shows that, at least in 1934, bonuses

[15]Iu. Artemov in *Voprosy Ekonomiki,* 1969, No. 5, pp. 33-34.
[16]In 1959, professional and managerial personnel working in the enterprise administration (as opposed to those in production departments) were transferred to a system under which they received bonuses according to quarterly results. In 1967, an option was given that they might be returned to a monthly bonus system. (*Sotsialisticheskii Trud,* 1968, No. 10, pp. 50-51.) No period longer than a quarter has ever been used, with the possible exception of years prior to the early 1930s.

Table 9.16 Variation in Earnings due to Bonuses for Soviet Managers

Total Variation in Earnings of Management (from the Average for that Enterprise over the Total Period Covered) as a Result of Bonuses	Quarters	
	Number	Percentage
By 20 percent or more	4	10
By 10-19 percent	9	22

were far from automatic for either top management or others, and that even the average bonus ran between 25 and 30 percent of total earnings for those receiving any bonus whatsoever in a given month; thus bonuses were of major financial significance to their recipients. These conditions pertained to a year when total bonuses as a proportion of earnings were only half as large as in any succeeding year for which data are available.

A second source provides data on a quarterly basis for nine Leningrad enterprises during 1960-1961.[17] A total of forty quarters are covered, ranging between four and six consecutive quarters for each enterprise. During this period, bonus rates for top management can be taken as roughly equivalent to the average in their enterprise for all professional and managerial employees. For the forty quarters, we find that in one-third of the quarters total managerial earnings varied, solely as a result of bonuses, by more than 10 percent from their average over the period as a whole (Table 9.16).

The remaining data (Table 9.17) consist of two separate samples of enterprises, with figures being presented only on an annual basis and covering six years. As one would expect, the variation in bonuses is less on an annual than on a quarterly or monthly basis, but it still appears to be substantial.

What is particularly interesting in these data is that bonus payments—and thus total earnings—move sharply downward as well as upward. No individual manager can feel reasonably sure of maintaining his earnings level throughout his tenure in post. Major fluctuations are common from month to month—or, at best, from quarter to quarter.

For individual enterprise managers, bonus payments have been substantial. Until 1959, it was not at all uncommon for bonus receipts to be equal to base salary. In 1958, top management personnel in enterprises under the Moscow City Council normally earned bonuses equal to 25 to 50 percent of their base

[17]B. M. Richman, *Soviet Management* (Prentice-Hall, Englewood Cliffs, N.J., 1965), p. 135. The data were collected by means of personal interviews.

Table 9.17 Change in Total Managerial Earnings in Twenty Soviet Enterprises as a Result of Bonuses (Annual Basis: Six Years)

	First Sample		Second Sample		Total	
	Number	Percentage	Number	Percentage	Number	Percentage
Coefficient of Variation						
Average of each enterprise's standard deviation/mean of annual earnings over the period		4.9		5.6		5.2
Variation of year's total earnings of management (from the average for that enterprise over the total period covered) as a result of bonuses						
Total number of years of variation by 8 percent or more	6	7.9	5	11.9	11	9.2
Enterprises affected by variations of 8 percent or more in one or more years	5	38.4	4	57.1	9	45.0
Sample size						
Number of enterprises	13		7		20	
Number of years	78		42		120	

Notes: The first sample is for the consecutive years 1959-1964. (N. S. Maslova, *Kollektivnye formy material'nogo stimulirovaniia v promyshlennosti SSSR*, Nauka, Moscow, 1966, p. 129. The second sample is for 1950, 1956, 1959-1962. (L. G. Lagvilava in L. S. Blakhman, ed., *Voprosy proizvoditel'nosti i oplaty truda v period stroitel'stva kommunisma*, Leningradskii universitet, Leningrad, 1964, p. 142.)

Table 9.17 (continued)

None of the enterprises in the two samples are the same.

Analysis of the 20 enterprises in the two samples does not suggest that any appreciable amount of the yearly variation for individual enterprises is caused by aggregative variation between the different years. In particular, 1960—as the first year of introduction of a new bonus system—might be expected to show bonuses sharply below those of 1959; indeed, this is suggested in the literature. But this did not occur in the enterprises studied here.

No analysis is presented as to deviation in bonuses between different enterprises because I do not know the grounds for selection of the enterprises in the two samples.

---

salaries.[18] Only since 1959 have peak bonuses been limited to 40 percent of base salary in most industries, and to 60 percent in the rest.

In the awarding of bonuses, fulfillment of the enterprise's plan for the period has generally been required for the payment of any bonuses, and the monetary difference between just missing and just achieving planned targets has been substantial for managerial personnel.[19] Thus in the middle 1950s, the director of one of the largest metal-fabricating enterprises received a 50 percent bonus in each month in which he reached the targeted output. In a minor plant of the same industry, the figure was 22 percent. In 1959, there was a sharp reduction in the bonuses paid for plan fulfillment alone: they were reduced to between 8 and 15 percent of base salary, depending upon the industry.[20] As late as 1968, the same rules applied to enterprises that had not yet been transferred to the new system of bonus awards.[21] But for the dominant group of enterprises that had been transferred, bonuses of 35 to 40 percent for plan fulfillment alone were quite common by 1969.[22]

It is true that evaluation of the individual's performance by his superior has always been relevant for the payment of bonuses: it is said that prior to 1959, half of the managerial and professional employees in enterprises (presumably mainly the junior managers) received bonuses that were determined by the enterprise director rather than by being firmly attached to specific measur-

[18]Granick, *The Red Executive,* p. 109.

[19]However, fulfillment of plan was not a critical point in the earning of bonuses in the iron and steel industry during the 1930s. See Shkurko, *Formy i sistemy,* p. 271. Even in 1959 in this industry, the difference between fulfilling the plan by 100 percent and by 99 percent was only 4 percent of total earnings for superintendents of production departments. See S. I. Shkurko in S. I. Shkurko, ed., *Sovershenstvovanie organizatsii zarabotnoi platy* (Research Institute of Labor, Moscow, 1961), pp. 70-71. This industry is the only one concerning which I have seen literature indicating that plan fulfillment had only a minor effect on bonus receipts.

[20]Shkurko, *Formy i sistemy,* pp. 278-279.

[21]I. D. Drize, G. A. Egiazarian, D. N. Karpukhin, *Fond material'nogo pooshchreniia* (Economika, Moscow, 1968), p. 28.

[22]Artemov in *Voprosy Ekonomiki,* pp. 33-34.

able indices of success.[23] But this subjective approach has always been frowned upon by Soviet authorities, and its use appears to have been reduced since 1959. As of 1968, individuals could have their bonuses increased or reduced by a maximum of only 25 percent of what had been "earned" according to the results of their production unit.[24] Bonuses could be eliminated completely only for specified offenses.

To sum up, Soviet bonuses appear to be at least as high as American. But payment of bonuses reaches much farther down into the ranks of lower management in Soviet enterprises. More significantly, bonus payments depend primarily upon the measured results of the individual subunit to which the manager is attached—in contrast with the American pattern in which, generally speaking, only the profits of the company as a whole are relevant. Most important of all, bonuses for even the director of the enterprise and for personnel in organizations supervising enterprises[25] are attached to very short-run results: monthly and quarterly. Unlike the usual situation in American companies, bonuses are paid out immediately rather than over a period of years. Thus the incentive system exercises its full force, since the manager feels the entire effect of variations, rather than receiving bonus payments which are an average of those earned over a long time span. Since there is nothing comparable to stock options in Soviet managerial rewards, the effect is to focus the attention of Soviet managers at all levels upon short-run results.

[23]Lutokhina, *Oplata truda*, p. 101.
[24]*Sotsialisticheskii Trud*, 1968, No. 7, pp. 132-133.
[25]F. Gorin in *Sotsialisticheskii Trud*, 1968, No. 7, pp. 20-24 and P. Tabalov in *Voprosy Ekonomiki*, 1969, No. 2, pp. 120-123.

Comparison of the Earnings
of Chief Executives in the
United States, Britain,
and France

Comparisons in Chapter 9 of the total monetary earnings of top management were limited to the lowest-salary category of top management. For the three western countries, I can add a comparison of the relative earnings of the single highest-paid executive in large companies (Table A.9A.1). As before, I shall compare these earnings (from salary plus bonus, but not including gains from stock options) with those of male manual workers in manufacturing in the case of Great Britain and France, and with all manual workers in manufacturing for the United States.

It is difficult, however, to draw conclusions from Table A.9A.1. In the case of the United States, a study of the compensation of the chief executives in the largest manufacturing companies showed that, if all sources of compensation had been taxed at the rate applied to salary and bonuses, and if the corporation had increased each form of compensation so as to provide the same posttax dollar amounts, salary and bonus would have constituted a mere 12 percent of total compensation during 1955-1963. Fifty-one percent would have been provided from stock options. Furthermore, the rank correlation

Table A. 9A. 1   Earnings of Highest-Paid Executives

Country	Average Earnings of Highest-Paid Executives	
	All manual workers = 100	Male manual workers = 100
United States:		
Median (1967)[a]	1891	
Great Britain:		
Mean (1967)[b]		1646
Median (1967)[c]		1385
France:		
Median (1967)[d]		1570

[a]Eighty-eight percent sample of the 762 manufacturing companies listed on the New York Stock Exchange. See Harland Fox, "Top Executive Compensation," in National Industrial Conference Board, *Studies in Personnel Policy*, No. 213 (N.Y., 1969), pp. 10-11.

[b]Eighty-seven percent response rate from a stratified sample of the private industrial and commercial firms among the three hundred largest companies in the private sector. See National Board for Prices and Incomes, Report No. 107, *Top Salaries in the Private Sector and Nationalized Industries* (Command Paper 3970, Her Majesty's Stationery Office, London, 1969), p. 51.

[c]Twenty-three percent response rate to questionnaires sent to the chief executives of the five hundred largest companies. See David J. Hall and G. Amado-Fischgrund, "Chief Executives in Britain," *European Business*, January 1969, pp. 28-29.

[d]Twenty-nine percent response rate to questionnaires sent to the chief executives of the five hundred largest companies. See D. Hall and H. C. de Bettignies, "The French Business Elite," *European Business*, October 1968, p. 10.

between salary and bonus and total compensation for the companies during the same period is only 0.6.[1] Thus a national comparison of chief executives which includes only salary and bonus is not particularly meaningful for the United States.

British and French comparisons are somewhat more meaningful, since stock options are unimportant in both countries. However, both the French and one British sample include nationalized firms and suffer from quite a poor response rate. Furthermore, since there is a fairly strong correlation between the size of a firm and the compensation of its chief executive officer, biases are built into our data toward a low French figure.

Nevertheless, it is interesting that no strong British-French differences emerge from this table. This provides weak confirmation for the vague impression which I have that British chief executives are quite highly paid relative to those immediately below them, and that the reverse is true of the French.

[1]Wilbur G. Lewellen, *Executive Compensation in Large Industrial Corporations* (National Bureau of Economic Research, New York, 1968), pp. 147 and 238. The sample includes fifty of the largest seventy-eight companies.

Bonus data are available for six French companies. In the first, upper and upper-middle management personnel (about 0.6 percent of the total number of employees) earn a bonus that is dependent upon their company grade, their seniority in the grade, and the profit declared for tax purposes to the government. In fact, however, the declared profits have been kept at a rather stable level from year to year, and thus the bonus was described as having in practice remained equal to the customary thirteenth-month salary with some allowance for seniority.

It is interesting that this company also has a bonus pot for manual workers and ordinary white-collar employees, and that this is formed as a share of declared profits in exactly the same fashion as is the case for that of top executives. The only difference between the two bonus systems is that the distribution of bonus among nonmanagers is dependent solely upon seniority, while for those in upper-middle management and above it is also dependent upon the managerial level.

The second company, a family-owned firm, provides a bonus only for its top manager. He is a nonfamily member, and the bonus is intended to give him a significant stake in the fortunes of the company. His bonus is attached to the profits earned by the firm in the previous year, these profits being defined contractually to depart in specified ways from the profit declared for purposes of company income tax. I have data as to his bonus award only for one quite prosperous year: it came to 35 percent of his base salary. There is no reason to doubt that bonus fluctuated considerably between years.

The third company, in theory, pays its *cadres* (9 percent of the labor force) a bonus of between one and two months' salary. The amount is not linked in any mathematical fashion to the earnings of the firm or to any other indicator of its success; no bonus pot is created, although in fact bonuses were reduced in a financially disastrous year. Presumably, the normal bonus has been one month's salary, i.e., 8.3 percent. A 5 percent bonus is paid out in monthly additions to salary, this being considered as an advance on the year's annual bonus payment.

The year before that of my final interviews was the first in which there was a large differential in the bonuses among different *cadres*—the differences in bonus percentage depending entirely upon managerial evaluation of the individual rather than upon his rank in the company. The reason for the differentiation in this year was partially the financial pressure to utilize all economies available to the company; thus the differentiation took the form of reducing the bonus received by some *cadres,* rather than of increasing that received by others. The differentiation was also motivated by the need of the company to reduce the numbers of its *cadres,* and the resultant top management desire to encourage resignations of the less desirable members.

In this extreme year, minimum bonus received was the amount advanced, i.e., 5 percent of salary. Normal bonus was 8.3 percent, and some received the full two months' supplement which was the maximum possible (16.7 percent). Thus the difference in bonus even in this year reached a maximum of only 12 percent of base salary between those being encouraged to resign and those who were most highly regarded.

In the fourth firm, all employees receive a bonus of 2 to 4 percent, which is based on a quite explicit and publicized formula expressing the productivity attained in the company as a whole, and another 2 percent or so depending on the company profits declared for tax purposes. An additional bonus is paid to all middle and senior *cadres* (6 percent of the company's total personnel).

The additional bonus for managerial personnel increases as a proportion of base salary; starting at 3 percent, it mounts to 12 percent for the top 0.5 percent of total personnel. Of the total amount set aside for these managerial bonuses, 20 percent is distributed according to individual merit. Thus, in fact, total bonus money available for distribution according to merit constitutes only 1.5 percent of the base salary of all managers.

The bonus is paid out of a bonus pot that is linked to the company's sales. However, the formula used is such as to lead to very little variation; over a period of years, the normal bonus for the top executives moved within the narrow range of 11.9 to 14.2 percent of base salary, and the same proportions held for the lower managers. It can be seen that neither individual merit nor company performance has had much of an effect upon bonus awards.

Company vice-presidents (*directeurs*) are paid on a different basis, their bonus pot being linked to the net profits declared for tax purposes. As in the first company, the pot has grown gradually but consistently. In one year, there was a reduction in the declared profits. However, as the personnel director of the company told me, it was inconceivable that the bonus pot for the vice-presidents should decline: the board of directors thus provided them with a "present" so that each would get the previous year's bonus.

In the fifth company, all *cadres* receive a salary supplement of a thirteenth month's pay. In addition, each subunit of the company receives a bonus pot equal to a given proportion of its managerial salaries; this percentage appears to be identical for all subunits and to be independent of the company's financial performance during the previous year.

The bonus pot is allocated among all *cadres* depending upon the evaluation of individuals; no more than 75 percent of the *cadres* in any subunit are permitted to receive any part of this bonus. For those participating in it, the average share is 4 to 5 percent of base salary; exceptional individuals receive no more than 10 percent.

In the sixth and last company, all *cadres* receive an annual supplemental percentage of base salary which varies hardly at all between individuals; while it may be raised very slightly for a given individual in order to reward particularly meritorious service, it would never be lowered. Bonuses, however, are reserved for the upper 11 percent of the *cadres* who constitute 1 percent of the total company labor force.

Of this upper managerial group eligible for the bonus, only some 5 percent receive it annually. Yet even for this small group of particularly meritorious managers, bonus payments have normally been only 5 to 10 percent of their annual earnings; in extreme cases, they might run as high as 15 or even 20 percent. Once such a bonus is given, it is incorporated as part of the manager's base salary for the coming year; thus no possibility of reduction in total compensation arises.

This chapter constitutes a synthesis of the materials presented in Chapters 7 and 8, although new information will also be provided. However, no attempt will be made here to relate the data concerning international differences in managerial education and careers to the behavior of managers, since this was done in Chapter 3.

The materials of Chapters 7 and 8 can be discussed in terms of the problem facing industrial organizations in all countries: how to select the personnel to man the various levels of managerial posts. The problem is inherently difficult for three reasons, all of which revolve around the grave objections to promoting people simply on the basis of their job records.

The first objection is that, with the exception of those showing clearly unsatisfactory performance, it is very difficult to evaluate the performance of managers, particularly those who have gone beyond the first levels. It is true that top management can often establish targets (i.e., plans) for the various subunits of the enterprise, and judge managers according to the performance of their subunits measured against these targets. But this procedure not only raises the issue of whether the various plans were in fact equally difficult to achieve under the conditions which prevailed during the relevant time period, but it also poses the problem of how to deal with those aspects of managerial performance which are not incorporated into plans.

For example, much of a sales manager's effort may have gone into the development and implementation of a sales strategy that is expected to have most of its effect in periods following the one-year time span for which the manager's record is to be evaluated. There is no way to judge these efforts objectively before their results have been achieved; yet clearly they cannot be ignored in the evaluation of the manager's accomplishments.

One American executive, in telling me of his own standards for evaluating the marketing managers under him, gave major importance to the question of whether the manager perceived which were his key problems and developed fruitful strategies for handling them. Even if he himself thought that the manager's objectives or strategy were poorly chosen, he believed in decentralization sufficiently so that—at least in theory—he would allow the manager to pursue his own course. However, unless the results proved that the manager had in fact been correct, the manager's poor choices (as the executive conceived them to be) would properly and inevitably go into the evaluation of the manager's performance. Since formal evaluations are made annually in this company, and in this short period of time many of the marketing objectives and strategies could not possibly bear fruit, a manager would necessarily be judged to a considerable degree on the basis of whether his concepts and prejudices coincided with those of his superior. It is no wonder that in this company a man would receive high performance ratings under one superior, only to see his performance ratings in the same post turn strongly negative when there was a change in the man holding the post above him.

In view of the problems involved in evaluation of performance, one can readily sympathize with the quip of the personnel head of one giant American company: that evaluations tell more about the person doing the evaluating than about the man being evaluated. In fact, as we shall see later in this chapter, a study of one American company showed a complete lack of correlation between a manager's performance record and his promotion record immediately thereafter. In a second American firm, there was very little or no correlation between a manager's performance rating and his readiness-for-advancement rating.

The second and even more serious objection to promotion on the basis of job record is that success in positions at higher managerial levels often rests primarily upon the possession of capabilities and personality traits that are largely irrelevant at lower levels, and which may even detract from the quality of performance there. Obviously, however, job performance is a useful criterion for promotion only to the degree that it is a good predictor of performance in the new position. Doubtless it is the lack of confidence in the validity of job performance as such a predictor that has led to widespread use of "potential" ratings for management; these are given, at least in theory, quite independently of performance ratings. Without some such alternative standard, a company would be completely at the mercy of Peter's law of promotion to the level of one's incompetence.[1]

The third objection is the considerable pressure existing in large organizations for the early selection of golden-haired boys. This is the case for two reasons. On the one hand, there is the fear that if potential executives are not given responsibility early and placed in positions providing opportunities for administrative creativity, they will have trained out of them the capacity needed for successful performance in higher posts. Second, a wide managerial experience at varying levels and with exposure to a variety of functions and organizational subdivisions can be an invaluable background for a senior executive. However, this can scarcely be provided to any manager unless he moves rapidly through the lower ranks. As precareer formal education has lengthened, and as the tendency has grown for the cutting short of even the

[1]L. J. Peter and R. Hull, *The Peter Principle* (William Morrow, New York, 1969).

chief executive's career at the age of sixty-five, the pressure has increased for very rapid advancement of those who are serious potential candidates for upper management. The larger the organization, and thus the more numerous the levels of management to pass through, the greater is such pressure.

But this early selection of managers destined for a fast track considerably increases the difficulty of promotion on the basis of job records. First, to the extent that there is early selection, it is only an exceptional job record during the first five or, at most, ten years which can be used for selection purposes— and it is precisely during this period that a manager is likely to be occupying posts whose requirements are most radically different from those of senior management. Second, and even more important, job change is likely to be so rapid that a man does not remain in a single post long enough to allow for a serious evaluation of his performance. Finally, many of the posts a man will be given are intended largely to prepare him for further advancement; competent but not really superior performance is all that can be expected from someone placed in charge of managing a function to which he has not previously been exposed. Certainly this is the pattern shown in Chapter 8 by many of the career paths of individual managers in large American firms.

Given these problems in depending upon job records, it seems inevitable that potential, however this may be evaluated by senior management, should be a major career determinant. In all four countries that we have examined, external indications of such potential appear to play a role. Formal education and social class in general, and Party status in the case of the Soviet Union, are obvious candidates. All play their part in reducing the number of potential candidates for middle and upper executive posts to manageable proportions.[2]

It is the French who take furthest the notion of preselection by external indicators: in their case, by success in formal education. Of the top executives of the very large firms in prestigious French industries in 1963, 42 percent were graduates of a single *grande école* (Polytechnique) that had graduated only 0.07 percent of the total French male population over the age of twenty-two. Seventy-one percent of these top executives had graduated from one of six *grandes écoles* or had had very prominent fathers. When one

[2]Professor J. Boddewyn has suggested an additional reason for the importance of these various external indicators of potential: that they appeal to "the eternally feudal in man." These status characteristics, once obtained by an individual, can never be taken away from him; performance, on the other hand, is subject to continuous reevaluation. Top managers in a company that places too high an emphasis on performance face the danger that this criterion may be applied to themselves as well.

considers the importance of family-dominated firms among these companies, and the extreme selectivity on academic grounds of these *grandes écoles,* this 71 percent figure is truly amazing. Of all the *polytechniciens* working in industry whose class ranking made them most highly eligible for top executive posts, 21 percent (of the appropriate age group) held one of the top 1.5 posts in one of the five hundred largest industrial companies in France. My examination of the education of managers in different hierarchical levels in individual large French industrial companies confirmed this picture of extreme selectivity on educational grounds.

One may question, as many French do, the degree to which academic achievement prior to the age of twenty is a good proxy for managerial potential, and whether it is sensible to allow these early nonmanagerial achievements to predetermine so heavily future managerial careers. In my opinion, however, a strong case can be made for the system. If one accepts the view that some type of early selection of serious candidates for top management is valuable in that it permits them to receive an on-the-job training which otherwise could not be made available, and if one also accepts the position that the possibilities for reasonable evaluation according to job performance are very limited, then one is forced into also holding that choice must be made according to some criterion of "managerial potential."

Yet the ability of companies to measure such potential is extremely limited. In Germany, there is considerable reliance upon graphology as such a measurement device.[3] Psychological testing of managerial recruits is employed in a few American companies, but the results still appear to be primarily experimental. In any case, they are not regarded as sufficiently reliable to replace normal methods of evaluating potential, despite the fact that the weaknesses of the customary evaluations are fully recognized.[4] The French method at least screens for a combination of a high degree of intelligence and ability to work intensively for long hours and over long periods at mentally taxing tasks, and for the willingness to apply these capacities to problems set by others. These constitute a set of characteristics that are far from the worst proxy for managerial potential, if such a proxy is indeed necessary.

The Americans and Russians are intermediate between the French and the British. It is true that higher education is the rule among industrial managers

[3]David Granick, *The European Executive* (Doubleday, Garden City, N. Y., 1962), Chapter 23.
[4]Cf. the articles on the Standard Oil Company of New Jersey by Harry Laurent and Harry D. Kolb in John A. Myers, ed., *Predicting Managerial Success* (Foundation for Research on Human Behavior, Ann Arbor, 1968).

in these two countries, particularly in the larger enterprises, and that possession of a degree clearly distinguishes between industrial managers and the mass of the male population. In the United States in the 1950s and 1960s, some eight to twelve times the proportion of top executives in large corporations had college degrees as was the case for all American males of their generation; doubtless the differential was even greater in large enterprises in the Soviet Union. Here is a degree of preselection which is significant. Further differentiation among degree holders according to whether they graduated from a prestige institution is also relevant in the United States. In seven samples, some 16 to 32 percent of those top executives in large companies who had attended any college had done their undergraduate work at one of three schools. The alumni of these three colleges reached such posts in proportions somewhere between 3.1 and 6.2 times that of alumni of American colleges as a whole. Yet, when all is said and done, the differentials in education between lower management and senior executives in American and Russian industrial organizations are a far cry from that which exists in French industry. Compared to the French, American and Soviet enterprises constitute relatively open organizations; a comparatively large share of the adult male population, and a much higher share of junior management personnel, have the type of education (and Party status in the case of the USSR) which leaves open the route to higher management positions.

Curiously, British industry is more open than that of any of the other three countries. Combining academic and social standards, only 38 percent of the upper managers in one good-sized sample were either university graduates or alumni of public schools. British industry is still full of early school leavers: in four samples of middle and upper managers, the average age at which current managers began work was eighteen to nineteen. Here, alone of the four countries, the man without higher education or family connections is still not weeded out at the start of the managerial-career race.

Clearly this peculiarity of British industry is not due to the openness of British society as a whole. Rather, it is a reflection of the lower social and economic status of industrial managerial careers in Britain than in the other countries, and the resultant difficulty of recruiting those with an elitist education into British industry. The situation would be entirely different if we were to look, for example, at merchant banking. Certainly British industry is changing in the direction of its American and Soviet counterparts, but it still stands in a world apart. Thus British industrial organizations, far more than those of other countries, are faced with a massive task of managerial selection that begins only after the entry into business life of the would-be managers.

Let me now turn to managerial careers, exploring through this medium how top management in different countries handles the problem of selecting middle and prospective top managers and how it prepares them for their future roles through on-the-job training. Given the differences in the emphasis placed upon precareer qualifications, one would expect national differences in career patterns as well.

Looking first at intercompany mobility of managers, one should not be surprised to see a high rate of such mobility between corporations in which promotion is relatively open. Large numbers of managers are qualified for consideration for promotion; when it is not forthcoming rapidly enough in one firm, transfer to another company is a natural response. Furthermore, a manager who may be held back from rapid promotion in one company because he does not fit in well with that company's "personality" and policies may do very well in another corporation with a different personality.

I have complete data for one large American chemical company as to the total number of managers and professionals (i.e., exempt personnel) who left the company during each year of a two-year period. Table 10.1 shows that 11 percent of the managerial staff left annually, very few because of retirement; even for those within the bonus level of management (1 percent of the labor force), the turnover rate was 8 percent. Since the managerial staff grew by 7 percent during these two years, it was not labor force contraction that caused these departures.

I do not have similar turnover data for British firms, but some figures do exist showing that change of companies is quite frequent for British managers

Table 10.1 Outward Mobility of Managers and Professionals in a Large American Chemical Company

Level (In Ascending Order)	Percentage of company's total labor force	Percentage Leaving Company, Annual Average	
		Total	Retirements only
1	6.2	9.6	0.9
2	6.9	14.0	0.6
3	3.7	10.0	0.5
4	2.2	7.9	0.8
5	1.3	8.1	0.4
Total[a]	22.4	11.2	0.7

[a]The total includes those who were not classified by level, but are reported to have been fairly randomly distributed among the five levels.

as well. Table 8.17 indicates that, although the average age at which the sample managers began work was eighteen to nineteen years, the average age at which they joined their present company was twenty-six to thirty; in fact, 25 to 40 percent joined after the age of thirty-five. In contrast, the composite average age of joining the company for the managers in the American Samples 1 and 2 is thirty-one years; 13 percent joined after the age of thirty-five.[5] In light of the fact that British managers must have begun work when they were at least three to four years younger than their American counterparts, this would suggest that British managerial turnover between companies is even greater than the American after the first few years of the individual's total career.

One would predict a much slower intercompany mobility of French *cadres* because promotion is so heavily predetermined by educational characteristics. Far more than in the United States or Britain, a manager can look forward to significant promotion or to career stagnation on the basis of things that happened to him prior to his ever beginning his working life. Particularly for that vast majority who are not graduates of the *grandes écoles,* promotion prospects are slim wherever they may work. Thus there is little point in a rapid transfer rate, particularly after the first few years when a man in any country may well welcome change simply for the sake of experience.

Figures as to the proportion of *cadres* leaving the company are available for two entire French companies and for one very large plant of a third firm (Table 10.2). Clearly, large French industrial firms appear to enjoy much greater stability within their managerial staffs than do American or British companies. The validity of this phenomenon is supported by the folklore in managerial circles in the three countries.

The same pattern of much higher job mobility in the open-promotion societies is similarly found in job changes within the organization. However, the USSR appears to be an exception to this rule.

The American and British sample data are extremely similar with regard to brevity of tenure in a single post. For middle and top managers in large companies, the average period spent in a single major post is as shown in Table 10.3.

---

[5]In case of mergers or takeovers, the American average is computed by using the age at which the manager joined the original company which was later merged with the present one. The same is true for Sample 4 and for at least most of the executives in Sample 2 of the British firms in Table 8.17; no information is available with regard to Sample 9. It would not appear that a distinction in methodology is responsible for the national differences.

Table 10.2   Outward Mobility of *Cadres* in French Companies

Company	Percentage of Total Labor Force in the Managerial Levels	Percentage of Managers Leaving Company, Annual Average		Period Covered by the Data (Years)
		Total	Retired or Died	
A	4.3	7.1	...	1.25[a]
B	8.2	3.2[b]	1.0	4
C (plant)	2.9	2.7[b]	1.4	5

[a]Average of two such periods.
[b]These annual averages are somewhat biased downward because the data available show only the proportion of *cadres* who were there in a given year and who left over a four-year and five-year period, respectively.

Table 10.3   Tenure in Single Posts: American and British Companies

Time in Post	American Companies		British Companies	
	Percentage	Number	Percentage	Number
All executives[a]				
Less than five years	85		83	
More than ten years	4		4	
Sample size		411		70
Plant managers[b]				
Less than five years	80		80	
Average number of years		3.6[c]		3.0
Sample size		94		15

[a]For the American companies, data relate to the number of years in which specified positions were held throughout the career in the company. Positions range from plant manager and regional sales manager through chairman of the board. Executives are those in the American Samples 1 and 2 of Chapter 8.
For the British companies, data relate to the number of years in which the current post was held by middle and top executives in large companies. Executives are those in the British Samples 2 and 7 of Chapter 8.
[b]The American companies' source and treatment is the same as above. For the British companies, the treatment is the same as that stated above, but the data are taken from only two companies.
[c]However, a figure of "just under five years" was obtained from a different sample of 414 plant managers of technically advanced factories with a high capital base in large manufacturing concerns. (Paul W. Hamelman, "Career Development Patterns of Plant Managers," *Industrial Management Review,* Fall 1966, pp. 79-80.)

Some skepticism may properly be indicated as to the brevity of tenure in post shown by the British sample. For one thing, the numbers of plant managers are fairly small. Second, conversations with a rather broad group of British managers reveal the impression of these interviewees that the speed of turnover shown by this sample is somewhat unrepresentative of large British companies as a whole.[6] Nevertheless, it would seem that British managerial turnover rates cannot be too much below the level indicated by the American rates.

French turnover rates between posts are markedly different. From data available for three companies, I found that one firm had 62 percent of its managers in the same post for five years or more and 54 percent of its higher managers in post for eight years or more. In a second company, higher managers had averaged eight years in each of their posts within the company. Only in one plant of a third company—a plant whose labor force doubled over the period studied—was the percentage of management in the same post for five years relatively low (37 percent), and even here it was twice as high as the proportion in the British samples.

How is this difference between the Anglo-American and French patterns to be explained? It may be posited that it is due to the differing requirements for the evaluation of managers which exist in open-promotion and in closed-promotion societies.

Where managers are to be promoted upon evaluation of their performance and potential as demonstrated by work within the company, the problem of judgment is eased if many individuals can share in this evaluation. The simplest way to assure this is to see that jobs are changed sufficiently frequently so that most managers have many different superiors over relatively brief periods of time. Two top personnel men in one large American oil company, who expressed considerable doubt about the validity of evaluations, stated this as an explicit reason for rapid managerial movement in their firm.

The second advantage of a system of rapid job movement for an open-promotion society is that each step-up in job level is relatively slight. Since

[6]A comparison of sixty English and one hundred five American managers in matched subunits of manufacturing enterprises showed the English to have a statistically significant 20 percent longer period in positions than the Americans. However, it is not clear whether this distinction is a product of sample inadequacy resulting from errors in design. (See J. H. K. Inkson, J. P. Schwitter, D. C. Pheysey, and D. J. Hickson, "A Comparison of Organizational Structure and Managerial Roles: Ohio, U.S.A., and the Midlands, England," *The Journal of Management Studies,* October 1970, pp. 356 and 360.)

the personal qualities needed for successful performance are different at varying managerial levels, this system of frequent but gradual promotions implies a greater probable relationship between the rating on one job and performance in the next than would be true if moves were fewer and the career step function correspondingly larger. In addition, a system of gradual promotions leaves a maximum of potential candidates for any higher position; this is because it is easier to skip a candidate over even a number of small steps than over one or two giant ones, particularly when the promotion pattern is not too systematized.

However, this Anglo-American pattern would seem to have its own two inherent disadvantages. The first is that a manager who is given a low evaluation grade at any of the multitude of career steps through which he must pass is unlikely to recover from this sufficiently rapidly to remain in the promotion race for a top management post. Now a manager with a strong personality and willingness to take sensible risks is quite likely either to antagonize one of his many immediate superiors or to fail in one of his risk ventures, thus running the serious danger of receiving a black mark. In this way, many of those with the greatest potential for creative top management may be weeded out by the selection process. This problem is handled differently by the British and American career evaluation systems, as shall be seen later.

The second disadvantage is that there are obvious costs to the company in rapid turnover of occupants of managerial posts. Since a large portion of managers' careers is of necessity spent in on-the-job training in their current posts, tasks are likely to be performed less effectively than if there were greater continuity of personnel.

The French pattern avoids these problems, since evaluation by many different managers is much less necessary in French companies. To the degree that there has been preselection of viable candidates both for middle and top management at the moment of entrance into the firm—preselection on the basis of education—continual review is less important. Thus French managers can be left much longer in each post.

In this regard, it is interesting to report a theme which I often heard repeated by French lower and middle managers who had visited the United States. They felt that, in comparison with French managers at the same organizational level, their American colleagues had highly specialized responsibilities and deeper—but much narrower—knowledge of their jobs.

This reportedly greater subdivision of lower and middle management tasks in the United States than in France is quite in line with the sort of division of labor which can make it possible for American managers to change posts frequently and yet remain effective. Just as with manual workers, there are advantages in reducing the cost of on-the-job training—this cost for a manager consisting of the loss of effectiveness in the operations of his subunit until the manager becomes familiar with the peculiarities of his new post; such reduction of cost is accomplished through job simplification. At the same time, the disadvantages of specialized knowledge without an awareness of the needs of surrounding functions is counteracted in the American environment by three phenomena: by the providing of a good deal of information concerning the division and company generally, by the organization of considerable lateral cooperation with other managers in other functions, and by the transfer of managers among functions and administrative levels of the company.

For French managers, none of these phenomena exist. Thus, in order for them to carry out their jobs properly, their positions must be defined more broadly than seems typical in American organizations. Nor are the costs of such broad definition exorbitant, since the losses from on-the-job training can be amortized over a relatively lengthy time period. Given a social environment in which access to information is restricted and in which lateral cooperation is limited, the French pattern is not a bad solution to the problems of managerial organization.

The explanation offered for the difference in mobility between posts in the United States and Britain on the one hand and France on the other would lead one to expect that Soviet job mobility would be quite rapid. For the Soviet is another open-promotion society.

Data of the 1930s for the USSR are quite in line with my hypothesis; in fact, job mobility then seems to have been even more rapid than American mobility today. But the early and middle 1960s presented a quite different picture. Fifty-two percent of Hough's sample of directors of important enterprises had held their post for more than five years, a figure that seems closer to the French than to the Anglo-American pattern. Similarly, a Soviet study of junior and middle management in one enterprise showed that 55 percent had been in the same position for more than five years. This lengthy tenure in recent times departs radically from what one would have predicted.

How is this to be explained? The primary explanation would appear to be the political purges of the 1930s and the absence of major purges since then.

As a result of the elimination of the older generation, the average age of the branch heads of industry and construction in June 1941 was forty. Twenty-four years later, the average date of birth had increased by only eight years. Essentially the same generation had remained in office for a quarter of a century. At lower levels such as that of factory director, the average age was presumably still lower in 1941; thus continuity in office at these levels might be expected to last even longer. The channels of promotion have been thoroughly clogged, and job mobility has thus been exceedingly low. One would expect this generational factor to disappear during the 1970s; indeed, some of the Russians with whom I spoke in 1967 reported a recent speeding up of job turnover at middle-management levels.

A second factor is probably the nature of the education of Soviet managers, which takes place in institutes specializing in engineering as applied to specific narrowly defined industries. As a result, the restrictions on mobility between industries is probably greater than in other countries. This may act as a serious constraint on the Soviet counterpart of the mobility between companies which is so prominent in Britain and in the United States.

The third factor is the narrowness of promotion possibilities above the level of the enterprise, i.e., in what is comparable to headquarters in capitalist firms. Positions of responsibility are few here, and responsible managers at the enterprise level seldom move to this organizational level except either to dead-end jobs or, alternatively, to one of the very few existing posts of minister, deputy minister or places immediately below. There is none of the plenitude of responsible positions in Soviet ministries which we find in American corporate headquarters, nor are promising young Soviet managers commonly sent there on interim tours of duty. The result is further clogging of the promotion channels.

Some relief is found in the transfer of Soviet industrial managers out of industry per se, and particularly to the Communist Party hierarchy. However, according to Jerry Hough, who has looked into this matter more than anyone else, it would seem that the transfers are primarily of managers who are not terribly successful in industry itself—rather than of those whose career prospects appear the most promising.

The first two factors preventing rapid job mobility are peculiar to the Soviet Union. But the third is probably also typical of large British companies, although I have no systematic information on this subject. The compensating feature in Britain, which does not seem to exist in the Soviet Union, is heavy interenterprise mobility.

Since it is American and British industry that alone share the common feature of high job mobility, it is important to see what the companies do with it. That there is plenty of room for maneuver is indicated by the fact that only 20 percent of the middle and upper American executives in our sample had averaged more than three years per post in their current company since they had reached the age of thirty-five.

The first major difference is with regard to the degree to which an executive changes functions during his career. British managers tend to remain in the same function throughout; when functions are divided up in a fourfold to sixfold classification system, 60 to 89 percent of the sample managers were seen never to have changed function.[7] This degree of functional change probably differs little from that of the French, despite the fact that the top French executives typically join their company four to six years later than do their British counterparts and change jobs within the firm much less frequently.

In contrast, using a fourteenfold classification system, 45 percent of the American executives who had been in their company for more than ten years had worked in at least three different functions.[8] In another study of 414 plant managers in technically advanced factories of large manufacturing companies, only 19 percent of the plant managers were found to have spent their entire career within the company in factory operations. (An eight-way division of functions was used here.) Of these plant managers, 39 percent came to the post directly from another function.[9]

The second major difference is with regard to movement among different organizational units within the company. Defining each division as composed of two such units (field and divisional headquarters), 44 percent of all American executives who had served in their company for more than twenty years had worked in four or more units. Furthermore, when we divide the company into three organizational levels (field, divisional headquarters, and corporate headquarters), 40 percent of the total number of moves between organiza-

[7]See Table 8.17. When a classification system much finer than that used for American managers is employed, the percentages are still 30 and 54—depending upon the level of management finally attained.
[8]It is unfortunate for purposes of comparison that the American and British statistics are compiled on a different basis. However, detailed examination of the functions involved in the American case shows that the national distinction would hold up if a similar classificatory system were used.
[9]P. W. Hamelman, "Career Development Patterns of Plant Managers," *Industrial Management Review,* Fall 1966, p. 84.

tional levels was downward; relatively few of these "downward" moves should be regarded as demotions or sidetracking of careers.

Thus normal career seasoning of American executives includes substantial functional change, substantial interdivisional change, and substantial movement in both directions between organizational levels. None of the three appears to apply to the British managers, any more than to the French or Russian.[10]

This American pattern of seasoning can be viewed as making three quite different kinds of contributions toward the selection of superior top executives. The first is an on-the-job training contribution: American executives acquire a breadth of experience (cross-functional, cross-unit, and cross-organizational level) which seems unparalleled elsewhere, and which one would expect to prove highly useful both in promoting fruitful cooperation with executives in other functions or units and in making for improved understanding of the several functions and units which they may later supervise.

The second is a socialization contribution. The literature of American industrial sociology is filled with accounts of conflict between different functions: sales with manufacturing, manufacturing with engineering, manufacturing and engineering with research and development, and the like. Yet cooperation between the executives in each of these functions, as well as between those at different organizational levels, is greatly striven for in American practice. Presumably the transfers between functions, units, and levels helps to reduce the parochialism of executives and so to lessen the strains preventing fruitful cooperation.[11]

The third contribution is in the selection process itself. The manager cannot make a successful career simply by pleasing his superior. Rather, he is operating in a marketplace that comprises all of the company's functions and organization units, and repeatedly throughout his career he must sell his abilities there. He does this in two ways: first and most important, through his contacts with other functions and company units both in committees and in

[10]Unfortunately, it has not been possible to collect any statistical data concerning interunit movement for countries other than the United States. However, general impressions leave little doubt as to the matter. The only modification of the statement in the text which is needed is with regard to the existence of interfunctional movement in the Soviet Union; while I have seen no indication of its widespread existence, I have no serious knowledge of the matter.

[11]The amount of time spent in secondary functions is very great: of executives who had been in their company for more than twenty years, 40 percent had worked in such functions for over ten years. Three-quarters of the same group of executives had worked consecutively within the same organizational unit for less than ten years.

daily cooperation. Second, he does it by developing a record—and not solely or even necessarily with his immediate superior—for success in a variety of business roles. In all of this, divisional and, even more, corporate headquarters play a leading role. It is the headquarters staff that is particularly involved in interfunctional and interunit relations, and thus inevitably in evaluation of the field managers with whom it comes into contact. It is this staff that is most frequently called upon for recommendations as to managerial candidates for posts in other functions and units. Finally, it is during the periods when a manager is himself assigned to headquarters that he can be most closely observed by the executives with power over his career. It is true that in some companies the personnel function is particularly important in guiding the careers of at least some particularly promising junior and middle managers, but managers in other staff functions almost always also have a weighty part to play.

It is this "marketplace" aspect of the large American corporation which goes far to reduce the danger that a risk-taking manager, or one with a strong personality, will be stopped in his career because of antagonizing one of the many immediate superiors encountered in the process of his movement upwards. The evaluation by the immediate superior just does not seem to be that important except, perhaps, for the most junior people.

The apparent unimportance of the opinion of the immediate superior can be shown statistically for the one large company of Sample 3. Here, managerial and professional employees at all levels are rated in a one-to-five classification system both for their job performance and for their potential for higher posts. Both ratings are given by the man's immediate superior, and are reviewed by his superior. The fact that there is no pressure to rate a manager if either he or the rater has been in his post for too short a time to permit of a judgment is shown by the fact that 46 percent of our sample were not rated for performance, and 52 percent were not rated for potential.

Taking as the sample all managerial and professional employees in this company who were either promoted or who changed subunits within a two-year period, the correlation was found between ratings immediately prior to the first move and the number of managerial levels advanced within the company during the two years. Since it seemed likely that the average number of levels advanced might vary depending on the original managerial level, this level was also introduced into the regression equation. Finally, since the function in which the manager originally worked might be relevant, this was inserted into one form of the regression equation as a dummy variable. After eliminating all those managers who either did not have original ratings or whose managerial level was unclassified either at the beginning or the end of the period, a sample of between seven hundred fifty and fifteen hundred were left.[12]

The striking result is that there was a zero (insignificantly negative) partial correlation between both the performance and potential ratings and the number of managerial levels advanced. The simple correlation ratios were also nonpositive. The only statistically significant relationship indicated was between the performance and potential ratings themselves.

Nor was this due to the fact that the raters did not take their task seriously and that they tended to give everyone the same rating. To the contrary, the rankings (particularly for potential) were surprisingly well distributed. This can be seen from the distribution of all those who were rated (Table 10.4).

In this company, then, there was absolutely no relationship between the evaluation of a manager by his immediate superior (as shown by the ratings given him) and the pace of the manager's advancement. Clearly, promotion was being determined by others than the immediate superior, and without any reference to the immediate superior's judgment.[13]

Doubtless, we have chanced upon a strange case in this company; in most corporations, one would expect some positive relationship between a man's rate of advancement and his evaluation by his immediate superior. But the data for this company (the only data available) do suggest that such a correlation is probably not too high.

---

[12]The figure is stated within this range so as to forestall identification of the company.
[13]Two objections might be made to this conclusion. The first is that we are dealing almost entirely with managers who were promoted (87 percent of our sample), and that the results might have been different if data had been available on those who were neither promoted nor transferred at all during this period. While admitting that this is a valid objection, I should point out that a reasonable distribution exists in our sample as to the number of levels advanced during the period.

Number of Management Levels Advanced:	0	1	2	3	4	5	6-9
Percentage of Sample:	13	52	25	7	2	1	0.4

The second objection is that superiors, in an effort to hold on to their best men, deliberately falsified their ratings; that this fact was recognized by higher executives; and that the latters' efforts to compensate for this falsification led to the observed results. Although this is possible, it would represent strangely perverse behavior on the part of the raters. In the first place, they would have difficulty getting proper salary increases for their good men who received low ratings, and so they would be likely to lose them through resignations. Second, it would imply that these raters were giving no consideration to the fact that they themselves were likely to be partially evaluated by their ability to develop managers under them, and that such development is best judged by the success of these men in other units.

Table 10.4   Distribution of Managerial Ratings in a Large American Company

	Level of Management	Rating (Percentage)				
		Highest	2nd	3rd	4th	Lowest
Performance	All	10	41	43	4	1
	Lowest	10	40	45	3	2
	Highest	6	41	35	11	6
Potential	All	13	37	26	11	13
	Lowest	9	36	24	9	20
	Highest	7	38	25	11	18

Rapid job mobility in British companies does not appear to share any of the characteristics of that mobility seen in American corporations. I have the impression that advancement is heavily within a single function and unit. The marketplace for jobs is essentially external to the company rather than internal to it.

Thus the British manager would seem peculiarly liable to career interruption because of antagonizing a single one of his many superiors. This is particularly the case because of the widespread decentralization which we observed in the British companies treated in the case studies of Part II. A British manager who is ambitious and receives a black mark from a superior has little choice but to leave the company; as we have seen, this is widely done. It seems likely that this organizational feature promotes the reluctance to engage in warranted risks which is observed in British companies.

The French promotion pattern, similar to the American but unlike the British, provides a solution to the danger of disqualifying risk takers and strong personalities. There are few enough managers with a truly elite education in any single company so that the *président* or *directeur général* himself can keep an eye on them, regardless of their current managerial level. The influence on their careers of judgment by intermediate superiors is likely to be relatively slight. Thus, until the *président's* retirement, these genuine candidates for top management need show little concern for the evaluations given by any but one man. As for those with a nonelite education, they appear in any case to be effectively cut off from the prospects of reaching top management. It is relatively unimportant for the company's future if the best men among them reach a level that is below their deserts, once their deserts are defined with due regard to the limits imposed by their education.

A potentially important educational distinction between industrial managers in the four countries relates to the nature of higher education. As was shown in Appendix B to Chapter 7, engineering and science education is over-whelmingly dominant in the Soviet Union and only slightly less so in France, while it plays a much less important role in American and British industry. One might expect that these national differences in type of education would lead to similar differences in the use of managerial manpower, and that a higher proportion of managerial personnel in the Soviet Union and in France would be engaged in technical functions which employ engineering and science skills. A top management that is primarily technically educated might be expected to place greater stress on developing the technical managerial functions than would a top management without this type of education.

No data are available concerning the proportion of managerial personnel in Soviet industry who are engaged in different functions. However, some such data do exist for France, the United States, and the United Kingdom. In earlier writing,[1] I presented evidence to the effect that French large enterprises do in fact employ a peculiarly high percentage of managerial personnel in technical functions. Further study of a somewhat larger sample of firms now indicates that, although the difference in national averages is substantial and in the predicted direction, it is not statistically significant at the 5 percent probability level as between large firms in different countries. The lack of significance is due to the high intraclass variance within the Anglo-American group of firms, and this variance seems quite unrelated to the nature of the firms' industries.

Data are available for six French, four American[2] and five British companies. A convenient way of posing the problem is to ask whether nontechnical staff comprise an unusually low percentage of staff in French industry. Since different branches have varying sales needs, and individual firms may make arrangements for the sale of their products by outside companies, it seems best to deduct sales and marketing staff from the total number of nontechnical staff. However, since the remaining nontechnical staff must service not only technical functions but also sales and marketing, these last two functions are kept in the denominator of total staff. Finally, executives who

---

[1] *The European Executive* (Doubleday, Garden City, N. Y., 1962), Chapter 22; and "Functional Divisions of Company Management: A Reflection of National 'Styles'," *Journal of Industrial Economics,* March 1962, pp. 100-117.
[2] The one American firm included in the article cited in the preceding footnote is excluded from the current sample on the ground that its data were for the 1930s. Data for the sample employed here all relate to the 1950s or 1960s.

Table A.10.1 Nontechnical Staff (Excluding Sales and Marketing) as a Proportion of Total Managerial Staff Excluding General Management (Unweighted Averages of Companies)

Statistical Measure	Country	Nontechnical Managerial Staff as Proportion of Total Managerial Staff after Exclusions (Percentage)	Managerial Staff Covered[a] as Proportion of the Company's Total Labor Force (Number of companies)				Sample Size (Number of companies)
			0.5 to 3.0%	3.1 to 6.0%	7.1 to 13.0%	33%	
Mean	France	22.1					
	Great Britain	27.6					
	United States	34.5					
	G.B. and U.S.	30.7					
	Total	27.2					
Standard error of mean	France	1.7					
	Great Britain	4.5					
	United States	7.4					
	G.B. and U.S.	4.0					
Count of companies	France		2	1	3		6
	Great Britain		3	1	1		5
	United States		3			1	4

Notes: Technical Staff: Production, engineering, maintenance, research and development, design, quality control, production control, etc.
Nontechnical Staff: Accounting and comptrollership, personnel, administration, purchasing, legal, etc.
[a]In each case, all managers above a certain hierarchical level are included. The proportion covered refers to the percentage of the labor force within these hierarchical levels, and includes sales, marketing, and general management personnel at these levels.

are designated as "general managers" are excluded from both numerator and denominator on the ground that they constitute an ambiguous category; fortunately, this last number was not very substantial as a proportion of the total in any of the firms studied.

The French firms include three steel and machinery, two electrical equipment, and one light producer goods firm. The American and British firms include five steel and machinery, one chemical, one other producer goods firm, and two consumer products companies. There is nothing in this industry mix which would lead us to expect a bias toward showing a low proportion of nontechnical personnel in the French firms.

The coverage of the various management levels differs by firm. While there is some independent indication that the proportion of managers in nontechnical functions rises with the level of management, the results do not appear to be sensitive to this feature of the sample.

Table A.10A.1 shows that the French firms all have a low proportion of nontechnical managerial staff but that the American and British enterprises display a wide scatter. There is thus no evidence that the differential character of national managerial education leads to systematic and major differences in the functions in which managers are employed in the different countries.

IV

Two Studies of National Behavioral Differences

Part IV brings us back to the main theme of the book: the analysis of national differences in managerial behavior and of the reasons for them. The principal explanatory variable relied upon is that of differences in managerial selection and promotion procedures.

Chapters 11 and 12, unlike earlier chapters, each concentrate upon a single economic problem. Chapter 11, however, is essentially limited to the presentation of national behavioral hypotheses that stem from the analytic framework developed earlier. Chapter 12, on the other hand, presents evidence for the existence of behavioral differences in the field studied.

11

Factory Investment and National Organizational Differences

Standard economic analysis treats the firm's short-run production function as one in which marginal costs typically vary with production, first declining and then /increasing. It is argued that a company management motivated either by profit or by growth maximization subject to a profit constraint will attempt to invest in such a fashion as to minimize long-run average costs. Thus one would expect such an enterprise normally to operate at some point on its short-run marginal cost curve where the marginal cost is increasing with output.

Yet the best study of the empirical data relating to British and American enterprises demonstrates that the weight of the evidence is strongly in favor of constant marginal costs, and thus declining average costs, over the relevant range of short-run fluctuations in output.[1] This conclusion as to constant short-run marginal costs is reinforced by the fact that businessmen usually describe their own production situation in terms of an expectation that average costs will vary in the short run in an inverse direction to changes in output. Similarly, cost-accounting systems are generally designed to distinguish between constant and variable costs, and to treat standard variable costs per unit of output as constant for any fairly brief future time period (such as one year).[2] Since variable costs may be considered as a proxy for marginal costs, this cost-accounting convention implies the expectation that short-run marginal costs will be invariant with respect to output.

[1]See J. Johnston, *Statistical Cost Analysis* (McGraw-Hill, New York, Toronto, and London, 1960). The data indicating the constancy of short-run marginal costs relate both to individual establishments and to enterprises but not to entire industries.

One might expect that the per unit monetary cost of production inputs would tend to fluctuate with the output of a typical firm, since the prices of major inputs into an industry will tend to rise with the demand from that industry. This hypothesis is not tested by Johnston's case studies, since he measures both output and inputs in constant prices. His treatment is perfectly correct conceptually, unless one were to assume that it is primarily the fluctuations in demand by the individual firm being studied which cause the changes in the prices of its inputs.

Johnston's case for constant short-run marginal costs is made in application to individual firms, but a number of the instances cited are really for establishments rather than for multiestablishment firms. Just as the national supply of a product may be increased by expansion in enterprises with higher marginal opportunity costs, so companies which are already producing the product may increase their output by using establishments not normally employed for this purpose. My use in this chapter of the hypothesis of constant short-run marginal costs takes it as holding at the establishment rather than necessarily at the enterprise level; thus I am using a rather weaker hypothesis than that of Johnston.

[2]Standard variable costs are considered as being stable in constant rather than in current prices. Thus the assumption (that marginal costs are constant) which is made in cost-accounting practice correctly ignores, just as does Johnston, any price movements related to output changes.

If we accept this evidence, then we face the troublesome problem of explaining the apparent constancy of short-run marginal costs. One line of approach is to hypothesize that there exists close to a zero short-run elasticity of substitution between factors which are respectively fixed and variable in the short run. But this explanation seems difficult to accept for industry in general (although a good case can be made for it in specific continuous-process branches), if only because the potential usually exists either for working overtime or for multishifts, and because either solution sharply increases the wage costs per hour of employment.

Various instances may be cited[3] when short-run marginal costs may be expected to decline with output for quite ordinary economic reasons. But while these instances counteract somewhat the normal tendency that can be predicted from economic theory—i.e., the increase of marginal costs with output—it is difficult to believe that they amount to much quantitatively. They can do no more than reduce somewhat the dimensions of the contradiction between theory and apparent fact.

Two other types of explanation remain. One is that organizational factors place rigid restraints on the allowable changes in marginal costs. The second is the existence of nonprofit managerial goals that place sharp limitations on the realization of technically feasible variations in marginal costs; combined constancy of employment in any given factory and stability of weekly hours worked per man is such a possible goal. It is clear that both of these explanations imply that managements typically choose to "misinvest" in the sense

[3]The first case is that of imperfect competition. Here it is conceivable that the marginal revenue curve has such a large negative slope that it intersects the marginal cost curve while the latter's slope is also still negative.

The second case is that linked to expectation by a firm's management of a secular growth trend in output over the lifetime of the plant and equipment it originally lays down. Here the size and degree of mechanization of the factory may be overbuilt for the average output produced during the early part of its life, and underbuilt for that part produced during its latter years. For plant where scale factors are important in determining variable costs, production in the early years is likely to be on the declining slope of the short-run marginal cost curve, and to be on the positive slope in the latter years. As an example, in a highly mechanized production line that is worked substantially below capacity, the lot size of each item produced is bound to be smaller than desired. This increases the cost per unit of changing jigs and fixtures; it also prevents the full utilization of the division of labor built into the fixed capital. In such a line, short-run marginal costs will move inversely to output.

The third case consists of worker responses to changes in the level of work orders placed by customers on the factory. When order levels are reduced, workers frequently react by reducing productivity in order that the available work may be stretched over a longer time period without dismissals or reduction in hours. On the other hand, even when they are paid by the hour, operators often work more intensively at times when the work to be done is temporarily greater than normal.

that the discounted expected value of average unit costs over the lifetime of the fixed investment will be higher than it need be.

It follows from these explanations that we would expect national distinctions to exist with regard to the forces at work in determining the combination of fixed and variable factors; where national similarities are observed, it is hypothesized that these result from the joint effect of different but counterbalancing factors.

Factory Suboptimization

In most companies, the plant manager plays an important role in determining both the amount and character of the fixed investment in his factory. This role is obvious if he is in charge either at the time of the original construction or when there is major reequipment due to obsolescence or to changes in the products produced. But it should be recognized that, even when such is not the case, the process of reequipment and of redesign of production processes is continous; moreover, expansion in the capacity of an existing plant is a commonplace of a plant manager's life.

It is quite true that investments of any significance require approval above the level of the factory manager. But initiation of requests generally occurs at the plant level; even when this is not so, and when it is the engineering department of the division or company which is responsible for making the requests, it is unlikely that specific types of equipment or expanded levels of mechanization would be forced upon an unwilling factory manager. Moreover, it appears that the most frequent company practice is to review individual conversion or expansion projects as a whole rather than in terms of each of their component parts; thus, even where the projects are subjected to a test as to return on capital, the plant manager has a great deal of free choice so long as the total project meets the necessary minimum criterion.

As a result of this importance of the plant manager in the determination of the specific fixed investments in his plant, it is important to ask whether his role leads him to any biases in the choice of such investments. To answer this question, let us first investigate how the plant manager is judged by his superiors.[4] Here I shall refer to an organizational pattern within private enterprise firms in which plant managers are judged according to their performance, and in which a major means of evaluating such performance is by

---

[4]The plant manager is treated here as a company executive who does not bear responsibility for the sale of his products. In enterprises where he does exercise such responsibility, it is the role of the plant production manager which we should investigate.

comparison with plan. Later I shall examine the degree to which enterprises in different countries correspond to this pattern.

In general, two criteria are basic. The first is that of meeting the demands of the sales department for output of the proper quality and mix. The prime responsibility of the factory manager is to turn out all the production that can be sold. Since this volume varies a good deal from one period to another, the plant manager is likely to favor a situation in which the capacity of his equipment is considerably above the modal output that he expects to be called upon to deliver.

The second criterion is the manager's ability to control variable expenses. Normally, he will be given an annual budget that has both fixed and variable components, and in which the variable expenditures are expected to be directly proportional to the level of his production. His task is to avoid negative variances (overexpenditures) from the budget, and it is such variances that lead to queries and attention from his superiors. On the other hand, positive variances appear to be treated rather matter-of-factly, and indeed to lead to tightening of the budget in the following year. Thus, from the point of view of the plant manager, the ideal production function is one that assures constant shortrun marginal costs over the entire range of possible output.[5]

[5]While I believe that this second criterion holds fairly well in its full generality, two modifications must be mentioned. The first is that if a plant manager expands output by operating obsolete facilities that are usually held idle (e.g., a high-cost furnace in a steel mill), the standard variable costs for this facility may well be computed separately by the company's comptrollership department and be set at a higher level than that for the facilities normally used. In this case, the plant manager is not penalized for using the obsolete facility, even though its operation raises the marginal costs of his total plant operation.

The most frequent exception to the constant-marginal-cost criterion is with regard to overtime and multiple-shift work. As was stated earlier, the budget is drawn up on the assumption that the prices of inputs will remain constant. When new wage agreements are signed during the course of the budgetary year, thus raising labor costs per hour, adjustments are made in the budget. The same is true with regard to the cost of materials, at least when purchasing is outside of the control of the individual plant manager. Since an extension in the use of overtime and/or of multiple-shift work increases the cost per labor hour, allowance is frequently made in the budget for these increases.

The difficulty with such a budgetary approach is that, if it were carried out fully, management would not be penalized for unnecessary use of overtime due to inefficiency or bad planning. The normal compromise appears to be that no increase in budgeted costs is made unless unbudgeted overtime work passes a certain previously unspecified point; but thereafter, a budgetary allowance is made. Thus, once overtime or multiple-shift work seriously surpasses the budgeted amount, it ceases to represent a negative variance to the plant manager. On the other hand, costs of transition must always be absorbed by him.

The significance for investment of these criteria for judging management would seem to be as follows:

1. The plant manager will strive for more capacity than is needed to produce the expected mean value of output, particularly where this capacity can be utilized without an increase in marginal costs of production. One means of realizing this is through pressing for excess factory space into which additional workers can be placed without overcrowding and thus without the factory suffering a rise in marginal costs. Additional assembly workers might be fitted into the factory; where normally there are several machines for each worker, to be used as the variety of operations requires, production workers might be added so as to utilize more fully the capacity of the equipment; finally, additional units of equipment might also be added in much less time than would be needed to add structures. The second means is by maintaining extra machinery which normally remains unutilized, but which can be operated in times of peak load by new employees without the worsening of production conditions.

To a degree, such efforts to maintain excess capacity of buildings and equipment in normal times is entirely consistent with the desire of top management to maximize profits. These efforts become a form of suboptimizing, however, when pushed beyond this point. The reason that we would expect such suboptimizing is that the plant manager is given much more of an interest in the stability of short-run marginal cost than in the level of average cost, since the necessary depreciation and maintenance of additional plant and equipment are written into his budget as extra allowances for fixed expenses.

2. Just as the foregoing measures lead to suboptimization by the plant manager in the light of possible excesses of production above the expected mean volume, so another measure can protect him against deficiencies. This is the rejection of the full degree of automation and mechanization which would lead to minimum expected average costs. From the point of view of maintaining a stable level of marginal costs, the objection to automation and mechanization is that they normally require much higher changeover costs than do less mechanized processes. When output is down, the ratio of changeover time to production time rises; for then the same variety of output is normally required (sometimes even more variation in order to encourage sales through greater variety of products) while the size of each lot of production is reduced. The more mechanized the process, the more the loss of such

production time, and thus the greater the increase in average variable costs as output falls.

Both the holding of excess capacity and the avoidance of full mechanization represent two aspects of the same policy: namely, a minimization in the variation of average variable costs as output rises or falls. An implication of both, of course, is a greater ability to meet unexpected increases in demand. (The larger the degree of automation, the higher are the fixed costs involved in holding excess capacity, and thus the less is the likelihood that higher management will agree to it.)

The methods employed in evaluating the performance of plant managers are thus seen to lead to an organizational bias on the part of these managers toward attaining a level and structure of fixed capital which assures a greater constancy of short-run marginal costs than would be the case if investment were determined purely on a profit-maximizing basis. For the reasons cited earlier, we would expect such a bias frequently to prove effective. To the extent that it does, this organizational phenomenon helps to reconcile profit-maximizing theory with the apparent fact of fairly constant marginal costs.

Why, however, are plant managers judged in terms of their variable costs rather than average costs? Why are the sorts of success criteria established which lead them to suboptimize to the detriment of the company as a whole?

Judgment according to costs rather than profits is not unreasonable, given the fact that plant managers are not responsible for sales decisions. To judge them according to the success of an activity over which they have no authority would be clearly unworkable, at least if the company management wishes to maintain a division of labor and authority between the production and the sales management. Similarly, evaluation according to a comparison between planned and realized average cost would imply taking no account of the effect of output variations upon per-unit fixed costs. If the sales rather than the production function is to be held responsible for the level of output required, then senior management can scarcely require that the plant manager bear the cost effects of a failure to achieve planned sales. Division of costs into fixed and variable items represents at least an attempt to eliminate the effect of sales success on the standard by which plant managers are evaluated.

Judgment according to an absolute standard of what average costs should be for a particular output level would be extremely difficult. The problem here would be that of knowing actual costs in other production units. Given the variations in product mix which are found in different plants, it is extremely difficult for most companies to use data even from their own plants to set such a standard. Data about plants of other companies seem almost never to be available in sufficient depth to be useful. Thus there seems little alternative to judging either by the standard of "plan" or of past experience in the given factory, and neither criterion can be employed without some method of wrestling with the cost effect of variations in output.

It now remains for us to inquire as to the degree to which management in the various countries corresponds to the pattern described above.

Britain is the country best represented by this organizational scheme. Managerial promotion above the level of plant manager is not predetermined by educational or class criteria, and thus plant managers can realistically strive for promotion. Evaluation of plant managers is carried out primarily within the production function itself, and performance on the job is the main standard used in most companies. Furthermore, cost accounting is quite well developed, at least for individual production units (although products are often aggregated together). While it is true that planning in general is quite weak in British firms, this applies least to the establishment of standard cost criteria for production units. Thus I would expect British industry to be particularly subject to this sort of suboptimizing behavior by plant managers.

Soviet enterprises also appear quite vulnerable to such suboptimizing, at least in recent years. The reason for this is that, while promotional opportunities for plant managers have not been great during the 1950s or 1960s, and demotion has not been an urgent problem, extraordinary bonuses by any international standard have been paid for short-run success as measured against plan. To the degree that plant managers are economic men, and it is clear from Soviet accounts that this is the case to a considerable degree, it is primarily through the earning of maximum bonuses that they can satisfy their desires. Moreover, it is by gaining high bonuses for the managerial and professional staff of the plant that managers can both satisfy their subordinates and build and maintain a managerial team that will make for future plant efficiency.

Since the end of 1959, success for bonus purposes has been primarily measured in terms of cost reduction or expansion of profits as well as by the meeting of output targets. Thus Soviet plant managers have been deeply concerned with assuring that average costs should not rise with output. But in fact they operate within a much more serious constraint. If wage and salary costs per unit of output rise above the level planned for the year, no bonus payments may be paid even if they have been earned. Thus success in obtaining bonuses virtually requires the maintenance of constant marginal labor costs, irrespective of whether the plant's annual plan calls for upward or downward movements of production.

American plant managers are less subject to these suboptimizing pressures, and for most of these managers such pressures would appear to be relatively weak. It is quite true that the managers' operational success is judged by the criteria described in our organizational model. But their length of tenure in any single plant is on the average quite brief, and often they are are moved elsewhere before they have had time to establish a performance record which will permit evaluation. The future careers of plant managers are determined much more by the judgments as to their potential made at divisional and corporate headwuarters, and there by executives in other functions as well as by those in production, than by the degree of their operational success—assuming, of course, that their operational performance meets minimal requirements.

The significance of this situation is that American plant managers and other production managers have a better probability of building a successful career by taking decisions that are really in the corporate interest, at least as this is evaluated by headquarters staff, than by suboptimizing. Their contribution to effective planning for their units, and not just to the execution of the plans, is a critical element in the evaluation of their potential.

The French business culture, however, is probably the least encouraging to suboptimizing investments. For one thing, cost accounting is least developed in France and thus variable cost standards are taken less seriously than in other countries. But much more significant is the fact that bonuses which vary with individual factory performance are quite rare (in contrast with the Russian situation), and that (unlike Britain) promotions are determined primarily on grounds other than job performance.

In France alone of the four countries we are examining, the likely limits of a managerial career in a company are to a considerable degree predetermined at the time of entrance into the firm by the nature of the education of the entrant. Graduates of the *grandes écoles* are sufficiently few so that there is little risk of their being lost from top-management view. Whatever degree of choice their company is in a position to make—among those with equal educational backgrounds—tends to be exercised far more by an evaluation of the individual's overall capacities for top management than by an examination of operational performance.

French plant managers who do not have the elite education normally considered necessary to equip them for top management have very little economic or career incentive either to optimize or to suboptimize, since they are usually fairly secure in their positions and quite unlikely to go further. They may indeed act in a suboptimizing fashion, but the particular form this takes will not be dictated by the organizational pattern described in our model; I doubt that it will have any particular bias with regard to choices of investment.

Managerial Goals and Hiring Constraints

A managerial goal that constrains the investment methods which would otherwise be used to attain profit or growth maximization is that of avoiding both layoffs of manual workers and sharp changes in the number of hours worked. This goal is given much higher priority in France and the Soviet Union than in England or the United States; within France, it has a much greater influence in provincial plants than in Parisian factories.

The American head of European operations of a major company reported that to him the single most striking feature in the value system of his French managerial subordinates was their great concern for avoiding any reductions of company employment. They were unwilling to engage in any actions which would lead to dismissals. This contrast in attitudes of American and French executives is quite frequently noted by American businessmen.

The effect of the French attitude can be seen in the remarks of a headquarters official of a large French industrial company with many similar tiny production units throughout the French provinces. He expressed the belief that, in his firm, labor productivity increased quite haphazardly within any individual unit. This was because both manual and white-collar workers would be retained in the location in which they were hired even when technical advances left them with no real work. Thus labor productivity could improve only when there was either an expansion of local sales or retirements or quits within the individual production unit.

On the other hand, plant managements operating in metropolitan Paris appear to be almost as willing as British or American firms to dismiss unneeded workers. The reason appears to be that Parisian managements believe that their workers can readily find jobs in their profession elsewhere, since the Parisian labor market is so large and the rate of unemployment very low. In contrast, provincial labor markets are much more restricted and thus dismissals are taken far more seriously.[6]

The avoidance of dismissals is an even more sacrosanct principle in the Soviet Union than in France, despite the fact that since 1966 the government has encouraged dismissals of unneeded workers in order to promote efficiency. Since dismissals can be, and do in fact normally seem to be, appealed through both the trade-union and legal systems,[7] managers are extremely reluctant to accept the costs in paper work, in managerial time spent in meetings on the subject, and in social opprobrium, which are involved in such staff reductions.[8]

Thus in the French provinces and the Soviet Union, wages and salaries are much more of a fixed cost for enterprises than is the case elsewhere. Expansion of employment tends to be restrained to a level which management believes can be maintained.

A profit-maximizing firm not subject to a labor force constraint would normally wish to have some excess buildings and machinery capacity available when producing at its expected average level. The long-run marginal cost of possessing such capacity would be the total additional fixed costs divided by the total additional output that will in fact be manufactured from such capacity and which could not otherwise be produced, plus the additional per-unit variable costs which are incurred only when the extra capacity is in fact utilized. But the firm subject to a labor-force constraint could not use

[6]One might expect that variations in the use of overtime would compensate for the lack of flexibility in employment. Indeed, with a legal workweek of forty hours, French workers in 1964 averaged six hours of overtime weekly. However, the permissible fluctuation of overtime is appreciably less. Generally speaking, workers are reluctant to work much less than forty-five hours weekly because of the effect on their paycheck of the loss of overtime; but they are similarly unwilling to go over forty-nine or, at the extreme, fifty-two hours.

For French manufacturing as a whole, the annual averages of hours worked weekly were kept within a range of 2.2 percent during the eleven years 1956-1966. In the specific companies I studied, no provincial plant had a range from one period to another of more than 6 to 9 percent.

[7]See Mary McAuley, *Labour Disputes in Soviet Russia 1957-1965* (Clarendon Press, Oxford, 1969), pp. 121-125, 160-162 and 210-235, and Emily Clark Brown, *Soviet Trade Unions and Labor Relations* (Harvard University Press, Cambridge, Mass., 1966), *passim* and especially fn. 35 on p. 369.

[8]Both the French and Soviet managerial reactions are reflections of attitudes common throughout the two societies. Partly these reactions occur because of the cost in energy and unpopularity of surmounting the administrative hurdles thrown up against dismissals. But the value system of executives themselves appears in both cases to be an even more weighty explanation.

this added capacity in periods of peak demand without incurring additional fixed labor costs. Thus such a firm might be expected to build less such excess capacity than would a traditional profit maximizer.

Similarly with regard to the level of automation and mechanization. A cost of such mechanization for an unconstrained profit maximizer is that the higher the level of mechanization, the more sharply does average variable cost rise as production changes in either direction from the rated capacity, i.e., the nature of the production function is increasingly constrained by the technology. A profit maximizer will be willing to buy some flexibility, in order to protect against sharp cost increases when output changes, by engaging in less mechanization than would be appropriate if the level of output could be exactly predicted and was not subject to variance. On the other hand, a firm operating under labor force constraints cannot change the size of its labor force very much in the short run, regardless of the nature of its equipment; there is no reason for it to pay for technological flexibility of which it cannot take advantage. Thus such a firm may be expected to engage in a greater degree of automation and mechanization than would an unconstrained profit-maximizing enterprise.

To the degree that Soviet and French provincial plant managers are influenced by the organizational consideration cited earlier, the labor-force constraint and the managerial organizational bias tend to neutralize each other with regard to their effect on the deviation of the production function chosen by management from what would be optimum in terms of an unrestrained profit-maximization goal. Thus, for them, the organizational bias is probably beneficial. In Britain and the United States, on the other hand, it clearly shifts production methods away from the optimum.

In addition to the two preceding behavioral reasons for departure from the optimum, there is a significant environmental feature that has a differential effect on the movement of short-run marginal costs in various geographic areas. This feature is the inability of all except a few industrial enterprises, which pay exceptionally high wages, to hire additional labor in periods when they wish to do so. Such a situation is quite general in England and also exists in the main cities of the Soviet Union, in contrast to the United States, France, and the rest of the Soviet Union. Companies facing such a constraint are both reluctant to dismiss labor for fear that it cannot be rehired when needed, and are unable to make use of excess equipment unless it is to be permanently manned. Thus their labor expenditures become relatively fixed costs, but for labor-market rather than managerial-behavior reasons.

British industry, particularly that portion of it whose demand peaks tend to be simultaneous with those of the general business cycle, suffers from this problem because of the low national rate of unemployment. Although the individual firm might solve its problems by bidding up wages in the jobs difficult to fill, the companies where I have interviewed have been reluctant to do so because of their belief that they could not keep such wage increases isolated to either particular jobs or skills. Thus all three of the British firms which I have studied in depth have suffered from the lack of one or another particular kind of labor.

This situation is greatly ameliorated in the United States both by the higher rate of unemployment, even at the peak of the business cycle, and by the regional mobility of labor and the greater willingness and ability of American workers to commute long distances. France has had a rate of unemployment very much like the British, but a large pool of agricultural labor has been available which can be easily drawn into industry as rapidly as is desired. Thus none of the French firms that I studied seemed ever to be concerned with labor shortages.

Most parts of Soviet industry are faced with much the same situation as the French, since collective-farm earnings are still well below industrial wages and the farm population is quite large relative to the industrial. However, plants located in such cities as Moscow, Leningrad, Kiev, and Kharkov are in a different position. The Soviet government has long attempted to restrain the population growth in these cities, and enterprises are legally prohibited from employing would-be migrants from other areas. For this reason, Soviet enterprises in the major cities face a similar restraint on hirings as that imposed on British firms, although for different reasons.

Conclusion

At this point we can summarize the effect of the factors already discussed in this chapter, plus one additional one (k), on the investment behavior of plant managers. The factors are symbolized as follows:

Behavioral factors

$x=$ The suboptimizing organizational factor which leads to the building of excess capacity and to the avoidance of mechanization and automation.

$y=$ The constraint on dismissing labor; this constraint makes labor a fairly fixed cost at output levels below "capacity," and prevents output from even temporarily rising much above capacity.

Environmental factors

$l=$ The inability to hire additional labor at peak-demand periods; it has the same effects as y.

$k=$ A relatively high price for labor compared to equipment, judged by standards of western Europe. This leads to an emphasis on mechanization and automation, and to an avoidance of excess equipment, and has the same effect as y.

A matrix of countries and regions on one axis and different degrees of short-run substitutability of factors can be drawn up as shown in Table 11.1. In the matrix of Table 11.1 the flexibility of technological coefficients of production is closely correlated both with a bias in investment choices toward the accumulation of excess equipment and away from mechanization and automation, and with a tendency to constancy of short-run marginal costs as output varies.

How can we test the foregoing hypotheses as to the effect of behavioral and environmental factors? A very weak test is provided by the fact that it is difficult to understand why short-run marginal costs should be invariant to output changes unless we introduce these or similar hypotheses. But certainly we should look for stronger tests.

It might appear that a cross-country comparison of the structure of equipment in identical industries would provide such a test, since the factors analyzed all provide a bias in investment choices. Unfortunately, as Table 11.1 shows, only in one case (the French provinces) do the relevant factors all operate to create the same bias. Thus no prediction can be made from my hypotheses unless it were possible to quantify the relative strengths of the factors involved. Since I am unable to do this, I can suggest no further test of the hypotheses.

Table 11.1   Direction in which Behavioral and Environmental Factors Act

	Technological Coefficients of Production	
Area	Flexibility	Rigidity
United Kingdom	x	l
Paris		
French provinces		y
United States	x(weak)	k
USSR, large cities	x	y, l
USSR, rest of country	x	y

Table 11.2 Direction in which Behavioral Factors Act

| Area | Technological Coefficients of Production | |
	Flexibility	Rigidity
United Kingdom	x	
Paris		
French provinces		y
United States	x(weak)	
USSR	x	y

The matrix of Table 11.1 presents the effects of both behavioral and environmental factors. But suppose that we restrict ourselves to a comparison of the actual technologies chosen with those that would be the outcome of the decisions of profit-maximizing managements? In that case, the environmental factors should be ignored, since their effects must be included in the determination of the optimum investment solutions. We are then left with the matrix of Table 11.2.

This matrix suggests that both behavioral factors x and y operate in the case of Soviet enterprises, but that they exert offsetting pressures toward shifting investment decisions from their optimum. Quite possibly, then, Soviet managers make better investment decisions than would be the case if either behavioral factor were to be eliminated without the other being simultaneously removed.

In the case of the United Kingdom and the French provinces, however, the x or y behavioral factor operates alone. Industrial enterprises in both countries suffer from the existence of one or the other of these factors, but they suffer from opposite kinds of distortion with regard to investment decisions.

In short, it is not the same behavioral factors in different countries that prevent enterprise managements from making investment decisions that are optimum in terms of maximizing profits. Moreover, in view of the potential counteracting influence of such factors, it is not at all obvious that the weakening of the influence of any one of these factors would represent a net gain from the point of view of a profit-maximizing top management. For certainly both the x and y factors operate to some degree in enterprises of all countries; a further weakening of the y factor in the United Kingdom, for example, would have negative consequences for the making of investment decisions.

12   Internal Transfer Prices

The establishment of prices attached to the transfer of goods or services between divisions or other units of large companies is virtually a necessity. Without such prices, cost accounting at the level of the individual administrative subunits would be impossible. So, too, would be the development of profit-and-loss statements for these subunits. Decisions or even sensible recommendations could not be made at this level with regard either to those investments or to those changes in production methods which economize on goods or services received from other units at the expense of expenditures made on the outside market. In short, decentralization in large-scale enterprises of capitalist countries depends upon financial accounting, which in turn requires a system of prices for transfers within the corporation.

Transfer prices fall into two categories. The first relates to transfers between major organizational subdivisions of a firm. These subdivisions may either be functional—manufacturing and sales are the most important—or they may consist of functionally integrated divisions that utilize one another's products. The second category relates to transfers between units within a single small organizational subdivision; usually, the sole purpose of this category of transfer prices is for cost-accounting purposes rather than to aid in decentralized decision making. Thus, within a given manufacturing division, semifinished goods may be transferred between vertically integrated shops according to some form of standard costing. This chapter will deal only with the first category of transfer prices. While I shall label these as interdivisional transfers, the names which the relevant organizational subunits bear may vary in status from that of departments to distinct legally constituted companies.

Customarily, interdivisional transfers are made at prices which are described within American and British companies as being "in principle" either equal to the open-market price of the transferred item, or as differing from it only sufficiently to take account of cost savings (in transport, packaging, and paper work) realized by one or the other of the divisions.[1] In fact, of course,

---

[1]See David Solomons, *Divisional Performance: Measurement and Control* (Financial Executives Research Foundation, New York, 1965), pp. 183-184. Solomons' conclusions are based upon a study of twenty-five divisionalized American corporations. My own interviews in Britain corroborate his work.

On the other hand, the National Industrial Conference Board, in its *Interdivisional Transfer Pricing,* (Studies in Business Policy, No. 122, 1967) reports that two-thirds of the American firms it studied use cost in some form in their transfer pricing; but much of this is apparently for transfers within single divisions. Over half of the firms queried use market-based prices for at least some of their transfers. The sample consists of 190 companies that "manufacture and sell a wide variety of products."

it is often extremely difficult to make operational this method of price determination; individual firms may also have specific reasons, such as tax minimization, for not trying too hard to do so. Nevertheless, it is generally intended that transfer prices be set so that the profit-and-loss statement of each division is unaffected by the fact that it is trading within the same company rather than with outside enterprises under separate ownership. Such independence of divisional profit results is usually bolstered by a broad ideological statement on the part of top management that divisions should bargain at arm's length and be allowed to buy or sell outside the company whenever they can get better terms than those offered in internal trading.

What is interesting about this commonly accepted corporate ideal for transfer prices is that it is in flat contradiction to that principle of transfer pricing which would lead to short-run divisional decisions that are optimal with regard to the maximization of the corporation's total profits. Optimal transfer prices would normally be those set to equate with short-run marginal cost.

Standard microeconomic theory indicates that a firm maximizes profits when it determines its combined pricing, sales and advertising, and capacity-utilization policy according to the criterion that short-run marginal cost should equal marginal revenue. Only in the case of firms operating in perfectly competitive markets does this come to the same thing as operating where short-run marginal cost equals the price of the final product.

The profit-maximizing rule in imperfectly competitive markets is frustrated if divisions selling to the outside market are allowed by the company to set their own prices and output levels, while they in turn purchase from other divisions of the company at market prices. For, in that case, the variation between company-wide short-run marginal cost and the price received from the outside buyer is higher, and the volume of sales is correspondingly lower, than would be optimum in order to maximize company profits. Similarly, choices as to the lowest-cost methods of production are biased by the fact that the decision-making division ignores the monopoly profits earned by other divisions within the corporation from materials it itself might buy internally in lieu of materials, equipment, or labor procured from outside the enterprise.

Of course, if there were completely centralized headquarters decisions as to the pricing of all sales to the outside, as to the quantities of final products produced for such sale, and as to the production functions to be used throughout the company, there would be no disadvantage in transfer prices that are set at the level of market prices. But if there is any degree of decentralization of such decisions (and such is virtually inevitable in corporations of substantial size), then these standard transfer prices result in inferior decisions.[2]

If short-run marginal costs in the various divisions varied sharply over the relevant range of outputs, then the criterion that transfer prices be set equal to marginal cost would be nonoperational when taken alone. It would also be necessary that either the buying or selling division indicate to the other its true demand or supply function for the relevant product, or that both functions be made available to corporate headquarters and that transfer prices be set there. If, on the other hand, short-run marginal costs are quite stable over the relevant production range, this problem does not arise. As we saw in Chapter 11, the latter situation seems to prevail—at least in Britain and the United States—both in the belief of industrial managers and in fact. If this is indeed so, the almost unenforceable requirement that divisions provide true information as to their demand or supply functions is not necessary.

We are now ready to face the puzzle that is inherent in internal transfer prices. Under normal conditions, there exists a readily apparent rule for establishing these prices in such a way as to promote optimum decentralized decision making. In fact, however, British and American managers attempt to set transfer prices according to quite a different procedure that leads to inferior decisions. Why this contradiction between optimal price setting and actual practice?

Leaving aside the problem of how marginal cost might be determined if it were desired for purposes of price setting,[3] there are four major disadvantages

---

[2]See Solomons, *Divisional Performance,* p. 160ff. and, especially, Jack Hirshleifer, "On the Economics of Transfer Pricing," *Journal of Business,* July 1956, pp. 172-184. As Hirshleifer points out, even marginal-cost transfer prices do not provide an optimal solution when there exists demand dependence, defined as meaning that an additional external sale by one division reduces the demand outside of the company for the products of another division. The same is true when there is technological dependence among the different divisions. See Hirshleifer, *"Economics of Transfer Pricing,"* and Hirshleifer, "Economics of the Divisionalized Firm," *Journal of Business,* April 1957, pp. 96-108. A linear programming solution to such dependence is provided by William J. Baumol and Tibor Fabian in "Decomposition, Pricing for Decentralization and External Economies," *Management Science,* September 1964, pp. 1-32.

However, demand or technological dependence is likely to be quite minor in most cases. Even when it is important, marginal-cost transfer prices will still often yield a better solution than will market-price transfer prices.

[3]Certainly, under the usual conditions of imperfect competition, one could readily find a closer proxy to marginal cost than open-market price.

of internal transfer prices based on short-run marginal cost. All disadvantages stem from organizational considerations.[4]

The first is that such pricing would make it extremely difficult for corporate management to evaluate the overall success of the individual divisions; this is because there would be no common denominator such as a meaningful profit figure by which to measure such success. Divisional management would have to be judged according to its success in each of the disparate areas of its work: cost reductions, sales to outside customers, improvements in the quality of its products, etc. Corporate management would have no external yardstick by which to weigh the importance of these various activities in the case of a given division, and thus would have to make a purely subjective evaluation of the divisional management's overall success.

Closely related to this is the fact that decentralization of decision making to the divisional level would be sharply reduced. It would be corporate rather than divisional management which would have to determine the proper trade-offs between the various measures of success of the individual functions, since their effect on profit could only be calculated at the corporate level. Thus cross-functional decisions would be pushed sharply upward in the hierarchy, reducing the possibilities for those quick and knowledgeable decisions which are a principal advantage of managerial decentralization.

Second, there would probably be a loss both in incentive and in managerial training at the divisional level. To the extent that managers are motivated to be profit seekers by the business culture in which they function, they might be frustrated to find that the goals of their division cannot be placed into a direct profit framework. When managers were promoted from the divisional to the corporate level, it would be found that they had not gained the proper experience in striving for profits.

Third, there would be a serious problem in determining queuing priorities between divisions and customers outside of the firm. While a division would promote its own profit position by giving priority with regard to delivery dates and attention to quality to orders coming from outside the company, the reverse might or might not be true with regard to the maximization of the profits of the firm as a whole. The producing division would be without information for deciding who should be treated as favored customers.

[4]See Joel Dean, "Decentralization and Intracompany Pricing," *Harvard Business Review,* July-August 1955, pp. 65-74, and Paul W. Cook, Jr., "Decentralization and the Transfer-Price Problem," *The Journal of Business,* April 1955, pp. 87-94 for a discussion of similar disadvantages.

Fourth, not only all decisions but even recommendations as to whether the corporation itself should produce or buy its intermediate products would have to be made at the corporate level. This would apply not only to decisions as to new needs for intermediate products but also to decisions for replacement and expansion of those existing facilities within the corporation which are required for the production of these intermediate goods. Since the producing division would sell internally at marginal cost, it would have no criterion for deciding whether such production is worthwhile. (Remember that we have assumed that marginal cost is not an increasing function of production volume.) Similarly, the purchasing division could provide no guidance through comparison of the price it paid internally with the price it would have to pay if it were to go to the external market. Only a comparison of the prospective average costs of production of the producing division, plus the corporation's expected cutoff rate of return on investment, with the expected costs of purchasing from outside would give a proper answer as to whether internal investments for the purpose of producing intermediate goods were worthwhile. But no incentives would exist to motivate either producing or consuming divisions to make accurate probabilistic estimates of either of these figures. Thus it would seem likely that such estimates would have to be made by corporate staff people, and this would further centralize the management of the company.

The setting of internal prices at the level of external market prices gets around all four of the preceding organizational problems, but only at the cost of nonoptimal final output quantities and final prices for the corporation's products which are sold on the outside market, as well as nonoptimal make versus buy decisions. Here is the inherent dilemma with which this chapter is concerned.

In the next two sections, I shall contrast the practices of internal transfer pricing found in a sample of six British and seven French firms and find that the median solution differs sharply between the two countries. We shall also examine in detail the practices in two large American firms where the two systems employed each bear a resemblance either to the typical British or to the French internal pricing mechanism, but nevertheless reflect a somewhat different reality. The final section of this chapter will examine national managerial differences as an explanation of why different solutions are adopted in the various countries. As we shall see, the organizational disadvantages of basing transfer prices on short-run marginal cost are much more applicable to British than to French firms. American companies appear to occupy an intermediate position in this regard.

British Firms and Their American Counterpart

The British Company B1 (described in Chapter 5) is the firm that comes closest to the transfer pricing practices recommended by Joel Dean: namely, prices determined by arm's-length bargaining between the divisions.[5] All units except service functions, whether trading within or between divisions, have in principle been free to make their own decisions as to whether or not to deal with other company units. This principle has indeed been realized to a remarkable degree.

Within the principal division, the individual factory managers sell their products to the sales department. As individual factories develop new styles, the sales department will ask whether a particular style can be supplied to the market at a specified price. Each of the factory managers is provided by headquarters with a targeted rate of profit, and himself determines whether or not to produce the new item at the price requested by sales. In making the decision, the factory manager naturally pays no attention to the amount of company profits that would be made at the level of the sales department. The sales department, on the other hand, is credited with a fixed percentage of the final sales price and thus—so long as the price elasticity of demand is substantially greater than unity, as has indeed generally been believed to be the case—has favored low sales prices for the division's products. The recognized bias of the sales department has made it a poor source of market information, and the factories have been loath to provide cost data to sales since such data might give sales a whip hand in pressing for lower prices. This has prevented all effective cooperation between sales and factory management in determining which features of a new style might have a high or low benefit-to-cost ratio in terms of additional sales to be reaped from supplemental production costs. The desired arm's-length relationship between the two functions has been attained at the cost of hoarding of relevant information by each of the separate functions.

The incentive to maintain arm's-length relationships between the various vertically integrated divisions has been even greater. This is because middle and upper management receive bonuses depending upon the profitability of their particular division rather than in accord with the results of the company as a whole.[6] By and large, as was shown by the illustration of interdivisional pricing cited in Chapter 5, company divisions have been treated exactly as

[5]Dean, "Decentralization and Intracompany Pricing."
[6]In contrast, attachment of managerial bonuses to divisional profits was found in only one American company, and partly in a second, out of a sample of seven.

any other purchasers—and they have paid high or low prices for their supplies depending upon the efficiency of their purchasing managers in price negotiations.

A major economy found by a newly appointed factory manager was in purchasing from another division. He discovered that his predecessor had been buying a major material at a high price simply because he took delivery only as the material was needed rather than ordering in bulk, and so paid a penalty charge exacted from all customers. He was able to change to bulk deliveries without tying up an exorbitant amount of either space or capital. If this change in interdivisional purchasing practices had not been instituted, the company might well have given up these product lines because of high production costs, and thus have sacrificed profits both in the supplying division and in the sales department. But the supplying division had never called the attention of the previous factory manager to the possibility for cost reduction, preferring to take its higher divisional profit and hoping that the factory manager would be able to maintain the lines in production by means of other economies.

In general, managers have had a great deal of freedom in deciding whether to buy supplies from other divisions within the company or to purchase from outside. Thus one factory manager followed a deliberate policy of taking half of his needs for certain major supplies from within the company, and half from outside. This policy was followed despite the fact that he paid an identical price for internal and for external purchases, both suppliers being members of a price-fixing ring. Similarly, when a supplying division developed a new semifinished product, it gave the company's principal division only a six-month monopoly of the new item before it began selling to outside competitors as well. In both cases, company profits were almost certainly sacrificed to divisional autonomy.

This company constitutes the only extreme case of arm's-length bargaining between divisions which I have encountered in any country. In particular, it is the only firm in which divisions and even some factory managers have had true freedom to buy and sell outside of the company at their own discretion.

A second British company differs sharply from the first in that interdivisional purchasing is heavily stressed. In fact, an aggressive acquisitions policy has been pursued primarily with the objective of promoting vertical integration toward the final consumer so as to increase the capacity utilization of early-stage divisions. Interdivisional transfers are in principle made at open-market prices, but business is not supposed to be given to suppliers outside the company so long as internal suppliers can meet the competition with regard to price and other conditions. One of the company's top executives pointed out to me that, indeed, some divisions are "naughty" and try to buy outside unnecessarily; he said that it was the task of the main board of the company to prevent such actions. These divisional efforts suggest that internal suppliers do not in fact always meet the terms of the competition.

Nevertheless, considerable stress is placed upon the importance of interdivisional transfers being at open-market prices so that the profit record of each division may be judged individually. Fear is expressed that deviation from this pricing system would provide managers with a solid excuse for low profits, and would seriously weaken their profit motivation.

Departures from open-market pricing do occur, but there is no indication that they are in the direction of marginal-cost prices. When one division opened a new plant, it contracted with another division for large-volume deliveries over an extended period. The price was lower than the market rate, but the supplying division was able to add a work shift in a major plant because of the extra orders. A year after the pricing agreement was made, neither the top executives of the company nor those of the supplying division were able to say whether the low transfer price was best interpreted as a subsidy to help the new plant to get started or simply as a reasonable concession for volume purchases. No comparison was possible with the terms which outside companies might have offered if the opportunity to bid had been presented to them.

A second instance of departure from open-market pricing was the development of a specialty and high-profit product by the research function in the company. Two different divisions were involved in the production of the product, and the transfer price between the two divisions was set by the comptroller in such a way as to "justly" apportion the monopoly profits between them. In this case, of course, the fact that the selling division paid a higher-than-market price for its principal supply, while at the same time the division was charged with setting the price for its final product, implied that the company both produced less of the product and made lower total profits than would have been the case if the division had gone outside of the company for its supplies.

A third instance was one in which the transfer price was set below the market level. Here, one subdivision received half of its supplies from within the company and half from a single outside supplier. The supplying division traditionally had received the same price as did the outside supplier. However, at one point when the outside supplier raised its price, the supplying division agreed to accept a price intermediate between the old level and the new. It was clear that a major reason for accepting this price was a reluctance to press for "overly high profits" at the expense of a fellow unit of the same company which would as a result be placed in difficult straits.

Even within a single major division, when goods are sold from one factory to another or to a wholesale house within the division, it is normally at market price. It is true that, when major orders from outside will be lost unless the first-stage factory accepts less than the market price, the decision as to the transfer price may be decided by the divisional chief. But it is interesting that no manager within the division except its chief is allowed to know the costs or profits of any function except his own. The divisional head gave two reasons for this secrecy. First, if the rate of return on capital of each unit within the division were known, each unit would be reluctant to trade with others except at a transfer price that assured it at least as high a return as the other unit was earning. Thus wider knowledge would lead each unit to "stick in its heels," and outside orders would be lost. Second, if the salesmen for the wholesale house knew that factories would be earning a good return on a given order, they would not fight as hard for a high price from the outside customers. The two reasons are, of course, contradictory; the first assumes that unit managers are interested only in unit profits, while the second assumes that they are primarily concerned with divisional profits. The effect of the secrecy, however, is clear; it is to assure that—except for the few cases which go to the divisional chief for decision—information is segmented at different points within the division so that no reasoned judgment can be made as to whether a given outside order is worth taking.

Thus this second British company, despite the fact that vertical integration was the prime motive for its acquisitions policy, nowhere used marginal-cost transfer prices between divisions.[7] Even for transfers within a given division, the segmentation of information made marginal cost pricing impracticable except in the few cases which went for decision to the head of the division.

The two foregoing firms differ sharply in the degree to which their divisions are free to purchase outside the company, but they share a strong emphasis upon the use of open-market prices as the basis for transfer pricing.

---

[7]At the time of my interviews, transfers between two divisions were being reorganized from a market-price basis to the basis of budgeted cost plus a fixed-percentage return on capital. This is the one departure from open-market prices not mentioned in the text, and it represents little, if any, move toward short-run marginal cost pricing.

The practices of the other four British firms in our sample are described in the appendix to this chapter. Summing up all six British companies, five base their transfer prices upon open-market prices and go a long way in ensuring arm's-length bargaining. To a surprising degree, both the divisions and the component units within a single division are operated as though they were separate firms. The sixth firm, which is our only exception, has reaped none of the potential advantages of being liberated from this sort of internal pricing system. To the contrary, it has suffered severely from the absence of this market type of coordination because there has been no informal managerial coordination that could function as a substitute. The result in this sixth firm has been simply a muddle.

The American firm whose system of internal pricing most closely resembles British practice is a large mass-production engineering company that is divisionalized along horizontal lines, with manufacturing divisions selling to one another as well as to the sales divisions. Engineering design is handled outside of these divisions. Manufacturing divisions produce almost entirely for sale within the corporation. Each division is a separate profit center, and the success of its top management is judged primarily according to its profit record. Thus the determination of internal transfer prices between divisions is very important to all divisions.

Manufactured items transferred between divisions are priced in three different ways, with the corporate finance staff determining the method of pricing applicable to each item.

The preferred method is the utilization of prices paid by the corporation for purchases made on the open market. The second method is that of "similar pricing," and is used when a product supplied by a division is similar but nonidentical to a product purchased from outside; in this case, the outside market price is modified to take account of those cost differences between the products which result from technological variations.

The third method, which is regarded by the company as least desirable but which nevertheless is used for the bulk of interdivisional transfers, is "formula pricing."[8] Here, prices are set on the basis of the average costs necessary for an "efficient operation"—and such costs may theoretically be lower than

[8]See Heflebower's statement that a situation in which there exists both an active external market and reliable reporting of prices is rare for products transferred between industrial divisions, except for some early stage processing of agricultural commodities. (R. B. Heflebower, "Observations on Decentralization in Large Enterprises," *Journal of Industrial Economics,* November 1960, p. 14.)

those of any plant within the corporation—plus a predetermined return on assets employed in the manufacturing process.

Prices established by all three methods are set by the corporate finance staff, with its judgment factor increasing in importance as it moves from applying method one to method three. But even the "market price" method leaves a good deal to judgment. This is because the outside market price will be used in its raw form only when the outside supplier is provided by the company with sufficient sales volume and a sufficiently long-term contract so that he can achieve the full economies of scale feasible, and when such prices are not regarded as abnormal either because of temporary shortages of the item on the outside market or because the outside supplier is trying to "buy its way in" to the corporation's business. Otherwise, the observed market price must be modified by the corporate staff before being applied to inter-divisional transfers. Thus, in fact, all three methods are variants of a "just price."

Once a product price is set, it is modified from year to year in three ways until eventually a complete revision is undertaken. The first adjustment is for changes in the prices of materials and labor that are used in producing the product. The second adjustment is a fixed annual percentage reduction in prices so as to reflect economies that the manufacturing divisions are expected to achieve.[9] The third adjustment, which is the only area of regular price negotiations between divisions, is intended to take account of the frequent engineering redesign of manufactured items; a new price for the redesigned item must be set on the basis of expected changes in cost compared to that of the item made obsolete.

An informant on the corporate finance staff believed that items whose transfer prices are set according to the open-market-price method are priced lower than are items valued by either of the other two methods. He based this statement partly on the fact that the one manufacturing division that sold primarily according to market price showed a lower return on assets than did the other three manufacturing divisions, while these three all had very similar profit rates. Second, he based it on an analysis which suggested that the average annual percentage reduction in prices[10] paid to outside suppliers was greater than the 3½ percent figure applied to internal transfers. His view

[9]An annual corporation-wide percentage reduction in internal prices of 2½ percent was used in the early 1960s, and of 3½ percent in the middle 1960s.
[10]This is after eliminating the effects of design changes and of the variation in the prices of material and labor inputs.

seemed to be substantiated for at least one manufacturing division which sold its products at "formula price" by the twin facts that it earned a much higher profit per unit of sales than did a major outside company producing rather similar items, and that this division regarded the outside company as selling at ruinously low prices.

Divisions that normally purchase from within the corporation have been severely limited in their efforts to obtain competitive bids from outside. This is because it has been fully recognized within the company that serious outside bids will not be made unless the company demonstrates that it is willing to place outside orders for quantities sufficient to provide full economies of scale and for periods long enough (two to four years were suggested) to make worthwhile the capture of such orders. Finally, it is believed essential, if the company is to receive genuine bids, that it place these orders outside whenever the price quoted is below the transfer price quoted internally *prior* to the receipt of the competitive bid.[11] However, since the short-run marginal cost to the division and company of producing an intermediate product is usually well below the transfer price, such placing of orders outside will often be injurious to total corporate profitability. The result is that divisions have been forbidden to ask for outside competitive bids on items which they normally buy internally, except with the permission of corporate headquarters.

It would appear that, although the theory of transfer pricing in this large American corporation calls for such prices to be set at the level of the outside market, they have in fact been set at even a higher figure. Thus decisions which would emanate from optimum decentralized decision making are departed from even more than would be the case if internal transfer prices were actually set at the level of open market prices. Yet this is a corporation that is nationally known for its imaginative use of internal financial controls.

However, there are efforts to prevent investments from being made within the corporation in order to produce goods which could be bought more cheaply outside. These efforts take the form of allowing a manufacturing division to contract out products which it is obligated to supply to another division at a fixed transfer price, and to count as a part of its divisional profit any favorable difference between the price it pays and the price it receives. Thus, if its average unit cost plus budgeted return on capital used is more than the price for which it can buy the product outside, the division will presumably not invest to make the product. Nevertheless, there are limits to

[11]See Heflebower, "Observations on Decentralization," p. 15 for an analogous viewpoint.

how successful such a corporate policy can be; for the divisional managers must be aware that, if such a contracting-out by their division became very major, it would doubtless be reflected in a lowering of the transfer prices received from other divisions.

The difficulties involved in setting transfer prices at a competitive level have their implications for the use of profitability in the evaluation of divisional managements. Several financial managers, both at the level of divisional and of corporate headquarters, have assured me that divisions are judged much less according to their absolute profits or to their return on assets than by the trend over time of their rate of return and by the comparison of their year's profits with the profits budgeted for that same year. The bonuses of the top managers of a division, for example, are closely linked to the division's profits; but the link is to profit performance compared both with the past year and with the budget for that year, rather than to rate of return relative to that of other divisions.

As a result, it is said that divisional managements are fairly indifferent to the absolute level of transfer prices that are established for their sales and purchases. But they are deeply concerned with the changes in these transfer prices, and interdivisional negotiations and disputes as to prices are concentrated on such changes. In practice, this means negotiation as to the prices of new items as well as of those items whose design has been modified.

Since the corporate financial staff establishes the rules for determining transfer prices, and since these prices are based upon cost-plus, divisional negotiations are concentrated on the determination of facts—primarily as to the prospective costs of production of the redesigned or new items. The selling division has a strong vested interest in seeing that the agreed-upon prospective costs (which will be treated as standard costs) are set at a high level, while the purchasing divisions wish to have them fixed low. Inasmuch as a transfer price is set as soon as the engineering design has been firmed up, and months before the item goes into production, there is clearly a good deal of room for legitimate disagreement as to these costs.

Once the item has been designed by the engineering department of the company, the producing division makes an analysis of how it will be made, on what equipment, and what quantities of materials and labor will be required. This analysis provides the producing division's estimate of prospective costs of production, and it is defined by the corporation as already including all the improvements in productivity which were to have been achieved by the division during the previous year and reflected in the annual percentage reduction in transfer prices. The producing division wishes the transfer price of the new item to be set on the basis of this cost analysis.

In fact, however, it is perfectly clear that the division will show further method improvements both before it puts the item into production and during the production run. This would be true if only because the original analysis represents the results of the first, rather than the final, grappling with the technical problems. The fact is that even after the original standard cost estimates are modified through negotiation, the individual plants normally show during the course of the year much more than the budgeted annual cost improvement factor on new and redesigned items, and less than budget on items which were in production during the previous year. In the divisional negotiations, the cards are stacked in favor of the producing divisions because it is they who have the most detailed information as to alternative production methods.

To sum up, the establishment of transfer prices between divisions of this American company is a highly complex process. But on the whole, transfer prices are above the level at which they would be set even on the usual oligopolistic open market. Thus they deviate even more sharply than do such market prices from what would be optimal from the point of view of maximizing the corporation's profits.

Clearly there are great similarities between the practices of this American company and the second British firm described earlier. But three differences are worthy of note between the American and most of the British companies. Central headquarters plays a much more active role in the setting of internal prices in the American company. Second, while relevant information is withheld from divisions in the companies of both countries, it is only in some of the British firms that it is withheld by central headquarters. The information withheld in the American firm is restricted to that possessed by a single division, and the withholding is contrary to rather than in accord with central policy. Third, the British divisions are vitally interested in the absolute profits which they earn; the American divisions are only concerned with the trend of their profit rate and with a comparison between their budgeted and realized profits. Thus the British divisions are interested in the absolute transfer prices which they receive or pay; the American divisions are motivated only by the difference between the negotiated transfer prices and those estimates which served as a basis for their annual profit plans. For this reason, interdivisional dispute in the American firm is concentrated upon the prices of new products, while it has a much broader base in the British companies.

French Firms and Their American Counterpart

The first French firm is a prime example of the use of short-run marginal costs as the basis for transfer pricing. Three of the seven firms in our French sample follow this practice.

This company is quite a large one, with a work force of between fifteen and twenty thousand employees. A considerable portion of its production is sold internally between the various production departments, most of which also sell in the external market. On the other hand, although the production and marketing departments are organized completely independently, no system of transfer prices is used between them.

The *directeur général* was of the opinion that the correct method of determining transfer prices is according to the short-run marginal costs of production. In fact, however, the general method that is used in principle is to price at 8 percent above the average cost to the plant—but excluding all amortization costs and headquarters charges from the definition of "average cost." Thus the theoretic level of transfer prices used by this firm is well below full average cost. Actual transfer prices are decided by executives who are above the level of the affected production departments, and these prices seem in general to have been set below the theoretic level.

A significant part of the internal transfers between plants has been carried out at a price equal to short-run marginal cost under an extremely strict definition of the latter. These transfers consist of products that are produced by both the purchasing and the selling factory, and for which headquarters has decided that a particular plant is the low-cost producer at the given level of utilization of total company capacity. Headquarters makes this decision on the basis of marginal costs of production at the two plants, and then credits the selling plant with receipts equal to these marginal costs. For this purpose, marginal costs are defined as the cost of raw materials, the cost of the jigs and fixtures required specifically for the order, and direct variable wage costs. The last item is subject to different interpretations depending on the specific case, the most extreme (which is used only exceptionally) being that variable wage costs should be considered to be zero, since employment would in any case be held constant in the short run.

The advantage of this system of transfer prices is twofold. First, the transfer-price system minimizes the obstacles in the way of concentrating production in those company facilities which have the lowest short-run marginal costs. Second, the general management of the company has been made aware of a reasonable proxy for marginal costs, and has accepted some orders (these have been exclusively for exports, so as not to interfere with the company's normal markets) at a price barely above the marginal cost of production defined so strictly as to exclude all wages. But the organizational harm has been considerable. Production units have had little choice as to whether to buy externally or internally, whether to produce for themselves or to buy or sell within the company, or even as to the plant within the company on which to place their orders. All of this is determined centrally. Second, the central management has shown little confidence in the consistency of the system of setting transfer prices, both in regard to the system's effects on the profitability of different departments and factories at a single moment of time and in regard to changes over time. Thus there has been a justified hesitancy on the part of top management in using profit figures as a significant means for judging the effectiveness of the managements of production units,[12] and a resultant lack of interest on the part of production managers in developing profitable products for sale outside.

Although the production and sales functions have been strictly separated organizationally, no system of transfer prices exists between the two functions. This absence of transfer prices has had the advantage of not interposing any obstacle to profit-maximizing pricing by the sales organization, but it has also deprived this organization of all interest in the sort of sales efforts and pricing policy which would have improved the profitability of the company. This negative effect may not have mattered too much in the case of the few major products whose evolution the three or four members of top management could follow closely, but it has been catastrophic for the host of minor products produced by the company. For these, the search for profitability has been severely handicapped by the inevitable lack of continuous attention by top management and by the lack of interest on the part of the intermediate and middle levels of sales management. Small wonder that it is these products which have proved the most unprofitable to the company, for they have been virtually ignored except in the narrow sense that functional specialists have tried to cut their production costs or increase their current sales or improve

[12]Partly this has been because transfer prices might be set at 108 percent of the theoretic level of average costs (excluding amortization and headquarters' charges), or might alternatively be established at one of several considerably lower levels. Partly it has been because departments might be instructed to supply goods at transfer prices when they could alternatively be sold externally. Finally, it has been because departments which sell part of their production at marginal-cost transfer prices are compelled to employ here engineering staff whose salaries are treated as fixed costs but who could otherwise have been used by the department in improving efficiency or in developing new products for an outside profitable market.

their design (in some sense undefined by any weighting of consumer attractiveness against costs of producing alternative designs). The company is far too large to be operated effectively in this highly centralized fashion.

Transfer pricing in the remaining six French companies is described in the appendix to this chapter. Summing up all seven firms, a radically different system is found than that seen in the British companies. For three of the seven French firms, the system of transfer prices leans heavily upon one or another proxy for marginal costs. The other four have operated on different principles, but one of them keeps transfer prices almost entirely isolated from the prices of the open market, and another has sharply restricted the influence of intermediate transfer prices on the final prices charged by the company to outside customers. Only two companies (the fifth and sixth) can be viewed as basing their transfer prices upon open market prices—as was the case for five of the six British concerns. Even in the case of these last two French firms, there was nothing approaching the arm's-length bargaining between divisions which we observed in five of the British companies.

A partial parallel to French transfer pricing is found in a large American food company. While here there is no transfer pricing at all in a formal sense, the result of the system employed is much the same as that of transfers at short-run marginal costs. What is interesting about the case is the set of managerial difficulties which it creates, and the particular organizational environment needed to render the situation viable.

In this company, there is very little transfer of goods or services between divisions but a good many transfers within each division. The division that we shall examine is a large one; at the time of study, it had some five thousand employees of whom twelve hundred were managerial and professional, and it produced at least a dozen major products. Thus the problem of coordinating managerial activities was quite serious.

Within the division, accounts are kept separately for the factories, the sales force, and the development and technical research operations. But all three of these are cost centers rather than profit centers, and are financed primarily from expense budgets allocated for the year. Of these cost centers, only the factories have a budget that varies with output, part of it being based upon a standard variable expense per unit of production. The factory managements are judged by their ability to live within these annual budgets, and thus are motivated to concern themselves entirely with costs and to prefer production volumes that minimize variable costs per unit. The sales managers are judged according to their total dollar volume of sales, with no regard being paid to the relative profits earned on the various products. Development and technical research is judged by its ability both to develop products which show future profitability and to reduce production costs through such methods as substituting cheaper for more expensive materials without affecting quality.

It is a fourth function, marketing, which plays the principal coordinating role. The division's profits are computed separately for each product line, and all production, sales, and development costs are charged against the gross revenues from the various lines. The advantage of this procedure is that marketing decisions are made quite explicitly on the basis of marginal cost.

Thus it is marketing that determines when to engage in special promotional activities. Since these involve additional packaging costs for the factories, the incremental factory costs of such promotions are borne by the marketing department—and these sums are added to the annual budgets of the factories. The same is true with regard to special projects for technical research.

Decisions with regard to the introduction of new products are particularly interesting, for costs again are treated on an incremental basis. Thus, if the products can be introduced into existing factories, only the depreciation of equipment that must be bought as a result of such introduction is charged against the new product line; if factories are currently working below capacity, these incremental costs may be very slight. A similar procedure is used for charging only incremental manpower costs against the new products. If a new product is judged to be potentially profitable under this system of costing, it will have passed the profit test (there are, of course, other criteria as well) for introduction.

Once introduced, new products are costed on this incremental basis until they reach a stage at which they are profitable under a full-costing criterion. At that point, they are no longer costed incrementally but rather must bear their full share of all overhead expenses.

From the point of view of rational divisional decision making, there appears to be only one serious objection to this procedure of incremental costing. This is that the order in which new products are examined becomes extremely important. A given factory may have excess capacity sufficient for the addition of either new product A or B but not of both. Under this circumstance, the product which is analyzed first will be charged with extremely low incremental capital charges, while the second must be charged with the full capital costs involved in building a new factory. For this reason, if only product A is under consideration at first, it is extremely important to judge the likelihood of the development in the near future of an alternative unknown product B that would be more profitable than product A. If such development is considered likely, then product A should be charged with the incremental costs of a new factory even if it is physically placed in an old one. The divisional comptroller must try to wrestle with this problem.

While the system of handling interfunctional transfers is highly conducive to rational decision making, the demands that it makes on organization within the division are serious. For the only functions that are directly concerned with profitability are marketing and, of course, comptrollership. But even the marketing product-group managers cannot be held responsible for profitability, since they exercise no control as such over the activities of any other line function. Similarly, the other line functions can scarcely be held completely responsible for performance even as judged by the individual success indicators developed for them.

Thus sales managers are judged according to the volume of their sales. But clearly such volume must depend heavily upon the success of the advertising and promotion campaigns, and these latter are under the control of the marketing rather than of the sales function. Similarly, inventories are a large proportion of the capital investment in the factories and, since factory costs are defined to include a budgeted return on capital, inventory volumes constitute an important constituent element in the costs incurred by factory managers. But factory managers are highly dependent upon prompt and correct information from the marketing product managers if they are to control inventory levels correctly. In its turn, development research hands over its products to marketing for the critical market tests and for the decisions as to marketing approaches; thus the development function can scarcely be held independently responsible for the degree of profitability obtained from the products which it has created.

Given this situation, the current divisional manager and his predecessor both told me that—unfortunately, in their opinion—managers are inevitably judged for promotion much more according to their personality traits than on the basis of the results of their activities. Both felt that the success of managers in cooperating successfully with other functions, and in avoiding rustling the feathers of their colleagues in these other functions, was a dominant element in the evaluation of the manager's own work.

As Charles Perrow has pointed out to me, judgment by personality traits does not necessarily imply either nepotism or the rewarding of blandness. Ability to cooperate with other managers is an important ingredient in a manager's execution of his proper functions, and thus quite properly plays a significant role in the evaluation of the manager's potential. A manager can also demonstrate the capability for getting things done long before it becomes clear whether he is doing things helpful or harmful to the company; this in itself is performance of a type.

Nevertheless, this latter type of performance seems similar to that by which Jones was judged in the British Company B3. Jones, we may recall from Chapter 5, was continually promoted for exceptional imagination and force-fulness; but the changes he instituted led only to a decline over an eleven-year period in his division's total productivity and profitability. It is this lack of necessary correlation between a manager's executive abilities and their effect on the economic characteristics of his enterprise which leads me to charac-terize evaluation of this sort of "performance" as really constituting judg-ment of personality traits.

Doubtless, the inability to attach independent responsibility to managers for the results of their function's activity has contributed to the determina-tion of promotions according to managerial traits. Similarly, the fact that short tenure in a given post would in any case have made it impracticable to judge managers by results has helped to reconcile top management to an organizational structure in which there is no independent personal respon-sibility. Given both features, the division can function effectively only to the degree that there is truly a high degree of effective cooperation among the managers in the various functions. This is the essential foundation for success-ful operations in the absence of a transfer-price system within the division.

In the light of this organizational environment, it should not be surprising that it has been the marketing function that has constituted the royal road to general management.[13] For it is the product managers in marketing who, of all people in the division, are most concerned with achieving profitability. Moreover, in an environment in which interfunctional cooperation is the very heart of the management problem, it is they who are responsible for guiding this cooperation. Thus it is the product managers who receive the only truly appropriate training for general management at either the divisional or corpo-rate level.

This situation, of course, sharply reduces the stock of managers from whom future general management can be chosen. Nevertheless, since there are a large number of product managers, and since these are either quickly pro-moted or gently eased out of the corporation, there exists a sufficient stock

[13]By "general management" is meant both the divisional general manager and his chief aid, and line personnel at a similar or higher level at corporate headquarters.

of candidates for general management so that there has been no embarrassment due to a paucity of choice.

To sum up, the method by which this division interrelates different functions is satisfactory only because of top management's acceptance of a situation in which an individual manager's results cannot be objectively evaluated, and where only a single function is regarded as the proper route to general management. Such acceptance is possible only because of the existence of an extreme degree of interfunctional cooperation. Other enterprises, with a different organizational environment, could scarcely accept similar handicaps. But once there is such acceptance, the gains are very real in rational decision making that promotes high profitability.

When we compare this company's situation with that of the French firms engaged in internal pricing at marginal costs, one major similarity and two differences appear. Both the American and the French companies have the same advantage of rationality in decision making. But the French companies suffer much less from the system's disadvantages for managerial evaluation and promotion; this is because their promotional structure is in any case based upon the advancement of *grande école* graduates. On the other hand, they find it impossible to realize the teamwork that is the bedrock of the American company's success.

Conclusion

Our examination of transfer-pricing practices in two American, six British, and seven French firms shows a considerable degree of similarity among large firms in the three countries. At the same time, however, it does indicate the existence of substantial national differences.

The British firms are striking for the degree to which transfer prices are based upon open-market prices, and for the extent to which arm's-length bargaining is utilized as a means of ensuring this. On the other hand, three of the French firms lean heavily upon one or another proxy for short-run marginal-cost transfer prices; only two have attempted to employ open-market prices, and these without the resort to arm's-length bargaining which alone is likely to make this approach really feasible. The one American firm that transfers goods extensively between divisions does so on the basis of planned-cost-plus, at prices seemingly above the open-market level, and with no attempt at arm's-length bargaining. The second American firm transfers goods and services only within divisions, and here the managerial determination of pricing and investment has been similar to what would have resulted from marginal-cost transfer pricing. Thus, if we consider only the method of transfer pricing (or the substitutes used for it, as in the case of the second American company), Britain stands at the opposite end of the continuum from France, with the United States in an intermediate position.[14]

While the British system of interdivisional transfers makes only minimal demands on cooperation among managers, use of marginal-cost transfer prices compels a choice between serious teamwork and a high degree of centralization. But French and American behavior patterns differ radically from one another with regard to the prevalence of lateral cooperation across functions; in this regard, the British and French stand together at the opposite end of the spectrum from the American managers. The French attempt to compensate for the absence of cooperation by extreme centralization of decision making at the top of the hierarchy. The British compensation takes the form of treating the various components of the company as though each were a separate enterprise.

When we turn to the attitude of middle managers toward the attainment of high profitability, the British and American managers are united in opposition to the French. The British companies are so structured that the middle managers can be effectively judged according to the profitability of their individual operations, and thus they emphasize it. Neither the American nor the French managers can be so evaluated. The French respond with a lack of concern, while the Americans develop close interfunctional cooperation so that informal, nonquantitative evaluations can be made of the contributions of the various managers.

American transfer prices generate information appropriate to decisions as to the maintenance or gradual abandonment of the production of intermediate

[14]Since our study includes only two American firms, this conclusion should probably be considered unreliable with regard to its generalization concerning American industry. I feel more comfortable with the British-French comparison.

Unfortunately, there has been little study of American transfer-pricing practices. The National Industrial Conference Board in its *Interdivisional Transfer Pricing* reported that only a few of the 190 manufacturing companies which it studied used direct variable costs as the basis for their transfer prices. This suggests a major distinction from the French concerns, but, since the second American firm in my sample would doubtless also, and correctly, deny that it transfers at variable cost, the Conference Board statement is not particularly helpful for our problem.

The few Harvard Business School cases that deal with transfer prices indicate a heavy reliance on open-market prices but also show that interdivisional bargaining is far from being at arm's length. If we can take these cases as being at all representative—and, of course, there is no necessary reason to do so—it would suggest a distinction from the British companies. (R. N. Anthony, J. Dearden, and R. F. Vancil, *Management Control Systems*, Richard D. Irwin, Homewood, Illinois, 1965, pp. 276-313.)

goods. French internal prices are less useful in this regard, being much better adapted to the making of short-run than long-run decisions. The acceptance of this situation by the French is closely linked to the attitude of senior management towards profitability. Since French top managers are more concerned with growth and are relatively unwilling to consider seriously renouncing the production of individual products, whether they be intermediate or final, information as to the relative advantages of making versus buying intermediate goods is of much less value to them than it is to British or American companies.

The foregoing is summed up in Figure 12.1 which shows the relative positions of large companies in the three countries along a scale that relates to four different attributes.

A useful way of viewing these differences among managerial practices in the three countries is to see the French and British behavior patterns as alternative responses to a common problem: namely, the relative absence of lateral cooperation among middle managers. The British response is to structure firms in an extremely decentralized fashion so that such cooperation is unnecessary. The disadvantage of this solution is that little attention can be paid to economies which are internal to the company but external to the individual decision-making subunits. The French response is to opt for extreme centralization in the hands of one or a few men, with a consequent reduction of the danger of suboptimization of profit objectives to the level of subunits. The difficulty with this approach is that it leads both to atrophy of the company's ability to make minor decisions sensibly and rapidly, and at the same time it sometimes results in anarchy (as in the first French firm treated in the appendix to this chapter) when the middle managers assert themselves.

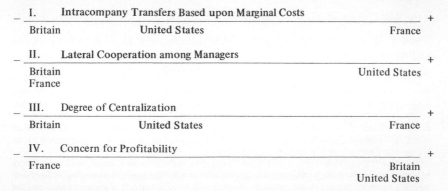

Figure 12.1   Relative positions of large companies in Britain, France, and the United States, with regard to four different attributes.

British Firms

Transfer pricing in two British firms has been described in the text. The remaining four companies will be treated here.

The third firm is similar to the American food company described in the text in that it relied upon product marketing managers to determine the company's choice of products and their prices. But in the British case, the product managers each represented an independent profit center in a chain of such vertically integrated centers and were totally cut off from information regarding earlier or later links. The product manager was given no information about costs at the factory level, and the factory managers had no information as to the demand schedule of the product manager. The product manager would ask the factory for a quotation for a given volume of products of a particular type, and on the basis of the single quotation would decide whether or not to order production. Even for major products, the company was organized so that no one possessed information as to the total profits that would be earned throughout the company. Each unit acted completely autonomously, despite the fact that their vertical links were such that each one was a complete monopolist, monopsonist, or both, in its dealings within the company.

A fourth company prices interdivisional sales at market prices (as well as these can be estimated), and sales within a single division at full average cost. In the division that I studied, even labor is primarily a fixed cost since the vast majority of it is employed in maintenance operations. Yet decisions both as to the production of new final products and as to the abandonment of old are made on the basis of the effect on profits earned only at the final-stage profit center.

On the other hand, the company does keep track of total profits earned on major final products and product groupings—for this purpose adding in the profits earned at the various early-stage production divisions. These calculations are used for purposes of investment decisions, and investment proposals are evaluated centrally by a comparison of the investments with the net additional revenue (additional company revenue minus additional costs, regardless of which division might incur these costs).

Thus, in this company, there has been a serious effort to evaluate investment decisions from the viewpoint of their effect on the profits of the company as a whole; but short-term decisions as to pricing, choice of inputs, and development of new products are made from the vantage point of the individual unit.

The result is a recognized dilemma. On the one hand, divisions are considered responsible for the return on capital they attain. As a consequence, a particular low-profitability division that I studied was outstanding within the company for its poor buildings and for its permanently low expenditures on training and education; this division was considered unable to "afford" what were normal expenditures elsewhere.

At the same time, since investment decisions are not made in terms of their effect on the profitability of any individual division, the division is unable to influence decisively its average profitability over any extended period of time. The consequence is that the gains from a feeling of decentralized managerial profit responsibility which were hoped for from the system of transfer prices have to a considerable degree been sacrificed by the method of investment decision making.

A fifth company employs transfer prices and makes investment decisions much in the same way as does the fourth company.

Of all six British companies studied, only the sixth departs radically from the system of basing transfer prices upon the open market. This is true with regard to transfers both between and within divisions.

A major semifabricate produced in one division is supplied to others at the list price for open-market sales. It was generally believed, both at one of the user divisions and at company headquarters, that lower prices would have been quoted by outside companies—but no quotations were requested. For a long time, at least one division asked to be permitted to purchase some 10 percent of its needs from outside the company; it was finally granted the right to buy a maximum of 3 percent outside—and most of this was of varieties not produced within the firm itself.

On the other hand, sales of capital equipment between divisions are in principle made at standard cost; this has been justified on tax grounds, to assure that the company did not pay profits tax on goods produced for investment purposes within the firm. One capital equipment subdivision in fact sold at what was probably a substantial loss, and its sales to another subdivision from which it had recently been separated were at a lower price than that charged to other subdivisions, and still lower than that charged to other divisions within the company. This subdivision sold to the favored subdivision at prices which were estimated to be only 50 percent of those which would have been charged by outside companies; when it was unable to make deliveries, it was obligated to buy the equipment from the outside and to deliver it at the low transfer price to the internal customers. The rather weak logic behind this pricing policy was that it would provide the capital equipment subdivision with a strong incentive to improve its production efficiency; no thought seems to have been given to the effect of this low-price policy on the investment decisions of the purchasing subdivisions and divisions.

Finally, the few services provided by company headquarters—such as operations research and programming and analysis for data processing—are provided the divisions without charge. The head of the company central services department defended this practice on the ground that the experience of consultants and of central service departments in other companies has shown that, when charges are made, divisions refuse to allow the advising service to implement its own suggestions. Only free implementation of advice was believed acceptable to the divisions, and so it was carried out on this basis. Here there was complete rejection of the market mechanism for determining which services company headquarters should provide.

From this description it can be seen that the pricing policy for interdivisional transfers in this company differs sharply, but in a totally nonsystematic fashion, from that of following the open-market prices.

Within the large division that I studied in this company, there were no transfer prices. True, the individual factories were instructed to earn the maximum possible profit on their products. But this factory profit was calculated without any deduction for the warehousing or distribution costs of the sales department. The sales department, which recommended prices and determined the size of the orders to place on the factories, did not have any separate profit account at all.

The result was a divisional operation which was highly centralized in form in the sense that no functions or other segments of the division were impelled by their financial budget structure toward actions that would promote their own interest at the expense of the division as a whole. There existed no set of intradivisional transfer prices that could lead to suboptimization. In this sense, the company was similar to the large American food company described in the text. However, such a system requires either a high degree of interfunctional coordination or centralization if it is to be efficient. Neither of these was present in this British firm.

No one in this company below the level of the divisional managing director had the authority to exercise coordination. It was noted in an official divisional report that the senior executives (i.e., the functional heads and the general manager) of the division never in seven years met together—apart from other managers—in a meeting where they could wrestle with problems of coordination. Heavy divisional investments were made in a geographic location which eventually turned out to be sorely lacking in labor force, and labor shortage ended up as the bottleneck to the full meeting of demand in boom times; but the divisional personnel director had never been called in to consult as to the geographic location of these investments. The production director made decisions as to double-shift operation of plants without inquiring of the personnel director as to the degree to which the multiple shifts could be manned. Lateral coordination of functions was similarly lacking at a lower level. Thus plant managers decided what specific machines should be purchased for expansion or replacement, and the purchasing department was then presented with an "order to buy" that specified the company with which to deal.

In short, of all the British companies studied, this division was outstanding for its lack of internal managerial coordination.

French Firms

The first French firm was treated in the text. The second is particularly interesting both because of the efforts of its *directeur général* to price along the lines of opportunity costs, and because of the reasons for the failure of these efforts. A large number of external price requests for custom-made products were received monthly, but these items were produced on a relatively small number of different kinds of machinery. Standard price quotations were written on the basis of expected average production costs for the order, plus a standard percentage markup to cover both nonproduction costs and profit. The salesmen, in determining the actual quotations to be offered, were permitted to deviate in either direction from these standard quotations; but the commission system was set so as to motivate them strongly against going below the standard price.

In employing this external pricing system, the *directeur général* treated his different kinds of machinery as the bottlenecks that should be subject to shadow-pricing when establishing the costs of production of the various orders. Thus he personally reviewed at regular intervals the utilization figures of each type of machinery, and monthly revised the "machine cost per hour" that was to be incorporated into the standard price; this machine charge was reduced when increased load for a particular type of machinery was desired, and was raised when abnormal demand would otherwise be threatened. If he wished to increase or decrease total demand for all products, regardless of which specific machine-

352 Part IV Two Studies of National Behavioral Differences

types were required to produce them, he would vary the markup. Thus he expected that the external prices would constitute a fairly good approximation to the opportunity costs of producing the various products.

This method of external pricing was designed to concentrate the key elements of the pricing system in the hands of the chief executive, while at the same time decentralizing the calculation of the actual price quotations. The individual salesmen were given a genuine if minor role in interpreting what the market would bear in deviations from the base price, thus permitting them to utilize detailed information that could scarcely be funneled up to the level of the chief executive. They also had it in their discretion to modify the standard prices for steady customers so that the prices charged them would not vary erratically from month to month. Strictly speaking, there was no system of transfer pricing in this company. But the external pricing system could be reasonably interpreted as a proxy for marginal (opportunity) cost pricing by the production department.

Unfortunately, the system of establishing standard prices appears to have been a dismal failure because of the inability of the *directeur général* to convince the pricing department of the reasonableness of the procedures. The people charged with working out the standard costs (from which the standard prices were derived through multiplication by a given markup) were convinced that no "real" standard cost could be calculated under this system. The result was extreme erraticism in their calculation of the amount of materials required for a given order, of the number of hours of machine time required, and even of the amount of packing materials needed.

The erraticism of calculation was indicated by an experiment in which an identical fictitious order was submitted for costing three times and at monthly intervals. But the experiment had been carried out for other reasons, and the variance of the costing estimates was not discovered until an outsider (myself) reviewed the detailed figures. Even after that, there were no attempts made to control the consistency of the estimates made in the pricing department. Nor was there any real effort by the *directeur général* to communicate to the pricing department the reasons for his system.

Thus this effort by the chief executive to use opportunity-cost pricing broke on the rock of resistance by middle and lower management. This situation appears to be a result of the minimum of cooperation or even face-to-face contact among professionals and managers which is so typical of France.

The third company (F6 of Chapter 6) is divided into departments that sell very extensively to one another; internal transfers reach a level of 45 percent of the company's external sales. Thus transfer prices are quite important to the operation of the company.

Two departments sell exclusively within the company, and their transfer prices are fixed on average at some 110 percent of direct variable cost. Since these two departments supply about one-half of total internal sales, and an even higher share of the total value-added of internal sales, one might fairly say that over half of the internal transfers have been priced at an approximation to short-run marginal cost. These transfer prices are set in this fashion despite the fact that the company purchases from outside sources a fair proportion of its needs for the services produced by these same two departments, and thus has had available to it information as to the market price of these items.

The other half of the interdepartmental transfers are comprised of goods that are also sold heavily on the outside market. Here, in principle, transfer prices are set 10 percent below the market prices charged to the most favored customers on the French market; this 10 percent differential is intended to represent both the cost of sales to the outside and the full profit made on sales. Thus these transfers are, in principle, to be made at full average cost.

Exports—which are important to the company—constitute a special case. Sales to countries outside of the Common Market have been made at an average of 20 to 22 percent below French prices and have represented an important share of the company's total sales. For these deliveries, the company headquarters computes a percentage reduction in normal transfer prices which applies uniformly to all departments except those selling at short-run marginal costs; this percentage is set at a different level for each major export transaction and depends upon the price received by the company.

As one might expect, given this system of transfer prices, there has been considerable centralization in determining the destination of the production of individual departments. The departments are not allowed to impinge on internal company deliveries in order to sell more on the outside at profitable prices; similarly, their external sales within France have been restricted by the imposition of quotas as to the output that must be devoted to exports. Because of this central interventionist policy, the company comptroller believed it to be impracticable to judge department managements by the level of their profits.

Of the seven French firms that I have studied, the previous three come the closest to using some approximation to marginal cost as the basis for transfer prices. But one of the remaining four has also made some efforts to prevent the system of transfer prices from diverting the company away from what would be profitable sales.

This fourth company (F2) functioned with one-third of its sales being made by a coordinating department that purchased very heavily from other departments. This department was allowed to operate at a loss, with its external sales prices being determined by the top managment of the company. Since transfer prices of products sold to this department included a profit, the company in this fashion attempted to avoid the rejection of orders which represented a net profit to the company but which would otherwise have involved a loss to some individual departments. This system was also intended to reduce the temptation for each department to keep secrets from the others in order to improve its own bargaining position.

A fifth company has normally tried to set its transfer prices at the level of market prices. However, since the early-stage fabricating departments have been relatively inefficient compared to their external competitors, this method of pricing has often resulted in these departments operating at fairly substantial losses. They have been allowed to sell internally at up to 10 percent more than the offers from external suppliers (on the ground that purchasing and materials-handling costs of external deliveries amount to this), but normally not at higher prices. Although the early-stage departments have been virtually guaranteed the business of the other company departments, they were selling at close to direct variable costs during the year when I first visited the company.

A sixth firm bases its system of transfer prices upon market prices. But its choice of this transfer-price system has been heavily influenced by the financial structure of the company. The supplying divisions are mostly separate companies, only partially owned by the parent firm. Given the division of ownership of the suppliers, any other system of pricing would have been difficult to arrange.

The last company (F3) has its transfer prices determined by bargaining between the individual factories and the separate sales depots, both being prohibited from going to the outside either for markets or for supplies of the goods produced by the company's own factories. Transfer prices are thus set on the basis of a market relationship among a number of different units of the company; but this internal market is virtually isolated from the external one, and the cost analyses of the factories are completely misleading due to an improper system of cost accounting.

V

Conclusions and Recent Developments

Chapter 13 sums up the book, linking national differences in career patterns, bonus schemes, and value systems to managerial behavior. Some macroeconomic data are presented which provide moderate empirical support for the analysis of Chapter 11 and which also indicate a likely important effect of British managerial decentralization on the national economy. Finally, two empirical hypotheses are presented on the basis of the analysis of the study as a whole.

Chapter 14 deals with developments from the early 1960s to the spring of 1971. Britain is regarded as displaying virtually no change, while France is seen as more affected by recent developments.

13

Chapter 1 began by indicating the historically slow tempo of equalization of the widely disparate per capita income levels among developed countries. Since all those countries examined have for a long time been fully capable of absorbing the latest technologies, it is the pace rather than the equalization itself which requires explanation. The explanatory hypothesis offered was the existence of a slower speed of adjustment to changing conditions in the other developed countries than in the United States.

The managerial function in a modern industrial society may be viewed as primarily that of adapting the enterprise to changing conditions. The quality of management can be judged primarily by its responses to changes in the technological, social, and market environment. Variations in the standard of management between countries have their most significant effect on the rate of productivity growth rather than upon the level of static efficiency reached at any moment.

Throughout this study, the effectiveness of managerial adaptation to change has been analyzed in terms of two systems of variables: managerial values on the one hand, and the characteristics of managerial organization on the other. Both determine the enterprise's state of readiness to implement successfully alternative projects.

Operation of these variables can be illustrated from French experience. Managements which give a high priority to the avoidance of any staff layoffs are hampered in their efforts to respond either to new technological or market possibilities. When such managements also give a low priority to the increase of profitability, there is a minimization of their incentive to take the psychologically painful decisions necessary for rapid adaptation to market changes.

With regard to organization, the successful design, production, and marketing of a large number of products that are individually of minor importance to the company probably requires the creation within the firm of small and decentralized decision-making units. Without such organization, adaptation to change is bound to be slow. Yet this type of organization is still not only generally absent but is also unwarranted in France, due to the fact that the competence of the middle-level managers who would head such units is distrusted by top management, and that these middle managers are themselves disinterested in the advancement of the goals of the company.

Part II explored the effect of the managerial variables on the rate of productivity change in nine large representative British and French industrial companies. Comparing these firms with one another, we saw in Chapter 4 that the managerial strengths and weaknesses were quite different in the two countries. The British firms were relatively strong at the lower and middle levels of management, but top management seemed incapable of taking and enforcing adaptive decisions. Each company operated as though it consisted of a host of small firms, with coordination lacking and suboptimization rampant. New investment was heavily concentrated in relatively unprofitable product markets because of the unwillingness of top management to depart from what they considered (often incorrectly) to be the areas of the company's managerial competence.

In contrast, top management decisions were extremely important in achieving the productivity improvements observed in the French firms. In four out of five relevant enterprises, central management proved capable of making and carrying through basic decisions when the affairs of the company or divisions were in crisis. On the other hand, middle management was unaggressive and ineffective; in five of the six firms, one could observe these managers acting in their own individual interests of professionalism rather than to achieve the goals of the company. Four of the six French companies seemed, under normal circumstances, to be quite out of control; middle management did not have the authority or incentive to take decisions, and top management did not receive enough information to make rational decisions.

Chapter 4 presented the case for believing that these firms are representative of large-scale industry in their respective countries. To the extent that this is so, one can appreciate why France has not made greater progress in catching up to the American productivity level and why Britain has made no progress whatsoever. Either of the European management systems might have worked effectively in a static situation; under changing conditions, the British proved capable only of successful minor action through lower- and middle-level managerial response, and the French only of major steps taken through drastic top management reorientation of policy. Neither was able to react to change with an effective managerial response at all levels of the hierarchy.

Chapter 12 illustrated in the field of internal transfer pricing the varying British and French approaches to centralization of management. The French, with their centralization of authority, are much more ready to use short-run marginal costs as a basis for internal transfers within the company; this practice promotes short-run efficiency, and the resultant absence of make versus buy information at middle managerial levels is not too serious a counterbalancing handicap under the circumstances. The British firms, on the other hand, use transfer prices that are as close as possible to external prices; this allows them to run their divisions as though they were independent companies but robs the parent firm of much of the advantage of vertical integration.

These observations about British decentralization may throw some light on what would otherwise appear to be a strange phenomenon: namely, the fact that despite French manufacturing establishments being considerably smaller than British, French labor productivity in manufacturing is still much the higher of the two.

Using data for 1954, and measuring the size of an establishment by the number of its employees, the median plant size of the twenty largest plants in each of thirty-four industries was 78 percent as high in the United Kingdom as in the United States, and 200 percent as high as in France.[1] Data of 1958 for all manufacturing establishments corroborate the position that British plants are larger than French.[2] Yet British industrial labor productivity in 1966 was only 65 to 75 percent of the French, depending on whether one uses American or European weights.[3]

Bain has argued that, in the United States, something like 70 to 90 percent of each industry's output is supplied by plants of reasonably efficient scale, and that countries with smaller size plants generally suffer from diseconomies arising out of suboptimal scale.[4] If this is even very roughly true, then Britain suffers in a fairly minor fashion from diseconomies of small scale, but French industry operates under a very serious handicap.

How, then, do we explain the substantially higher productivity in French than in British manufacturing? One possible explanation, of course, is that French industry is sufficiently more efficient as to reverse the relationship that relative scale would lead us to expect. But an alternative explanation is that British establishments are so organized internally as to fail to reap the cost benefits of their larger size.

The second explanation is particularly suggested by a comparison of British and West German industry. In 1958, the average British plant was only slightly (11 percent) larger than the average German one. The same is true

[1]Joe S. Bain, *International Differences in Industrial Structure* (Yale University Press, New Haven and London, 1966), p. 39.
[2]G. F. Ray, "The Size of Plant: A Comparison," *National Institute Economic Review,* November 1966, p. 63.
[3]Table 1.2.
[4]Bain, *International Differences,* pp. 57-60 and 144.

Table 13.1 Labor Productivity in Establishments of More than One Thousand Employees

Industry	Index of Labor Productivity (Labor Productivity in Plants of 200-500 Employees in the Respective Countries = 100)	
	Britain	Germany
All manufacturing	113	127
Chemicals and allied industries	103	120[a]
Engineering, shipbuilding, and electrical goods	93	108
Vehicles	108[b] [c]	121

Source: G. F. Ray, "The Size of Plant: A Comparison," *National Institute Economic Review*, November 1966, p. 65.
[a]Plants of 100 to 500 employees = 100.
[b]Plants of 300 to 500 employees = 100.
[c]The index is for establishments with 1,500 and more employees.

(there is a 10 percent differential) for a comparison of plants in both countries restricted to those with more than 1,000 employees.[5] Thus manufacturing in these two countries seems to have much the same size distribution of plants.

Where they differ markedly, however, is in the rise in labor productivity that accompanies larger plant size. Data for 1954 are shown in Table 13.1. German labor productivity in manufacturing as a whole was 27 percent larger in plants with more than 1,000 employees than in those with between 200 and 500, while the British increase was only 13 percent. Clearly, German industry appears to realize economies of plant scale that are unrealizable in the United Kingdom.

It may be hypothesized that the explanation lies in the extreme form of British decentralization. In the case study of Company B1, for example, it was seen that this firm has built some good-sized factories; but they are mostly operated through the establishment of vertically integrated production sections within the factory which are virtual replicas of one another and in which diseconomies of scale are fairly obvious. To the extent that British executives attempt to establish small and relatively independent management units, economies of scale at the establishment as well as at the corporate level are lost. It is a matter of relative unimportance whether these units are

[5]Ray, "The Size of Plant," pp. 63-64.

grouped together in a single factory area or are distributed among different plant sites.

Another piece of macroeconomic information that my analysis of managerial behavior may help to explain is the difference in incremental capital-output ratios between Britain and France. In Chapter 11, we examined the effect of suboptimizing behavior by plant managers on the amount and type of fixed investment. The bias arises primarily from the incentive given to British, but not to French, plant managers to strive for a quantity and mix of fixed capital that will permit them to maintain marginal costs at a fairly stable level when sales vary in the short run. This leads to a clear tendency in Britain toward overinvestment (judged from a profit-maximizing standpoint) through the accumulation of excess equipment.

It is true that the situation is complicated by differential national influences toward avoiding the rigidity of technological coefficients of production which is implied by mechanization and automation. But the net behavioral and environmental effect would appear to favor higher incremental capital-output ratios in Britain than in France.

National data as to these ratios exist for the 1950s and early 1960s, with output lagged one year later than investment. Two of the various possible measures seem the most interesting. The first, called ICOR, relates gross investment (excluding investment in residential building) to the increase in output. The second, called ICOR (L'), is similar except that it excludes from the increase in output the product of the growth in employment multiplied by the share of wages in national income (Table 13.2). All of these indices indicate that the incremental capital-output ratio was substantially less for France than for the United Kingdom or the United States, and the 1956-1962 data show the ratio to be higher for the United Kingdom than for the United States.[6] While there are various possible alternative explanations for these national differences (including both the slower British growth in production and the possible success of French planning in restraining the amount of "wasteful" investment), at least the differences in ratios are in the predicted direction.

For reasons given in Chapter 4, it is not possible to go very far in indicating with macroeconomic data the effect of the managerial variables on the quality of national adjustment to changing conditions. No great claims are made for the significance of the two sets of data cited here as a test of my

[6]Wilfred Beckerman and Associates, *The British Economy in 1975* (Cambridge University Press, Cambridge, 1965), pp. 27-39.

Table 13.2 Marginal Capital-Output Ratios

| Countries | Gross National Product | | | | Manufacturing Output 1957-1962 | |
| | 1940-1959 | 1956-1962 | | | | |
	ICOR(L′)	ICOR	ICOR(L′)		ICOR	ICOR(L′)
France	2.37	3.26	3.37		2.34	2.34
United Kingdom	4.44	4.88	5.82		4.84	4.84
United States	5.00	4.17	5.37		. . .	. . .

hypotheses. Primary reliance in hypothesis testing must be laid on the micro-economic data that were presented in the case studies.

Behavioral Effects of Differences in Careers and Bonuses

The most important set of variables used in this study to explain national differences in managerial behavior are those stemming from variations in managerial careers. This set of variables was described in Chapters 7, 8, and 10, and its influence was expounded in Chapter 3.

The British is the extreme form of an "open promotion" system, while the French have a "closed promotion" structure. In Britain, there is little pre-selection before entrance into the firm of those who will reach management positions. The French, on the other hand, preselect sharply on the basis of education, and in fact preselect for the individual strata of management. The American and Soviet patterns are intermediate. In determining promotion, the British appear to lay a particularly heavy stress on success in the present position, and career lines tend to lie fairly narrowly within the same function. Because of their educational preselection, the French are in no position to rely on the success criterion. The high turnover between managerial positions in American companies, as well as the frequent transfers between functions, makes it extremely difficult for American top management to set reasonable standards for judging job success. The very low promotional opportunities in Soviet industry since the Second World War have tended to deprive the entire managerial-career issue of the importance that it has in Britain and in the United States.

An ancillary variable to that of careers is the short-run financial incentive to management provided by bonuses. Chapter 9 demonstrated that these are most important in the Soviet Union and in the United States. But while managerial bonuses represent as large, or almost as large, a share of managerial compensation in the United States as in the Soviet Union, they play an entirely different role in the two countries. In the Soviet Union they are based on monthly or quarterly specified performance indices of the enterprise or of its subunits, depending on the position of the manager concerned. In the United States, to the contrary, they are generally not linked to any specific performance criteria, except for the profits of the organization as a whole rather than that of its constituent parts. To the degree that the performance of an individual manager is relevant at all to the size of his bonus, it is performance as judged subjectively by his superiors. There is very little effort to use objective criteria for determining individual bonuses.

This fundamental distinction between the Russian and American bonus systems reflects quite a different psychological approach to the problem of managing managers. The Soviet emphasis is placed entirely upon the encouragement of greater immediate inputs of effort and imagination, and a high payoff is provided for these. But this emphasis exacts its own price: namely, it strongly encourages managers to suboptimize in terms of the specific performance criteria used in determining their bonuses. While the Soviets clearly recognize the nature of the price that is paid, they have chosen to give priority to inducing intensity of effort—regardless of what this effort is directed toward.

American firms, to the contrary, seem to take effort for granted. They are much more willing to live with subjectivity and uncertainty in their evaluation of managerial performance, rather than trust to objective standards which are of necessity narrowly limited in scope. It seems probable that the radical differences between these approaches are partially accounted for by the fact that the average manager in the two countries comes to his post with different life experiences and thus would not react identically to similar incentives and stimuli. But be this as it may, the result appears to be a sharp difference in the degree of suboptimization and in its economic effects.

The complementary variables of careers and short-run financial rewards seem to lead to a high degree of suboptimization in both British and Soviet industry. It is the career factor that is determining in the British case, and the bonus factor in the Russian; but the effect is similar.

Why, then, do the negative results in Britain appear to be less serious than in the Soviet Union? I would suggest that the answer lies essentially in the fact that industry does not attract the quality of man in Britain that it does in the USSR, the United States, or France. Moreover, those who do enter industry have their self-confidence diminished by the very fact that they were forced to pursue this career line.[7] Precisely because industrial management is not a prestigious career in Britain as it is elsewhere, less vigor, inventiveness, and risk taking is shown by British managers. While the net effect is probably unfavorable for the performance of British industry, a major positive effect is that suboptimizing behavior is pursued less strenuously and creatively than in the Soviet Union.

Three other factors reinforce this national distinction. The first was pointed to in Chapter 10, and consists of the fact that British managers have rapid job mobility and can find their upward movement within a company blocked through antagonizing any one of the many superiors under whom they work at various stages of their career. This phenomenon promotes a reluctance to engage in risk taking, and this must have an effect on suboptimization as well as on other behavior.

The second factor is the level of compensation paid to British industrial management. As seen in Chapter 9, total compensation of the lowest earners within the top 1 percent of income recipients in large industrial organizations relative to that of male manual workers in the same country is considerably lower in Britain—even pretax—than in France or the United States. Taking into account tax considerations, the relative position of British managers falls even lower and is also considerably poorer than that of Soviet managers. One would expect that the paucity of managerial rewards would have its effect upon the vigor with which British managers scramble for promotion, and that this in turn would affect not only functional but also dysfunctional behavior.

The third factor is that the British have to a large extent structured their firms as though each was composed of a number of small independent companies. In short, they have accepted suboptimization and built it into the management system. The Russians, on the other hand, are engaged in a permanent if unsuccessful struggle against it. It is perhaps not surprising that a managerial system constructed in line with a national fact of life has less difficulty in reconciling itself with it than has the Soviet system.

It should be remembered that, prior to the Second World War, promotion and demotion of managers were exceedingly rapid in the Soviet Union. This fact leads to a historical hypothesis: namely, that the macroeconomic problems associated with suboptimization were considerably less severe in the Soviet Union during the period of the 1930s than they have been since. The hypothesis stems from the presumption that, at a time when Soviet managers

---

[7]See David Granick, *The European Executive* (Doubleday, Garden City, N.Y., 1962), Chapter 9, for an elaboration.

had a high statistical probability of moving sharply upwards or downwards, their behavior was much more influenced by the subjective and more comprehensive criteria of performance which helped determine their promotion or demotion. Presumably, the narrowly objective criteria applicable to bonus awards had less of an influence.

This hypothesis would be extremely difficult to test because of the large degree of change that has occurred in the Soviet Union, particularly as a result of economic development, in a wide variety of other variables which also affect economic performance. A serious attempt to test it would constitute another full-blown study. I can only say that, on the basis of wide reading in the Soviet industrial literature, I do not find this hypothesis unreasonable.

French industry escapes the British-Soviet suboptimization. Since top management posts are virtually reserved for graduates of the few truly *grandes écoles,* and since no system of bonuses exists, graduates of the lesser *écoles* are preserved from suboptimizing behavior because it is not worth their trouble. Graduates of the *grandes écoles* are sufficiently few in number that they can be assured of the direct attention of the company *président;* because of this fact and the managerial level to which they can legitimately aspire, suboptimizing behavior would be self-defeating for them.

But the price for French companies is high. Because middle-management graduates of lesser *écoles* feel stripped of the possibility of satisfying their career ambitions, and because they are reasonably sheltered from dismissal by the traditions of French management, they are in a position to ignore the goals of top management and to exercise their functions in the fashion most appealing to their professional pride. This professional ethos is best observed in the engineering and the research and development fields, where these graduates are most highly concentrated. Here they feel relatively free to follow the ethos of high quality, engineering perfectionism, and technical progressiveness with which they had been imbued during the years of formal education. There is little reason for them to pursue profit goals in their engineering work—i.e., to strive for technological improvement only so long as its marginal financial returns to the enterprise are greater than its costs. Nor, in development, is there any reason for them to be particularly guided by marketing considerations. The rejection of a profit goal is quite in line both with their professional viewpoint and with the ideology of the French intelligentsia.

Michel Crozier, writing of a large state enterprise with many factories, describes another aspect of the behavior of these middle managers. Cut off within this enterprise from all possibility of becoming a plant director (a post that was reserved for *polytechniciens*), the plant engineering personnel successfully prevented any rationalization of maintenance. For, so long as this work remained unsystematized, the smooth flow of mass production continued to be uncertain, and it was they who were left in possession of the genuine power in the factory.[8]

While such behavior bears a family resemblance to suboptimization, I believe that it would be a serious mistake to confuse the two. Suboptimization, as observed in Soviet and British industry, consists of striving to attain a narrowly defined success record for the individual subunit and its managers which leads to their being rewarded either through bonuses or promotions. French middle-management behavior, on the other hand, ignores the rewards at the disposal of top management and concentrates upon individualistic goals of the managers. The latter approach, of course, provides far more independence.

One result of this approach is a severe separation between the various managerial functions and a minimum of face-to-face contact and cooperation among the managers engaged in them. Crozier's case is an example of such behavior. In my own case studies, it was clearly observable in companies F1 and F3, and in the second French company of Chapter 12 (described in the appendix to that chapter).

With regard to the public service and state enterprises, Crozier holds that "individual isolation and strata isolation . . . allow some part of *bon plaisir* (acting at one's own discretion, although within the rules) to everyone, although largely in a negative sense. People are protected against interference from above." The people on top cannot interfere with the subordinate strata and cannot provide real leadership on a daily basis. "If they want to introduce change, they must go through the long and difficult ordeal of a crisis. Thus, although they are all-powerful because they are at the apex of the whole centralized system, they are made so weak by the pattern of resistance of the different isolated strata that they can use their power only in truly exceptional circumstances."[9]

It is true that Laurence W. Wylie describes this as a general phenomenon of French life. For example, he believes that every group within a hierarchy

[8]M. Crozier, *The Bureaucratic Phenomenon* (University of Chicago Press, Chicago, 1964), especially pp. 118-142 and 153-156.
[9]*Ibid.*, pp. 223-225.

barricades itself behind its "acquired rights." Jesse R. Pitts, writing of the French child, says that "when face-to-face encounters do not result in the formation of a preferential relationship, hostility is likely to follow; the other person is (considered) unjust and (as giving) a preference to someone else." The adult abstains from face-to-face contacts that do not include such preference.[10]

Nevertheless, even if it is indeed the case that the general pattern of French training and of its cultural values provides a basis for such noncooperative behavior, it is the peculiar conditions of work of the French middle *cadres* which render this a feasible approach in large industrial companies.

The middle managers in line production and in nontechnical functions pursue these individualistic objectives much less vigorously. This is because a considerably higher proportion of them consists of people who have been promoted from non-*cadre* positions and who thus do not have the biases instilled by the minor *écoles*. Much of their work career has been spent in striving for a *cadre* post, and in this effort they have had to accept efficiency values. They have reached in middle management the pinnacle of career success to which they could ever have legitimately aspired, and they are not only grateful men but also managers who have been shaped by their long non-*cadre* work experience. One would expect them to show less personal independence of values than the managers from the lesser *écoles* who started out in management posts.

Since the main middle tier of management pursues neither subunit nor company goals and chooses instead to employ its own professional rather than business standards, it is small wonder that French companies operate in a highly centralized fashion. Top management can scarcely give more decision-making power than necessary to a middle management that follows its own goals rather than those of the company. Of course, such centralization also fits well with the traditional prejudices and love of secrecy in "his" affairs of the French *président*. The reinforcing effects of the two phenomena are obvious.

While the French seem almost entirely to escape the British-Soviet problems of suboptimization, but only by paying a fearful price, American companies preserve an "open promotion" system but go a long way in minimizing the

---

[10]See Lawrence W. Wylie and Jesse R. Pitts in *In Search of France* (Harvard University Press, Cambridge, Mass., 1963), especially pp. 223-224 and 251. See also Wylie, *A Village in the Vaucluse* (Harvard University Press, Cambridge, Mass., 1957), especially Chapter 9, for a similar treatment taken from rural France.

resultant difficulties. This is accomplished first by very frequent transfers of executives both between functions and between units within the company, and second by the imaginative use of headquarters as both an evaluating and socializing force. The rotation of managers through either or both divisional and company headquarters at an early stage in their careers—a phenomenon that is not seen in any of the other three countries—plays a major role in this regard.

But the American solution is also costly. Because of the speedy rotation of managers, they are constantly learning on the job and are unlikely to have fully mastered their position before they are transferred. Second, the rapid job turnover makes it extremely difficult to evaluate properly the results actually achieved by an executive in a specific position. Thus promotions must be determined on relatively subjective grounds, and American executives are probably made more sensitive to company politics than are managers in other countries.

Up to this point, I have approached the national differences in managerial approaches in terms of a suboptimizing framework. An interesting supplementary one, however, is that of Lawrence and Lorsch, who, on the basis of a study of ten American manufacturing organizations, view successful management as dependent upon the development of a system which combines both differentiation of functional roles of individual managers and cooperation among the various functions. While the differentiation of roles is perceived as being in conflict with cooperation among functions, a successful management must achieve at least a threshhold amount of each.[11]

The narrowly functional career lines followed in Britain and the Soviet Union lead to a rich degree of differentiation of roles among managers. Managers are quite specialized in experience and in their attitude. But cooperation among functions suffers badly as a result.

In the United States, to the contrary, the emphasis is placed upon cooperation. The multifunction experience of most managers is an important aid in this. While it is true that differentiation of functions must suffer, the relative narrowness of tasks executed while in a particular managerial post (compared to the French, for example) helps to compensate for this and to provide the necessary specialization of roles.

[11]Paul R. Lawrence and Jay W. Lorsch, *Organization and Environment* (Harvard University Graduate School of Business Administration, Boston, 1967). Differentiation of roles is defined both as the holding of attitudes and interests that focus clearly on departmental goals, and as the presence of time horizons that are consistent with the departmental tasks.

Only the French managers vary sharply depending upon their level. Those from the lesser *écoles* or the universities, as well as those who have worked their way up into *cadre* positions, have highly specialized careers and thus exercise quite differentiated roles; but cooperation, as we have seen, is minimal. On the other hand, the truly *grande école* executives will have had far less functionally differentiated careers and are in a relatively good position to carry out cooperation among functions. The result is that integration of functions can really be carried out by only the top managers, who—unlike their British or Russian counterparts—have the necessary background to do so. Such a situation, of course, necessitates considerable centralization of authority if integration is to be carried out at all; and this is precisely what we find.

As to the differentiation of functions, the French *grande école* executives do not do badly in engineering, research, or even operational manufacturing posts; for the nature of their higher education is well specialized along these lines. But the matter is quite different when one looks at their performance in nontechnical functions such as marketing, comptrollership, and finance. Indeed, it is precisely these functions that have proved most troublesome for large-scale French industrial companies.[12]

Thus the Lawrence-Lorsch analytic system provides us with a basis for analyzing national managerial behavior which fits in well with the suboptimizing framework first used; the results are quite complementary and overlapping.

National Value Systems

In addition to the variables of managerial careers and bonuses discussed in the preceding section, this study has also examined the effect on managerial behavior of national value systems. This was done both in Chapter 2 and through the case studies of Part II. The connection between values on the one hand and careers and incentive systems on the other is particularly worthy of attention.

Both the United States and the Soviet Union share an ideology that careers should be open to all with talent, a belief in the key importance of economic effectiveness, and a faith that the two are closely connected. Despite the restrictive interpretations that are given to this ideology, it serves as the basis

[12]For corroboration of the last fact, see John H. McArthur and B. R. Scott, *Industrial Planning in France* (Harvard University Graduate School of Business Administration, Boston, 1969).

for their "open promotion" systems. In contrast, the French "closed promotion" system stems on the one hand from the values of a much more traditional class society, and on the other from confidence in trained intellect as attested to by success in a school environment. While Britain fully shares the traditional class emphasis of France, the low prestige of industrial management as an upper-class career shields industry from this influence.

The low prestige of industrial management in Britain is probably of major importance in explaining the weakness of the role of its top management. The industrial managerial career probably does not attract as highly talented individuals as is the case in the other countries, and those who do select it have their self-confidence diminished by that very fact. Certainly the breadth of training and experience of top managers is far less in Britain than elsewhere. Under these circumstances, it is not surprising that British top managers play a quite modest role in their companies and encourage the most extreme decentralization found in any of the four countries.

Compared to managers in the other three countries, one has the impression that British managers compensate for their low incomes by taking considerable leisure on the job. The demand for results that American managers expect would be resented by British managers just as bitterly as the imposition of an American work pace on the factory floor would be resented by blue-collar workers. British managers share in the national value system of placing great importance on preserving the workplace from speedup.

The career lines of French top management personnel have an important effect upon the values adopted by French companies. The most prestigious career line is that of the *grande école* graduate who works for a period in the civil service before entering private business. Not surprisingly, these executives tend to take on the values of the *grand corps* civil servants—for they were themselves educated for such posts and served the first part of their careers in these functions. Furthermore, it is not surprising that the values of these most prestigious top executives of large private industrial firms should be widely accepted by other top executives who did not have the opportunity to follow similar educational and career paths. Thus the nature of career patterns of top management provides considerable socialization to the values of the top civil servants of France.

The result of this socialization process is seen most particularly in the acceptance of the advancement of the *gloire* of France as an operational goal for large private companies. The great attention to rapid growth in output and to the avoidance of dismissals of employees stems to a considerable degree from this. The antiprofit mystique of much of top management similarly arises from the same socialization to the values of the civil service, with the socialist ideology that permeates the French civil service neatly reinforcing the traditional ethos of the aristocracy.[13]

A supplementary effect is the bolstering of the position of middle *cadres* in rejecting a market orientation for their activities, and instead substituting a technological bias. The "acquired rights" principle of French society, and the tradition of avoidance of face-to-face encounters, add further support to the posture taken by the middle *cadres*.

Soviet emphasis has been placed upon short-run rewards for effort throughout the economy. This is seen not only in the nature and great importance of managerial bonuses but in the traditional major role of piecework in the payment system for manual workers. It is as though effectiveness were viewed as a simple function of intensity of effort, and as if it were assumed that this would not be forthcoming unless it were paid for immediately and in an assured fashion.

As we saw in Chapter 2, this emphasis finds its expression in the sharp contrast between planning in the Soviet Union and in American companies. Russian planning emphasizes overfulfillment and places little stress upon coordination and long-run effects. Such a negative by-product as the slowness to introduce new products has long been noted but has led to no fundamental changes. To the contrary, American company planners are willing to live with "satisficing" and with the failure to overfulfill divisional profit plans even when this is plainly feasible. American attention is much more firmly fixed on the long-run implications of actions. Perhaps this is because American companies are in a position to take individual effort for granted in a fashion which would be quite unrealistic in the Soviet environment.

American companies, compared to those in other countries, lean very heavily in their operations upon regular coordination between managers in different functions, in the field and at headquarters, and at different levels of the hierarchy. Career development is considerably dependent upon the judgment of executives who are more interested in the manager's willingness and ability to consider and serve the needs of other subunits in addition to his

[13]McArthur and Scott quote from a *polytechnicien* and top business executive whom they interviewed, and who reports that there is little respect among the *polytechniciens* for a graduate who is solely interested in making money. Highly regarded by his fellows, however, is the type of *polytechnicien* who "doesn't enter business with the idea of making his business as profitable as possible [but rather] accepts a role in the community, responsibility for maintaining employment, and so on." (*Ibid.* p. 238.)

own than they are in his performance as judged by the narrow criteria most relevant to his specific subunit. In fact, for the one company for which I have such data, there is absolutely no correlation between a manager's rate of promotion and his performance as judged by his immediate superior.

All of this depends upon a national spirit of teamwork which seems much more developed in the United States than in any other of the countries examined.

Prediction

The test of theory is its ability to predict. Let me then end this chapter with a specific prediction as to future developments in France and Britain, even though this is a prediction that will be difficult to verify.

Both British and French executives have been impressed with the greater size of American corporations, and since the middle of the 1960s they have tried to emulate them through extensive mergers. This has been done under the slogan of achieving economies of scale. My analysis would suggest, however, that the great expectations from these mergers will be frustrated.

It is true that three advantages from larger scale operations do seem likely to be realized. The first of these is in research and development, where such overhead costs can be spread over a larger volume. The second is financial: greater size of company may result in lower costs of raising both debt and equity capital; larger sums can be invested in a single product if the company is willing to concentrate its investment expenditures for a period of a few years; greater diversity of products may make feasible the taking of larger risks with regard to any individual product or product group, since the insurance principle will be working on a larger scale. The third advantage lies in the realm of market power: existing oligopolistic positions can be better protected, and the oligopolistic positions of other firms more readily invaded, the greater are the financial resources of the enterprise.

Presumably the strong tendency toward extreme decentralization in British management would allow these economies to be realized (except, perhaps, the second) with very little offsetting costs—although the advantages (for example, of pooling R&D) may be lower than expected. But the high degree of French centralization should make the diseconomies of scale quite substantial.

However, there is one major scale economy of company size found in American management practice which is most unlikely to be realized in either country, and which can be expected to make both the gross and net advantages of scale appreciably less in Europe than in the United States.

We have seen that the promotion patterns of management in large American corporations, as well as the means by which suboptimization is combated, are heavily dependent upon the existence of substantial functional staffs at headquarters. These staffs—consisting as they do of highly paid executives as well as of other managers—represent an overhead burden that can be economically borne only when the total sales of the company are sizable. The advantageous features of American managerial practice in large firms are a benefit obtained from the large size which makes these headquarters staffs supportable.

But neither British nor French managerial practices require substantial headquarters staffs, nor is there any reason to believe that expansion of company size would lead to an alteration of career practice. Headquarters staffs might remain small or, even if they expand substantially, there should be no expectation that such expansion would lead to a change of managerial patterns in the American direction.

Thus a major economy of company scale which exists in the United States is not present in Britain or France. All of the American diseconomies, however, remain. The net effect should be much less favorable in Europe than one would predict without giving attention to the managerial considerations.

Epilogue: Recent Developments
in Britain and France

All of the preceding chapters have been based upon research conducted during the middle 1960s or earlier. In the case of British and French management, my field work occurred during 1963–1965 with a supplementary period in 1967. The purpose of this chapter is to report briefly on developments up to March-April 1971, when I returned to England and France for a quick survey of the management scene.

Britain

The basic impression received in Britain was one of absence of change. Thus, despite a continuous decline over the last two decades in the per capita income ranking of Britain among the northwest European countries, and apparently a widespread awareness of this phenomenon, no one indicated that this was a matter of serious concern either among business executives or among the general public. Entrance into the Common Market—which was clearly the key economic decision then facing Britain—aroused no strong emotions among either the proponents or opponents with whom I talked. Nowhere in either business or popular circles did there seem to be a feeling of long-run economic crisis that demanded a different response than had been customary during the previous decades. To my surprise, none of the businessmen with whom I talked suggested that the Conservative Government's quite courageous actions of the previous few months represented such a response.

As the tendency has continued for a sharply rising proportion of British youth to attend universities, doubtless the composition of management is becoming increasingly university trained. But there appears to be no break in the tradition that most graduates enter business because of a lack of viable alternatives. While it is the Oxford and Cambridge arts and social studies courses that are the most prestigious, Table 14.1 demonstrates that it is primarily the science graduates who go into business. Unlike the French *grande école* graduates, British science and engineering graduates seem essentially directed toward technology rather than toward business management. Moreover, entrance into business seems particularly rare among those British arts and social studies graduates who earn a first class honors degree. As can be seen from Table 14.1, only 5 percent of them go directly into business after graduation; although no statistics exist as to the proportion who enter business after first taking a higher degree, knowledgeable Britishers suggest that the figure is very small.

It is true that two prestigious business schools have been developed during the second half of the 1960s: at London and at Manchester. Moreover, while

Table 14.1   Proportion of British Male Graduates Going into Business

| | 1968/69 Graduates from | | | |
| | Oxford | | All British Universities | |
Categories of Graduates	Arts and Social Studies	Physical Sciences	Arts and Social Studies	Physical Sciences
A. Estimated percentage of first-degree graduates taking jobs in Great Britain or continuing their studies who eventually enter industry or commerce[a]	...	...	29	67
B. Percentage of first-degree graduates taking jobs in Great Britain or continuing their studies who directly entered industry or commerce:				
All graduates	20	36	23	48
Graduates with first class honors	5	17	5	29
C. Percentage of all higher degree graduates taking jobs in Great Britain who directly entered:				
Manufacturing	...	...	14	41
All areas of industry and commerce	17	56	28	56
First class honors degrees as a percentage of all first degrees	9	16	5	11

[a]For physical science students, the assumption is made that the same proportion of 1969 first-degree graduates who went on for further study will eventually enter business as was the case for those receiving higher degrees in 1969. If the same assumption were made for arts and social studies students, the estimated figure for them would be 31 percent. However, 35 percent of those taking higher degrees in arts or social studies in 1969 who thereafter went into business had taken their higher degree in some form of business study. Since a high proportion of business school students begin these studies only after having first worked for a few years in business, this introduces a considerable degree of double counting. This fact accounts for my having reduced the estimated proportion of those eventually entering business from 31 to 29 percent.

in 1967 British graduates of the better American graduate business schools were offered no more salary than they would have received if they had not attended the master's program, this situation had radically changed by 1971. Then, graduates with a first degree and no experience were receiving £1,500, while London master's degree graduates (with an average of three years' prior experience) were being offered £3,500. London, at least, recruits a student body which is heavily both Oxford or Cambridge and of good family: in short, traditional pillars of the Establishment. Here is one institutional starting point for the notion of management as a profession rather than as simply the top rung of all the functional ladders.

But the significance of these business schools for the future of British business should not be exaggerated. The two schools together award only about two hundred degrees annually. At least at London, the graduates go into a wide range of business occupations; it is merchant banking—the traditional upper-class point of entry into business—rather than industry which is their first choice. Already by 1971 there were rumblings in the business community of discontent with these new schools and a demand that they should be more "practical"—shades of the traditional British industrial emphasis on the early school leaver with training in the firm!

The hope of the middle 1960s that mergers under the aegis of a few talented managers could do much to turn around the British industrial scene was meeting with much skepticism by 1971. A sign of this was the winding down of the Government's Industrial Reorganization Corporation, which had been intended to promote exactly such mergers with the help of government money.

The only behavioral difference that was noted by those British experts with whom I talked was an increased willingness to dismiss employees—at all levels including higher management—under pressure of hard times. But, as seen in earlier chapters, the absence of labor turnover in British industry was never a problem that approached the dimensions of that in French industry.

France
Changes in French industry have been much more marked than in British throughout the middle and late 1960s. Primarily, this can be taken as a response to the growing winds of competition associated with the development of the Common Market. By 1968, exports of manufactured goods per person engaged in manufacturing were substantially higher from France than from Britain.

For our purposes, the most important effect of this growing competition is the change in the managerial value system. Profitability of the enterprise has received ever-increasing attention. Even middle management has come partially to accept it, motivated heavily by the well-publicized wave of mergers and by the fear of unemployment if their company should go under.

The least important change resulting from the increased competitiveness is in the education of management. Despite a great deal of talk about the need for democratization of the sources of managerial recruitment, there is nothing to indicate any alteration in the role of the *grandes écoles* in serving as a selection base. There has, however, been an explosion of interest in management studies. Partly this took the form of the creation in the late 1960s of the two-year master's program at the Institut Supérieur des Affaires. More strikingly, it has been expressed in the proliferation of short courses—mostly of only two or three days—offered by consulting firms.

A more significant accompaniment of this change of values has been an increased willingness by top management to engage in dismissals both of workers and of managerial personnel, and a greater willingness on the part of the French government to see this occur. In fact, the government has even encouraged a policy of dismissals in some branches (especially iron and steel) as an adjunct of mergers, viewing this as a key means of increasing productivity and making French firms more competitive. An aspect of this shift in viewpoint has been the greater emphasis on improving adaptation of workers to changing employment: the creation both of a substantially improved government employment service and the beginning of a system of "permanent retraining."

It is true that it would be easy to exaggerate the significance of this alteration in attitude toward dismissals. Some of my French contacts insist that the change is more reflected in talk than in action. A vice-president of a large metal firm that has been closing two or three plants annually for the last three to four years estimates that his firm spends (both in compensation and in efforts to arrange alternative employment) some 10,000 new francs per worker dismissed. Nevertheless, it is clear that something is happening in this regard in the mores of French industry.

Another aspect of the search for greater competitiveness has been the expansion since the early 1960s of mergers of large enterprises.[1] The major

[1] Annual data for 1961-1967 suggest, however, that the increase in mergers of large enterprises has been fully equaled by a decline in mergers affecting smaller firms. (Institut National de la Statistique et des Etudes Economiques (INSEE), Département

industries of electrical equipment, iron and steel, glass and chemicals, construction materials, and oil, have been virtually transformed. Accompanying these mergers of larger firms has been the growth in the importance and activity of business banks and of financial holdings.

The combination of a change in managerial values toward dismissals and of the merger movement in large enterprises has resulted in an entirely new phenomenon for postwar France: namely, the beginning of the unemployment of *cadres*. Up until the middle of the 1960s, unemployment of *cadres* was virtually unknown in France. By 1970 (probably the high point), it had reached about 1 percent. This unemployment seems to be particularly concentrated among *cadres* in administrative and commercial, rather than in technical functions; dismissals have been strongly associated with the restructuring of enterprises, particularly of headquarter establishments as a result of mergers.

While the unemployment among *cadres* is totally insignificant statistically, it has clearly represented a major psychological shock to the French management world. Primarily this is because of its novelty. But it is also because of the seriousness of such unemployment to the person concerned. The Frenchman best in a position to know guesses that four-fifths of the unemployed find a new position only at a salary lower than that which they had previously earned. Furthermore, the period of unemployment is long: of those searching for employment through an official agency, the period of search for those still registered at the end of July 1970 was as follows: over twenty-one months, 15 percent; twelve to twenty-one months, 18 percent; and six to twelve months, 25 percent.[2]

The development of unemployment among the *cadres,* and particularly the sharpness of its consciousness, has created a new psychological environment for lower and middle management. In earlier chapters, I have stressed that those *cadres* who are not graduates of *grandes écoles* work without either the carrot of promotion or the whip of dismissal, and thus that they are free to

Entreprises, Division Etude des Entreprises, "Documents Statistiques sur l' Industrie Française," October 1969, pp. II–22 and II–23.) A well-informed observer suggested to me that mergers of smaller firms seem to have speeded up since 1967; but there are no statistics as to this.
[2]Association pour le Placement de Cadres, "Etudes & Informations," September 1970, Document No. 9 (mimeographed). The figures include *cadres* who are currently working and looking for a change of employment, but these comprise only 9 percent of the total. It is estimated that about three-quarters of unemployed *cadres* in France are registered with A.P.E.C. It should be noted that the average age of those registered is approximately the same as that of French *cadres* taken as a whole.

pursue in their work their own private objectives rather than those of top management. While there do not seem to have been any changes in recent years in the situation with regard to promotion, the fear of dismissal has now been introduced. How much this will change the attitude toward adopting the objectives of top management is, however, unclear. Obviously, this cannot occur overnight; on the other hand, in a longer period, the *cadres'* perception of the degree of risk of their own dismissal which is implied in a 1 percent national unemployment rate of *cadres* will presumably become more realistic.

The general strike of May 1968 introduced a new factor into the French managerial situation. For, while it is clear that a mjaority of the *cadres* proved loyal to their employers, a sizable minority showed a strong sympathy with the sit-ins and even participated in them. Nor, unlike the blue-collar workers, were their demands primarily economic; many even supported the position of the Condéfération Française Démocratique du Travail trade union that the income gap between workers and *cadres* should be reduced. The interpretation of the events of May as a "crisis of civilization" was widespread among them.[3] Top management, perhaps overreacting, was left with the feeling which persisted in 1971 that it did not know what the *cadres* wanted and that it could not predict their behavior in case of another crisis like that of May 1968.

What was perhaps as disturbing as anything else was the fact that the younger *cadres* from the *grandes écoles* (Polytechnique, Mines, and Centrale) were perhaps quite as affected as the mass of *cadres:* for these constituted the most intellectual groups and the ones that felt the closest links with the student movement. Older *polytechniciens* in top management complain that they no longer have anything in common with the new graduates; the old school ties have been severely strained.

Top management has responded to this *cadre* crisis by sharply increasing the amount of information given to the *cadres* as well as by increasing their opportunities for further education. This reaction was observed in all of the enterprises I visited. It is by adopting these "American" methods that they hope better to reintegrate the *cadres* into the management structure and to make them once again feel that they are the "collaborators" of the *patron.*

[3]For a treatment of the role of *cadres* in May 1968, see the following: Renaud DuLong, "Les cadres et le mouvement ouvrier" in Pierre Dubois and others, *Grèves Revendicatives ou Grèves Politiques?* (Anthropos, Paris, 1971); Marc Maurice, Roger Cornu, et J. C. Garnier, "Les Cadres en Mai-Juin 1968 dans la Région d'Aix-Marseille" (Rapport préliminaire), (Centre National de la Recherche Scientifique, January 1970); papers by Alfred Willener, Catherine Gajdos and Georges Benguigui in Fondation Royaumont, *Les Cadres en Mouvement* (Editions de l'Epi, Paris, 1969).

But two problems can be seen in this approach. The first is that the solution appears to have been more imposed from above than demanded from below; it was the increase of unemployment among *cadres* which seems to have been most responsible for the *cadres'* participation in the May events.[4] The second is that the providing of significant information and the participation of middle management in the making of important decisions requires a confidence on the part of top managers that junior and middle managers share top management's definitions of the objectives of the enterprise and are ready to work for these goals. But the events of May helped to remove what little underpinning had existed for such a belief. The social framework for an "American solution" simply does not seem to exist.

At least for the present, the two management goals of increased competitiveness of the enterprise and of increased integration of the *cadres* can be taken as contradictory. The younger *cadres* insist to a substantial degree on social goals for the enterprise—as opposed to that of profitability—in the same fashion that the older generation had done. As the French economic milieu has become more economically liberal and more open to the outside world, French technocracy has turned to the left. It is not an accident that a sixty-year-old French friend with an exceptionally wide *grande école* acquaintance in large industrial enterprises reports that he has great difficulty in communicating with the managers of thirty-five to fifty years of age. Men of his generation were turned to social objectives by events of 1936 and of the Second World War; the younger generation has turned in the same direction, and he and they can understand one another; but the intermediate generation of managers places its emphasis on enterprise efficiency, competitiveness, and profitability. The unrelenting pursuit of profitability by this intermediate generation is not easy when its members are pressed both by their elders and by their juniors in management for more attention to traditional French values.

From a material standpoint, the position of French *cadres* relative to blue-collar workers remains excellent by international standards. As of 1966, total costs to the employer in manufacturing industry in the five countries of the Common Market were as shown in Table 14.2. French white-collar employees (and this means *cadres* in particular) were the highest paid in the Common Market, while blue-collar workers were paid less than in any of the other countries except Italy.

[4]See DuLong, "Les cadres et le mouvement ouvrier," p. 172.

Table 14.2   White-Collar versus Blue-Collar Earnings, 1966 (Index: France = 100)

	Germany	Holland	Belgium	Italy
Total hourly costs	103.4	99.0	98.4	87.1
Hourly cost for blue-collar workers	117.1	106.6	110.8	94.8
Hourly cost for white-collar employees	80.0	82.1	93.0	91.0

Source: INSEE, "Documents Statistiques sur l'Industrie Française," p. VI-10. The indices reflect official rates of exchange.

While the situation changed somewhat in favor of blue-collar workers as a result of the June 1968 raising of the minimum wage, *cadres* again made some headway between September 1968 and September 1969. If we take each group's nominal weekly earnings in September 1967 as 100, earnings in September 1969 were approximately: blue-collar workers, 125; and cadres, 119.[5] Thus virtually no narrowing has occurred in the extraordinary income differential between workers and managers which exists in France in comparison with Britain, the Soviet Union and the United States.

From all of the foregoing we can conclude that, while certainly there has been change in French large-scale industry since the early 1960s—primarily as a result of the increased competition within the Common Market, but also as a result of the events of May 1968—it would be wrong to exaggerate it. The forces of conservatism and *dirigisme* are found on both sides of the political balance and are strong both among the very young and the older *cadres;* they are not likely to allow change in management mores to occur too rapidly.

But the vigor of French industry has been astonishing, particularly if one takes Britain as the point of comparison. This can best be seen in the response to the events of May.

Between 1963 and 1967, hourly real wages in the private sector increased in each year by 3 to 4 percent per annum. In 1968, it increased by 10 percent. One might well have expected a compensating decline thereafter, but in fact 1969 and 1970 saw a return to the customary 3 to 4 percent advance. Moreover, 1969 was a highly profitable year for French industry.[6] The rate of inflation doubled as compared with the previous three years but was still no more than a total of 16 percent over the three years of 1968-1970.

What helped to make this accomplishment possible was a sharp rise in

[5]M. Perrot in *Economie & Statistique,* February 1971, pp. 15–21.
[6]A contributing factor here was the abolition as of the end of 1968 of the 5 percent tax on wages which had been levied on business.

industrial labor productivity around the period of the events of May. Whether this increase began before May 1968 is a matter of dispute,[7] but in any case it continued for at least two quarters beyond these events. Clearly, workers responded to their economic gains with increased work effort. There was a quite successful effort to make it possible for most of the nominal wage improvement to be preserved in real terms.

Thus both industrial management and workers responded magnificently to the economic challenge implicit in the wage increases of May. As we had seen in the company histories for earlier periods, French industry proved quite capable of meeting the challenges set before it.

[7]One article dates this rise as occurring from the fourth quarter of 1967 through the fourth quarter of 1968. *(Economie & Statistique,* June 1970, pp. 17 and 19.) An influential French business economist dates it as occurring from the third quarter of 1968 through the second quarter of 1969, if one ignores changes occurring as a result of variations in the volume of industrial production.

Glossary

Education
Ecoles
This term refers only to French higher education and includes all of the schools of engineering and some of the nontechnical institutions. It does not include the universities.

Grandes écoles
This term is used in its more restrictive sense to include only the three French peak engineering *écoles* (Polytechnique, les Ecoles des Mines, and l'Ecole Centrale des Arts et Manufactures) and four nonengineering *écoles* which also partially service industry (Ecole des Hautes Etudes Commerciales, Ecole Normale Supérieure, St. Cyr, and Ecole Nationale d'Administration).

The *grande école* pattern of management refers particularly to the three engineering schools, which together have graduated only five hundred forty to seven hundred ninety students per annum during the last four decades. (The total number of graduates for five selected years were: 1924—669; 1934—624; 1948—594; 1954—540; 1965—790.)

Public School
These are British nonstate and fee-paying secondary schools that are members of the Headmasters' Conference. At the time when current upper executives attended school, there were about one hundred twenty public schools in Britain.

French Governmental Careers
Corps
This term refers to elitist branches of the French civilian and military engineering services, as well as to a few nonengineering branches of the civil service. Membership in the *corps* is restricted to those granted permanent managerial positions in these services.

Grands corps
These are defined very restrictively as including only the Corps des Mines, the Inspection des Finances, the Conseil d'Etat, and the Cour des Comptes.

Managerial Terms
Cadres
French managerial and professional employees above the level of foreman.

Président-directeur général
Chief executive officer of a French company.

Managing director
Chief executive officer of a British company.

Directeur général
Senior vice-president of a French company; there are sometimes one or more of these directly under the *président-directeur général.*

Directeur
Vice-president of a French company. He is not a member of the board of directors.

Director
Member of a British company's board of directors. A full-time director is comparable to an American company vice-president.

Index

Absenteeism, 144
Accounting firms, 212, 213
Accounting systems: and investment decisions, 28-29, 30-31, 33; and satisficing, 35-36; French, 45; B2, 108; F3, 136-37, 140; and pricing, 341. *See also* Cost-accounting
Acquisitions policy: outside vs. internal suppliers, 328, 331-33, 335, 349-50, 358; U.S., 335, 336. *See also* Subcontracting; Transfers, interdivisional
Adjustment to change: in the U.S., 13; value of speed of, 16; and balance of trade, 18-19; components of, 19-22; resistance to, in British firms, 42-43; and long-run planning, 48-49; influences growth in factor productivity, 69-70; managerial function and, 357, 361
Advertising and promotion: and profits, 36, 51*n*, 326; B1, 97; U.S., 342, 343
Advertising firms, 212, 213
Age of managers: British, 174*n*, 180, 226, 228-29, 295; Soviet, 192, 193, 194, 239, 300; U.S., 212, 213, 214, 215, 224, 249, 295; French, 233, 235, 256
Amortization, rapid: in profit-maximizing matrix, 30; in French tax system, 45, 147
Automation: costs of, and investment policy, 315-16, 321, 322, 323; British attitudes toward, 361

Backwardness, economic: advantage of, 11-13, 17; determining degree of, 16*n*; and adjustment to change, 19, 20
Bain, Joe S., 359
Balance of trade, 18-19
Banking: British careers in, 376
Belgium, 15, 381
Blue-collar workers: productivity growth of (F5), 150-51, 153-54, 155; wages of, 379, 380, 381
Bonus system: Soviet, 39, 52, 53-55, 261, 277-83, 317-18, 362-63, 365, 371; and short-run success, 53-55, 317-18, 362, 371; for French management, 59-60, 147 (F4), 276-77, 286-88, 318, 365, 366; British, 109 (B2), 273-76, 330 (B1); for sales personnel (F3), 138-39, 140; incentive function of, 258; in U.S., 264-73, 283, 337, 362-63
Bourse, 78, 90, 91, 92
Britain: production of, 14-15; value of speed of adjustment in, 16; balance of

trade in, 18, 19; government promotion of mergers, 376
Buildings: investment in, 30; depreciation rates for, 85. *See also* Facilities

Cadres. See Management, French
Cambridge University, 174*n*, 175, 179, 180, 210, 374, 376
Capital, fixed: valuation of, 45; sample data on, 72-73; in calculating capital input, 84; depreciation rates for, 85; and plant manager, 313-14. *See also* Equipment; Facilities
Capital, intangible: in profit maximizing matrix, 30-35, 37-38, 40, 48; in U.S., 62, 63
Capital, invested: ratio of, to national income, 12; in model of economic development, 13, 16, 17, 18, 19, 21; rate of return on British, 27-28, 88; and French tax system, 45-46, 144; rate of return on samples, 73; in productivity calculations, 83-84, 86-87; in low profit sector (F6), 161; national ratio of, to output, 361, 362. *See also* Investment policy
Capital productivity: calculating, 83-84, 86-87; B1, 95; B2, 112; F1, 122; F2, 131; F3, 135; F4, 142; F5, 150; F6, 157
Case study approach, 67-76
Centrale des Arts et Manufactures, 183, 185, 189, 190, 199, 200, 203, 204, 379, 383
Centralization. *See* Organization, enterprise
Clarendon Schools, 174*n*
Columbia University, 170
Common Market: and French attitude, 43-44*n*, 376, 381; and British attitude, 374
Communist Party: management membership in, 167, 191-93, 194, 196-97, 291, 293; *oblast* secretaries' tenure in, 238; management experience in hierarchy, 240, 241, 243, 244-45, 300
Company personality: described, 23; in financial planning, 24-26, 37-38; trend toward national standardization of, 49; and promotion, 294. *See also* Policy, company
Compensation, managerial. *See* Bonus system; Salary and compensation of management; Stock options
Competition: response to, 127 (F1), 146, 148 (F4); and divisional autonomy, 331; and internal transfers, 336